# "I CANNOT. . .
# I WILL NOT. . . RECANT!
# HERE I STAND. . . .

**"If anyone despise my fraternal warning, I am free from his blood in the last judgment. It is better that I should die a thousand times than retract one syllable of the condemned articles. And as they excommunicated me for the sacrilege of heresy, so I excommunicated them in the name of the sacred truth of God. Christ will judge whose excommunication will stand. Amen."**

Martin Luther spoke these fateful words as he took his unyielding position against the abuses of the medieval church. In this outstanding modern contribution to religious literature, Roland H. Bainton has created a vivid portrait of the man who, because of his unshakable faith in his God, helped bring about the Protestant Reformation.

ROLAND H. BAINTON was a minister, theologian, and Titus Street Professor of Ecclesiastical History at Yale Divinity School.

*A Life of Martin Luther*

# HERE I STAND

*Roland H. Bainton*

A MERIDIAN BOOK

MERIDIAN
Published by the Penguin Group
Penguin Books USA Inc., 375 Hudson Street,
New York, New York 10014, U.S.A.
Penguin Books Ltd, 27 Wrights Lane, London W8 5TZ, England
Penguin Books Australia Ltd, Ringwood, Victoria, Australia
Penguin Books Canada Ltd, 10 Alcorn Avenue,
Toronto, Ontario, Canada M4V 3B2
Penguin Books (N.Z.) Ltd, 182–190 Wairau Road, Auckland 10, New Zealand

Penguin Books Ltd, Registered Offices: Harmondsworth, Middlesex, England

Published by Meridian, an imprint of Dutton Signet,
a division of Penguin Books USA Inc.
Previously published in a Mentor edition.
Published by arrangement with Abingdon Press. For information address
Abingdon Press, 201 Eighth Avenue South, Nashville, Tennessee 37203.

A hardcover library edition of this book is published by Abingdon Press.

First Mentor Printing, February, 1955
First Meridian Printing, January, 1995
20  19  18  17

 REGISTERED TRADEMARK—MARCA REGISTRADA

ISBN 0-452-01146-9

Printed in the United States of America

TO

*My Partner*

IN THE

*"School for Character"*

# ACKNOWLEDGMENTS

PORTIONS OF THIS BOOK have been delivered as the Nathaniel Taylor lectures at the Yale Divinity School, the Carew Lectures at the Hartford Seminary Foundation, and the Hein Lectures at the Wartburg Seminary and Capital University, as well as at the Bonebrake Theological Seminary, the Gettysburg Theological Seminary, and the Divinity School of Howard University. For many courtesies on the part of these institutions I am indebted.

I also thank the firm of J. C. B. Mohr at Tübingen for permission to reprint as Chapter XXI the article which appeared in the *Gerhard Ritter Festschrift*, and the Westminster Press for permission to use in condensed form certain portions from my *Martin Luther Christmas Book*.

Extensive travel and borrowing for this work have not been necessary because the Yale library is so richly supplied and so generous in acquiring new material. Especially to Mr. Babb, Mr. Wing, and Mr. Tinker hearty thanks are tendered by Martin Luther.

# CONTENTS

I. THE VOW     15

    AT HOME AND SCHOOL
    RELIGIOUS DISQUIET
    THE HAVEN OF THE COWL

II. THE CLOISTER     27

    THE TERROR OF THE HOLY
    THE WAY OF SELF-HELP
    THE MERITS OF THE SAINTS
    THE TRIP TO ROME

III. THE GOSPEL     39

    THE FAILURE OF CONFESSION
    THE MYSTIC LADDER
    THE EVANGELICAL EXPERIENCE

IV. THE ONSLAUGHT     51

    THE INDULGENCE FOR ST. PETER'S
    THE NINETY-FIVE THESES

V. THE SON OF INIQUITY     64

    THE DOMINICAN ASSAULT
    THE CASE TRANSFERRED TO GERMANY
    THE INTERVIEWS WITH CAJETAN
    THREATENING EXILE

VI. THE SAXON HUS     78

    THE GAUNTLET OF ECK
    THE LEIPZIG DEBATE
    THE ENDORSEMENT OF HUS

VII. THE GERMAN HERCULES     93

    THE HUMANISTS: ERASMUS
    MELANCHTHON AND DÜRER
    THE NATIONALISTS: HUTTEN AND SICKINGEN

VIII. THE WILD BOAR IN THE VINEYARD     105
    THE SACRAMENTS AND THE THEORY OF THE
      CHURCH
    PROSECUTION RESUMED
    THE BULL "EXSURGE"
    THE BULL SEEKS LUTHER

IX. THE APPEAL TO CAESAR     116
    PUBLICATION OF THE BULL
    AGAINST THE EXECRABLE BULL OF ANTICHRIST
    THE FREEDOM OF THE CHRISTIAN MAN

X. HERE I STAND     129
    A HEARING PROMISED AND RECALLED
    THE EMPEROR ASSUMES RESPONSIBILITY
    INVITATION TO LUTHER RENEWED
    LUTHER BEFORE THE DIET
    THE EDICT OF WORMS

XI. MY PATMOS     148
    AT THE WARTBURG
    THE REFORMATION AT WITTENBERG:
      MONASTICISM
    THE MASS
    THE OUTBREAK OF VIOLENCE

XII. THE RETURN OF THE EXILE     158
    TURMOIL
    THE INVITATION TO COME BACK
    THE RETURN TO WITTENBERG

XIII. NO OTHER FOUNDATION     166
    NATURE, HISTORY, AND PHILOSOPHY
    CHRIST THE SOLE REVEALER
    THE WORD AND THE SACRAMENTS
    THE MENACE TO MORALS
    THE GROUND OF GOODNESS

XIV. REBUILDING THE WALLS     179
    THE CALLINGS
    ECONOMICS
    POLITICS
    CHURCH AND STATE

XV. THE MIDDLE WAY     191
    HOSTILITY OF THE REFORMED PAPACY
    RECOIL OF THE MODERATE CATHOLICS: ERASMUS
    DEFECTION OF THE PURITANS: CARLSTADT
    THE REVOLUTIONARY SAINTS: MÜNTZER
    BANISHMENT OF THE AGITATORS

XVI. BEHEMOTH, LEVIATHAN, AND THE GREAT WATERS 205
 RIVALS: ZWINGLI AND THE ANABAPTISTS
 RELIGION AND SOCIAL UNREST
 LUTHER AND THE PEASANTS
 MÜNTZER FOMENTS REBELLION
 THE DEBACLE AND THE EFFECT ON THE
 REFORMATION

XVII. THE SCHOOL FOR CHARACTER 223
 KATHERINE VON BORA
 DOMESTICITY
 CHILDREN AND TABLE TALK
 VIEWS OF MARRIAGE
 CONSOLATIONS OF HOME

XVIII. THE CHURCH TERRITORIAL 238
 DISSEMINATION OF THE REFORM
 PRACTICAL CHURCH PROBLEMS
 THE GODLY PRINCE
 THE PROTEST
 PROTESTANT ALLIANCE: THE MARBURG COLLOQUY
 THE AUGSBURG CONFESSION

XIX. THE CHURCH TUTORIAL 254
 THE BIBLE TRANSLATION
 DOCTRINAL PROBLEMS IN TRANSLATION
 CATECHISMS
 LITURGY
 MUSIC
 HYMNBOOK

XX. THE CHURCH MINISTERIAL 272
 PREACHING
 SERMON ON THE NATIVITY
 EXPOSITION OF JONAH
 PRAYER

XXI. THE STRUGGLE FOR FAITH 281
 LUTHER'S PERSISTENT STRUGGLE
 HIS DEPRESSIONS
 THE WAY OF INDIRECTION
 WRESTLING WITH THE ANGEL
 THE ROCK OF SCRIPTURE

XXII. THE MEASURE OF THE MAN 292
 THE BIGAMY OF THE LANDGRAVE
 ATTITUDE TO THE ANABAPTISTS
 ATTITUDE TO THE JEWS
 THE PAPISTS AND THE EMPEROR
 THE MEASURE OF THE MAN

BIBLIOGRAPHY 303
REFERENCES 315
SOURCES OF ILLUSTRATIONS 325
INDEX 327

# LIST OF ILLUSTRATIONS

Luther as the Evangelist Matthew
   Translating the Scriptures           Inside front cover
Dürer's "Melancolia"                 Inside back cover
Woodcuts of School Scenes of Luther's Day   16–17
A Student Wearing the Donkey Mask   17
Hans and Margaretta Luther by Cranach   19
Fiends Tempting a Dying Man to Abandon Hope   21
Christ the Judge Sitting upon the Rainbow   23
View of the City of Erfurt   24
Sixteenth-Century Monks in a Choir   26
The Augustinian Cloister Luther Entered as a Monk   28
Celebrating the Mass in Luther's Time   29
Illustration from Luther's Bible of 1522   32
Monks of the Sixteenth Century   34–37
Wittenberg in 1627   40
Illustrated Title Page of Luther's Bible of 1541   46
Cranach's "Frederick the Wise Adoring the Virgin and Child"   52
A Holbein Cartoon Showing True and False Repentance   54–55
Portrait of Albert of Brandenburg   57
Cartoon Showing the Hawking of Indulgences   58
The Vendor and His Indulgences   59
The Castle Church at Wittenberg   61
Cartoon Showing Forgiveness of Christ Outweighing
   Indulgences from the Pope   62
Spalatin and the Crucified Christ   69
1556 Woodcut of Luther's Interview with Cajetan   72
The Pope as an Ass Playing Bagpipes   74
Reversible Cartoon of Cardinal and Fool   74
Portrait of Philip Melanchthon by Aldegrever   81
Portrait of John Eck   82
Fifteenth-Century Cartoon of Antichrist   85
Woodcut of the Leipzig Debate by a Contemporary   87
Luther and Hus Administer the Bread and Wine to the
   House of Saxony   91
Luther Depicted as the German Hercules by Holbein   94
Luther and Hutten as Companions in Arms   100
Cartoon Showing Luther and Hutten Bowling Against the Pope   101
The Ebernburg   102
Title Page of the Bull Against Luther   113
Title Page of Luther's *Address to the German Nobility*   118
"The Passion of Christ and Antichrist"   120
Title Page of Hutten's Protest *Against the Burning of
   Luther's Books at Mainz*   123

Luther Burning the Papal Bull 128
Title Page of Hutten's *Satire on the Bull Against Luther* 131
The Diet of Worms and the Public Peace 133
Portrait of Aleander 134
Luther with a Dove Above His Head 135
Luther's First Hearing at Worms 142
Luther's Second Hearing at Worms 145
The Wartburg 150
Luther as Junker George at the Wartburg 151
Marriage of Bishops, Monks, and Nuns 154
A Cartoon Against the Image Breakers 160
Portrait of Frederick the Wise 163
Portrait of Luther 172
Title Page of Luther's Tract *On the Freedom of the
   Christian Man* 177
Rebuilding the Walls of Jerusalem 180
A Father of a Household at Work 182
From the Title Page of Luther's Tract *On Usury* 183
Frederick the Wise and Luther Kneeling Before the
   Crucified Christ 192
Portrait of Duke George 194
Portrait of Thomas Müntzer 202
Peasants Swearing Allegiance to the Bund 210
A Prophecy of Convulsion in 1524 211
Peasants Plundering a Cloister 214
Peasants About to Take Over a Cloister 215
Title Page of Luther's Tract *Against the Murderous and
   Thieving Hordes of Peasants* 217
Surrender of the Upper Swabian Peasants 218–19
Luther Instructs the Peasants 221
Luther in Armor Prepares to Put on the Peasants' Boot 222
A Peasant Taxes Luther as Double-Tongued 222
A Wedding Party in Front of the Church 225
Katherine and Martin in the Year of Their Marriage 227
The Luther Household at Table 230
Cartoon of 1529 Showing Luther as a Seven-Headed Monster 232
Christ Disarms the Pope 240
Luther and Lucifer in League 240
The Devil Delivers a Declaration of War to Luther 241
The Signatures at the Marlburg Colloquy 251
Cranach's "Jacob Wrestling with the Angel" 256
Lemberger's "Jacob Wrestling with the Angel" 257
The Whore of Babylon in Three Editions of Luther's Bible 259–60
Four Cuts Illustrating the Catechism 264–65
Sample of Luther's Hymnbook 268
Songs Praising Luther and Melanchthon 270
Evangelical and Catholic Services Contrasted 273
Illustration of the Nativity from Luther's Bible 277
Martyrdom of Heinrich of Zuetphen 282
Devil and Death Harass a Soul in an Unfinished
   Cranach Drawing 285
Luther from the Copper Plate by Daniel Hopfer (1523) 287
"A Mighty Fortress" in Luther's Hand 291
"The Anabaptist Preacher" Adapted from the Title Page of
   Hosea in Luther's Bible 294
The Lower Magistrate: John Frederick, Elector of Saxony 298
Luther in the Year of His Death 300

# CHRONOLOGY

| | | |
|---|---|---|
| 1483 | November 10 | Birth of Martin Luther at Eisleben |
| 1484 | early summer | Family moved to Mansfeld |
| 1497 | about Easter | Luther goes to school at Magdeburg |
| 1498 | | Luther goes to school at Eisenach |
| 1501 | May | Matriculation at Erfurt |
| 1502 | September 29 | Bachelor of Arts |
| 1505 | January 7 | Master of Arts |
| | July 2 | Thunderstorm and vow |
| | July 17 | Enters Augustinian cloister at Erfurt |
| 1507 | May 2 | First mass |
| 1508 | winter | Teaches one semester at Wittenberg |
| 1509 | October | Return to Erfurt |
| 1510 | November | Journey to Rome |
| 1511 | early April | Return to Erfurt; transfer to Wittenberg |
| 1512 | October 19 | Doctor of Theology |
| 1513 | August 16 | Lectures on Psalms begin |
| 1515 | April | Lectures on Romans begin |
| 1516 | September 7 | Lectures on Romans end |
| | October 27 | Lectures on Galatians begin |
| 1517 | October 31 | Posting the ninety-five theses |
| 1518 | April 26 | Disputation at Heidelberg |
| | July | Prierias attacks Luther |
| | August 5 | Maximilian writes to the pope |
| | August 7 | The pope cites Luther to Rome |
| | August 8 | Luther appeals to Frederick |
| | August 25 | Melanchthon arrives |
| | August 31 | Luther's reply to Prierias |
| | September 26 | Luther starts for Augsburg |
| | October 12–14 | Interview with Cajetan |
| | October 20–21 | Flight from Augsburg |
| | October 30 | Back in Wittenberg |
| | November 8 | The bull *Cum Postquam* |
| | November 28 | Luther appeals to a general council |
| | December 2 | Ready to go into exile |
| | December 18 | Frederick will not banish Luther |
| 1519 | January 4–6 | Interview of Luther with Miltitz |
| | January 12 | Death of Emperor Maximilian |
| | June 28 | Election of Charles V |
| | July 4–14 | Leipzig debate between Luther and Eck |
| 1520 | January | Hutten and Sickingen offer Luther help |
| | May | *Sermon on Good Works* |
| | June 11 | Offer of protection from one hundred knights; *The Papacy at Rome* |

| | | |
|---|---|---|
| | June 15 | *Exsurge Domine* gives Luther sixty days to submit |
| | August | *Address to the German Nobility* |
| | October 6 | *Babylonian Captivity* |
| | October 10 | Luther receives the pope's bull |
| | November 4 | Charles at Cologne promises a hearing |
| | November 12 | Burning of Luther's books at Cologne |
| | November | *Against the Execrable Bull of Antichrist; On the Freedom of the Christian Man* |
| | November 28 | Luther invited to Worms |
| | December 10 | Burning by Luther of the pope's bull |
| | December 17 | Invitation to Worms rescinded |
| 1521 | January 3 | The bull *Decet Romanum Pontificum* again Luther is read |
| | January 5 | Frederick arrives at Worms |
| | January 27 | The diet of Worms opens |
| | February 10 | The bull against Luther reaches Aleander |
| | February 13 | Aleander's three-hour speech; the bull is sent back |
| | February 14 | Glapion's attempts at mediation |
| | February 17 | Draft of an edict against Luther |
| | February 19 | Intense opposition |
| | February 22 | Decision to summon Luther |
| | March 2 | Second draft of an edict |
| | March 6 | Invitation to Luther |
| | March 8 | Edict for sequestration of Luther's books read |
| | March 26 | Edict issued |
| | April 10 | Glapion reports failure of mission to Hutten and Sickingen |
| | April 16 | Luther in Worms |
| | April 17 | First hearing |
| | April 18 | Second hearing |
| | April 19 | The emperor announces his decision |
| | April 20 | Diet requests a committee |
| | April 23–24 | Hearings before the committee |
| | April 26 | Luther leaves Worms |
| | May 4 | Luther arrives at the Wartburg |
| | May 8 | Edict of Worms ready |
| | May 26 | Edict of Worms actually issued |
| | September 22 | Melanchthon celebrates an evangelical Lord's Supper |
| | November 12 | Thirteen monks leave the Augustinian cloister |
| | December 3–4 | Tumult at Wittenberg; Luther's flying trip home and return |
| | December | Commencement of the New Testament translation; work on the Sermon Postils |
| | December 25 | Carlstadt gives wine in the mass to laity |
| | December 27 | Zwickau prophets in Wittenberg |
| 1522 | January 6 | Disbanding of the Augustinian Congregation at Wittenberg |
| | February 26 | Justus Jonas, minister of the Castle Church at Wittenberg, marries |
| | March 1–6 | Luther's return to Wittenberg |
| | September— May, 1523 | Sickingen's campaign against Trier |

| | September | Luther's German New Testament published |
|---|---|---|
| | September 14 | Hadrian VI elected pope |
| 1523 | March 6 | Edict of the Diet of Nürnberg deferring action |
| | March | *On Civil Government* |
| | Pentecost | *On the Order of Worship* |
| | July 1 | Burning of the first martyrs of the Reformation at Brussels |
| | August 23 | Death of Hutten |
| | September | Clement VII elected pope |
| 1524 | | Hymnbook |
| | January—February | *To the Councilman . . . Christian Schools* |
| | April 18 | Edict of the second diet of Nürnberg |
| | September | Erasmus, *On the Freedom of the Will* |
| 1525 | January | *Against the Heavenly Prophets* |
| | March | Twelve articles of the peasants |
| | April 19 | *Admonition to Peace* |
| | May 5 | Death of Frederick the Wise |
| | May 5 | *Against the Robbing and Murdering Horde* |
| | May 15 | Battle of Frankenhausen; capture of Müntzer |
| | May—June | Crushing of the peasants |
| | June 13 | Luther's betrothal to Katherine von Bora |
| | July | *Open Letter Concerning the Hard Book Against the Peasants* |
| | before Christmas | *The German Mass* |
| | December | *On the Enslaved Will* |
| 1526 | June 25—August 27 | Diet of Speyer defers action on the Edict of Worms |
| | | *Exposition of Jonah* |
| 1527 | January | *Whether Soldiers Too May Be Saved* |
| | April | *Whether These Words: This Is My Body* |
| | summer | Sickness, intense depression |
| | | Composition of "A Mighty Fortress" |
| 1528 | March 22 | *Instruction for the Visitors* |
| | March 28 | *Confession of the Lord's Supper* |
| 1529 | April 19 | Protest at the Diet of Speyer |
| | October 1–4 | Marburg Colloquy; German catechism |
| 1530 | April 16 | Luther at the Coburg |
| | June 25 | Presentation of the Augsburg Confession |
| | | *Exposition of the Eighty-Second Psalm* (Death penalty for sedition and blasphemy) |
| 1531 | | *Warning to His Beloved Germans* |
| 1534 | | Publication of the complete German Bible |
| 1536 | | Wittenberg Concord with the Swiss |
| | | Outbreak of Anabaptists at Münster |
| | | Melanchthon's memorandum on the death penalty for peaceful Anabaptists |
| 1539 | | Bigamy of the Landgrave Philip |
| 1543 | January 4 | *Against the Jews* |
| | July | Publication of the Genesis Commentary (lectures delivered from 1535–1545) |
| 1545 | March 25 | *Against the Papacy at Rome Founded by the Devil* |
| 1546 | February 18 | Luther's death at Eisleben |

CHAPTER ONE

# THE VOW

N A SULTRY DAY in July of the year 1505 a lonely traveler was trudging over a parched road on the outskirts of the Saxon village of Stotternheim. He was a young man, short but sturdy, and wore the dress of a university student. As he approached the village, the sky became overcast. Suddenly there was a shower, then a crashing storm. A bolt of lightning rived the gloom and knocked the man to the ground. Struggling to rise, he cried in terror, "St. Anne help me! I will become a monk."

The man who thus called upon a saint was later to repudiate the cult of the saints. He who vowed to become a monk was later to renounce monasticism. A loyal son of the Catholic Church, he was later to shatter the structure of medieval Catholicism. A devoted servant of the pope, he was later to identify the popes with Antichrist. For this young man was Martin Luther.

His demolition was the more devastating because it reinforced disintegrations already in progress. Nationalism was in process of breaking the political unities when the Reformation destroyed the religious. Yet this paradoxical figure revived the Christian consciousness of Europe. In his day, as Catholic historians all agree, the popes of the Renaissance were secularized, flippant, frivolous, sensual, magnificent, and unscrupulous. The intelligentsia did not revolt against the Church because the Church was so much of their mind and mood as scarcely to warrant a revolt. Politics were emancipated from any concern for the faith to such a degree that the Most Christian King of France and His Holiness the Pope did not disdain a military alliance with the Sultan against the Holy Roman Empire. Luther changed all this. Religion became again a dominant factor even in politics for another century and a half. Men cared enough for the faith to die for it and to kill for it. If there is any sense remaining of Christian civilization in the West, this man Luther in no small measure deserves the credit.

15

Very naturally he is a controversial figure. The multitudinous portrayals fall into certain broad types already delineated in his own generation. His followers hailed him as the prophet of the Lord and the deliverer of Germany. His opponents on the Catholic side called him the son of perdition and the demolisher of Christendom. The agrarian agitators branded him as the sycophant of the princes, and the radical sectaries compared him to Moses, who led the children of Israel out of Egypt and left them to perish in the wilderness. But such judgments belong to an epilogue rather than a prologue. The first endeavor must be to understand the man.

One will not move far in this direction unless one recognizes at the outset that Luther was above all else a man of religion. The great outward crises of his life which bedazzle the eyes of dramatic biographers were to Luther himself trivial in comparison with the inner upheavals of his questing after God. For that reason this study may appropriately begin with his first acute religious crisis in 1505 rather than with his birth in 1483. Childhood and youth will be drawn upon only to explain the entry into the monastery.

### AT HOME AND SCHOOL

The vow requires interpretation because even at this early point in Luther's career judgments diverge. Those who deplore his subsequent repudiation of the vow explain his defection on the ground that he ought never to have taken it. Had he ever been a true monk, he would not have abandoned the cowl. His critique of monasticism is made to recoil upon himself in that he is painted as a monk without vocation, and the vow is interpreted, not as a genuine call, but rather as the resolution of an inner conflict, an escape from maladjustment at home and at school.

A few sparse items of evidence are adduced in favor of this explanation. They are not of the highest reliability because they are all taken from the conversation of the older Luther as recorded, often inaccurately, by his students; and even if they are genuine, they cannot be accepted at face value because the Protestant Luther was no longer in a position to recall objectively the motives of his Catholic period. Really there is only one saying which connects the taking of the cowl with resentment against parental discipline. Luther is reported to have said, "My mother caned me for stealing a nut, until the blood came. Such strict discipline drove me to the monastery, although she meant it well." This saying is reinforced by two others: "My father once whipped me so that I ran away and felt ugly toward him until he was at pains to win me back." "[At school] I was caned in a single morning fifteen times for nothing at all. I was required to decline and conjugate and hadn't learned my lesson."

Unquestionably the young were roughly handled in those days, and Luther may be correctly reported as having cited these instances in order to bespeak a more humane treatment, but there is no indication that such severity produced more than a flash of resentment. Luther was highly esteemed at home. His parents looked to him as a lad of brilliant parts who should become a jurist, make a prosperous marriage, and support them in their old age. When Luther became a Master of Arts, his father presented him with a copy of the *Corpus Juris* and addressed him no longer with the familiar *Du* but with the polite *Ihr*. Luther always exhibited an extraordinary devotion

THE ASINUS

to his father and was grievously disturbed over parental dis-
approval of his entry into the monastery. When his father died,
Luther was too unnerved to work for several days. The attachment to the mother appears to have been less marked; but
even of the thrashing he said that it was well intended, and
he recalled affectionately a little ditty she used to sing:

> If folk don't like you and me,
> The fault with us is like to be.

The schools also were not tender, but neither were they
brutal. The object was to impart a spoken knowledge of the
Latin tongue. The boys did not resent this because Latin was
useful—the language of the Church, of law, diplomacy, international relations, scholarship, and travel. The teaching was
by drill punctuated with the rod. One scholar, called a *lupus*
or wolf, was appointed to spy on the others and report lapses
into German. The poorest scholar in the class every noon was
given a donkey mask, hence called the *asinus,* which he wore
until he caught another talking German. Demerits were accu-
mulated and accounted for by birching at the end of the week.
Thus one might have fifteen strokes on a single day.

But, despite all the severities, the boys did learn Latin and
loved it. Luther, far from being alienated, was devoted to his
studies and became highly proficient. The teachers were no
brutes. One of them, Trebonius, on entering the classroom
always bared his head in the presence of so many future bur-
gomasters, chancellors, doctors, and regents. Luther respected
his teachers and was grieved when they did not approve of
his subsequent course.

Nor was he prevailingly depressed, but ordinarily rollicking,
fond of music, proficient on the lute, and enamored of the
beauty of the German landscape. How fair in retrospect was
Erfurt! The woods came down to the fringes of the village
to be continued by orchards and vineyards, and then the fields
which supplied the dye industry of Germany with plantings
of indigo, blue-flowered flax, and yellow saffron; and nestling
within the brilliant rows lay the walls, the gates, the steeples
of many-spired Erfurt. Luther called her a new Bethlehem.

### RELIGIOUS DISQUIET

Yet Luther was at times severely depressed, and the reason
lay not in any personal frictions but in the malaise of existence
intensified by religion. This man was no son of the Italian
Renaissance, but a German born in remote Thuringia, where
men of piety still reared churches with arches and spires strain-
ing after the illimitable. Luther was himself so much a gothic
figure that his faith may be called the last great flowering of

the religion of the Middle Ages. And he came from the most
religiously conservative element of the population, the peasants. His father, Hans Luther, and his mother, Margaretta,
were sturdy, stocky, swarthy German *Bauern*. They were not
indeed actually engaged in the tilling of the soil because as
a son without inheritance Hans had moved from the farm to
the mines. In the bowels of the earth he had prospered with
the help of St. Anne, the patroness of miners, until he had

HANS LUTHER                    MARGARETTA LUTHER

come to be the owner of half a dozen foundries; yet he was not
unduly affluent, and his wife had still to go to the forest and
drag home the wood. The atmosphere of the family was that
of the peasantry: rugged, rough, at times coarse, credulous,
and devout. Old Hans prayed at the bedside of his son, and
Margaretta was a woman of prayer.

Certain elements even of old German paganism were
blended with Christian mythology in the beliefs of these untutored folk. For them the woods and winds and water were
peopled by elves, gnomes, fairies, mermen and mermaids,
sprites and witches. Sinister spirits would release storms, floods,
and pestilence, and would seduce mankind to sin and melan-
cholia. Luther's mother believed that they played such minor
pranks as stealing eggs, milk, and butter; and Luther himself
was never emancipated from such beliefs. "Many regions are
inhabited," said he, "by devils. Prussia is full of them, and
Lapland of witches. In my native country on the top of a high
mountain called the Pubelsberg is a lake into which if a stone
be thrown a tempest will arise over the whole region because
the waters are the abode of captive demons."

The education in the schools brought no emancipation but rather reinforced the training of the home. In the elementary schools the children were instructed in sacred song. They learned by heart the *Sanctus,* the *Benedictus,* the *Agnus Dei,* and the *Confiteor.* They were trained to sing psalms and hymns. How Luther loved the *Magnificat!* They attended masses and vespers, and took part in the colorful processions of the holy days. Each town in which Luther went to school was full of churches and monasteries. Everywhere it was the same: steeples, spires, cloisters, priests, monks of the various orders, collections of relics, ringing of bells, proclaiming of indulgences, religious processions, cures at shrines. Daily at Mansfeld the sick were stationed beside a convent in the hope of cure at the tolling of the vesper bell. Luther remembered seeing a devil actually depart from one possessed.

The University of Erfurt brought no change. The institution at that time had not yet been invaded by Renaissance influences. The classics in the curriculum, such as Vergil, had always been favorites in the Middle Ages. Aristotelian physics was regarded as an exercise in thinking God's thoughts after him, and the natural explanations of earthquakes and thunderstorms did not preclude occasional direct divine causation. The studies all impinged on theology, and the Master's degree for which Luther was preparing for the law could have equipped him equally for the cloth. The entire training of home, school, and university was designed to instill fear of God and reverence for the Church.

In all this there is nothing whatever to set Luther off from his contemporaries, let alone to explain why later on he should have revolted against so much of medieval religion. There is just one respect in which Luther appears to have been different from other youths of his time, namely, in that he was extraordinarily sensitive and subject to recurrent periods of exaltation and depression of spirit. This oscillation of mood plagued him throughout his life. He testified that it began in his youth and that the depressions had been acute in the six months prior to his entry into the monastery. One cannot dismiss these states as occasioned merely by adolescence, since he was then twenty-one and similar experiences continued throughout his adult years. Neither can one blithely write off the case as an example of manic depression, since the patient exhibited a prodigious and continuous capacity for work of a high order.

The explanation lies rather in the tensions which medieval religion deliberately induced, playing alternately upon fear and hope. Hell was stoked, not because men lived in perpetual dread, but precisely because they did not, and in order to instill enough fear to drive them to the sacraments of the Church. If they were petrified with terror, purgatory was introduced by way of mitigation as an intermediate place where those not bad enough for hell nor good enough for heaven might make further expiation. If this alleviation inspired complacency, the temperature was advanced on purgatory, and then the pressure was again relaxed through indulgences.

Even more disconcerting than the fluctuation of the temperature of the afterlife was the <u>oscillation</u> between wrath and mercy on the part of the members of the <u>divine hierarchy.</u> God was portrayed now as the Father, now as the wielder of the thunder. He might be softened by the intercession of his kindlier Son, who again was delineated as an implacable judge unless mollified by his mother, who, being a woman, was not above cheating alike God and the Devil on behalf of her suppliants; and if she were remote, one could enlist her mother, St. Anne.

How these themes were presented is graphically illustrated in the most popular handbooks in the very age of the Renaissance. The theme was death; and the best sellers gave instructions, not on how to pay the income tax, but on how to escape hell. Manuals entitled *On the Art of Dying* depicted in lurid woodcuts the departing spirit surrounded by fiends who tempted him to commit the irrevocable sin of abandoning hope in God's mercy. To convince him that he was already beyond pardon he was confronted by the woman with whom he had committed adultery or the beggar he had failed to feed. A companion woodcut then gave encouragement by presenting the figures of forgiven sinners: Peter with his cock, Mary Magdalene with her cruse, the penitent thief, and Saul the persecutor, with the concluding brief caption, "Never despair."

FIENDS TEMPTING A DYING
MAN TO ABANDON HOPE

If this conclusion ministered to complacency, other presentations invoked dread. A book strikingly illustrative of the prevailing mood is a history of the world published by Hartmann Schedel in Nürnberg in 1493. The massive folios, after recounting the history of mankind from Adam to the humanist Conrad Celtes, conclude with a meditation on the brevity of human existence accompanied by a woodcut of the dance of death. The final scene displays the day of judgment. A full-page woodcut portrays Christ the Judge sitting upon a rainbow. A lily extends from his right ear, signifying the redeemed, who below are being ushered by angels into paradise. From his left ear protrudes a sword, symbolizing the doom of the damned, whom the devils drag by the hair from the tombs and cast into the flames of hell. How strange, comments a modern editor, that a chronicle published in the year 1493 should end with the judgment day instead of the discovery of America! Dr. Schedel had finished his manuscript in June. Columbus had returned the previous March. The news presumably had not yet reached Nürnberg. By so narrow a margin Dr. Schedel missed this amazing scoop. "What an extraordinary value surviving copies of the Chronicle would have today if it had recorded the great event!"

So writes the modern editor. But old Dr. Schedel, had he known, might not have considered the finding of a new world worthy of record. He could scarcely have failed to know of the discovery of the Cape of Good Hope in 1488. Yet he never mentioned it. The reason is that he did not think of history as the record of humanity expanding upon earth and craving as the highest good more earth in which to expand. He thought of history as the sum of countless pilgrimages through a vale of tears to the heavenly Jerusalem. Every one of those now dead would some day rise and stand with the innumerable host of the departed before the judgment seat to hear the words, "Well done," or, "Depart from me into everlasting fire." The Christ upon the rainbow with the lily and the sword was a most familiar figure in the illustrated books of the period. Luther had seen pictures such as these and testified that he was utterly terror-stricken at the sight of Christ the Judge.

### THE HAVEN OF THE COWL

Like everyone else in the Middle Ages he knew what to do about his plight. The Church taught that no sensible person would wait until his deathbed to make an act of contrition and plead for grace. From beginning to end the only secure course was to lay hold of every help the Church had to offer: sacraments, pilgrimages, indulgences, the intercession of the saints. Yet foolish was the man who relied solely on the good offices of the heavenly intercessors if he had done nothing to insure their favor!

CHRIST THE JUDGE SITTING UPON THE RAINBOW

And what better could he do than take the cowl? Men believed the end of the world already had been postponed for the sake of the Cistercian monks. Christ had just "bidden the

ERFURT

angel blow his trumpet for the Last Judgment, when the
Mother of Mercy fell at the feet of her Son and besought Him
to spare awhile, 'at least for my friends of the Cistercian
Order, that they may prepare themselves.' " The very devils
complained of St. Benedict as a robber who had stolen souls
out of their hands. He who died in the cowl would receive
preferential treatment in heaven because of his habit. Once
a Cistercian in a high fever cast off his frock and so died.
Arriving at the gate of Paradise he was denied entry by St.
Benedict because of the lack of uniform. He could only walk
around the walls and peep in through the windows to see how
the brethren fared, until one of them interceded for him, and
St. Benedict granted a reprieve to earth for the missing garment. All this was of course popular piety. However much
such crude notions might be deprecated by reputable theologians, this was what the common man believed, and Luther
was a common man. Yet even St. Thomas Aquinas himself
declared the taking of the cowl to be second baptism, restor-
ing the sinner to the state of innocence which he enjoyed when
first baptized. The opinion was popular that if the monk should
sin thereafter, he was peculiarly privileged because in his case
repentance would bring restoration to the state of innocence.
Monasticism was the way par excellence to heaven.

Luther knew all this. Any lad with eyes in his head understood what monasticism was all about. Living examples were
to be seen on the streets of Erfurt. Here were young

Carthusians, mere lads, already aged by their austerities. At Magdeburg, Luther looked upon the emaciated Prince William of Anhalt, who had forsaken the halls of the nobility to become a begging friar and walk the streets carrying the sack of the mendicant. Like any other brother he did the manual work of the cloister. "With my own eyes I saw him," said Luther. "I was fourteen years old at Magdeburg. I saw him carrying the sack like a donkey. He had so worn himself down by fasting and vigil that he looked like a deaths'-head, mere bone and skin. No one could look upon him without feeling ashamed of his own life."

Luther knew perfectly well why youths should make themselves old and nobles should make themselves abased. This life is only a brief period of training for the life to come, where the saved will enjoy an eternity of bliss and the damned will suffer everlasting torment. With their eyes they will behold the despair which can never experience the mercy of extinction. With their ears they will hear the moans of the damned. They will inhale sulphurous fumes and writhe in incandescent but unconsuming flame. All this will last forever and forever and forever.

These were the ideas on which Luther had been nurtured. There was nothing peculiar in his beliefs or his responses save their intensity. His depression over the prospect of death was acute but by no means singular. The man who was later to revolt against monasticism became a monk for exactly the same reason as thousands of others, namely, in order to save his soul. The immediate occasion of his resolve to enter the cloister was the unexpected encounter with death on that sultry July day in 1505. He was then twenty-one and a student at the University of Erfurt. As he returned to school after a visit with his parents, sudden lightning struck him to earth. In that single flash he saw the denouement of the drama of existence. There was God the all-terrible, Christ the inexorable, and all the leering fiends springing from their lurking places in pond and wood that with sardonic cachinnations they might seize his shock of curly hair and bolt him into hell. It was no wonder that he cried out to his father's saint, patroness of miners, "St. Anne help me! I will become a monk."

Luther himself repeatedly averred that he believed himself to have been summoned by a call from heaven to which he could not be disobedient. Whether or not he could have been absolved from his vow, he conceived himself to be bound by it. Against his own inclination, under divine constraint, he took the cowl. Two weeks were required to arrange his affairs and to decide what monastery to enter. He chose a strict one, the reformed congregation of the Augustinians. After a farewell party with a few friends he presented himself at the monastery

gates. News was then sent to his father, who was highly enraged. This was the son, educated in stringency, who should
have supported his parents in their old age. The father was
utterly unreconciled until he saw in the deaths of two other
sons a chastisement for his rebellion.

Luther presented himself as a novice. From no direct evidence but from the liturgy of the Augustinians we are able to
reconstruct the scene of his reception. As the prior stood upon
the steps of the altar, the candidate prostrated himself. The
prior asked, "What seekest thou?" The answer came, "God's
grace and thy mercy." Then the prior raised him up and inquired whether he was married, a bondsman, or afflicted with
secret disease. The answer being negative, the prior described
the rigors of the life to be undertaken: the renunciation of
self-will, the scant diet, rough clothing, vigils by night and
labors by day, mortification of the flesh, the reproach of
poverty, the shame of begging, and the distastefulness of
cloistered existence. Was he ready to take upon himself these
burdens? "Yes, with God's help," was the answer, "and in
so far as human frailty allows." Then he was admitted to a
year of probation. As the choir chanted, the head was tonsured. Civilian clothes were exchanged for the habit of the
novice. The initiate bowed the knee. "Bless thou thy servant,"
intoned the prior. "Hear, O Lord, our heartfelt pleas and deign
to confer thy blessing on this thy servant, whom in thy holy
name we have clad in the habit of a monk, that he may continue with thy help faithful in thy Church and merit eternal
life through Jesus Christ our Lord. Amen." During the singing
of the closing hymn Luther prostrated himself with arms
extended in the form of a cross. He was then received into

SIXTEENTH-CENTURY MONKS IN A CHOIR

*[handwritten: salvation depended on enduring to the end]*

the convent by the brethren with the kiss of peace and again admonished by the prior with the words, "Not he that hath begun but he that endureth to the end shall be saved."

The meaning of Luther's entry into the monastery is simply this, that the great revolt against the medieval Church arose from a desperate attempt to follow the way by her prescribed. Just as Abraham overcame human sacrifice only through his willingness to lift the sacrificial knife against Isaac, just as Paul was emancipated from Jewish legalism only because as a Hebrew of the Hebrews he had sought to fulfill all righteousness, so Luther rebelled out of a more than ordinary devotion. To the monastery he went like others, and even more than others, in order to make his peace with God.

<br>

## CHAPTER TWO

# THE CLOISTER

 UTHER in later life remarked that during the first year in the monastery the Devil is very quiet. We have every reason to believe that his own inner tempest subsided and that during his novitiate he was relatively placid. This may be inferred from the mere fact that at the end of the year he was permitted to make his profession. The probationary period was intended to give the candidate an opportunity to test himself and to be tested. He was instructed to search his heart and declare any misgivings as to his fitness for the monastic calling. If his companions and superiors believed him to have no vocation, they would reject him. Since Luther was accepted, we may safely assume that neither he nor his brethren saw any reason to suppose that he was not adapted to the monastic life.

His days as a novice were occupied with those religious exercises designed to suffuse the soul with peace. Prayers came seven times daily. After eight hours of sleep the monks were awakened between one and two in the morning by the ringing of the cloister bell. At the first summons they sprang up, made the sign of the cross, and pulled on the white robe and the scapular without which the brother was never to leave his cell. At the second bell each came reverently to the church, sprinkled himself with holy water, and knelt before the high altar with a prayer of devotion to the Saviour of the world. Then all took their places in the choir. Matins lasted three quarters of an hour. Each of the seven periods of the day ended with the chanting by the cantor of the *Salve Regina:* "Save, O Queen, Thou Mother of mercy, our life, our delight, and our hope. To Thee we exiled sons of Eve lift up our cry. To Thee we sigh as we languish in this vale of tears. Be Thou our advocate. Sweet Virgin Mary, pray for us. Thou holy Mother of God." After the *Ave Maria* and the *Pater Noster* the brothers in pairs silently filed out of the church.

With such exercises the day was filled. Brother Martin was sure that he was walking in the path the saints had trod. The occasion of his profession filled him with joy that the brothers had found him worthy of continuing. At the foot of the prior he made his dedication and heard the prayer, "Lord Jesus Christ, who didst deign to clothe thyself in our mortality, we beseech thee out of thine immeasurable goodness to bless the habit which the holy fathers have chosen as a sign of innocence and renunciation. May this thy servant, Martin Luther, who takes the habit, be clothed also in thine immortality, O thou who livest and reignest with God the Father and the Holy Ghost, God from eternity to eternity. Amen."

THE COURTYARD OF THE AUGUSTINIAN CLOISTER

The solemn vow had been taken. He was a monk, as innocent as a child newly baptized. Luther gave himself over with confidence to the life which the Church regarded as the surest way of salvation. He was content to spend his days in prayer, in song, in meditation and quiet companionship, in disciplined and moderate austerity.

### THE TERROR OF THE HOLY

Thus he might have continued had he not been overtaken by another thunderstorm, this time of the spirit. The occasion was the saying of his first mass. He had been selected for the priesthood by his superior and commenced his functions with this initial celebration.

The occasion was always an ordeal because the mass is the focal point of the Church's means of grace. Here on the altar bread and wine become the flesh and blood of God, and the sacrifice of Calvary is re-enacted. The priest who performs the miracle of transforming the elements enjoys a power and privilege denied even to angels. The whole difference between the clergy and the laity rests on this. The superiority of the Church over the state likewise is rooted here, for what king or emperor ever conferred upon mankind a boon comparable to that bestowed by the humblest minister at the altar?

Well might the young priest tremble to perform a rite by which God would appear in human form. But many had done it, and the experience of the centuries enabled the manuals to

**THE MASS**

foresee all possible tremors and prescribe the safeguards. The celebrant must be concerned, though not unduly, about the forms. The vestments must be correct; the recitation must be correct, in a low voice and without stammering. The state of the priest's soul must be correct. Before approaching the altar he must have confessed and received absolution of all his sins. He might easily worry lest he transgress any of these conditions, and Luther testified that a mistake as to the vestments was considered worse than the seven deadly sins. But the manuals encouraged the trainee to regard no mistake as fatal because the efficacy of the sacrament depends only on the right intention to perform it. Even should the priest recall during the celebration a deadly sin unconfessed and unabsolved, he should not flee from the altar but finish the rite, and absolution would be forthcoming afterward. And if nervousness should so assail him that he could not continue, an older priest would be at his side to carry on. No insuperable difficulties faced the celebrant, and we have no reason to suppose that Luther approached his first mass with uncommon dread. The postponement of the date for a month was not due to any serious misgivings.

The reason was rather a very joyous one. He wanted his father to be present, and the date was set to suit his convenience. The son and the father had not seen each other since the university days when old Hans presented Martin with a copy of the Roman law and addressed him in the polite speech. The father had been vehemently opposed to his entry into the monastery, but now he appeared to have overcome all resentment and was willing, like other parents, to make a gala day of the occasion. With a company of twenty horsemen Hans Luther came riding in and made a handsome contribution to the monastery. The day began with the chiming of the cloister bells and the chanting of the psalm, "O sing unto the Lord a new song." Luther took his place before the altar and began to recite the introductory portion of the mass until he came to the words, "We offer unto thee, the living, the true, the eternal God." He related afterward:

At these words I was utterly stupefied and terror-stricken. I thought to myself, "With what tongue shall I address such Majesty, seeing that all men ought to tremble in the presence of even an earthly prince? Who am I, that I should lift up mine eyes or raise my hands to the divine Majesty? The angels surround him. At his nod the earth trembles. And shall I, a miserable little pygmy, say 'I want this, I ask for that'? For I am dust and ashes and full of sin and I am speaking to the living, eternal and the true God."

The terror of the Holy, the horrors of Infinitude, smote him like a new lightning bolt, and only through a fearful restraint could he hold himself at the altar to the end.

The man of our secularized generation may have difficulty
in understanding the tremors of his medieval forebear. There
are indeed elements in the religion of Luther of a very primitive character, which hark back to the childhood of the race.
He suffered from the savage's fear of a malevolent deity, the
enemy of men, capricious, easily and unwittingly offended if
sacred places be violated or magical formulas mispronounced.
His was the fear of ancient Israel before the ark of the Lord's
presence. Luther felt similarly toward the sacred host of the
Saviour's body; and when it was carried in procession, panic
took hold of him. His God was the God who inhabited the
storm clouds brooding on the brow of Sinai, into whose presence Moses could not enter with unveiled face and live.
Luther's experience, however, far exceeds the primitive and
should not be so unintelligible to the modern man who, gazing
upon the uncharted nebulae through instruments of his own
devising, recoils with a sense of abject littleness.

Luther's tremor was augmented by the recognition of unworthiness, "I am dust and ashes and full of sin." Creatureli-
ness and imperfection alike oppressed him. Toward God he
was at once attracted and repelled. Only in harmony with the
Ultimate could he find peace. But how could a pigmy stand
before divine Majesty; how could a transgressor confront divine
Holiness? Before God the high and God the holy Luther was
stupefied. For such an experience he had a word which has
as much right to be carried over into English as *Blitzkrieg.*
The word he used was *Anfechtung,* for which there is no
English equivalent. It may be a trial sent by God to test man,
or an assault by the Devil to destroy man. It is all the doubt,
turmoil, pang, tremor, panic, despair, desolation, and desperation which invade the spirit of man.

Utterly limp, he came from the altar to the table where his
father and the guests would make merry with the brothers.
After shuddering at the unapproachableness of the heavenly
Father he now craved some word of assurance from the
earthly father. How his heart would be warmed to hear from
the lips of old Hans that his resentment had entirely passed,
and that he was now cordially in accord with his son's decision! They sat down to meat together, and Martin, as if he
were still a little child, turned and said, "Dear father, why
were you so contrary to my becoming a monk? And perhaps
you are not quite satisfied even now. The life is so quiet and
godly."

This was too much for old Hans, who had been doing his
best to smother his rebellion. He flared up before all the doctors and the masters and the guests, "You learned scholar,
have you never read in the Bible that you should honor your
father and your mother? And here you have left me and your
dear mother to look after ourselves in our old age."

Luther had not expected this. But he knew the answer. All the manuals recalled the gospel injunction to forsake father and mother, wife and child, and pointed out the greater benefits to be conferred in the spiritual sphere. Luther answered, "But, father, I could do you more good by prayers than if I

"AND WHEN I SAW HIM, I FELL AT HIS FEET AS DEAD"

had stayed in the world." And then he must have added what to him was the clinching argument, that he had been called by a voice from heaven out of the thunder cloud.

"God grant," said the old Hans, "it was not an apparition of the Devil."

There was the weak spot of all medieval religion. In this day of skepticism we look back with nostalgia to the age of faith. How fair it would have been to have lived in an atmosphere of naïve assurance, where heaven lay about the infancy of man, and doubt had not arisen to torment the spirit! Such a picture of the Middle Ages is sheer romanticism. The medieval man entertained no doubt of the supernatural world, but that world itself was divided. There were saints, and there were demons. There was God, and there was the Devil. And the Devil could disguise himself as an angel of light. Had Luther, then, been right to follow a vision which might after all have been of the arch fiend, in preference to the plain clear word of Scripture to honor father and mother? The day which began with the ringing of the cloister chime and the psalm "O sing unto the Lord a new song" ended with the horror of the Holy and doubt whether that first thunderstorm had been a vision of God or an apparition of Satan.

### THE WAY OF SELF-HELP

This second upheaval of the spirit set up in Luther an inner turmoil which was to end in the abandonment of the cowl, but not until after a long interval. In fact he continued to wear the monastic habit for three years after his excommunication. Altogether he was garbed as a monk for nineteen years. His development was gradual, and we are not to imagine him in perpetual torment and never able to say mass without terror. He pulled himself together and went on with the appointed round and with whatever new duties were assigned. The prior, for example, informed him that he should resume his university studies in order to qualify for the post of lector in the Augustinian order. He took all such assignments in stride.

But the problem of the alienation of man from God had been renewed in altered form. Not merely in the hour of death but daily at the altar the priest stood in the presence of the All High and the All Holy. How could man abide God's presence unless he were himself holy? Luther set himself to the pursuit of holiness. Monasticism constituted such a quest; and while Luther was in the world, he had looked upon the cloister in any form as the higher righteousness. But after becoming a monk he discovered levels within monasticism itself. Some monks were easygoing; some were strict. Those Carthusian lads prematurely old; that prince of Anhalt, mere animated bones—these were not typical examples. They were the rigorists, heroic athletes, seeking to take heaven by storm. Whether Luther's call to the monastery had been prompted by God or the Devil, he was now a monk, and a monk he would be to the uttermost. One of the privileges of the monastic life was that it emancipated the sinner from all distractions and freed him to save his soul by practicing the counsels of perfection—not simply charity, sobriety, and love, but chastity, poverty, obedience, fastings, vigils, and mortifications of the flesh. Whatever good works a man might do to save himself, these Luther was resolved to perform.

He fasted, sometimes three days on end without a crumb. The seasons of fasting were more consoling to him than those of feasting. Lent was more comforting than Easter. He laid upon himself vigils and prayers in excess of those stipulated by the rule. He cast off the blankets permitted him and well-nigh froze himself to death. At times he was proud of his sanctity and would say, "I have done nothing wrong today." Then misgivings would arise. "Have you fasted enough? Are you poor enough?" He would then strip himself of all save that which decency required. He believed in later life that his austerities had done permanent damage to his digestion.

I was a good monk, and I kept the rule of my order so strictly that I may say that if ever a monk got to heaven by his monkery it was I. All my brothers in the monastery who knew me will bear me out. If I had kept on any longer, I should have killed myself with vigils, prayers, reading, and other work.

All such drastic methods gave no sense of inner tranquillity. The purpose of his striving was to compensate for his sins, but he could never feel that the ledger was balanced. Some historians have therefore asserted that he must have been a very great sinner, and that in all likelihood his sins had to do with sex, where offenses are the least capable of any rectification. But Luther himself declared that this was not a particular problem. He had been chaste. While at Erfurt he had never heard a woman in confession. And later at Wittenberg he had confessed only three women, and these he had not seen. Of course he was no wood carving, but sexual temptation beset him no more than any other problem of the moral life.

The trouble was that he could not satisfy God at any point. Commenting in later life on the Sermon on the Mount, Luther gave searching expression to his disillusionment. Referring to the precepts of Jesus he said:

This word is too high and too hard that anyone should fulfill it. This is proved, not merely by our Lord's word, but by our own experience and feeling. Take any upright man or woman. He will get along very nicely with those who do not provoke him, but let someone proffer only the slightest irritation and he will flare up in anger, . . . if not against friends, then against enemies. Flesh and blood cannot rise above it.

Luther simply had not the capacity to fulfill the conditions.

### THE MERITS OF THE SAINTS

But if he could not, others might. The Church, while taking an individualistic view of sin, takes a corporate view of goodness. Sins must be accounted for one by one, but goodness can be pooled; and there is something to pool because the saints, the Blessed Virgin, and the Son of God were better than they needed to be for their own salvation. Christ in particular, being both sinless and God, is possessed of an unbounded store. These superfluous merits of the righteous constitute a treasury which is transferable to those whose accounts are in arrears. The transfer is effected through the Church and, particularly, through the pope, to whom as the successor of St. Peter have been committed the keys to bind and loose. Such a transfer of credit was called an indulgence.

Precisely how much good it would do had not been definitely defined, but the common folk were disposed to believe the most extravagant claims. No one questioned that the pope could draw on the treasury in order to remit penalties for sin imposed by himself on earth. In fact one would suppose that he could do this by mere fiat without any transfer. The important question was whether or not he could mitigate the pangs of purgatory. During the decade in which Luther was born a pope had declared that the efficacy of indulgences extended to purgatory for the benefit of the living and the dead alike. In the case of the living there was no assurance of avoiding purgatory entirely because God alone knew the extent of the unexpiated guilt and the consequent length of the sentence, but the Church could tell to the year and the day by how much the term could be reduced, whatever it was. And in the case of those already dead and in purgatory, the sum of whose wickedness was complete and known, an immediate release could be offered. Some bulls of indulgence went still further and applied not merely to reduction of penalty but even to the forgiveness of sins. They offered a plenary remission and reconciliation with the Most High.

There were places in which these signal mercies were more accessible than in others. For no theological reason but in the interest of advertising, the Church associated the dispensing of the merits of the saints with visitation upon the relics of the saints. Popes frequently specified precisely how much benefit could be derived from viewing each holy bone. Every relic of the saints in Halle, for example, was endowed by Pope Leo X with an indulgence for the reduction of purgatory by four thousand years. The greatest storehouse for such treasures was Rome. Here in the single crypt of St. Callistus forty popes were buried and 76,000 martyrs. Rome had a piece of Moses' burning bush and three hundred particles of the Holy Innocents. Rome had the portrait of Christ on the napkin of St. Veronica. Rome had the chains of St. Paul and the scissors with which Emperor Domitian clipped the hair of St. John. The walls of Rome near the Appian gate showed the white spots left by the stones which turned to snowballs when hurled by the mob against St. Peter before his time was come. A church in Rome had the crucifix which leaned over to talk to St. Brigitta. Another had a coin paid to Judas for betraying our Lord. Its value had greatly increased, for now it was able to confer an indulgence of fourteen hundred years. The amount of indulgences to be obtained between the Lateran and St. Peter's was greater than that afforded by a pilgrimage to the Holy Land. Still another church in Rome possessed the twelve-foot beam on which Judas hanged himself. This, however, was not strictly a relic, and doubt was permitted as to its authenticity. In front of the Lateran were the *Scala Sancta*, twenty-eight stairs, supposedly those which once stood in

front of Pilate's palace. He who crawled up them on hands and knees, repeating a *Pater Noster* for each one, could thereby release a soul from purgatory. Above all, Rome had the entire bodies of St. Peter and St. Paul. They had been divided to distribute the benefits among the churches. The heads were in the Lateran, and one half of the body of each had been deposited in their respective churches. No city on earth was so plentifully supplied with holy relics, and no city on earth was so richly endowed with spiritual indulgences as Holy Rome.

### THE TRIP TO ROME

Luther felt himself to be highly privileged when an opportunity presented itself to make a trip to the Eternal City. A dispute had arisen in the Augustinian order calling for settlement by the pope. Two brothers were sent to the holy city to represent the chapter at Erfurt. One of the brothers was Martin Luther. This was in the year 1510.

The trip to Rome is very revealing of the character of Martin Luther. What he saw, and what he did not care to see, throw light upon him. He was not interested in the art of the Renaissance. Of course, the great treasures were not yet visible.

The piers for the new basilica of St. Peter's had only just been laid, and the Sistine Chapel was not yet completed. But the frescoes of Pinturicchio were in view and might have awakened his admiration had he not been more interested in a painting of the Virgin Mary attributed to Luke the Evangelist than in all the Madonnas of the Renaissance. Again, the ruins of antiquity evoked no enthusiasm but served only to point the moral that the city founded on fratricide and stained with the blood of martyrs had been overthrown by divine justice like the Tower of Babel.

Neither the Rome of the Renaissance nor the Rome of antiquity interested Luther so much as the Rome of the saints. The business of the order would not be too time-consuming to prevent taking advantage of the unusual opportunities to save his soul. Luther's mood was that of a pilgrim who at the first sight of the Eternal City cried, "Hail, holy Rome!" He would seek to appropriate for himself and his relatives all the enormous spiritual benefits available only there. He had but a month in which to do it. The time was strenuously spent. He must of course perform the daily devotions of the Augustinian cloister in which he was lodged, but there remained sufficient hours to enable him to say the general confession, to celebrate mass at sacred shrines, to visit the catacombs and the basilicas, to venerate the bones, the shrines, and every holy relic.

Disillusionments of various sorts set in at once. Some of them were irrelevant to his immediate problem but were concomitants in his total distress. On making his general confession he was dismayed by the incompetence of the confessor. The abysmal ignorance, frivolity, and levity of the Italian priests stupefied him. They could rattle through six or seven masses while he was saying one. And when he was only at the Gospel, they had finished and would say to him, *"Passa! Passa!"*—"Get a move on!" The same sort of thing Luther could have discovered in Germany if he had emerged from the cloister to visit mass priests, whose assignment it was to repeat a specified number of masses a day, not for communicants but in behalf of the dead. Such a practice lent itself to irreverence. Some of the Italian clergy, however, were flippantly unbelieving and would address the sacrament saying, "Bread art thou and bread thou wilt remain, and wine art thou and wine thou wilt remain." To a devout believer from the unsophisticated Northland such disclosures were truly shocking. They need not have made him despondent in regard to the validity of his own quest because the Church had long taught that the efficacy of the sacraments did not depend on the character of the ministrants.

By a like token the stories that came to Luther's ears of the immorality of the Roman clergy should not logically have undermined his faith in the capacity of Holy Rome to confer spiritual benefits. At the same time he was horrified to hear that if there were a hell Rome was built upon it. He need not have been a scandalmonger to know that the district of ill fame was frequented by ecclesiastics. He heard there were those who considered themselves virtuous because they confined themselves to women. The unsavory memory of Pope Alexander VI was still a stench. Catholic historians recognize candidly the scandal of the Renaissance popes, and the Catholic Reformation was as greatly concerned as the Protestant to eradicate such abuses.

Yet all these sorry disclosures did not shatter Luther's confidence in the genuine goodness of the faithful. The question was whether they had any superfluous merit which could be conveyed to him or to his family, and whether the merit was so attached to sacred places that visits would confer benefit. This was the point at which doubt overtook him. He was climbing Pilate's stairs on hands and knees repeating a *Pater Noster* for each one and kissing each step for good measure in the hope of delivering a soul from purgatory. Luther regretted that his own father and mother were not yet dead and in purgatory so that he might confer on them so signal a favor. Failing that, he had resolved to release Grandpa Heine. The stairs were climbed, the *Pater Nosters* were repeated, the steps were kissed. At the top Luther raised himself and exclaimed, not as legend would have it, "The just shall live by faith!"—he was not yet that far advanced. What he said was, "Who knows whether it is so?"

That was the truly disconcerting doubt. The priests might be guilty of levity and the popes of lechery—all this would not matter so long as the Church had valid means of grace. But if crawling up the very stairs on which Christ stood and repeating all the prescribed prayers would be of no avail, then another of the great grounds of hope had proved to be illusory. Luther commented that he had gone to Rome with onions and had returned with garlic.

*[Handwritten marginal and bottom notes:]*

*Questions Voiced*

*1. priest - levity*
*2. popes - lechery — not answer to forgiveness*
*3. holy grounds*

## CHAPTER THREE

# THE GOSPEL

 ETURNING from Rome, Luther came under new influences due to a change of residence. He was transferred from Erfurt to Wittenberg, where he was to pass the remainder of his days. In comparison with Erfurt, Wittenberg was but a village with a population of only 2,000 to 2,500. The whole length of the town was only nine tenths of a mile. Contemporaries variously described it as "the gem of Thuringia" and "a stinking sand dune." It was built on a sand belt and for that reason was called the White Hillock, *Witten-Berg.* Luther never rhapsodized over the place, and he addressed to it this ditty:

> Little land, little land,
> You are but a heap of sand.
> If I dig you, the soil is light;
> If I reap you, the yield is slight.

But as a matter of fact it was not unproductive. Grain, vegetables, and fruit abounded, and the near-by woods provided game. The river Elbe flowed on one side, and a moat surrounded the town on the other. Two brooks were introduced by wooden aqueducts through the walls on the upper side and flowed without a covering down the two main streets of the town until they united at the mill. Open sluggish water was at once convenient and offensive. Luther lived in the Augustinian cloister at the opposite end from the Castle Church.

The chief glory of the village was the university, the darling of the elector, Frederick the Wise, who sought in this newly founded academy to rival the prestige of the century-old University of Leipzig. The new foundation had not flourished according to hope, and the elector endeavored to secure better teachers by inviting the Augustinians and Franciscans to supply three new professors. One of them was Luther. This was in 1511.

By reason of the move he came to know well a man who was to exercise a determinative influence upon his development, the vicar of the Augustinian order, Johann von Staupitz.

No one better could have been found as a spiritual guide. The vicar knew all the cures prescribed by the schoolmen for spiritual ailments, and besides had a warm religious life of his own with a sympathetic appreciation of the distress of another. "If it had not been for Dr. Staupitz," said Luther, "I should have sunk in hell."

Luther's difficulties persisted. A precise delineation of their course eludes us. His tremors cannot be said to have mounted in unbroken crescendo to a single crisis. Rather he passed through a series of crises to a relative stability. The stages defy

WITTENBERG IN 1627

localization as to time, place, or logical sequence. Yet this is clear. Luther probed every resource of contemporary Catholicism for assuaging the anguish of a spirit alienated from God. He tried the way of good works and discovered that he could never do enough to save himself. He endeavored to avail himself of the merits of the saints and ended with a doubt, not a very serious or persistent doubt for the moment, but sufficient to destroy his assurance.

### THE FAILURE OF CONFESSION

He sought at the same time to explore other ways, and Catholicism had much more to offer. Salvation was never made to rest solely nor even primarily upon human achievement. The whole sacramental system of the Church was designed to mediate to man God's help and favor. Particularly the sacrament of penance afforded solace, not to saints but to sinners. This only was required of them, that they should confess all their wrongdoing and seek absolution. Luther endeavored unremittingly to avail himself of this signal mercy. Without confession, he testified, the Devil would have devoured him long ago. He confessed frequently, often daily, and for as long as six hours on a single occasion. Every sin in order to be absolved was to be confessed. Therefore the soul must be searched and the memory ransacked and the motives probed. As an aid the penitent ran through the seven deadly sins and the Ten Commandments. Luther would repeat a confession and, to be sure of including everything, would review his entire life until the confessor grew weary and exclaimed, "Man, God is not angry with you. You are angry with God. Don't you know that God commands you to hope?"

This assiduous confessing certainly succeeded in clearing up any major transgressions. The leftovers with which Luther kept trotting in appeared to Staupitz to be only the scruples of a sick soul. "Look here," said he, "if you expect Christ to forgive you, come in with something to forgive—parricide, blasphemy, adultery—instead of all these peccadilloes."

But Luther's question was not whether his sins were big or little, but whether they had been confessed. The great difficulty which he encountered was to be sure that everything had been recalled. He learned from experience the cleverness of memory in protecting the ego, and he was frightened when after six hours of confessing he could still go out and think of something else which had eluded his most conscientious scrutiny. Still more disconcerting was the discovery that some of man's misdemeanors are not even recognized, let alone remembered. Sinners often sin without compunction. Adam and Eve, after tasting of the fruit of the forbidden tree, went blithely for a walk in the cool of the day; and Jonah, after fleeing from the Lord's commission, slept soundly in the hold of the ship. Only when each was confronted by an accuser was there any consciousness of guilt. Frequently, too, when man is reproached he will still justify himself like Adam, who replied, "The woman whom thou gavest to be with me"—as if to say to God, "She tempted me; you gave her to me; you are to blame."

There is, according to Luther, something much more drastically wrong with man than any particular list of offenses which can be enumerated, confessed, and forgiven. The very nature of man is corrupt. The penitential system fails because it is directed to particular lapses. Luther had come to perceive that the entire man is in need of forgiveness. In the course of this quest he had wrought himself into a state of emotional disturbance passing the bounds of objectivity. When, then, his confessor said that he was magnifying his misdemeanors, Luther could only conclude that the consultant did not understand the case and that none of the proffered consolations was of any avail.

In consequence the most frightful insecurities beset him. Panic invaded his spirit. The conscience became so disquieted as to start and tremble at the stirring of a wind-blown leaf. The horror of nightmare gripped the soul, the dread of one waking in the dusk to look into the eyes of him who has come to take his life. The heavenly champions all withdrew; the fiend beckoned with leering summons to the impotent soul. These were the torments which Luther repeatedly testified were far worse than any physical ailment that he had ever endured.

His description tallies so well with a recognized type of mental malady that again one is tempted to wonder whether his disturbance should be regarded as arising from authentic religious difficulties or from gastric or glandular deficiencies. The question can better be faced when more data become available from other periods of his life. Suffice it for the moment to observe that no malady ever impaired his stupendous capacity for work; that the problems with which he wrestled were not imaginary but implicit in the religion on which he had been reared; that his emotional reactions were excessive, as he would himself recognize after emerging from a depression; that he did make headway in exhausting one by one the helps proffered by medieval religion.

*He tried all the avenues offered by medieval church*

He had arrived at a valid impasse. Sins to be forgiven must be confessed. To be confessed they must be recognized and remembered. If they are not recognized and remembered, they cannot be confessed. If they are not confessed, they cannot be forgiven. The only way out is to deny the premise. But that Luther was not yet ready to do. Staupitz at this point offered real help by seeking to divert his attention from individual sins to the nature of man. Luther later on formulated what he had learned by saying that the physician does not need to probe each pustule to know that the patient has smallpox, nor is the disease to be cured scab by scab. To focus on particular offenses is a counsel of despair. When Peter started to count the waves, he sank. The whole nature of man needs to be changed.

## THE MYSTIC LADDER

This was the insight of the mystics. Staupitz was a mystic. Although the mystics did not reject the penitential system, their way of salvation was essentially different, directed to man as a whole. Since man is weak, let him cease to strive; let him surrender himself to the being and the love of God.

The new life, they said, calls for a period of preparation which consists in overcoming all the assertiveness of the ego, all arrogance, pride, self-seeking, everything connected with the I, the me, and the my. Luther's very effort to achieve merit was a form of assertiveness. Instead of striving he must yield and sink himself in God. The end of the mystic way is the absorption of the creature in the creator, of the drop in the ocean, of the candle flame in the glare of the sun. The struggler overcomes his restlessness, ceases his battering, surrenders himself to the Everlasting, and in the abyss of Being finds his peace.

Luther tried this way. At times he was lifted up as if he were amid choirs of angels, but the sense of alienation would return. The mystics knew this too. They called it the dark night of the soul, the dryness, the withdrawing of the fire from under the pot until it no longer bubbles. They counseled waiting until exaltation would return. For Luther it did not return because the enmity between man and God is too great. For all his impotence, man is a rebel against his Maker.

The acuteness of Luther's distress arose from his sensitivity at once to all the difficulties by which man has ever been beset. Could he have taken them one at a time, each might the more readily have been assuaged. For those who are troubled by particular sins the Church offers forgiveness through the penitential system, but pardon is made contingent upon conditions which Luther found unattainable. For those too weak to meet the tests there is the mystic way of ceasing to strive and of losing oneself in the abyss of the Godhead. But Luther could not envisage God as an abyss hospitable to man the impure. God is holy, majestic, devastating, consuming.

Do you not know that God dwells in light inaccessible? We weak and ignorant creatures want to probe and understand the incomprehensible majesty of the unfathomable light of the wonder of God. We approach; we prepare ourselves to approach. What wonder then that his majesty overpowers us and shatters!

So acute had Luther's distress become that even the simplest helps of religion failed to bring him heartsease. Not even prayer could quiet his tremors; for when he was on his knees, the Tempter would come and say, "Dear fellow, what are you praying for? Just see how quiet it is about you here. Do you think that God hears your prayer and pays any attention?"

Staupitz tried to bring Luther to see that he was making religion altogether too difficult. There is just one thing needful, and that is to love God. This was another favorite counsel of the mystics, but the intended word of comfort pierced like an arrow. How could anyone love a God who is a consuming fire? The psalm says, "Serve the Lord with fear." Who, then, can love a God angry, judging, and damning? Who can love a Christ sitting on a rainbow, consigning the damned souls to the flames of hell? The mere sight of a crucifix was to Luther like a stroke of lightning. He would flee, then, from the angry

Son to the merciful Mother. He would appeal to the saints—twenty-one of them he had selected as his especial patrons, three for each day of the week. All to no avail, for of what use is any intercession if God remains angry?

The final and the most devastating doubt of all assailed the young man. Perhaps not even God himself is just. This misgiving arose in two forms, depending on the view of God's character and behavior. Basic to both is the view that God is too absolute to be conditioned by considerations of human justice. The late scholastics, among whom Luther had been trained, thought that God is so unconditioned that he is bound by no rules save those of his own making. He is under no obligation to confer reward on man's achievements, no matter how meritorious. Normally God may be expected to do so, but there is no positive certitude. For Luther this meant that God is capricious and man's fate is unpredictable. The second view was more disconcerting because it held that man's destiny is already determined, perhaps adversely. God is so absolute that nothing can be contingent. Man's fate has been decreed since the foundation of the world, and in large measure also man's character is already fixed. This view commended itself all the more to Luther because it had been espoused by the founder of his order, St. Augustine, who, following Paul, held that God has already chosen some vessels for honor and some for dishonor, regardless of their deserts. The lost are lost, do what they can; the saved are saved, do what they may. To those who think they are saved this is an unspeakable comfort, but to those who think they are damned it is a hideous torment.

Luther exclaimed:

Is it not against all natural reason that God out of his mere whim deserts men, hardens them, damns them, as if he delighted in sins and in such torments of the wretched for eternity, he who is said to be of such mercy and goodness? This appears iniquitous, cruel, and intolerable in God, by which very many have been offended in all ages. And who would not be? I was myself more than once driven to the very abyss of despair so that I wished I had never been created. Love God? I hated him!

The word of blasphemy had been spoken. And blasphemy is the supreme sin because it is an offense against the most exalted of all beings, God the majestic. Luther reported to Staupitz, and his answer was *"Ich verstehe es nicht!"*—"I don't understand it!" Was, then, Luther the only one in all the world who had been so plagued? Had Staupitz himself never experienced such trials? "No," said he, "but I think they are your meat and drink." Evidently he suspected Luther of thriving on his disturbances. The only word of reassurance he could give was a reminder that the blood of Christ was shed for the remission of sins. But Luther was too obsessed with the picture of Christ the avenger to be consoled with the thought of Christ the redeemer.

Staupitz then cast about for some effective cure for this tormented spirit. He recognized in him a man of moral earnestness, religious sensitivity, and unusual gifts. Why his difficulties should be so enormous and so persistent was baffling. Plainly argument and consolation did no good. Some other way must be found. One day under the pear tree in the garden of the Augustinian cloister—Luther always treasured that pear tree—the vicar informed Brother Martin that he should study for his doctor's degree, that he should undertake preaching and assume the chair of Bible at the university. Luther gasped, stammered out fifteen reasons why he could do nothing of the sort. The sum of it all was that so much work would kill him. "Quite all right," said Staupitz. "God has plenty of work for clever men to do in heaven."

Luther might well gasp, for the proposal of Staupitz was audacious if not reckless. A young man on the verge of a nervous collapse over religious problems was to be commissioned as a teacher, preacher, and counselor to sick souls. Staupitz was practically saying, "Physician, cure thyself by curing others." He must have felt that Luther was fundamentally sound and that if he was entrusted with the cure of souls he would be disposed for their sakes to turn from threats to promises, and some of the grace which he would claim for them might fall also to himself.

Staupitz knew likewise that Luther would be helped by the subject matter of his teaching. The chair designed for him was the one which Staupitz himself had occupied, the chair of Bible. One is tempted to surmise that he retired in order unobtrusively to drive this agonizing brother to wrestle with the source book of his religion. One may wonder why Luther had not thought of this himself. The reason is not that the Bible was inaccessible, but that Luther was following a prescribed course and the Bible was not the staple of theological education.

Yet anyone who seeks to discover the secret of Christianity is inevitably driven to the Bible, because Christianity is based on something which happened in the past, the incarnation of God in Christ at a definite point in history. The Bible records this event.

### THE EVANGELICAL EXPERIENCE

Luther set himself to learn and expound the Scriptures. On August 1, 1513, he commenced his lectures on the book of Psalms. In the fall of 1515 he was lecturing on St. Paul's Epistle to the Romans. The Epistle to the Galatians was treated throughout 1516-17. These studies proved to be for Luther the Damascus road. The third great religious crisis which resolved his turmoil was as the still small voice compared to the earthquake of the first upheaval in the thunderstorm at

LUTHER'S BIBLE

Stotternheim and the fire of the second tremor which consumed him at the saying of his first mass. No *coup de foudre*, no heavenly apparition, no religious ceremony, precipitated the third crisis. The place was no lonely road in a blinding storm, nor even the holy altar, but simply the study in the tower of the Augustinian monastery. The solution to Luther's problems came in the midst of the performance of the daily task.

His first lectures were on the book of Psalms. We must bear in mind his method of reading the Psalms and the Old Testament as a whole. For him, as for his time, it was a Christian book foreshadowing the life and death of the Redeemer.

The reference to Christ was unmistakable when he came to the twenty-second psalm, the first verse of which was recited by Christ as he expired upon the cross. "My God, my God, why hast thou forsaken me?" What could be the meaning of this? Christ evidently felt himself to be forsaken, abandoned by God, deserted. Christ too had *Anfechtungen*. The utter desolation which Luther said he could not endure for more than a tenth of an hour and live had been experienced by Christ himself as he died. Rejected of men, he was rejected also of God. How much worse this must have been than the scourging, the thorns, the nails! In the garden he sweat blood as he did not upon the cross. Christ's descent into hell was nothing other than this sense of alienation from God. Christ had suffered what Luther suffered, or rather Luther was finding himself in what Christ had suffered, even as Albrecht Dürer painted himself as the Man of Sorrows.

Why should Christ have known such desperation? Luther knew perfectly well why he himself had had them: he was weak in the presence of the Mighty; he was impure in the presence of the Holy; he had blasphemed the Divine Majesty. But Christ was not weak; Christ was not impure; Christ was not impious. Why then should he have been so overwhelmed with desolation? The only answer must be that Christ took to himself the iniquity of us all. He who was without sin for our sakes became sin and so identified himself with us as to participate in our alienation. He who was truly man so sensed his solidarity with humanity as to feel himself along with mankind estranged from the All Holy. What a new picture this is of Christ! Where, then, is the judge, sitting upon the rainbow to condemn sinners? He is still the judge. He must judge, as truth judges error and light darkness; but in judging he suffers with those whom he must condemn and feels himself with them subject to condemnation. The judge upon the rainbow has become the derelict upon the cross.

A new view also of God is here. The All Terrible is the All Merciful too. Wrath and love fuse upon the cross. The hideousness of sin cannot be denied or forgotten; but God, who desires not that a sinner should die but that he should turn and live, has found the reconciliation in the pangs of bitter death. It is not that the Son by his sacrifice has placated the irate Father; it is not primarily that the Master by his self-abandoning goodness has made up for our deficiency. It is that in some inexplicable way, in the utter desolation of the forsaken Christ, God was able to reconcile the world to himself. This does not mean that all the mystery is clear. God is still shrouded at times in thick darkness. There are almost two Gods, the inscrutable God whose ways are past finding out and the God made known to us in Christ. He is still a consuming fire, but he burns that he may purge and chasten and heal. He is not a God of idle whim, because the cross is not the last word. He who gave his Son unto death also raised him up and will raise us with him, if with him we die to sin that we may rise to newness of life.

Who can understand this? Philosophy is unequal to it. Only faith can grasp so high a mystery. This is the foolishness of the cross which is hid from the wise and prudent. Reason must retire. She cannot understand that "God hides his power in weakness, his wisdom in folly, his goodness in severity, his justice in sins, his mercy in anger."

How amazing that God in Christ should do all this; that the Most High, the Most Holy should be the All Loving too; that the ineffable Majesty should stoop to take upon himself our flesh, subject to hunger and cold, death and desperation. We see him lying in the feedbox of a donkey, laboring in a carpenter's shop, dying a derelict under the sins of the world. The gospel is not so much a miracle as a marvel, and every line is suffused with wonder.

What God first worked in Christ, that he must work also in us. If he who had done no wrong was forsaken on the cross, we who are truly alienated from God must suffer a deep hurt. We are not for that reason to upbraid, since the hurt is for our healing.

Repentance which is occupied with thoughts of peace is hypocrisy. There must be a great earnestness about it and a deep hurt if the old man is to be put off. When lightning strikes a tree or a man, it does two things at once—it rends the tree and swiftly slays the man. But it also turns the face of the dead man and the broken branches of the tree itself toward heaven. . . . We seek to be saved, and God in order that he may save rather damns. . . . They are damned who flee damnation, for Christ was of all the saints the most damned and forsaken.

The contemplation of the cross had convinced Luther that God is neither malicious nor capricious. If, like the Samaritan, God must first pour into our wounds the wine that smarts, it is that he may thereafter use the oil that soothes. But there still remains the problem of the justice of God. Wrath can melt into mercy, and God will be all the more the Christian God; but if justice be dissolved in leniency, how can he be the just God whom Scripture describes? The study of the apostle Paul proved at this point of inestimable value to Luther and at the same time confronted him with the final stumbling block because Paul unequivocally speaks of the justice of God. At the very expression Luther trembled. Yet he persisted in grappling with Paul, who plainly had agonized over precisely his problem and had found a solution. Light broke at last through the examination of exact shades of meaning in the Greek language. One understands why Luther could never join those who discarded the humanist tools of scholarship. In the Greek of the Pauline epistle the word "justice" has a double sense, rendered in English by "justice" and "justification." The former is a strict enforcement of the law, as when a judge pronounces the appropriate sentence. Justification is a process of the sort which sometimes takes place if the judge suspends the sentence, places the prisoner on parole, expresses confidence and personal interest in him, and thereby instills such resolve that the man is reclaimed and justice itself ultimately better conserved than by the exaction of a pound of flesh. Similarly the moral improvement issuing from the Christian experience of regeneration, even though it falls far short of perfection, yet can be regarded as a vindication of the justice of God.

But from here on any human analogy breaks down. God does not condition his forgiveness upon the expectation of future fulfillment. And man is not put right with God by any achievement, whether present or foreseen. On man's side the one requisite is faith, which means belief that God was in Christ seeking to save; trust that God will keep his promises; and commitment to his will and way. Faith is not an achievement. It is a gift. Yet it comes only through the hearing and study of the Word. In this respect Luther's own experience was made normative. For the whole process of being made new Luther took over from Paul the terminology of "justification by faith."

These are Luther's own words:

I greatly longed to understand Paul's Epistle to the Romans and nothing stood in the way but that one expression, "the justice of God," because I took it to mean that justice whereby God is just and deals justly in punishing the unjust. My situation was that, although an impeccable monk, I stood before God as a sinner troubled in conscience, and I had no confidence that my merit would assuage him. Therefore I did not love a just and angry God, but rather hated and murmured against him. Yet I clung to the dear Paul and had a great yearning to know what he meant.
Night and day I pondered until I saw the connection between the justice of God and the statement that "the just shall live by his faith." Then I grasped that the justice of God is that righteousness by which through grace and sheer mercy God justifies us through faith. Thereupon I felt myself to be reborn and to have gone through open doors into paradise. The whole of Scripture took on

a new meaning, and whereas before the "justice of God" had filled me with hate, now it became to me inexpressibly sweet in greater love. This passage of Paul became to me a gate to heaven. . . .

If you have a true faith that Christ is your Saviour, then at once you have a gracious God, for faith leads you in and opens up God's heart and will, that you should see pure grace and overflowing love. This it is to behold God in faith that you should look upon his fatherly, friendly heart, in which there is no anger nor ungraciousness. He who sees God as angry does not see him rightly but looks only on a curtain, as if a dark cloud had been drawn across his face.

Luther had come into a new view of Christ and a new view of God. He had come to love the suffering Redeemer and the God unveiled on Calvary. But were they after all powerful enough to deliver him from all the hosts of hell? The cross had resolved the conflict between the wrath and the mercy of God, and Paul had reconciled for him the inconsistency of the justice and the forgiveness of God, but what of the conflict between God and the Devil? Is God lord of all, or is he himself impeded by demonic hordes? Such questions a few years ago would have seemed to modern man but relics of medievalism, and fear of demons was dispelled simply by denying their existence. Today so much of the sinister has engulfed us that we are prone to wonder whether perhaps there may not be malignant forces in the heavenly places. All those who have known the torments of mental disorder well understand the imagery of satanic hands clutching to pull them to their doom. Luther's answer was not scientific but religious. He did not dissipate the demons by turning on an electric light, because for him they had long ago been routed when the veil of the temple was rent and the earth quaked and darkness descended upon the face of the land. Christ in his utter anguish had fused the wrath and the mercy of God, and put to flight all the legions of Satan.

In Luther's hymns one hears the tramp of marshaled hordes, the shouts of battle, and the triumph song.

> In devil's dungeon chained I lay
> > The pangs of death swept o'er me.
> My sin devoured me night and day
> > In which my mother bore me.
> My anguish ever grew more rife,
> I took no pleasure in my life
> > And sin had made me crazy.

> Then was the Father troubled sore
> > To see me ever languish.
> The Everlasting Pity swore
> > To save me from my anguish.

He turned to me his father heart
And chose himself a bitter part,
   His Dearest did it cost him.

Thus spoke the Son, "Hold thou to me,
   From now on thou wilt make it.
I gave my very life for thee
   And for thee I will stake it.
For I am thine and thou art mine,
And where I am our lives entwine,
   The Old Fiend cannot shake it."

CHAPTER FOUR

# THE ONSLAUGHT

 UTHER'S new insights contained already the marrow of his mature theology. The salient ideas were present in the lectures on Psalms and Romans from 1513 to 1516. What came after was but commentary and sharpening to obviate misconstruction. The center about which all the petals clustered was the affirmation of the forgiveness of sins through the *concise gospel* utterly unmerited grace of God made possible by the cross of Christ, which reconciled wrath and mercy, routed the hosts of hell, triumphed over sin and death, and by the resurrection manifested that power which enables man to die to sin and rise to newness of life. This was of course the theology of Paul, heightened, intensified, and clarified. Beyond these cardinal tenets Luther was never to go.

His development lay rather on the positive side in the drawing of practical inferences for his theory of the sacraments and the Church, and on the negative side by way of discovering discrepancies from contemporary Catholicism. At the start Luther envisaged no reform other than that of theological education with the stress on the Bible rather than on the decretals and the scholastics. Not that he was indifferent to the evils of the Church! In his notes for the lectures on Romans he lashed out repeatedly against the luxury, avarice, ignorance, and greed of the clergy and upbraided explicitly the chicanery of that warrior-pope Julius II. Yet whether these strictures were ever actually delivered is doubtful; for no record of them appears in the student notes on the lectures.

Luther was, in fact, less impelled to voice a protest against immoral abuses in the Church than were some of his contemporaries.

For one reason he was too busy. In October, 1516, he wrote to a friend:

I could use two secretaries. I do almost nothing during the day but write letters. I am a conventual preacher, reader at meals,

FREDERICK THE WISE ADORING THE VIRGIN AND CHILD

parochial preacher, director of studies, overseer of eleven monasteries, superintendent of the fish pond at Litzkau, referee of the
squabble at Torgau, lecturer on Paul, collector of material for a
commentary on the Psalms, and then, as I said, I am overwhelmed
with letters. I rarely have full time for the canonical hours and
for saying mass, not to mention my own temptations with the
world, the flesh, and the Devil. You see how lazy I am.

But out of just such labors arose his activities as a reformer.

As a parish priest in a village church he was responsible for
the spiritual welfare of his flock. They were procuring indulgences as he had once done himself. Rome was not the
only place in which such favors were available, for the popes
delegated to many churches in Christendom the privilege of
dispensing indulgences, and the Castle Church at Wittenberg
was the recipient of a very unusual concession granting full
remission of all sins. The day selected for the proclamation
was the first of November, the day of All Saints, whose merits
provided the ground of the indulgences and whose relics were
then on display. Frederick the Wise, the elector of Saxony,
Luther's prince, was a man of simple and sincere piety who
had devoted a lifetime to making Wittenberg the Rome of
Germany as a depository of sacred relics. He had made a
journey to all parts of Europe, and diplomatic negotiations
were facilitated by an exchange of relics. The king of Denmark, for example, sent him fragments of King Canute and
St. Brigitta.

The collection had as its nucleus a genuine thorn from the
crown of Christ, certified to have pierced the Saviour's brow.
Frederick so built up the collection from this inherited treasure that the catalogue illustrated by Lucas Cranach in 1509
listed 5,005 particles, to which were attached indulgences
calculated to reduce purgatory by 1,443 years. The collection
included one tooth of St. Jerome, of St. Chrysostom four pieces,
of St. Bernard six, and of St. Augustine four; of Our Lady
four hairs, three pieces of her cloak, four from her girdle, and
seven from the veil sprinkled with the blood of Christ. The
relics of Christ included one piece from his swaddling clothes,
thirteen from his crib, one wisp of straw, one piece of the
gold brought by the Wise Men and three of the myrrh, one
strand of Jesus' beard, one of the nails driven into his hands,
one piece of bread eaten at the Last Supper, one piece of
the stone on which Jesus stood to ascend into heaven, and
one twig of Moses' burning bush. By 1520 the collection had
mounted to 19,013 holy bones. Those who viewed these relics
on the designated day and made the stipulated contributions
might receive from the pope indulgences for the reduction of
purgatory, either for themselves or others, to the extent of
1,902,202 years and 270 days. These were the treasures made
available on the day of All Saints.

Three times during his sermons of the year 1516 Luther spoke critically of these indulgences. The third of these occasions was Halloween, the eve of All Saints. Luther spoke moderately and without certainty on all points. But on some he was perfectly assured. No one, he declared, can know whether the remission of sins is complete, because complete remission is granted only to those who exhibit worthy contrition and confession, and no one can know whether contrition and confession are perfectly worthy. To assert that the pope can deliver souls from purgatory is audacious. If he can do so, then he is cruel not to release them all. But if he possesses this ability, he is in a position to do more for the dead than for the living. The purchasing of indulgences in any case is highly dangerous and likely to induce complacency. Indulgences can remit only those private satisfactions imposed by the Church, and may easily militate against interior penance, which consists in true contrition, true confession, and true satisfaction in spirit.

Luther records that the elector took this sermon amiss. Well he might, because indulgences served not merely to dispense the merits of the saints but also to raise revenues. They were

the bingo of the sixteenth century. The practice grew out of the crusades. At first indulgences were conferred on those who sacrificed or risked their lives in fighting against the infidel, and then were extended to those who, unable to go to the Holy Land, made contributions to the enterprise. The device proved so lucrative that it was speedily extended to cover the construction of churches, monasteries, and hospitals. The gothic cathedrals were financed in this way. Frederick the Wise was using an indulgence to reconstruct a bridge across the

Elbe. Indulgences, to be sure, had not degenerated into sheer mercenariness. Conscientious preachers sought to evoke a sense of sin, and presumably only those genuinely concerned made the purchases. Nevertheless, the Church today readily concedes that the indulgence traffic was a scandal, so much so that a contemporary preacher phrased the requisites as three: contrition, confession, and contribution.

A cartoon by Holbein makes the point that the handing over of the indulgence letter was so timed as not to anticipate the dropping of the money into the coffer. We see in this cartoon a chamber with the pope enthroned. He is probably Leo X because the arms of the Medici appear frequently about the walls. The pope is handing a letter of indulgence to a kneeling Dominican. In the choir stalls on either side are seated a number of church dignitaries. On the right one of them lays his hand upon the head of a kneeling youth and with a stick points to a large ironbound chest for the contributions, into which a woman is dropping her mite. At the table on the left various Dominicans are preparing and dispensing indulgences. One of them repulses a beggar who has nothing to give in exchange, while another is carefully check-

ing the money and withholding the indulgences until the full amount has been received. In contrast he shows on the left the true repentence of David, Manasseh, and a notorious sinner, who address themselves only to God.

The indulgences dispensed at Wittenberg served to support the Castle Church and the university. Luther's attack, in other words, struck at the revenue of his own institution. This first blow was certainly not the rebellion of an exploited German against the mulcting of his country by the greedy Italian

papacy. However much in after years Luther's followers may
have been motivated by such considerations, his first onslaught
was not so prompted. He was a priest responsible for the
eternal welfare of his parishioners. He must warn them against
spiritual pitfalls, no matter what might happen to the Castle
Church and the university.

## THE INDULGENCE FOR ST. PETER'S

In 1517, the year following, his attention was called to
another instance of the indulgence traffic fraught with far-
reaching ramifications. The affair rose out of the pretensions
of the house of Hohenzollern to control the ecclesiastical and
civil life of Germany. An accumulation of ecclesiastical bene-
fices in one family was an excellent expedient, because every
bishop controlled vast revenues, and some bishops were princes
besides. Albert of Brandenburg, of the house of Hohenzollern,
when not old enough to be a bishop at all, held already the
sees of Halberstadt and Magdeburg, and aspired to the arch-
bishopric of Mainz, which would make him the primate of
Germany.

He knew that he would have to pay well for his office. The
installation fee was ten thousand ducats, and the parish could
not afford it, being already depleted through the deaths of
three archbishops in a decade. One of them apologized for
dying after an incumbency of only four years, thereby so soon
involving his flock in the fee for his successor. The diocese
offered the post to Albert if he would discharge the fee himself. He realized that he would have to pay the pope in addition for the irregularity of holding three sees at once and probably still more to counteract the pressures of the rival house
of Hapsburg on the papacy.

Yet Albert was confident that money would speak, because
the pope needed it so badly. The pontiff at the moment was
Leo X, of the house of Medici, as elegant and as indolent as
a Persian cat. His chief pre-eminence lay in his ability to
squander the resources of the Holy See on carnivals, war,
gambling, and the chase. The duties of his holy office were
seldom suffered to interfere with sport. He wore long hunting
boots which impeded the kissing of his toe. The resources of
three papacies were dissipated by his profligacy: the goods
of his predecessors, himself, and his successor. The Catholic
historian Ludwig von Pastor declared that the ascent of this
man in an hour of crisis to the chair of St. Peter, "a man who
scarcely so much as understood the obligations of his high
office, was one of the most severe trials to which God ever
subjected his Church."

Leo at the moment was particularly in need of funds
to complete a project commenced by his predecessor,

the building of the new St.
Peter's. The old wooden basilica, constructed in the age
of Constantine, had been
condemned, and the titanic
Pope Julius II had overawed
the consistory into approv-
ing the grandiose scheme of
throwing a dome as large as
the Pantheon over the re-
mains of the apostles Peter
and Paul. The piers were laid;
Julius died; the work lagged;
weeds sprouted from the pillars; Leo took over; he needed
money.

The negotiations of Albert
with the pope were conducted
through the mediation of the
German banking house of
Fugger, which had a monop-

ALBERT OF BRANDENBURG

oly on papal finances in Germany. When the Church needed
funds in advance of her revenues, she borrowed at usurious
rates from the sixteenth-century Rothschilds or Morgans.
Indulgences were issued in order to repay the debts, and the
Fuggers supervised the collection.

Knowing the role they would ultimately play, Albert turned
to them for the initial negotiations. He was informed that the
pope demanded twelve thousand ducats for the twelve apostles.
Albert offered seven thousand for the seven deadly sins. They
compromised on ten thousand, presumably not for the Ten
Commandments. Albert had to pay the money down before he
could secure his appointment, and he borrowed the sum from
the Fuggers.

Then the pope, to enable Albert to reimburse himself,
granted the privilege of dispensing an indulgence in his territories for the period of eight years. One half of the return,
in addition to the ten thousand ducats already paid, should
go to the pope for the building of the new St. Peter's; the
other half should go to reimburse the Fuggers.

These indulgences were not actually offered in Luther's
parish because the Church could not introduce an indulgence
without the consent of the civil authorities, and Frederick
the Wise would not grant permission in his lands because he
did not wish the indulgence of St. Peter to encroach upon
the indulgences of All Saints at Wittenberg. Consequently
the vendors did not enter electoral Saxony, but they came
close enough so that Luther's parishioners could go over the
border and return with the most amazing concessions.

In briefing the vendors Albert reached the pinnacle of pretensions as to the spiritual benefits to be conferred by indulgences. He made no reference whatever to the repayment of his debt to the Fuggers. The instructions declared that a plenary indulgence had been issued by His Holiness Pope Leo X to defray the expenses of remedying the sad state of the blessed apostles Peter and Paul and the innumerable martyrs and saints whose bones lay moldering, subject to constant desecration from rain and hail. Subscribers would enjoy a plenary and perfect remission of all sins. They would be restored to the state of innocence which they enjoyed in baptism and would be relieved of all the pains of purgatory, including those incurred by an offense to the Divine Majesty. Those securing indulgences on behalf of the dead already in purgatory need not themselves be contrite and confess their sins.

Then let the cross of Christ, continued the instructions, and the arms of the pope be planted at preaching stations that all might contribute according to their capacity. Kings and queens, archbishops and bishops, and other great princes were expected to give twenty-five gold florins. Abbots, cathedral prelates, counts, barons, and other great nobles and their wives were put down for twenty. Other prelates and lower nobility should give six. The rate for burghers and

HAWKING INDULGENCES

*So much money is going into the coffer of the vendor that new coins have to be minted on the spot.*

merchants was three. For those more moderately circumstanced, one.

And since we are concerned for the salvation of souls quite as much as for the construction of this building, none shall be turned empty away. The very poor may contribute by prayers and fastings, for the Kingdom of Heaven belongs not only to the rich but also to the poor.

The proclamation of this indulgence was entrusted to the Dominican Tetzel, an experienced vendor. As he approached a town, he was met by the dignitaries, who then entered with him in solemn procession. A cross bearing the papal arms preceded him, and the pope's bull of indulgence was borne aloft on a gold-embroidered velvet cushion. The cross was solemnly planted in the market place, and the sermon began.

*Pagentry*

Listen now, God and St. Peter call you. Consider the salvation of your souls and those of your loved ones departed. You priest, you noble, you merchant, you virgin, you matron, you youth, you old man, enter now into your church, which is the Church of St. Peter. Visit the most holy cross erected before you and ever imploring you. Have you considered that you are lashed in a furious tempest amid the temptations and dangers of the world, and that you do not know whether you can reach the haven, not of your mortal body, but of your immortal soul? Consider that all who are contrite and have confessed and made contribution

THE VENDOR

will receive complete remission of all their sins. Listen to the voices of your dear dead relatives and friends, beseeching you and saying, "Pity us, pity us. We are in dire torment from which you can redeem us for a pittance." Do you not wish to? Open your ears. Hear the father saying to his son, the mother to her daughter, "We bore you, nourished you, brought you up, left you our fortunes, and you are so cruel and hard that now you are not willing for so little to set us free. Will you let us lie here in flames? Will you delay our promised glory?"

Remember that you are able to release them, for

> As soon as the coin in the coffer rings,
> The soul from purgatory springs.

Will you not then for a quarter of a florin receive these letters of indulgence through which you are able to lead a divine and immortal soul into the fatherland of paradise?

Such harangues were not being delivered in Wittenberg because of the prohibition of Frederick the Wise, but Tetzel was just over the border, not too far away for Luther's parishioners to make the journey and return with the pardons. They even reported Tetzel to have said that papal indulgences could absolve a man who had violated the Mother of God, and that the cross emblazoned with the papal arms set up by the indulgence sellers was equal to the cross of Christ. A cartoon published somewhat later by one of Luther's followers showed the cross in the center empty of all save the nail holes and the crown of thorns. More prominent beside it stood the papal arms with the balls of the Medici, while in the foreground the vendor hawked his wares.

## THE NINETY-FIVE THESES

This was too much. Again on the eve of All Saints, when Frederick the Wise would offer his indulgences, Luther spoke, this time in writing, by posting in accord with current practice on the door of the Castle Church a printed placard in the Latin language consisting of ninety-five theses for debate. Presumably at the time Luther did not know all the sordid details of Albert's transaction. He must have known that Albert would get half the returns, but he directed his attack solely against Tetzel's reputed sermon and Albert's printed instructions, which marked the apex of unbridled pretensions as to the efficacy of indulgences. Sixtus IV in 1476 had promised immediate release to souls in purgatory. Tetzel's jingle thus rested on papal authority. And Leo X in 1513 had promised crusaders plenary remission of all sins and reconciliation with the Most High. Albert assembled the previous pretensions and in addition dispensed explicitly with contrition on the part of those who purchased on behalf of the dead in purgatory.

Luther's *Theses* differed from the ordinary propositions for debate because they were forged in anger. The ninety-five affirmations are crisp, bold, unqualified. In the ensuing discussion he explained his meaning more fully. The following summary draws alike on the *Theses* and the subsequent explications. There were three main points: an objection to the avowed object of the expenditure, a denial of the powers of the pope over purgatory, and a consideration of the welfare of the sinner.

The attack focused first on the ostensible intent to spend the money in order to shelter the bones of St. Peter beneath a universal shrine of Christendom. Luther retorted:

THE CASTLE CHURCH

The revenues of all Christendom are being sucked into this insatiable basilica. The Germans laugh at calling this the common treasure of Christendom. Before long all the churches, palaces, walls, and bridges of Rome will be built out of our money. First of all we should rear living temples, not local churches, and only last of all St. Peter's, which is not necessary for us. We Germans cannot attend St. Peter's. Better that it should never be built than that our parochial churches should be despoiled. The pope would do better to appoint one good pastor to a church than to confer indulgences upon them all. Why doesn't the pope build the basilica of St. Peter out of his own money? He is richer than Croesus. He would do better to sell St. Peter's and give the money to the poor folk who are being fleeced by the hawkers of indulgences. If the pope knew the exactions of these vendors, he would rather that St. Peter's should lie in ashes than that it should be built out of the blood and hide of his sheep.

This polemic would evoke a deep *Ja wohl* among the Germans, who for some time had been suffering from a sense of grievance against the venality of the Italian *curia* and often quite overlooked the venality of the German confederates. Luther lent himself to this distortion by accepting Albert's picture of the money going all to Rome rather than to the coffers of the Fuggers. Yet in a sense Albert's picture was right. He was only being reimbursed for money which had already gone to Rome. In any case, however, the financial aspect was the least in Luther's eyes. He was ready to undercut the entire practice even though not a gulden left Wittenberg.

His second point denied the power of the pope over purgatory for the remission of either sin or penalty. The absolution of sin is given to the contrite in the sacrament of penance.

Papal indulgences do not remove guilt. Beware of those who say that indulgences effect reconciliation with God. The power of the keys cannot make attrition into contrition. He who is contrite has plenary remission of guilt and penalty without indulgences. The pope can remove only those penalties which he himself has imposed on earth, for Christ did not say, "Whatsoever I have bound in heaven you may loose on earth."

*Pope does not have the transfer powers*

The penalties of purgatory the pope cannot reduce because these have been imposed by God, and the pope does not have at his disposal a treasury of credits available for transfer.

The saints have no extra credits. Every saint is bound to love God to the utmost. There is no such thing as supererogation. If there were any superfluous credits, they could not be stored up for subsequent use. The Holy Spirit would have used them fully long ago. Christ indeed had merits, but until I am better instructed I deny that they are indulgences. His merits are freely available without the keys of the pope.

Therefore I claim that the pope has no jurisdiction over purgatory. I am willing to reverse this judgment if the Church so pronounces. If the

FORGIVENESS FROM CHRIST
OUTWEIGHS INDULGENCES
FROM THE POPE

pope does have the power to release anyone from purgatory, why in the name of love does he not abolish purgatory by letting everyone out? If for the sake of miserable money he released uncounted souls, why should he not for the sake of most holy love empty the place? To say that souls are liberated from purgatory is audacious. To say they are released as soon as the coin in the coffer rings is to incite avarice. The pope would do better to give away everything without charge. The only power which the pope has over purgatory is that of making intercession on behalf of souls, and this power is exercised by any priest or curate in his parish.

Luther's attack thus far could in no sense be regarded as heretical or original. Even though Albert's instructions rested on papal bulls, there had as yet been no definitive pronouncement, and many theologians would have endorsed Luther's claims.

But he had a more devastating word:

*Danger of indulgence*

Indulgences are positively harmful to the recipient because they impede salvation by diverting charity and inducing a false sense of security. Christians should be taught that he who gives to the poor is better than he who receives a pardon. He who spends his money for indulgences instead of relieving want receives not the indulgence of the pope but the indignation of God. We are told that money should be given by preference to the poor only in the case of extreme necessity. I suppose we are not to clothe the naked and visit the sick. What is extreme necessity? Why, I ask, does natural humanity have such goodness that it gives itself freely and does not calculate necessity but is rather solicitous that there should not be any necessity? And will the charity of God, which is incomparably kinder, do none of these things? Did Christ say, "Let him that has a cloak sell it and buy an indulgence"? Love covers a multitude of sins and is better than all the pardons of Jerusalem and Rome.

Indulgences are most pernicious because they induce complacency and thereby imperil salvation. Those persons are damned who think that letters of indulgence make them certain of salvation. God works by contraries so that a man feels himself to be lost in the very moment when he is on the point of being saved. When God is about to justify a man, he damns him. Whom he would make alive he must first kill. God's favor is so communicated in the form of wrath that it seems farthest when it is at hand. Man must first cry out that there is no health in him. He must be consumed with horror. This is the pain of purgatory. I do not know where it is located, but I do know that it can be experienced in this life. I know a man who has gone through such pains that had they lasted for one tenth of an hour he would have been reduced to ashes. In this disturbance salvation begins. When a man believes himself to be utterly lost, light breaks. Peace comes in the word of Christ through faith. He who does not have this is lost even though he be absolved a million times by the pope, and he who does have it may not wish to be released from purgatory, for true contrition seeks penalty. Christians should be encouraged to bear the cross. He who is baptized into Christ must be as a sheep for the slaughter. The merits of Christ are vastly more potent when they bring crosses than when they bring remissions.

Luther's *Ninety-Five Theses* ranged all the way from the complaints of aggrieved Germans to the cries of a wrestler in the night watches. One portion demanded financial relief, the other called for the crucifixion of the self. The masses could grasp the first. Only a few elect spirits would ever comprehend the full import of the second, and yet in the second lay all the power to create a popular revolution. Complaints of financial extortion had been voiced for over a century without visible effect. Men were stirred to deeds only by one who regarded indulgences not merely as venal but as blasphemy against the holiness and mercy of God.

Luther took no steps to spread his theses among the people. He was merely inviting scholars to dispute and dignitaries to define, but others surreptitiously translated the theses into German and gave them to the press. In short order they became the talk of Germany. What Karl Barth said of his own unexpected emergence as a reformer could be said equally of Luther, that he was like a man climbing in the darkness a winding staircase in the steeple of an ancient cathedral. In the blackness he reached out to steady himself, and his hand laid hold of a rope. He was startled to hear the clanging of a bell.

## CHAPTER FIVE

# THE SON OF INIQUITY

ENERAL dissemination was not in Luther's mind when he posted the theses. He meant them for those concerned. A copy was sent to Albert of Mainz along with the following letter:

Father in Christ and Most Illustrious Prince, forgive me that I, the scum of the earth, should dare to approach Your Sublimity. The Lord Jesus is my witness that I am well aware of my insignificance and my unworthiness. I make so bold because of the office of fidelity which I owe to Your Paternity. May Your Highness look upon this speck of dust and hear my plea for clemency from you and from the pope.

Luther then reports what he had heard about Tetzel's preaching that through indulgences men are promised remission, not only of penalty but also of guilt.

God on high, is this the way the souls entrusted to your care are prepared for death? It is high time that you looked into this matter. I can be silent no longer. In fear and trembling we must work out our salvation. Indulgences can offer no security but only the remission of external canonical penalties. Works of piety and charity are infinitely better than indulgences. Christ did not command the preaching of indulgences but of the gospel, and what a horror it is, what a peril to a bishop, if he never gives the gospel to his people except along with the racket of indulgences. In the instructions of Your Paternity to the indulgence sellers, issued without your knowledge and consent [Luther offers him a way out], indulgences are called the inestimable gift of God for the reconciliation of man to God and the emptying of purgatory. Contrition is declared to be unnecessary. What shall I do, Illustrious Prince, if not to beseech Your Paternity through Jesus Christ our Lord to suppress utterly these instructions lest someone arise to confute this book and to bring Your Illustrious Sublimity into obloquy, which I dread but fear if something is not done speedily? May Your Paternity accept my faithful admonition. I, too, am one of your sheep. May the Lord Jesus guard you forever. Amen.

WITTENBERG, 1517, on the eve of All Saints

If you will look over my theses, you will see how dubious is the doctrine of indulgences, which is so confidently proclaimed.

MARTIN LUTHER, Augustinian Doctor of Theology

Albert forwarded the theses to Rome. Pope Leo is credited with two comments. In all likelihood neither is authentic, yet each is revealing. The first was this: "Luther is a drunken German. He will feel different when he is sober." And the second: "Friar Martin is a brilliant chap. The whole row is due to the envy of the monks."

Both comments, wherever they originated, contain a measure of truth. If Luther was not a drunken German who would feel different when sober, he was an irate German who might be amenable if mollified. If at once the pope had issued the bull of a year later, clearly defining the doctrine of indulgences and correcting the most glaring abuses, Luther might have subsided. On many points he was not yet fully persuaded in his own mind, and he was prompted by no itch for controversy. Repeatedly he was ready to withdraw if his opponents would abandon the fray. During the four years while his case was pending his letters reveal surprisingly little preoccupation with the public dispute. He was engrossed in his duties as a professor and a parish priest, and much more concerned to find a suitable incumbent for the chair of Hebrew at the University of Wittenberg than to knock a layer from the papal tiara. Prompt and straightforward action might have allayed the outburst.

But the pope preferred to extinguish the friar with a clandestine snuffer and appointed a new general of the Augustinians that he might "quench a monk of his order, Martin Luther by name, and thus smother the fire before it should become a conflagration." The first opportunity came the next May at the regular triennial gathering of the chapter, meeting in that year at Heidelberg. Luther was scheduled to report on the completion of his term as vicar and was likewise to defend the theology of the father of the order, St. Augustine, concerning human depravity. The question of indulgences was not on the docket, but the Augustinian theology had provided the ground for Luther's attack.

He had reason to fear the occasion. Warnings of danger came from many sources. His enemies were boasting, some that he would be burned within a month, some within two weeks. He was warned of the possibility of assassination on the road to Heidelberg. "Nevertheless," wrote Luther, "I will obey. I am going on foot. Our Prince [Frederick the Wise] quite unsolicited has undertaken to see that under no circum-

stances I shall be taken to Rome." Yet as a precaution Luther
traveled incognito. After four days of tramping he wrote back,
"I am properly contrite for going on foot. Since my contrition is perfect, full penance has already been done, and no indulgence is needed."

To his amazement he was received at Heidelberg as a guest
of honor. The Count Palatine invited him, along with Staupitz
and others, to dinner and personally conducted them on a tour
to see the ornaments of the chapel and the armor. Before the
chapter Luther defended the Augustinian view that even outwardly upright acts may be mortal sins in the eyes of God.

"If the peasants heard you say that, they would stone you,"
was the frank comment of one hearer, but the company roared.
Acrimonious letters against Luther were presented before the
chapter, but there were no repercussions. The older men did
no more than shake their heads, and the younger were enthusiastic. "I have great hope," Luther said, "that as Christ,
when rejected by the Jews, went over to the Gentiles, so this
true theology, rejected by opinionated old men, will pass over
to the younger generation." Among those young men were
several later to be prominent as leaders in the Lutheran movement. There were John Brenz, the reformer of Wuerttemburg,
and Martin Bucer, the leader at Strassburg. He was a Dominican who was permitted to attend the public session. "Luther,"
he reported, "has a marvelous graciousness in response and
unconquerable patience in listening. In argument he shows the
acumen of the apostle Paul. That which Erasmus insinuates
he speaks openly and freely."

Far from being shunned by the brothers Luther was invited
to ride home with the Nürnberg delegation until their ways
diverged. Then he was transferred to the wagon of the Er-
furters, where he found himself beside his old teacher, Dr.
Usingen. "I talked with him," said Luther, "and tried to
persuade him, but I do not know with what success. I left him
pensive and dazed." On the whole Luther felt that he was returning from a triumph. He summed it all up with the comment, "I went on foot. I came back in a wagon."

### THE DOMINICAN ASSAULT

The Augustinians were conceivably the more loath to suppress their obstreperous brother because their rivals, the
Dominicans, were pressing him hard. This is the truth of the
second comment attributed to Pope Leo. The Dominicans
rallied to the aid of Tetzel, who was granted a doctor's degree
that he might be in a position to publish. At his promotion he
roundly defended the jingle,

> As soon as the coin in the coffer rings,
> The soul from purgatory springs.

His theses were printed. The students at Wittenberg by theft or purchase collected eight hundred copies and, unbeknown to the elector, the university, or to Luther, committed them to a bonfire. Luther was highly embarrassed by their impetuosity. To Tetzel he did not deign a reply.

But he did feel constrained to declare himself more fully to the general public. The *Ninety-Five Theses* had been given by the printer to all Germany, though intended only for professional theologians. The many bald assertions called for explanation and clarification, but Luther could never confine himself to a mere reproduction or explication of what he had said previously. The sermons written out by request on Monday do not correspond to the notes taken by hearers on Sunday. Ideas were so churning within him that new butter always came out of the vat. The *Resolutions Concerning the Ninety-Five Theses* contain some new points. Luther had made the discovery that the biblical text from the Latin Vulgate, used to support the sacrament of penance, was a mistranslation. The Latin for Matt. 4:17 read *penitentiam agite,* "do penance," but from the Greek New Testament of Erasmus, Luther had learned that the original meant simply "be penitent." The literal sense was "change your mind." "Fortified with this passage," wrote Luther to Staupitz in the dedication of the *Resolutions,* "I venture to say they are wrong who make more of the act in Latin than of the change of heart in Greek." This was what Luther himself called a "glowing" discovery. In this crucial instance a sacrament of the Church did not rest on the institution of Scripture.

In a very casual way Luther threw off another remark for which he was to be severely pressed. "Suppose," said he, "that the Roman Church were as once it was before the days of Gregory I, when it was not above the other churches, at least not above the Greek." This was to say that the primacy of the Roman Church was a historical development due rather to the exigencies of history than to divine ordination reaching back to the very founding of the Church.

Declarations of such sweeping import soon raised the controversy far above a mere strife of the orders, and every fresh stage served to elicit the radicalism implicit in Luther's presuppositions. He was soon prompted to deny not only the pope's power to release from, but also his ability to consign to, purgatory. Hearing that he was under the ban, Luther had the temerity to preach on the ban, declaring, according to the reports of hostile hearers, that excommunication and reconciliation affect only the external fellowship of the Church on earth and not the grace of God. Bishops are impious who excommunicate over money matters, and they should be disobeyed. These alleged statements were printed by opponents and shown at the imperial diet to the papal legates, who were

rumored to have sent them to Rome. Luther was informed
that they had done him inestimable damage. To put himself
in the clear he wrote out for the press what he could remember
of the sermon, but his attempt to conciliate was hardly felicitous. If Mother Church errs in her censures, said he, we
should still honor her as Christ honored Caiaphas, Annas, and
Pilate. Excommunications apply only to the outward communion of the sacraments, to burial, and to public prayers.
The ban does not commit a man to the Devil unless he is
already consigned. Only God can sever spiritual communion.
No creature can separate us from the love of Christ. We need
not fear to die in a state of excommunication. If the sentence
is just, the condemned man, if contrite, can still be saved; and
if it is unjust, he is blessed.

The printed sermon was not off the press until the end
of August. In the meantime the more provocative version of
his critics took effect. The pope would no longer dally. From
the unco-operative Augustinians he turned to the Dominicans. Sylvester Prierias, of the Order of St. Dominic, Master
of the Sacred Palace at Rome, was commissioned to draft a
reply to Luther. He produced it in short order. The opening
paragraph shifted the focus from indulgences to the ban and
the prerogatives of the pope. Prierias declared that the universal Church is virtually the Roman Church. The Roman
Church consists representatively in the cardinals, but virtually
in the pope. Just as the universal Church cannot err on faith
and morals, nor can a true council, neither can the Roman
Church nor the pope when speaking in his official capacity.
Whoever does not accept the doctrine of the Roman Church
and of the Roman pontiff as the infallible rule of faith from
which sacred Scripture derives strength and authority is a
heretic, and he who declares that in the matter of indulgences
the Roman Church cannot do what actually it does is a heretic.
Then Prierias proceeded to refute Luther's errors, describing
him on the way as a leper with a brain of brass and a nose of
iron.

Luther retorted:

I am sorry now that I despised Tetzel. Ridiculous as he was, he
was more acute than you. You cite no Scripture. You give no reasons. Like an insidious devil you pervert the Scriptures. You say
that the Church consists virtually in the pope. What abominations
will you not have to regard as the deeds of the Church? Look at
the ghastly shedding of blood by Julius II. Look at the outrageous
tyranny of Boniface VIII, who, as the proverb declares, "came in
as a wolf, reigned as a lion, and died as a dog." If the Church
consists representatively in the cardinals, what do you make of a
general council of the whole Church? You call me a leper because
I mingle truth with error. I am glad you admit there is some truth.
You make the pope into an emperor in power and violence. The
Emperor Maximilian and the Germans will not tolerate this.

The radicalism of this tract lies not in its invective but in its affirmation that the pope might err and a council might err and that only Scripture is the final authority. Prior to the appearance of this declaration the pope had already taken action. On the seventh of August, Luther received a citation to appear at Rome to answer to charges of heresy and contumacy. He was given sixty days in which to make his appearance. On the following day Luther wrote to the elector to remind him of his previous assurance that the case would not be taken to Rome. Then began a tortuous series of negotiations culminating in Luther's hearing before the Diet of Worms. The significance of that occasion is that an assembly of the German nation came to function as a council of the Catholic Church. The popes were doing their best to stifle or control councils. The result was that a secular assembly assumed conciliar functions, but not until after many other devices had first been tried.

### THE CASE TRANSFERRED TO GERMANY

The initial step toward a hearing before a German diet was the transfer of Luther's trial from Rome to Germany. To this end on August 8 he besought the intervention of the elector. The plea was addressed not directly to him but to the court chaplain, George Spalatin, who from now on played a large role as the intermediary between the professor and the prince. Frederick was eager that his right hand might plausibly claim ignorance of the left, and was very chary of appearing to endorse Luther's opinions or of backing his person beyond the due of any subject. The elector protested not to have spoken with Luther more than twenty words in all his life. Now in response to the plea transmitted by Spalatin, Frederick opened negotiations with Cardinal Cajetan, the papal legate, to give Luther a personal hearing in connection with the forthcoming meeting of the imperial diet at Augsburg. The hearing was to be private and not before the diet, but would at least be on German soil. The gain on this score was offset, however, by the competence and character of Cardinal Cajetan, a high

**SPALATIN**

papalist of integrity and erudition. He could scarcely tolerate Luther's *Reply to Prierias* or the *Sermon on the Ban*, and would be less inclined to moderation because Emperor Maximilian had been incensed by the excerpts from the reputed sermon and had himself taken the initiative on the fifth of August in writing to the pope "to set a stop to the most perilous attack of Martin Luther on indulgences lest not only the people but even the princess be seduced." With the emperor, the pope, and the cardinal against him Luther had but slender hope of escaping the stake.

He started for Augsburg with grave misgiving. The danger was vastly greater than three years later when he went to Worms as the champion of an aroused nation. At this time he was only an Augustinian eremite suspected of heresy. He saw ahead the stake and said to himself, "Now I must die. What a disgrace I shall be to my parents!" On the road he contracted an intestinal infection and well-nigh fainted. Even more disconcerting was the recurring doubt whether the taunt of his critics might after all be right, "Are you alone wise and all the ages in error?" Luther's friends had advised him not to enter Augsburg without a safe conduct, and Frederick at length obtained one from Emperor Maximilian. Cajetan, on being consulted, was incensed. "If you don't trust me," he said, "why do you ask my opinion, and if you do why is a safe conduct necessary?"

But the cardinal was in a much more complacent mood than Luther had reason to know. The diet was already over, and during its course he had learned much. His mission had been to rally the north for a great new crusade against the Turk. The Bohemian heretics should be reconciled in order that they might participate in the enterprise; a tax should be levied for the purpose; important persons were to be enlisted by emoluments and distinctions. The Archbishop of Mainz was to be elevated to the purple, and Emperor Maximilian to be decorated with a helmet and dagger as the Protector of the Faith. Incidentally the tares were to be weeded from the vineyard of the Lord.

The diet opened with characteristic medieval pageantry and etiquette. All due deference was shown to the cardinal. Albert of Mainz received the purple with becoming blushes, and the emperor accepted the dagger without demur. But when the business began, the princes were not ready to fight the Turk under the auspices of the Church. They were through with crusades and averred their inability to raise a tax after being so exploited by the Church. The grievances of the German nation were presented, as on many previous occasions, but this time with fangs. The document declared:

These sons of Nimrod grab cloisters, abbeys, prebends, canonates.

and parish churches, and they leave these churches without pastors, the people without shepherds. Annates and indulgences increase. In cases before the ecclesiastical courts the Roman Church smiles on both sides for a little palm grease. German money in violation of nature flies over the Alps. The pastors given to us are shepherds only in name. They care for nothing but fleece and batten on the sins of the people. Endowed masses are neglected, the pious founders cry for vengeance. Let the Holy Pope Leo stop these abuses.

Cajetan failed in all his large objectives. The crusade and the tax had been rejected. Could he succeed better with the weed in the vineyard of the Lord? He sensed that he must tread warily, but he was shackled by papal instructions which allowed him only to reconcile Luther to the Church in case he recanted, and, in case he did not, to send him bound to Rome. The aid of the secular arm should be invoked, particularly of Emperor Maxilimian, whose remonstrance may well have prompted the pope's instructions.

The genuineness of this papal document was first impugned by Luther and subsequently by modern historians on the ground that the pope would not take such summary action before the expiration of the sixty days allowed in the citation. But the pope had merely given Luther sixty days in which to appear, and had made no promises in case he did not. Besides, as Cardinal de Medici wrote to Cajetan on the seventh of October, "In cases of notorious heresy no further ceremony or citation needs to be observed."

The genuineness of these instructions cannot be absolutely established because the original is not extant. The Vatican archives contain, however, the manuscript of another letter written on the very same day by the pope to Frederick, which is no less peremptory.

Beloved son, the apostolic benediction be upon you. We recall that the chief ornament of your most noble family has been devotion to the faith of God and to the honor and dignity of the Holy See. Now we hear that a son of iniquity, Brother Martin Luther of the Augustinian eremites, hurling himself upon the Church of God, has your support. Even though we know it to be false, we must urge you to clear the reputation of your noble family from such calumny. Having been advised by the Master of the Sacred Palace that Luther's teaching contains heresy, we have cited him to appear before Cardinal Cajetan. We call upon you to see that Luther is placed in the hands and under the jurisdiction of this Holy See lest future generations reproach you with having fostered the rise of a most pernicious heresy against the Church of God.

### THE INTERVIEWS WITH CAJETAN

In the light of this letter the instructions to Cajetan need not be doubted on the score of the content. Obviously they cur-

Cajetan — a cardinal, papal legate

tailed his freedom, and a fresh memorandum limited him to
inquiry as to Luther's teaching. There should be no discussion.
Three interviews took place—on Tuesday, Wednesday, and
Thursday the twelfth through the fourteenth of October,
1518. Staupitz was among those present. On the first day
Luther prostrated himself in all humility, and the cardinal

THE INTERVIEW WITH CAJETAN

raised him up in all paternity and then informed him that he
must recant. Luther answered that he had not made the arduous journey to Augsburg to do what he could have done quite
as well at Wittenberg. He would like to be instructed as to his
errors.

The cardinal replied that the chief was the denial of the
Church's treasury of merit clearly enunciated in the bull
*Unigenitus* of Pope Clement VI in the year 1343. "Here," said
Cajetan, "you have a statement by the pope that the merits
of Christ are a treasure of indulgences." Luther, who knew
the text well, answered that he would recant if it said so.
Cajetan chuckled, leafed through the page to the spot where
it said Christ by his sacrifice acquired a treasure. "Oh, yes,"
said Luther, "but you said that the merits of Christ *are* a treasure. This says he *acquired* a treasure. To *be* and to *acquire*
do not mean the same thing. You need not think we Germans
are ignorant of grammar."

The reply was both rude and irrelevant. Luther blustered
because he was cornered. Any unprejudiced reader would have
said that the cardinal correctly paraphrased the sense of the

decretal which declares that Christ by his sacrifice acquired a treasure which through the power of the keys has been placed at the disposal of Peter and his successors in order to release the faithful from temporal penalties. This treasure has been increased by the merits of the Blessed Virgin and the saints. The pope dispenses this store as a treasury to those who visit Rome in the jubilee year 1350, when to those penitent and confessed may be given full remission of all their sins.

The whole concept of the treasury of the surplus merits of Christ and the saints is unmistakably here, but Luther was trapped because he must recant or reject the decretal or interpret it in an acceptable sense. He tried the latter and, realizing the delicacy of the task, requested to be allowed to submit a statement in writing, remarking *en passant* that they had "wrangled quite enough." The cardinal was nettled, for he realized that he had gone beyond his instructions in debating with Luther. "My son," he snapped, "I did not wrangle with you. I am ready to reconcile you with the Roman Church." But since reconciliation was possible only through recantation, Luther protested that he ought not to be condemned unheard and unrefuted. "I am not conscious," said he, "of going against Scripture, the fathers, the decretals, or right reason. I may be in error. I will submit to the judgment of the universities of Basel, Freiburg, Louvain, and, if need be, of Paris." This was a most undiplomatic attempt to evade the cardinal's jurisdiction.

The written statement was only a more ingenious and labored effort to place a favorable construction on the decretal. Cajetan must have impressed this upon Luther, for he shifted ground and came out with a blunt rejection of the decretal and of the authority of the pope who formulated it. "I am not so audacious that for the sake of a single obscure and ambiguous decretal of a human pope I would recede from so many and such clear testimonies of divine Scripture. For, as one of the canon lawyers has said, 'in a matter of faith not only is a council above a pope but any one of the faithful, if armed with better authority and reason.' " The cardinal reminded Luther that Scripture has itself to be interpreted. The pope is the interpreter. The pope is above a council, above everything in the Church. "His Holiness abuses Scripture," retorted Luther. "I deny that he is above Scripture." The cardinal flared up and bellowed that Luther should leave and never come back unless he was ready to say, *"Revoco"*—"I recant."

Luther wrote home that the cardinal was no more fitted to handle the case than an ass to play on a harp. The cartoonists before long took up the theme and pictured the pope himself in this pose.

Cajetan promptly cooled off and had dinner with Staupitz,

urging him to induce Luther to recant and insisting that Luther had no better friend than he. Staupitz answered, "I have often tried, but I am not equal to him in ability and command of Scripture. You are the pope's representative. It is up to you."

"I am not going to talk with him any more," said the cardinal. "His eyes are as deep as a lake, and there are amazing speculations in his head."

Staupitz released Luther from his vow of obedience to the order. He may have wished to relieve the Augustinians of the onus, or he may have sought to unfetter the friar, but Luther felt that he had been disclaimed. "I was excommunicated three times," he said later, "first by Staupitz, secondly by the pope, and thirdly by the emperor."

THE POPE AS AN ASS PLAYING BAGPIPES

He waited until the next week in Augsburg to see whether he would be summoned further, then posted an appeal from Cajetan to the pope, pointing out that since the doctrine of indulgences had never been officially declared, a debate on dubious questions should not be regarded as heresy, especially on points unessential for salvation. Luther complained of the citation to Rome which would submit him to the Dominicans. Besides, Rome would not be a safe place even with a safe conduct. In Rome not even Pope Leo himself was safe. The reference was to a conspiracy, lately disclosed, among the very cardinals to poison His Holiness. In any case Luther as a mendicant had no funds for the journey. He had been graciously received by Cajetan, but instead of being allowed to debate had been given only an opportunity to recant. The proposal to submit the case to the universities had been spurned. "I feel that I have not had justice because I teach nothing save what is in Scripture. Therefore I appeal from Leo badly informed to Leo better informed."

THE CARDINAL-FOOL

Rumor then reached Luther that the cardinal was empowered to arrest him. The gates of the city were being guarded.

With the connivance of friendly citizens Luther escaped by night, fleeing in such haste that he had to ride horseback in his cowl without breeches, spurs, stirrups, or a sword. He arrived in Nürnberg and there was shown the pope's instructions to Cajetan. Luther questioned the authenticity but at the same time contemplated an appeal from the pope to a general council. On the thirtieth day of October he was back in Wittenberg.

### THREATENING EXILE

His tenure there became highly precarious. Cajetan sent his report of the interview to Frederick the Wise, declaring that what Luther had said with regard to the papal decretal was not fit to put on paper. Let Frederick either send Luther bound to Rome or else banish him from his territories. The elector showed this to Luther, who made the matter still more difficult for his prince by publishing a version of the interview with Cajetan strengthened by subsequent reflection. There was no longer any attempt to explain the papal decretal in a favorable sense. Instead it was called emphatically false. The ambiguous decretal of a mortal pope was contrasted with the clear testimonies of holy Scripture. Luther continued:

You are not a bad Christian if you deny the decretal. But if you deny the gospel, you are a heretic. I damn and detest this decretal. The Apostolic Legate opposed me with the thunder of his majesty and told me to recant. I told him the pope abused Scripture. I will honor the sanctity of the pope, but I will adore the sanctity of Christ and the truth. I do not deny this new monarchy of the Roman Church which has arisen in our generation, but I deny that you cannot be a Christian without being subject to the decrees of the Roman pontiff. As for the decretal, I deny that the merits of Christ are a treasure of indulgences because his merits convey grace apart from the pope. The merits of Christ take away sins and increase merits. Indulgences take away merits and leave sins. These adulators put the pope above Scripture and say that he cannot err. In that case Scripture perishes, and nothing is left in the Church save the word of man. I resist those who in the name of the Roman Church wish to institute Babylon.

On the twenty-eighth of November, Luther lodged with a notary an appeal from the pope to a general council, declaring that such a council, legitimately called in the Holy Spirit, represents the Catholic Church, and is above the pope, who, being a man, is able to err, sin, and lie. Not even St. Peter was above this infirmity. If the pope orders anything against divine mandates, he is not to be obeyed.

Therefore from Leo badly advised and from his excommunication, suspension, interdict, censures, sentences, and fines, and what-

soever denunciations and declarations of heresy and apostasy,
which I esteem as null, nay, as iniquitous and tyrannical, I appeal
to a general council in a safe place.

Luther had the appeal printed and requested that all the
copies be committed to him to be released only if he was
actually banned, but the printer disregarded the injunction
and gave them at once to the public. This put Luther in a most
exposed position because Pope Julius II had ruled that an
appeal without papal consent to a council would itself constitute heresy.

Frederick the Wise was doubly embarrassed. He was a most
Catholic prince, addicted to the cult of relics, devoted to indulgences, quite sincere in his claim that he was not in a position
to judge Luther's teaching. On such matters he craved guidance. That was why he had founded the University of Wittenberg and why he so often turned to it for advice on matters jur-
istic and theological. Luther was one of the doctors of that university, commissioned to instruct his prince in matters of faith.
Was the prince to believe that his doctor of Holy Scripture
was in error? Of course, if the pope declared him to be a
heretic, that would settle the matter, but the pope had not yet
passed sentence. The theological faculty at Wittenberg had not
repudiated Luther. Many scholars throughout Germany believed him to be right. If Frederick should take action prior
to papal condemnation, might he not be resisting the word of
God? On the other hand, the pope had urged that Luther be
taken into custody and had called him a "son of iniquity."
Might not a refusal to comply mean the harboring of a heretic?
Such questions troubled Frederick. He differed from other
princes of his time in that he never asked how to extend his
boundaries nor even how to preserve his dignities. His only
question was, "What is my duty as a Christian prince?" At this
juncture he was gravely disturbed and would take no action
beyond writing on the nineteenth of November beseeching the
emperor either to drop the case or to grant a hearing before
unimpeachable judges in Germany.

Luther wrote to the elector:

I am sorry that the legate blames you. He is trying to bring the
whole House of Saxony into disrepute. He suggests that you send
me to Rome or banish me. What am I, a poor monk, to expect if
I am banished? Since I am in danger enough in your territory, what
would it be outside? But lest Your Honor suffer on my account I
will gladly leave your dominions.

To Staupitz, Luther wrote:

The prince opposed the publication of my version of the interview but has at length given his consent. The legate has asked him

to send me to Rome or banish me. The prince is very solicitous for
me, but he would be happier if I were somewhere else. I told
Spalatin if the ban came I would leave. He dissuaded me from
precipitant flight to France.

When at Augsburg one of the Italians had asked Luther where
he would go if abandoned by the prince, he had answered,
"Under the open sky."

On the twenty-fifth of November he sent word to Spalatin:

I am expecting the curses of Rome any day. I have everything in
readiness. When they come, I am girded like Abraham to go I
know not where, but sure of this, that God is everywhere.

*If*

*banned*

Staupitz wrote Luther from Salzburg in Austria:

The world hates the truth. By such hate Christ was crucified, and
what there is in store for you today if not the cross I do not know.
You have few friends, and would that they were not hidden for
fear of the adversary. Leave Wittenberg and come to me that we
may live and die together. The prince [Frederick] is in accord.
Deserted let us follow the deserted Christ.

Luther told his congregation that he was not saying good-by;
but if they should find him gone, then let this be his farewell.
He entertained a few friends at supper. In another two hours
he would have left had not a letter come from Spalatin saying
that the prince wished him to stay. Precisely what had happened we shall never know. Years afterward Luther declared
that the prince had in mind a plan to hide him, but a few
weeks after the event Luther wrote, "At first the prince would
have been willing not to have me here." Two years later Fred-
rick justified himself before Rome for taking no action against
Luther on the ground that he had been ready to accept Luther's
offer to leave when word came from the papal nuncio advising
that Luther would be much less dangerous under surveillance
than at large. Frederick of course might have said this after
the event, even though secretly he had entertained the design
of spiriting Luther to some hide-out. Yet it is equally possible
that for a moment Frederick was ready to yield but delayed
until after the pope had made his move. At any rate on the
eighteenth of December, Frederick sent to Cajetan the only
document he ever addressed to the Roman *curia* on Luther's
behalf:

We are sure that you acted paternally toward Luther, but we
understand that he was not shown sufficient cause to revoke. There
are learned men in the universities who hold that his teaching has
not been shown to be unjust, unchristian, or heretical. The few who
think so are jealous of his attainments. If we understood his doctrine to be impious or untenable, we would not defend it. Our

*Prince Frederick writes to Pope
on Luther's Behalf*

whole purpose is to fulfill the office of a Christian prince. Therefore we hope that Rome will pronounce on the question. As for sending him to Rome or banishing him, that we will do only after he has been convicted of heresy. His offer to debate and submit to the judgment of the universities ought to be considered. He should be shown in what respect he is a heretic and not condemned in advance. We will not lightly permit ourselves to be drawn into error nor to be made disobedient to the Holy See. We wish you to know that the University of Wittenberg has recently written on his behalf. A copy is appended.

Luther commented to Spalatin:

I have seen the admirable words of our Most Illustrious Prince to our Lord the Legate of Rome. Good God, with what joy I read them and read them over again!

## CHAPTER SIX

# THE SAXON HUS

RESUMABLY the shift in papal policy was due in part to the discerning reports of Cardinal Cajetan. He well knew that a man may be a vexation without being a heretic, because heresy involves a rejection of the established dogma of the Church, and the doctrine of indulgences had not yet received an official papal definition. The pope must first speak; and only then, if Luther refused to submit, could he properly be placed under the ban. A papal declaration was at last forthcoming, composed in all likelihood by Cajetan himself. On November 9, 1518, the bull *Cum Postquam* definitely clarified many of the disputed points. Indulgences were declared to apply only to penalty and not to guilt, which must first have been remitted through the sacrament of penance. Not the eternal pains of hell but only the temporal penalties of earth and purgatory might be diminished. Over the penalties imposed on earth by himself, the pope of course exercised complete jurisdiction by virtue of the power of absolution. But in the case of the penalties of purgatory he could do no more than present to God the treasury of the superfluous merits of Christ and the saints by way of petition. This decretal terminated some of the worst abuses.

Had it appeared earlier, the controversy might conceivably have been terminated, but in the interim Luther had attacked

*(handwritten margin notes: "Pope defines indulgences", "some end abuses", "But Luther continues the attack")*

not only the papal power to loose but also the power to bind through the ban. He had further declared the pope and councils to be capable of error. He had undercut the biblical text used to support the sacrament of penance and had rejected a portion of the canon law as incompatible with Scripture. The Dominicans had called him a notorious heretic, and the pope had referred to him as a son of iniquity.

But how was he to be handled? The conciliatory policy commenced in December, 1518, was prompted by considerations of politics. The pope knew that the plan for a crusade had been repudiated, that the tax had been refused, that the grievances of the German nation were recriminatory. There was a more serious consideration. Emperor Maximilian died on the twelfth of January. An election to the office of Holy Roman Emperor was thereby precipitated, and for some time earlier Maximilian was known to have been scheming to ensure the election of his grandson Charles as his successor.

The empire was a waning but still imposing legacy from the Middle Ages. The office of emperor was elective, and any European prince was eligible. The electors were, however, preponderantly German and preferred a German. Yet they were realistic enough to perceive that no German had sufficient strength in his own right to sustain the office. For that reason they were ready to accept the head of one of the great powers, and the choice lay between Francis of France and Charles of Spain. The pope objected, however, to either because an accretion of power on one side or the other would destroy that balance on which papal security depended. When the Germans despaired of a German, the pope threw his support to Frederick the Wise. Under such circumstances his wishes with regard to Martin Luther could not lightly be disregarded. The situation of course was altered when Frederick, sensible of his inadequacy, defeated himself by voting for the Hapsburg who on June 28, 1519, was chosen as Charles V of the Holy Roman Empire. Yet the situation did not so greatly alter, because for fully a year and a half thereafter Charles was too occupied in Spain to concern himself with Germany, and Frederick remained the pivotal figure. The pope still could not afford to alienate him unduly over Luther.

Papal policy became conciliatory; and Cajetan was assigned an assistant, a German related to Frederick the Wise, Carl von Miltitz by name, whose assignment was to curry the favor of the elector and to keep Luther quiet until the election was settled. For these ends Miltitz was equipped with every arrow in the quiver of the Vatican, from indulgences to interdicts. In order to soften Frederick he brought new privileges for the Castle Church at Wittenberg, whereby to those who made appropriate contributions purgatory might be reduced by a hundred years for every bone of the saints in Frederick's famous collection. He was further honored by a long-coveted distinction, the gift of a golden rose from the hand of the pope. In conferring this honor Leo X wrote to him:

Beloved son, the most holy golden rose was consecrated by us on the fourteenth day of the holy fast. It was anointed with holy oil and sprinkled with fragrant incense with the papal benediction. It will be presented to you by our most beloved son, Carl von Miltitz, of noble blood and noble manners. This rose is the symbol of the most precious blood of our Saviour, by which we are redeemed. The rose is a flower among flowers, the fairest and most fragrant on earth. Therefore, dear son, permit the divine fragrance to enter the innermost heart of Your Excellency, that you may fulfill whatever the aforementioned Carl von Miltitz shall show you.

No little delay occurred in the delivery of the rose, because it was deposited for safekeeping in the bank of the Fuggers at Augsburg.

Frederick suggested another reason for the delay. "Miltitz," he said, "may refuse to give me the golden rose unless I banish the monk and pronounce him a heretic." Luther heard that Miltitz was armed with a papal brief which made the gift of the rose conditional on his extradition, but that Miltitz was deterred from taking this course by the prudence of a cardinal who exclaimed, "You are a pack of fools if you think you can buy the monk from the prince." Miltitz was most certainly preceded by letters from the pope and the *curia* to Frederick urging all to assist against that "child of Satan, son of perdition, scrofulous sheep, and tare in the vineyard, Martin Luther." Brother Martin fully expected to be arrested, and Miltitz may have started out with that intent. "I learned afterwards," wrote Luther to Staupitz, "at the court of the prince, that Miltitz came armed with seventy apostolic briefs, that he might take me to the Jerusalem which kills the prophets, the purple Bayblon." Miltitz boasted in Germany that he had the friar in his pocket, but he was made quickly aware that too peremptory a course would not be discreet. In the inns on the way he questioned the people and discovered that for every one in favor of the pope there were three for Luther. He frankly confessed that no case had so plagued the Church in a thousand years, and Rome would gladly pay ten thousand ducats to have it out of the way. The *curia* was prepared to do even more than that. Frederick the Wise was given to understand that if he were compliant he might be permitted to name a cardinal. He took this to mean that the dignity might be conferred on Luther.

Miltitz arrived full of blandishments. In one interview he said to Luther, "We'll have it all fixed up in no time." He asked of Luther that he should subscribe to the new papal decretal on indulgences. Luther replied that there was not a word in it from Scripture. Then Miltitz required of him but one thing, that he should refrain from debate and publication if his opponents would observe the same condition. Luther promised. Miltitz wept. "Crocodile tears," commented Luther.

Tetzel was made the scapegoat. Miltitz summoned him to a hearing and charged that he was extravagant in traveling with two horses and a carriage, and that he had two illegitimate children. Tetzel retired to a convent to die of chagrin. Luther wrote to him, "Don't take it too hard. You didn't start this racket. The child had another father." The elector in the meantime took advantage of his singular position to use Miltitz for a plan of his own. Let Luther's case be referred to a commission of German ecclesiastics under the chairmanship of the Archbishop of Trier, Richard of Greiffenklau, who might please the Germans because he was an elector, the pope because he was an archbishop, and Luther because in the election he was opposing the papal candidate. Cajetan was won for the scheme, and Richard expressed his willingness. Frederick arranged with him that the hearing take place at the forthcoming meeting of the Diet of Worms. But the pope neither authorized nor disavowed the proposal, and for the moment nothing came of it.

**PHILIP MELANCHTHON**

Luther in the meantime became involved in further debate. He had agreed to refrain from controversy only if his opponents also observed the truce, and they did not. The universities were becoming involved. The University of Wittenberg was coming to be regarded as a Lutheran institution. Prominent among the faculty were Carlstadt and Melanchthon. The former was Luther's senior and had conferred on him the doctor's hood. Carlstadt was erudite but devoid of the caution which learning sometimes induces. He was sensitive, impressionable, impetuous, and at times tumultuous. His espousal of Luther's teachings prompted him to indulge in such blasts against critics that Luther himself was prone at times to wince.

Melanchthon was gentler, younger—only twenty-one—a prodigy of learning, enjoying already a European reputation. In appearance he was not prepossessing, as he had an impediment of speech and a hitch in the shoulder when he walked.

Luther once, when asked how he envisaged the appearance of the apostle Paul, answered with an affectionate guffaw, "I think he was a scrawny shrimp like Melanchthon." But when the stripling opened his mouth, he was like the boy Jesus in the temple. He came as professor of Greek, not of theology, and without any commitment to Luther; but soon he succumbed to his spell. His conversion stemmed from no travail of spirit but from agreement with Luther's interpretation of the apostle Paul. These were the leaders of the Wittenberg phalanx.

### THE GAUNTLET OF ECK

The Goliath of the Philistines who stepped forth to taunt Israel was a professor from the University of Ingolstadt, John Eck by name. On the appearance of Luther's theses he had leveled against them an attack under the title *Obelisks*, the word used to designate interpolations in Homer. Luther replied with *Asterisks*. Eck's attack was galling to Luther because he was an old friend, not a mendicant but a humanist, not "a perfidious Italian" but a German, and not the least because he was formidable. Despite his butcher's face and bull's voice he was a man of prodigious memory, torrential fluency, and uncanny acumen—a professional disputant who would post to Vienna or Bologna to debate the works of the Trinity, the substance of angels, or the contract of usury. Particularly exasperating was his propensity for clothing the opprobrious with plausibility and driving an opponent to incriminating conclusions.

Eck succeeded in inducing, not his own institution, but the University of Leipzig to enter the lists as the challenger of Wittenberg. Thereby old jealousies were brought into alignment with the new conflict, because Wittenberg and Leipzig represented the rival sections of electoral and ducal Saxony. Eck approached the patron of Leipzig, Duke George the Bearded—all the Saxon princes were bearded, but George left it to the others to be known as the Wise, the Steadfast, and the Magnanimous. He agreed that Eck should debate at Leipzig with Carlstadt, who in Luther's defense had already launched at Eck a virulent attack. But Eck had no mind

**JOHN ECK**

to fence with the second. He openly baited Luther by challenging his alleged assertions that the Roman Church in the days of Constantine was not above the others, and that the occupant of the see of Peter had not always been recognized as the successor of Peter and the vicar of Christ—in other words, that the papacy was of recent and therefore human origin. Luther retorted:

Let it be understood that when I say the authority of the Roman pontiff rests on a human decree I am not counseling disobedience. But we cannot admit that all the sheep of Christ were committed to Peter. What, then, was given to Paul? When Christ said to Peter, "Feed my sheep," he did not mean, did he, that no one else can feed them without Peter's permission? Nor can I agree that the Roman pontiffs cannot err or that they alone can interpret Scripture. The papal decretal by a new grammar turns the words of Christ, "Thou art Peter" into "Thou art the primate." By the decretals the gospel is extinguished. I can hardly restrain myself against the most impious and perverse blasphemy of this decretal.

Plainly the debate was between Eck and Luther, but to bring a man stigmatized by the pope as a "son of iniquity" out into the open in a public debate under the auspices of the orthodox University of Leipzig was daring. The bishop of the region interposed a prohibition. But Duke George rallied. He was later to become Luther's most implacable opponent, but at the moment he really wanted to know whether

As soon as the the coin in the coffer rings,
The soul from purgatory springs.

He reminded the bishop: "Disputations have been allowed from ancient times, even concerning the Holy Trinity. What good is a soldier if he is not allowed to fight, a sheep dog if he may not bark, and a theologian if he may not debate? Better spend money to support old women who can knit than theologians who cannot discuss." Duke George had his way. Luther was given a safe conduct to debate at Leipzig. "If that isn't the very devil!" commented Tetzel from his enforced retirement.

Luther set himself to prepare for the debate. Since he had asserted that only in the decretals of the previous four hundred years could the claims of papal primacy be established, he must devote himself to a study of the decretals. As he worked, his conclusions grew ever more radical. To a friend he wrote in February:

Eck is fomenting new wars against me. He may yet drive me to a serious attack upon the Romanists. So far I have been merely trifling.

In March, Luther confided to Spalatin:

I am sending Eck's letters in which he already boasts of having won the Olympic. I am studying the papal decretals for my debate. I whisper this in your ear, "I do not know whether the pope is Antichrist or his apostle, so does he in his decretals corrupt and crucify Christ, that is, the truth."

The reference to Antichrist was ominous. Luther was to find it easier to convince men that the pope was Antichrist than that the just shall live by faith. The suspicion which Luther did not yet dare breathe in the open links him unwittingly with the medieval sectaries who had revived and transformed the theme of Antichrist, a figure invented by the Jews in their captivity to derive comfort from calamity on the ground that the coming of Messiah is retarded by the machinations of an Anti-Messiah, whose raging must reach a peak before the Saviour should come. The gloomiest picture of the present thus became the most encouraging for the future. The book of Revelation made of the Anti-Messiah an Antichrist and added the details that before the end two witnesses must testify and suffer martyrdom. Then would appear Michael the Archangel and a figure with eyes of flame upon a white horse to cast the beast into the abyss. How the theme was handled in Luther's day is graphically shown in a woodcut from the *Nürnberg Chronicle*. Below on the left a very plausible Antichrist beguiles the people, while on the right the two witnesses from a pulpit instruct the throng. The hillock in the center is the Mount of Olives, from which Christ ascended into heaven and from which Antichrist is to be cast into hell. At the top Michael smites with his sword.

The theme became very popular in the late Middle Ages among the Fraticelli, Wycliffites, and Hussites, who identified the popes with the Antichrist soon to be overthrown. Luther was unwittingly in line with these sectaries, with one significant difference, however. Whereas they identified particular popes, because of their evil lives, with Antichrist, Luther held that every pope was Antichrist even though personally exemplary, because Antichrist is collective: an institution, the papacy, a system which corrupts the truth of Christ. That was why Luther could repeatedly address Leo X in terms of personal respect only a week or so after blasting him as Antichrist. But all this was yet to come. On the eve of the Leipzig debate Luther was frightened by his own thoughts. To one who had been so devoted to the Holy Father as the vicar of Christ the very suggestion that he might be, after all, the great opponent of Christ was ghastly. At the same time the thought was comforting, for the doom of Antichrist was sure. If Luther should fall like the two witnesses, his assailant would early be demolished by the hand of God. It was no longer a fight merely with

*Antichrist at the top is smitten by Michael and dragged by devils toward hell. The hillock is the Mount of Olives, from which Christ ascended into heaven and from which Antichrist is cast down. In the foreground at the left Antichrist with a devil speaking into his ear is beguiling the people. On the right the two witnesses give their testimony.*

men, but against the principalities and the powers and the world ruler of this darkness in the heavenly places.

### THE LEIPZIG DEBATE

The debate was held in Leipzig in the month of July. Eck came early and strode in a chasuble in the *Corpus Christi* procession. The Wittenbergers arrived a few days later, Luther, Carlstadt, Melanchthon, and other doctors with two hundred students armed with battle-axes. Eck was provided by the town council with a bodyguard of seventy-six men to protect him day and night from the Wittenbergers and the Bohemians whom he believed to be among them. Morning and evening a guard marched with streaming banners to fife and drum, and stationed themselves at the castle gate. The debate had been scheduled to be held in the aula of the university; but so great was the concourse of abbots, counts, Knights of the Golden Fleece, learned and unlearned, that Duke George placed at their disposal the auditorium of the castle. Chairs and benches were decorated with tapestries, those of the Wittenbergers with the emblem of St. Martin and Eck's with the insigne of the dragon killer, St. George.

On the opening day the assembly attended mass at six in the morning in St. Thomas Church. The liturgy was sung by a choir of twelve voices under the leadership of George Rhaw, later to be the printer of Luther's music at Wittenberg. The assembly then transferred itself to the castle. The session was opened with a Latin address of two hours by Duke George's secretary on the proper mode of conducting a theological discussion with decorum. "A grand address," said Duke George, "though I marvel that theologians should need such advice." Then the choir rendered the *Veni, Sancte Spiritus* while the town piper blew lustily. By then it was dinnertime. Duke George had an eye for the delicacies of the table. To Eck he sent a deer, to Carlstadt a roe, and wine all round.

In the afternoon began the preliminary skirmish over the rules of the tournament. The first question was whether to have stenographers. Eck said no, because taking them into account would chill the passionate heat of the debate. "The truth might fare better at a lower temperature," commented Melanchthon. Eck lost. The next question was whether to have judges. Luther said no. Frederick was arranging to have his case heard by the Archbishop of Trier, and he did not wish at this juncture to give the appearance of interjecting a rival plan. But Duke George was insistent. Luther lost. The universities of Erfurt and Paris were chosen. This was a reversion to the method several times previously proposed for the handling of his case. When Paris accepted, Luther demanded that the entire faculty be invited and not merely the theologians, whom he had come to distrust. "Why then," blurted Eck, "don't you refer the case to shoemakers and tailors?" The third question was whether to admit any books to the arena. Eck said no. Carlstadt, he charged, on the opening days lugged in tomes and read the audience to sleep. The Leipzigers in particular had to be awakened for dinner. Carlstadt accused Eck of wishing to befuddle the audience by a torrent of erudition. Carlstadt lost. By common consent the notes of the debate were not to be published until after the judges had submitted their verdict. The discussion proper then began.

An eyewitness has left us a description of the contestants.

Martin is of middle height, emaciated from care and study, so that you can almost count his bones through his skin. He is in the vigor of manhood and has a clear, penetrating voice. He is learned and has the Scripture at his fingers' ends. He knows Greek and Hebrew sufficiently to judge of the interpretations. A perfect forest of words and ideas stands at his command. He is affable and friendly, in no sense dour or arrogant. He is equal to anything. In company he is vivacious, jocose, always cheerful and gay no matter how hard his adversaries press him. Everyone chides him for the fault of being a little too insolent in his reproaches and more caustic than is prudent for an innovator in religion or becoming to a theologian. Much the same can be said of Carlstadt, though in a lesser degree. He is smaller than Luther, with a complexion of smoked herring. His voice is thick and unpleasant. He is slower in memory and quicker in anger. Eck is a heavy, square-set fellow with a full German voice supported by a hefty chest. He would make a tragedian or town crier, but his voice is rather rough than clear. His eyes and mouth and his whole face remind one more of a butcher than a theologian.

THE LEIPZIG DEBATE

After Carlstadt and Eck had wrestled for a week over the depravity of man, Luther entered to discuss the antiquity of the papal and the Roman primacy, together with the question whether it was of human or divine institution. "What does it all matter," inquired Duke George, "whether the pope is by divine right or by human right? He remains the pope just the same." "Perfectly right," said Luther, who insisted that by denying the divine origin of the papacy he was not counseling a withdrawal of obedience. But Eck saw more clearly than Luther the subversiveness of his assertions. The claim of the pope to unquestioning obedience rests on the belief that his office is divinely instituted. Luther revealed how lightly after all he esteemed the office when he exclaimed, "Even if there were ten popes or a thousand popes there would be no schism. The unity of Christendom could be preserved under numerous heads just as the separated nations under different sovereigns dwell in concord."

"I marvel," sniffed Eck, "that the Reverend Father should forget the everlasting dissension of the English and the French, the inveterate hatred of the French for the Spaniards, and all the Christian blood spilled over the Kingdom of Naples. As for me, I confess one faith, one Lord Jesus Christ, and I venerate the Roman pontiff as Christ's vicar."

But to prove that Luther's views were subversive was not to prove that they were false. The contestants had to come to grips with history. Eck asserted that the primacy of the Roman see and the Roman bishop as the successor of Peter went back to the very earliest days of the Church. By way of proof he introduced letters ascribed to a bishop of Rome in the first century affirming, "The Holy Roman and Apostolic Church obtained the primacy not from the apostles but from our Lord and Saviour himself, and it enjoys pre-eminence of power above all of the churches and the whole flock of Christian people"; and again, "The sacerdotal order commenced in the period of the New Testament directly after our Lord Christ, when to Peter was committed the pontificate previously exercised in the Church by Christ himself." Both of these statements had been incorporated into the canon law.

"I impugn these decretals," cried Luther. "No one will ever persuade me that the holy pope and martyr said that." Luther was right. They are today universally recognized by Catholic authorities as belonging to the spurious Isidorian decretals. Luther had done an excellent piece of historical criticism, and without the help of Lorenzo Valla, whose work he had not yet seen. Luther pointed out that actually in the early centuries bishops beyond Rome were not confirmed by nor subject to Rome, and the Greeks never accepted the Roman primacy. Surely the saints of the Greek Church were not on that account to be regarded as damned.

### THE ENDORSEMENT OF HUS

"I see," said Eck, "that you are following the damned and pestiferous errors of John Wyclif, who said, 'It is not necessary for salvation to believe that the Roman Church is above all others.' And you are espousing the pestilent errors of John Hus, who claimed that Peter neither was nor is the head of the Holy Catholic Church."

"I repulse the charge of Bohemianism," roared Luther. "I have never approved of their schism. Even though they had divine right on their side, they ought not to have withdrawn from the Church, because the highest divine right is unity and charity."

Eck was driving Luther onto ground especially treacherous at Leipzig, because Bohemia was near by and within living memory the Bohemian Hussites, the followers of John Hus, burned for heresy at Constance, had invaded and ravaged the Saxon lands. The assembly took time out for lunch. Luther availed himself of the interlude to go to the university library and read the acts of the Council of Constance, by which Hus had been condemned. To his amazement he discovered among the reproved articles the following: "The one holy universal Church is the company of the predestined," and again, "The universal Holy Church is one, as the number of the elect is one." The second of these statements he recognized as deriving directly from St. Augustine. When the assembly reconvened at two o'clock, Luther declared, "Among the articles of John Hus, I find many which are plainly Christian and evangelical, which the universal Church cannot condemn." Duke George at these words jabbed his elbows into his ribs and muttered audibly, "The plague!" His mind conjured up the Hussite hordes ravaging the Saxon lands. Eck had scored.

Luther continued. "As for the article of Hus that 'it is not necessary for salvation to believe the Roman Church superior to all others' I do not care whether this comes from Wyclif or from Hus. I know that innumerable Greeks have been saved though they never heard this article. It is not in the power of the Roman pontiff or of the Inquisition to construct new articles of faith. No believing Christian can be coerced beyond holy writ. By divine law we are forbidden to believe anything which is not established by divine Scripture or manifest revelation. One of the canon lawyers has said that the opinion of a single private man has more weight than that of a Roman pontiff or an ecclesiastical council if grounded on a better authority or reason. I cannot believe that the Council of Constance would condemn these propositions of Hus. Perhaps this section in the acts has been interpolated."

"They are recorded," stated Eck, "in the reliable history of

Jerome of Croatia, and their authenticity has never been impugned by the Hussites."

"Even so," replied Luther, "the council did not say that all the articles of Hus were heretical. It said that 'some were heretical, some erroneous, some blasphemous, some presumptuous, some seditious, and some offensive to pious ears respectively.' You should differentiate and tell us which were which."

"Whichever they were," retorted Eck, "none of them was called most christian and evangelical; and if you defend them, then you are heretical, erroneous, blasphemous, presumptuous, seditious, and offensive to pious ears respectively."

"Let me talk German," demanded Luther. "I am being misunderstood by the people. I assert that a council has sometimes erred and may sometimes err. Nor has a council authority to establish new articles of faith. A council cannot make divine right out of that which by nature is not divine right. Councils have contradicted each other, for the recent Lateran Council has reversed the claim of the councils of Constance and Basel that a council is above a pope. A simple layman armed with Scripture is to be believed above a pope or a council without it. As for the pope's decretal on indulgences I say that neither the Church nor the pope can establish articles of faith. These must come from Scripture. For the sake of Scripture we should reject pope and councils."

"But this," said Eck, "is the Bohemian virus, to attach more weight to one's own interpretation of Scripture than to that of the popes and councils, the doctors and the universities. When Brother Luther says that this is the true meaning of the text, the pope and councils say, 'No, the brother has not understood it correctly.' Then I will take the council and let the brother go. Otherwise all the heresies will be renewed. They have all appealed to Scripture and have believed their interpretation to be correct, and have claimed that the popes and the councils were mistaken, as Luther now does. It is rancid to say that those gathered in a council, being men, are able to err. This is horrible, that the Reverend Father against the holy Council of Constance and the consensus of all Christians does not fear to call certain articles of Hus and Wyclif most Christian and evangelical. I tell you, Reverend Father, if you reject the Council of Constance, if you say a council, legitimately called, errs and has erred, be then to me as a Gentile and a publican."

Luther answered, "If you won't hold me for a Christian, at least listen to my reasons and authorities as you would to a Turk and infidel."

Eck did. They went on to discuss purgatory. Eck cited the famous passage from II Maccabees 12:45, "Wherefore he made the propitiation for them that had died, that they might be released from their sin." Luther objected that the book of II Maccabees belongs to the Apocrypha and not to the canon-

ical Old Testament, and is devoid of authority. This was the
third time during the debate that he had impugned the rele-
vance of the documentary buttresses of papal claims.

**LUTHER AND HUS ADMINISTER THE BREAD AND WINE
TO THE HOUSE OF SAXONY**

First he had denied the genuineness of papal decretals of the
first century, and he was right. Next he questioned the acts of
the Council of Constance, and he was wrong. This time he
rejected the authority of the Old Testament Apocrypha, which
is, of course, a matter of judgment.

Then they took up indulgences, and there was scarcely any
debate. Eck declared that if Luther had not assailed the papal
primacy, their differences could easily have been composed.
On the subject of penance, however, Eck kept pressing Luther
with the query, "Are you the only one that knows anything?
Except for you is all the Church in error?"

"I answer," replied Luther, "that God once spoke through the mouth of an ass. I will tell you straight what I think. I am a Christian theologian; and I am bound, not only to assert, but to defend the truth with my blood and death. I want to believe freely and be a slave to the authority of no one, whether council, university, or pope. I will confidently confess what appears to me to be true, whether it has been asserted by a Catholic or a heretic, whether it has been approved or reproved by a council."

The debate lasted eighteen days and "might have gone forever," said a contemporary, "had not Duke George intervened." He had not learned much about what happens when the coin in the coffer rings, and he needed the assembly hall for the entertainment of the Margrave of Brandenburg, on his way home from the imperial election. Both sides continued the controversy in a pamphlet war. The agreement to wait for the judgment of the universities before publishing the notes was not observed, because Erfurt never reported at all, and Paris not for two years.

Before leaving the debate a minor incident is worth recording because it is so revealing of the coarseness and insensitivity of that whole generation. Duke George had a one-eyed court fool. A comic interlude in the disputation was staged when Eck and Luther debated whether this fool should be allowed a wife, Luther pro and Eck con. Eck was so opprobrious that the fool took offense; and whenever subsequently Eck entered the hall, the fool made grimaces. Eck retaliated by mimicking the blind eye, at which the fool ripped out a volley of bitter profanity. The audience roared.

After the debate Eck came upon a new fagot for Luther's pyre. "At any rate," he crowed, "no one is hailing me as the Saxon Hus." Two letters to Luther had ben intercepted, from John Paduška and Wenzel Roždalowski, Hussites of Prague, in which they said, "What Hus was once in Bohemia you, Martin, are in Saxony. Stand firm." When these letters did reach Luther, they were accompanied by a copy of Hus's work *On the Church.* "I agree now," said Luther, "with more articles of Hus than I did at Leipzig." By February, 1520, he was ready to say, "We are all Hussites without knowing it." By that time Eck was in Rome informing the pope that the son of iniquity was also the Saxon Hus.

## CHAPTER SEVEN

# THE GERMAN HERCULES

N THE early years of the Reform a cartoon appeared portraying Luther as "the German Hercules." The pope is suspended in derision from his nose. Beneath his hand cowers the inquisitor Hochstraten, and about him sprawl the scholastic theologians. The caption reveals that Luther had become a national figure. Such prominence came to him only after the Leipzig debate. Why the debate should of itself have so contributed to his reputation is puzzling. He had said very little at Leipzig which he had not said before, and the partial endorsement of Hus might rather have brought opprobrium than acclaim. Perhaps the very fact that an insurgent heretic had been allowed to debate at all was what attracted public notice.

A more important factor, however, may have been the dissemination of Luther's writings. John Froben, that hardy printer of Basel, had collected and brought out in a single edition the *Ninety-Five Theses*, the *Resolutions*, the *Answer to Prierias*, the sermon *On Penitence*, and the sermon *On the Eucharist*. In February, 1519, he was able to report to Luther that only ten copies were left, and that no issue from his press had ever been so quickly exhausted. The copies had gone not only to Germany but also to other lands, making of Luther not only a national but also an international figure. Six hundred had been sent to France and to Spain, others to Brabant and England. Zwingli, the reformer of Switzerland, ordered several hundred in order that a colporteur on horseback might circulate them among the people. Even from Rome came a letter to Luther written by a former fellow student, informing him that disciples at the peril of their lives were spreading his tracts under the shadow of the Vatican. He deserved a statue as the father of his country.

Such acclaim speedily made Luther the head of a movement which has come to be known as the Reformation. As it took on shape, it was bound to come into relation with the two other great movements of the day, the Renaissance and nationalism.

*From a cartoon attributed to Holbein and assigned to the
year 1522. The pope is suspended from Luther's nose. Jakob
von Hochstraten, the inquisitor, is under his hand. Among the
vanquished are St. Thomas, Duns Scotus, Robert Holcot, William of Occam, Nicholas of Lyra, Aristotle, and Peter Lombard in the immediate foreground with the title of his Sentences upside down. The devil disguised as a monk is fleeing
in the background.*

The Renaissance was a many-sided phenomenon in which a central place was occupied by the ideal commonly called Humanism. It was basically an attitude to life, the view that the proper interest of mankind is man, who should bring every area of the earth within his compass, every domain of knowledge within his ken, and every discipline of life within his rational control. War should be reduced to strategy, politics to diplomacy, art to perspective, and business to bookkeeping. The individual should seek to comprise within his grasp all the exploits and all the skills of which man is capable. The *uomo universale,* the universal man, should be courtier, politician, explorer, artist, scientist, financier, and quite possibly divine as well. The literature and languages of classical antiquity were pursued with avidity as a part of the quest for universal knowledge, and because the Hellenic attitude to life had been similar.

This program entailed no overt breach with the Church, since the secularized popes of the Renaissance became its patrons, and because a synthesis between the classical and the Christian had already been achieved by St. Augustine. At the same time a menace to Christianity was implicit in the movement because it was centered on man, because the quest for truth in any quarter might lead to relativity, and because the philosophies of antiquity had no place for the distinctive tenets of Christianity: the Incarnation and the Cross.

Yet only one overt clash occurred between the Humanists and the Church. The issue was over freedom of scholarship, and the scene was Germany. Here a fanatical Jewish convert, Pfefferkorn by name, sought to have all the Hebrew books destroyed. He was resisted by the great German Hebraist, Reuchlin, the great-uncle of Melanchthon. The obscurantists enlisted the aid of the inquisitor Jacob von Hochstraten, who in the cartoon lies beneath Luther's hand, and of Sylvester Prierias as the prosecutor. The upshot was a compromise. Reuchlin was permitted to continue his teaching, though saddled with the costs of the trial. Essentially he had won.

At several points Humanism and the Reformation could form an alliance. Both demanded the right of free investigation. The Humanists included the Bible and the biblical languages in their program of the revival of antiquity, and Luther's battle for the right understanding of Paul appeared to them and to Luther himself as a continuation of the Reuchlin affair. The opponents were the same, Hochstraten and Prierias; and the aim was the same, unimpeded inquiry. The Humanist of Nürnberg, Willibald Pirkheimer, lampooned Eck by portraying him as unable to secure a doctor in the Humanist cities of Augsburg and Nürnberg and under the necessity, therefore, of turning to Leipzig, the scene of his recent "triumph" over Luther. The message was sent by a witch who, to make her goat mount the air, pronounced the magic words *Tartshoh Nerokreffefp,* which in reverse give the names of the principals in the Reuchlin case, Pfefferkor(e)n and Ho(c)hstrat(en).

Luther's exposure of the spuriousness of papal documents appeared to the Humanists as to him to be entirely on a par with Lorenzo Valla's demonstration that the *Donation of Constantine* was a forgery. For different reasons Humanism as well as the Reformation attacked indulgences. What the one called blasphemy the other ridiculed as silly superstition.

The deepest affinity appeared at that point where Renaissance man was not sure of himself, when he began to wonder whether his valor might not be thwarted by the goddess Fortuna or whether his destiny had not already been determined by the stars. Here was Luther's problem of God the capricious and God the adverse. Renaissance man, confronted by this enigma and having no deep religion of his own, was commonly disposed to find solace less in Luther's stupefying irrationalities than in the venerable authority of the Church.

But reactions were diverse. Many early admirers of Luther, like Pirkheimer, recoiled and made their peace with Rome. Three examples well illustrate the varied courses taken by others: Erasmus passed from discriminating support of Luther to querulous opposition; Melanchthon became the most devoted and the most disconcerting of colleagues; Dürer might have become the artist of the Reformation had not death intervened not too long after his crisis of the spirit.

### THE HUMANISTS: ERASMUS

Erasmus was closer to Luther than many another figure of the Renaissance because he was so Christian. The major portion of his literary labors was devoted, not to the classics, but to the New Testament and the Fathers. His ideal, like that of Luther, was to revive the Christian consciousness of Europe through the dissemination of the sacred writings, and to that end Erasmus first made available in print the New Testament in the original Greek. From the press of Froben in 1516 was issued a handsome volume, the Greek type reminiscent of manuscripts, the text accompanied by a literal translation and illumined by annotations. The volume reached Wittenberg as Luther was lecturing on the ninth chapter of Romans, and thereafter became his working tool. From the accompanying translation he learned the inaccuracy of the Vulgate rendering of "do penance" instead of "be penitent." Erasmus throughout his life continued to improve the tools of biblical scholarship. Luther prized his efforts and in his lectures on Galatians in 1519 declared that he would have been happier to have waited for a commentary from the pen of Erasmus. The first letter of Luther to Erasmus was adulatory. The prince of the

Humanists was called "Our delight and our hope. Who has not learned from him?" In the years 1517-1519 Luther was so sensible of his affinity with the Humanists as to adopt their fad of Hellenizing vernacular names. He called himself Eleutherius, the free man.

Luther and Erasmus did have much in common. Both insisted that the Church of their day had relapsed into the Judaistic legalism castigated by the apostle Paul. Christianity, said Erasmus, has been made to consist not in loving one's neighbor but in abstaining from butter and cheese during Lent. What are pilgrimages, he demanded, but outward feats, often at the expense of family responsibility? What good are indulgences to those who do not mend their ways? The costly votive offerings which bedeck the tomb of St. Thomas at Canterbury might better be devoted to the charity dear to the saint. Those who never in their lives endeavored to imitate St. Francis desire to die in his cowl. Erasmus scoffed at those who to forfend the fiends trusted to a garment incapable of killing lice.

Both men had a quarrel with the pope, Luther because the pontiffs imperiled the salvation of souls, Erasmus because they fostered external ceremonies and impeded at times free investigation. Erasmus went out of his way to interpolate in new editions of his works passages which could scarcely be interpreted other than as abetting Luther. The *Annotations on the New Testament* in the edition of 1519 introduced this passage:

By how many human regulations has the sacrament of penitence and confession been impeded? The bolt of excommunication is ever in readiness. The sacred authority of the Roman pontiff is so abused by absolutions, dispensations, and the like that the godly cannot see it without a sigh. Aristotle is so in vogue that there is scarcely time in the churches to interpret the gospel.

Again, the edition of the *Ratio Theologiae* in 1520 inserted this interpolation:

There are those who, not content with the observance of confession as a rite of the Church, superimpose the dogma that it was instituted not merely by the apostles but by Christ himself, nor will they suffer one sacrament to be added or subtracted from the number of the seven although they are perfectly willing to commit to one man the power to abolish purgatory. Some assert that the universal body of the Church has been contracted into a single Roman pontiff, who cannot err on faith and morals, thus ascribing to the pope more than he claims for himself, though they do not hesitate to dispute his judgment if he interferes with their purses or their prospects. Is not this to open the door to tyranny in case such power were wielded by an impious and pestilent man? The same may be said of vows, tithes, restitutions, remissions, and confessions by which the simple and superstitious are beguiled.

During the years after the attack on indulgences and before
the assault on the sacraments Erasmus and Luther appeared to
contemporaries to be preaching so nearly the same gospel that
the first apology for Luther issued in the German tongue and
composed in 1519 by the Humanist secretary of Nürnberg,
Lazarus Spengler, lauded him as the emancipator from
rosaries, psalters, pilgrimages, holy water, confession, food
and fast laws, the misuse of the ban, and the pomp of indulgences. Erasmus could have said every word of that.

But there were differences; and the most fundamental was
that Erasmus was after all a man of the Renaissance, desirous
of bringing religion itself within the compass of man's understanding. He sought to do so, not like the scholastics by rearing an imposing edifice of rationally integrated theology, but
rather by relegating to the judgment day the discussion of
difficult points and couching Christian teaching in terms simple enough to be understood by the Aztecs, for whom his devotional tracts were translated. His patron saint was ever the
penitent thief because he was saved with so little theology.

For another reason also Erasmus was diffident of unreserved
support to Luther. Erasmus was nostalgic for the vanishing
unities of Europe. His dream was that Christian Humanism
might serve as a check upon nationalism. In dedicating his
commentary on the four Gospels to four sovereigns of the
new national states—Henry of England, Francis of France,
Charles of Spain, and Ferdinand of Austria—he voiced the
hope that as their names were linked with the evangelists, so
might their hearts be welded by the evangel. The threat of
division and war implicit in the Reformation frightened him.

Most decisive of all was his own inner need. That simple
philosophy of Christ which he so vaunted did not allay ultimate doubts, and that very program of scholarship which he
trusted to redeem the world was not immune to wistful scoff-
ing. Why inflict upon oneself pallor, invalidism, sore eyes, and
premature age in the making of books when perchance wisdom lies with babes? He who could so query the utility of his
life's endeavor needed anchorage—if not with Luther, then
with Rome.

Such a man simply could not give Luther unqualified endorsement without a violation of his own integrity. Erasmus
chose his course with circumspection and held to it with more
tenacity and courage than are usually credited to him. He
would defend the man rather than the opinions. If he endorsed
an idea, it would be as an idea and not as Luther's. He would
champion the right of the man to speak and to be heard.
Erasmus pretended even not to know what Luther was saying.
There had been no time, he affirmed, to read Luther's books,
save perhaps a few lines of the Latin works, and of the German nothing at all, through ignorance of the language—

though two letters of Erasmus to Frederick the Wise in German are extant. After such disclaimers he would then over and over again betray acquaintance even with the German works. But his point was sound enough. He was confining the defense to questions of civil and religious liberty. Luther was a man of irreproachable life. He was ready to submit to correction. He had asked for impartial judges. He should be accorded a hearing, and a real hearing, to determine whether his interpretation of Scripture was sound. The battle was for freedom of investigation. Even if Luther was mistaken, he should be corrected fraternally and not by bolts from Rome. Erasmus was by conviction a neutral in an age intolerant of neutrality.

### MELANCHTHON AND DÜRER

Others among the Humanists went over to Luther unreservedly, among them Melanchthon, who as a Humanist scholar had been convinced that Luther correctly interpreted the apostle Paul. Melanchthon therefore became the colleague and the ally. Yet he continued to occupy a position at once so mediating and so ambiguous as to provoke questioning to this day whether he was the defender or the perverter of Luther's gospel. The fact that to the end Melanchthon preserved the unbroken friendship of Erasmus would not of itself be particularly significant were it not that he was ever ready to place upon Luther's teaching an alien nuance. After Luther's death Melanchthon translated the Augsburg Confession into Greek for the patriarch at Constantinople and in so doing actually transmuted Luther's teaching of justification by faith into the Greek concept of the deification of man through sacramental union with the incorruptible Christ. Humanism was a dubious ally.

One wonders whether Luther was not better understood by that German Humanist who in his early years was the typical Renaissance figure. The artist Albrecht Dürer was a fine example of the *uomo universale,* experimenting with all techniques and seeking to comprehend all mysteries in esoteric symbolism; given sometimes to a touch of levity, as in the "Madonna of the Parrot"; subject also to profound disquiet over the futility of all human endeavor. Those exuberant horsemen of the Renaissance reined up before the chasms of destiny. Their plight is poignantly displayed in Dürer's *Melancolia*. There sits a winged woman of high intelligence in torpid idleness amid all the tools and symbols of man's highest skills. Unused about her lie the compass of the draftsman, the scales of the chemist, the plane of the carpenter, the inkwell of the author; unused at her belt the keys of power, the purse of wealth; unused beside her the ladder of construction. The perfect sphere and the chiseled rhomboid inspire no new endeavor. Above her head the sands in the hourglass sink, and the magic square no matter how computed yields no larger sum. The bell above is ready to toll. Yet in sable gloom she broods, because the issues of destiny strive in the celestial sphere. In the sky the rainbow arches, sign of the covenant sworn by God to Noah, never to bring again the waters upon the earth; but within the rainbow glimmers a comet, portent of impending disaster. Beside Melancolia, perched upon a millstone, sits a scribbling cherub alone active because insouciant of the forces at play. Is the point again, as with Erasmus, that wisdom lies with the simplicity of childhood, and man might better lay aside his skills until the gods have decided the issues of the day?

What a parallel have we here in quite other terms to Luther's agonizing quest for the ultimate meaning of life! His language was different; his symbols were different; but the Renaissance could encompass a shift of symbols. When Dürer heard that man is saved by faith, he comprehended that the comet had been drawn into the rainbow, and desired with God's help to see Martin Luther and to engrave his portrait "as a lasting memorial of the Christian man who has helped me out of great anxiety." Thereafter Dürer's art abandoned the secular for the evangelical. From "scintillating splendor" he passed to a "forbidding yet strangely impassioned austerity."

### THE NATIONALISTS: HUTTEN AND SICKINGEN

The second great movement to relate itself to the Reformation was German nationalism. The movement was itself inchoate in Luther's day because Germany was retarded in na-

LUTHER AND HUTTEN AS COMPANIONS IN ARMS

tional unification as compared with Spain, France, and England. Germany had no centralized government. The Holy Roman Empire no more than approximated a German national state because it was at once too large, since any European prince was eligible to the highest office, and too small, because actually the Hapsburg dynasty was dominant. Germany was segmented into small and overlapping jurisdictions of princes

and bishops. The free cities twinkled in the murky way of entangling alliances. The knights were a restive class seeking to arrest the waning of their power, and the peasants were likewise restive because desirous of a political role commensurate with their economic importance. No government, and no class, was able to weld Germany into one. Dismembered and retarded, she was derided by the Italians and treated by the papacy as a private cow. Resentment against Rome was more intense than in countries where national governments curbed papal exploitation.

**HUTTEN AND LUTHER
BOWLING AGAINST THE POPE**

The representatives of German nationalism who for several years in some measure affected Luther's career were Ulrich von Hutten and Franz von Sickingen. Hutten was himself both a knight and a Humanist, fond of parading both in armor and laurel. He illustrates again the diversities of Humanism, which could be international in Erasmus and national in him. Hutten did much to create the concept of German nationalism and to construct the picture of the ideal German, who should repel the enemies of the fatherland and erect a culture able to vie with the Italian.

The first enemy to be repulsed was the Church, responsible so often for the division and the mulcting of Germany. Hutten wielded the pen of the Humanist to blast the *curia* with the most virulent invective. In a tract called *The Roman Trinity* he catalogued in a crescendo of triplets all the sins of Rome: "Three things are sold in Rome: Christ, the priesthood, and women. Three things are hateful to Rome: a general council, the reformation of the church, and the opening of German eyes. There ills I pray for Rome: pestilence, famine, and war. This be my trinity."

The man who wrote this did not at first applaud Luther. In the opening stages of the skirmish with Eck, Hutten looked on the controversy as a squabble of monks and rejoiced that they would devour each other, but after the Leipzig debate he perceived that Luther's words had the ring of his own. Luther, too, resented the fleecing of Germany, Italian chicanery and superciliousness. Luther wished that St. Peter's might lie in ashes rather than that Germany should be despoiled. Hutten's picture of the romantic German could be enriched by Luther's

THE EBERNBURG

concept of a mystical depth in the German soul exceeding that of other people's. In 1516 Luther had discovered an anonymous manuscript emanating from the Friends of God and had published it under the title of *A German Theology,* declaring in the preface that he had learned from it more than any writing save the Bible and the works of St. Augustine. These words imply no narrow nationalism, for St. Augustine was a Latin, but certainly Luther meant that the Germans should be rated above those by whom they were despised. The similarity between Hutten and Luther became all the more marked when Hutten grew evangelical and shifted his idiom from Athens to Galilee.

The practical question for Hutten was how to implement his program for the emancipation of Germany. He looked first to Emperor Maximilian to curb the Church and consolidate the nation, but Maximilian died. Next Hutten hoped that Albert of Mainz, as the primate of Germany, might be induced to head a genuinely national church, but Albert owed too much to Rome.

One class alone in Germany responded to Hutten's pleas, and that was his own, the knights. Among them the most outstanding figure was Franz von Sickingen, who did so much to effect the imperial election by throwing his troops around Frankfurt. Sickingen was trying to obviate the extinction of his class by giving to Germany a system of justice after the manner of Robin Hood. He announced himself as the vindicator of the oppressed, and since his troops lived off the land, he was always seeking more oppressed to vindicate. Hutten saw a chance to enlist him for the vindication alike of Germany and Luther. During the warless winter Hutten established himself at Sickingen's castle called the Ebernburg, and there the poet laureate of Germany read to the illiterate swordsman from the German works of the Wittenberg prophet. Sickingen's foot and fist stamped assent, as he resolved to champion the poor and the sufferers for the gospel. Popular pamphlets began to picture him as the vindicator of the peasants and of Martin Luther. In one of these manifestoes a peasant, having paid half of his fine to the Church, cannot produce the remainder. Sickingen advises him that he should not have paid the first half and cites the word of Christ to the disciples to take neither scrip nor purse. The peasant inquires where these words are to be found, and Sickingen replies, "In Matthew 10, also in Mark 6, and Luke 9 and 10."

"Sir Knight," exclaims the astonished peasant, "how did you learn so much Scripture?"

Sickingen answers that he learned from Luther's books as read to him by Hutten at the Ebernburg.

The picture of Sickingen as the vindicator of the oppressed was not altogether fantastic. He did permit himself to be enlisted by Hutten to embark on a minor crusade for Humanism and the Reform. Reuchlin was thereby relieved of his fine, and fugitives for the gospel were harbored at the Ebernburg. Among them was that young Dominican, Martin Bucer, who had been so enthusiastic about Luther at the Heidelberg conference and now, having abandoned his own cowl, had fled to the gentlemen of the greenwood tree. Luther was made to know that he, too, would be welcome. What he replied we do not know, but we can infer his answer from the response to a similar overture on the part of a knight who informed him that, should the elector fail, one hundred knights could be mustered for his protection, so long as he was not confuted by irreproachable judges. To such offers Luther was noncommittal. "I do not despise them," he confided to Spalatin, "but I will not make use of them unless Christ, my protector, be willing, who has perhaps inspired the knight."

But Luther was ready to utilize the letters he had received for diplomatic purposes, and instructed Spalatin if it was not improper to show them to Cardinal Riario. Let the *curia* know that if by their fulminations he was expelled from Saxony, he would not go to Bohemia but would find an asylum in Germany itself, where he might be more obnoxious than when under the surveillance of the prince and fully occupied with the duties of teaching. The mood of the letter was truculent. "For me the die is cast," he said. "I despise alike Roman fury and Roman favor. I will not be reconciled nor communicate with them. They damn and burn my books. Unless I am unable to get hold of a fire, I will publicly burn the whole canon law."

In August, 1520, Luther intimated that because he had been delivered by these knights from the fear of men he would attack the papacy as Antichrist. But he had already done that; and while the assurance of protection undoubtedly heartened and emboldened him, the source of his courage was not to be found in a sense of immunity. One of his friends was fearful that Luther might retreat before the impending danger. He answered:

You ask how I am getting on. I do not know. Satan was never so furious against me. I can say this, that I have never sought goods, honor, and glory, and I am not cast down by the hostility of the masses. In fact, the more they rage the more I am filled with the spirit. But, and this may surprise you, I am scarcely able to resist the smallest wave of inner despair, and that is why the least tremor of this kind expels the greatest of the other sort. You need not fear that I shall desert the standards.

The most intrepid revolutionary is the one who has a fear greater than anything his opponents can inflict upon him. Luther, who had so trembled before the face of God, had no fear before the face of man.

As the issue became more plainly drawn, it was clear that he would have no violence either for himself or for the gospel. To Spalatin he wrote in January, 1521:

You see what Hutten asks. I am not willing to fight for the gospel with bloodshed. In this sense I have written to him. The world is conquered by the Word, and by the Word the Church is served and rebuilt. As Antichrist arose without the hand of man, so without the hand of man will he fall.

## CHAPTER EIGHT

# THE WILD BOAR
# IN THE VINEYARD

ECAUSE Luther relied at long last on the arm of the Lord outstretched from heaven, he was not for that reason remiss in doing what might be done on earth. The delay of a year and a half in his trial gave him an opportunity to elaborate his views and to declare his findings. His theology, as we have seen, was already mature before the breach with Rome as to the essential nature of God and Christ and as to the way of salvation. On these points Luther had been brought to see that he was in some respects at variance with the Church. But he had not as yet thought through the practical implications of his theology for the theory of the Church, her rites, her composition, and her relation to society. Neither had he addressed himself to the problems of moral conduct. The interlude during which he was unmolested, from the conference with Cajetan in October of 1518 to the arrival of the papal bull in October of 1520, provided the opportunity. Luther availed himself feverishly of the respite, not knowing of course how long it would last. During the summer of 1520 he delivered to the printer a sheaf of tracts which are still referred to as his primary works: *The Sermon on Good Works* in May, *The Papacy at Rome* in June, and *The Address to the German Nobility* in August, *The Babylonian Captivity* in September, and *The Freedom of the Christian Man* in November. The latter three pertain more immediately to the controversy and will alone engage us for the moment.

The most radical of them all in the eyes of contemporaries was the one dealing with the sacraments, entitled *The Babylonian Captivity*, with reference to the enslavement of the sacraments by the Church. This assault on Catholic teaching was more devastating than anything that had preceded; and when Erasmus read the tract, he ejaculated, "The breach is irreparable." The reason was that the pretensions of the

Roman Catholic Church rest so completely upon the sacraments as the exclusive channels of grace and upon the prerogatives of the clergy, by whom the sacraments are exclusively administered. If sacramentalism is undercut, then sacerdotalism is bound to fall. Luther with one stroke reduced the number of the sacraments from seven to two. Confirmation, marriage, ordination, penance, and extreme unction were eliminated. The Lord's Supper and baptism alone remained. The principle which dictated this reduction was that a sacrament must have been directly instituted by Christ and must be distinctively Christian.

The removal of confirmation and extreme unction was not of tremendous import save that it diminished the control of the Church over youth and death. The elimination of penance was much more serious because this is the rite of the forgiveness of sins. Luther in this instance did not abolish it utterly. Of the three ingredients of penance he recognized of course the need for contrition and looked upon confession as useful, provided it was not institutionalized. The drastic point was with regard to absolution, which he said is only a declaration by man of what God has decreed in heaven and not a ratification by God of what man has ruled on earth.

The repudiation of ordination as a sacrament demolished the caste system of clericalism and provided a sound basis for the priesthood of all believers, since according to Luther ordination is simply a rite of the Church by which a minister is installed to discharge a particular office. He receives no indelible character, is not exempt from the jurisdiction of the civil courts, and is not empowered by ordination to perform the other sacraments. At this point what the priest does any Christian may do, if commissioned by the congregation, because all Christians are priests. The fabrication of ordination as a sacrament

was designed to engender implacable discord whereby the clergy and the laity should be separated farther than heaven and earth, to the incredible injury of baptismal grace and to the confusion of evangelical fellowship. This is the source of that detestable tyranny over the laity by the clergy who, relying on the external anointing of their hands, the tonsure and the vestments, not only exalt themselves above lay Christians, anointed by the Holy Spirit, but even regard them as dogs, unworthy to be included with them in the Church. . . . Here Christian brotherhood has expired and shepherds have become wolves. All of us who have been baptized are priests without distinction, but those whom we call priests are ministers. chosen from among us that they should do all things in our name and their priesthood is nothing but a ministry. The sacrament of ordination, therefore, can be nothing other than a certain rite of choosing a preacher in the Church.

But Luther's rejection of the five sacraments might even have been tolerated had it not been for the radical transformation which he effected in the two which he retained. From his view of baptism he was to infer a repudiation of monasticism on the ground that it is not a second baptism, and no vow should ever be taken beyond the baptismal vow.

Most serious of all was Luther's reduction of the mass to the Lord's Supper. The mass is central for the entire Roman Catholic system because the mass is believed to be a repetition of the Incarnation and the Crucifixion. When the bread and wine are transubstantiated, God again becomes flesh and Christ again dies upon the altar. This wonder can be performed only by priests empowered through ordination. Inasmuch as this means of grace is administered exclusively by their hands, they occupy a unique place within the Church; and because the Church is the custodian of the body of Christ, she occupies a unique place in society.

Luther did not attack the mass in order to undermine the priests. His concerns were always primarily religious and only incidentally ecclesiastical or sociological. His first insistence was that the sacrament of the mass must be not magical but mystical, not the performance of a rite but the experience of a presence. This point was one of several discussed with Cajetan at the interview. The cardinal complained of Luther's view that the efficacy of the sacrament depends upon the faith of the recipient. The teaching of the Church is that the sacraments cannot be impaired by any human weakness, be it the unworthiness of the performer or the indifference of the receiver. The sacrament operates by virtue of a power within itself *ex opere operato*. In Luther's eyes such a view made the sacrament mechanical and magical. He, too, had no mind to subject it to human frailty and would not concede that he had done so by positing the necessity of faith, since faith is itself a gift of God, but this faith is given by God when, where, and to whom he will and even without the sacrament is efficacious; whereas the reverse is not true, that the sacrament is of efficacy without faith. "I may be wrong on indulgences," declared Luther, "but as to the need for faith in the sacraments I will die before I will recant." This insistence upon faith diminished the role of the priests who may place a wafer in the mouth but cannot engender faith in the heart.

The second point made by Luther was that the priest is not in a position to do that which the Church claims in the celebration of the mass. He does not "make God," and he does not "sacrifice Christ." The simplest way of negating this view would have been to say that God is not present and Christ is not sacrificed, but Luther was ready to affirm only the latter. Christ is not sacrificed because his sacrifice was made once and for all upon the cross, but God is present in the elements because Christ, being God, declared, "This is my body." The repetition of these words by the priest, however, does not transform the bread and wine into the body and blood of God, as the Catholic Church holds. The view called transubstantiation was that the elements retain their accidents of shape, taste, color, and so on, but lose their substance, for which is substituted the substance of God. Luther rejected this position less on rational than on biblical grounds. Both Erasmus and Melanchthon before him had pointed out that the concept of substance is not biblical but a scholastic sophistication. For that reason Luther was averse to its use at all, and his own view should not be called consubstantiation. The sacrament for him was not a chunk of God fallen like a meteorite from heaven. God does not need to fall from heaven because he is everywhere present throughout his creation as a sustaining and animating force, and Christ as God is likewise universal, but his presence is hid from human eyes. For that reason God has chosen to declare himself unto mankind at three loci of revelation. The first is Christ, in whom the Word was made flesh. The second is Scripture, where the Word uttered is recorded. The third is the sacrament, in which the Word is manifest in food and drink. The sacrament does not conjure up God as the witch of Endor but reveals him where he is.

*sacrament reveals God - where He is.*

To the degree that the powers of the priest were diminished, his prerogatives also were curtailed. In Catholic practice one of the distinctions between the clergy and the laity is that only the priest drinks the wine at the mass. The restriction arose out of the fear that the laity in clumsiness might spill some of the blood of God. Luther felt no less reverence for the sacrament, but he would not safeguard it at the expense of a caste system within the Church. Despite the risk, the cup should be given to all believers. This pronouncement in his day had an uncommon ring of radicalism because the chalice for the laity was the cry of the Bohemian Hussites. They justified their practice on the ground that Christ said, "Drink ye all of it." Catholic interpreters explain these words as addressed only to the apostles, who were all priests. Luther agreed, but retorted that all believers were priests.

### THE SACRAMENTS AND THE THEORY OF THE CHURCH

Such a view was fraught with far-reaching consequences for the theory of the Church, and Luther's own view of the Church was derivative from his theory of the sacraments. His deductions, however, were not clear-cut in this area, because his view of the Lord's Supper pointed in one direction and his view of baptism in another. That is why he could be at once to a degree the father of the congregationalism of the

Anabaptists and of the territorial church of the later Lutherans.

His view of the Lord's Supper made for the gathered church of convinced believers only, because he declared that the sacrament depends for its efficacy upon the faith of the recipient. That must of necessity make it highly individual because faith is individual. Every soul, insisted Luther, stands in naked confirmation before its Maker. No one can die in the place of another; everyone must wrestle with the pangs of death for himself alone. "Then I shall not be with you, nor you with me. Everyone must answer for himself." Similarly, "The mass is a divine promise which can help no one, be applied for no one, intercede for no one, and be communicated to none save him only who believes with a faith of his own. Who can accept or apply for another the promise of God which requires faith of each individually?"

Here we are introduced to the very core of Luther's individualism. It is not the individualism of the Renaissance, seeking the fulfillment of the individual's capacities; it is not the individualism of the late scholastic, who on metaphysical grounds declared that reality consists only of individuals, and that aggregates like Church and state are not entities but simply the sum of their components. Luther was not concerned to philosophize about the structure of Church and state; his insistence was simply that every man must answer for himself to God. That was the extent of his individualism. The faith requisite for the sacrament must be one's own. From such a theory the obvious inference is that the Church should consist only of those possessed of a warm personal faith; and since the number of such persons is never large, the Church would have to be a comparatively small conventicle. Luther not infrequently spoke precisely as if this were his meaning. Especially in his earlier lectures he had delineated a view of the Church as a remnant because the elect are few. This must be so, he held, because the Word of God goes counter to all the desires of the natural man, abasing pride, crushing arrogance, and leaving all human pretensions in dust and ashes. Such a work is unpalatable, and few will receive it. Those who do will be stones rejected by the builders. Derision and persecution will be their lot. Every Abel is bound to have his Cain, and every Christ his Caiaphas. Therefore the true Church will be despised and rejected of men and will lie hidden in the midst of the world. These words of Luther might readily issue in the substitution for the Catholic monastery of the segregated Protestant community.

But Luther was not willing to take this road because the sacrament of baptism pointed for him in another direction. He could readily enough have accommodated baptism to the preceding view, had he been willing, like the Anabaptists, to regard baptism as the outward sign of an inner experience of regeneration appropriate only to adults and not infants. But this he would not do. Luther stood with the Catholic Church on the score of infant baptism because children must be snatched at birth from the power of Satan. But what then becomes of his formula that the efficacy of the sacrament depends upon the faith of the recipient? He strove hard to retain it by the figment of an implicit faith in the baby comparable to the faith of a man in sleep. But again Luther would shift from the faith of the child to the faith of the sponsor by which the infant is undergirded. Birth for him was not so isolated as death. One cannot die for another, but one can in a sense be initiated for another into a Christian community. For that reason baptism rather than the Lord's Supper is the sacrament which links the Church to society. It is the sociological sacrament. For the medieval community every child outside the ghetto was by birth a citizen and by baptism a Christian. Regardless of personal conviction the same persons constituted the state and the Church. An alliance of the two institutions was thus natural. Here was a basis for a Christian society. The greatness and the tragedy of Luther was that he could never relinquish either the individualism of the eucharistic cup or the corporateness of the baptismal font. He would have been a troubled spirit in a tranquil age.

### PROSECUTION RESUMED

But his age was not tranquil. Rome had not forgotten him. The lifting of the pressure was merely opportunist; and as the time approached when the Most Catholic Emperor would come from Spain to Germany, the papacy was prepared to resume the prosecution. Even before the publication of the assault on the sacraments, which in the eyes of Erasmus made the breach irreparable, Luther had said quite enough to warrant drastic action. The assertions of the indulgence controversy had been augmented by the more devastating attack upon the divine origin and rule of the papacy at the Leipzig debate. His offense was so glaring that a member of the *curia* deprecated waiting until the arrival of the emperor. Then came Eck to Rome, armed not only with the notes on Leipzig but also with condemnations of Luther's teaching by the universities of Cologne and Louvain. When Erfurt had declined and Paris had failed to report on the disputation between Luther and Eck, these two other universities stepped unsolicited into the breach. The judgment of Cologne, dominated by the Dominicans, was more severe. Louvain was slightly tinctured with Erasmianism. Both were agreed in condemning Luther's views on human depravity, penance, purgatory, and indulgences. Louvain was silent with regard to the attack on the papacy, whereas Cologne complained of heretical notions as to the primacy and derogation from the power of the keys.

Luther retorted that neither cited against him any proof from the Scripture.

Why do we not abolish the gospel and turn instead to them? Strange that handworkers give sounder judgments than theologians! How seriously should one take those who condemned Reuchlin? If they burn my books, I will repeat what I have said. In this I am so bold that for it I will suffer death. When Christ was filled with scorn against the Pharisees and Paul was outraged by the blindness of the Athenians, what, I beg you, shall I do?

Nothing further of the prosecution is on record until March, when the attempt was resumed to suppress Luther quietly through the Augustinian order. The general wrote to Staupitz:

The order, never previously suspected of heresy, is becoming odious. We beg you in the bonds of love to do your utmost to restrain Luther from speaking against the Holy Roman Church and her indulgences. Urge him to stop writing. Let him save our order from infamy.

Staupitz extricated himself by resigning as vicar.

Another approach was made through Frederick the Wise. Cardinal Riario, lately pardoned for his complicity in an attempt on the life of the pope, wrote to Frederick:

Most illustrious noble lord and brother, when I recall the splendor of your house and the devotion ever displayed by your progenitors and yourself toward the Holy See, I think it the part of friendship to write to you concerning the common good of Christendom and the everlasting honor of yourself. I am sure you are not ignorant of the rancor, contempt, and license with which Martin Luther rails against the Roman pontiff and the whole *curia*. Wherefore I exhort you, bring this man to reject his error. You can if you will; with just one little pebble the puny David killed the mighty Goliath.

Frederick replied that the case had been referred to his most dear friend, the Archbishop of Trier, Elector of the Holy Roman Empire, Richard of Greiffenklau.

In May dallying ended. Four meetings of the consistory were held, on May 21, 23, 26, and June 1. The pope on the evening of the twenty-second retired to his hunting lodge at Magliana, *a soliti piaceri*. The cardinals, the canonists, and the theologians carried on. There may have been some forty in attendance. Eck was the only German. The three great monastic orders were represented, the Dominicans, the Franciscans, and the Augustinians. No longer could one speak of a monk's squabble. Luther's own general was there, not to mention his old opponents Prierias and Cajetan. Three questions were to be settled: what to do with Luther's opinions, what to do with his books, and what to do with his person. Lively differences of opinion ensued. Some in the first session questioned the expediency of issuing a bull at all in view of the exacerbated state of Germany. The theologians were for condemning Luther outright. The canonists contended that he should be given a hearing like Adam, for even though God knew him to be guilty he gave him an opportunity to defend himself when he said, "Where art thou?" A compromise was reached whereby Luther was not to have a hearing but should be given sixty days in which to make his submission.

With regard to his teaching there were debates, though by whom and about what can only be surmised. Reports at second or third hand suggest the differences within the consistory. The Italian Cardinal Accolti is said to have called Tetzel a *"porcaccio"* and to have given Prierias a *rabbuffo* for composing in three days a reply to Luther which might better have taken three months. Cajetan is reported to have sniffed on Eck's arrival in Rome, "Who let in that beast?" Spanish Cardinal Carvajal, a conciliarist, is said to have opposed vehemently the action against Luther. In the end unanimity was attained for the condemnation of forty-one articles. The previous strictures of Louvain and Cologne were combined and amplified.

### THE BULL "EXSURGE"

Anyone acquainted with Luther's mature position will feel that the bull was exceedingly sparse in its reproof. Luther's views on the mass were condemned only at the point of the cup to the laity. No other of the seven sacraments received notice, save penance. There was nothing about monastic vows, only a disavowal of Luther's desire that princes and prelates might suppress the sacks of the mendicants. There was nothing about the priesthood of all believers. The articles centered on Luther's disparagement of human capacity even after baptism, on his derogation from the power of the pope to bind and loose penalties and sins, from the power of the pope and councils to declare doctrine, from the primacy of the pope and of the Roman Church. At one point the condemnation of Luther conflicted with the recent pronouncement of the pope on indulgences. Luther was reproved for reserving the remission of penalties imposed by divine justice to God alone, whereas the pope himself had just declared that in such cases the treasury of merits could be applied only by way of intercession, not of jurisdiction. The charge of Bohemianism against Luther had plainly lodged, because he was condemned on the score of introducing certain of the articles of John Hus. Two characteristically Erasmian tenets received strictures, that to burn heretics is against the will of the Spirit and that war

Bulla contra errores Martini Lutheri z sequacium.

THE BULL AGAINST LUTHER

against the Turks is resistance to God's visitation. The forty-one articles were not pronounced uniformly heretical but were condemned as "heretical, or scandalous, or false, or offensive to pious ears, or seductive of simple minds, or repugnant to Catholic truth, respectively." Some suspected at the time that this formula was adopted because the consistory was not able to make up its mind which were which, and therefore, like the triumvirs, proscribed the enemies of each though they might be friends of the rest. One may doubt, however, whether this was the case, because the formula was stereotyped and had been used in the condemnation of John Hus.

The completed bull was presented to the pope for a preface and conclusion. In keeping with the surroundings of his hunting lodge at Magliana he commenced:

Arise, O Lord, and judge thy cause. A wild boar has invaded thy vineyard. Arise, O Peter, and consider the case of the Holy Roman Church, the mother of all churches, consecrated by thy blood. Arise, O Paul, who by thy teaching and death hast and dost illumine the Church. Arise, all ye saints, and the whole universal Church, whose interpretation of Scripture has been assailed. We can scarcely express our grief over the ancient heresies which have been revived in Germany. We are the more downcast because she was always in the forefront of the war on heresy. Our pastoral office can no longer tolerate the pestiferous virus of the following forty-one errors. [They are enumerated.] We can no longer suffer the serpent to creep through the field of the Lord. The books of Martin Luther which contain these errors are to be examined and burned. As for Martin himself, good God, what office of paternal love have we omitted in order to recall him from his errors? Have we not offered him a safe conduct and money for the journey? [Such an offer never reached Luther.] And he has had the temerity to appeal to a future council although our predecessors, Pius II and Julius II, subjected such appeals to the penalties of heresy. Now therefore we give Martin sixty days in which to submit, dating from the time of the publication of this bull in his district. Anyone who presumes to infringe our excommunication and anathema will stand under the wrath of Almighty God and of the apostles Peter and Paul.

Dated on the 15th day of June, 1520.

This bull is known by its opening words, which are *Exsurge Domine*.

A few weeks later the pope wrote to Frederick the Wise:

Beloved son, we rejoice that you have never shown any favor to that son of iniquity, Martin Luther. We do not know whether to credit this the more to your sagacity or to your piety. This Luther favors the Bohemians and the Turks, deplores the punishment of heretics, spurns the writings of the holy doctors, the decrees of the ecumenical councils, and the ordinances of the Roman pontiffs, and gives credence to the opinions of none save himself alone, which no heretic before ever presumed to do. We cannot suffer the scabby sheep longer to infect the flock. Wherefore we have summoned a conclave of venerable brethren. The Holy Spirit also was present, for in such cases he is never absent from our Holy See. We have composed a bull, sealed with lead, in which out of the innumerable errors of this man we have selected those in which he perverts the faith, seduces the simple, and relaxes the bonds of obedience, continence, and humility. The abuses which he has vaunted against our Holy See we leave to God. We exhort you to induce him to return to sanity and receive our clemency. If he persists in his madness, take him captive.

Given under the seal of the Fisherman's ring on the 8th of July, 1520, and in the eighth year of our pontificate.

### THE BULL SEEKS LUTHER

The papal bull took three months to find Luther, but there were early rumors that it was on the way. Hutten wrote to him on July 4, 1520:

You are said to be under excommunication. If it be true, how mighty you are. In you the words of the psalm are fulfilled, "They have condemned innocent blood, but the Lord our God will render to them their iniquity and destroy them in their malice." This is our hope; be this our faith. There are plots against me also. If they use force, they will be met with force. I wish they would condemn me. Stand firm. Do not waver. But why should I admonish you? I will stand by, whatever come. Let us vindicate the common liberty. Let us liberate the oppressed fatherland. God will be on our side; and if God is with us, who can be against us?

This was the time when renewed offers came from Sickingen and from a hundred knights besides. Luther was not unmoved, yet he scarcely knew whether to rely on the arm of man or solely on the Lord. During that summer of 1520, when the papal bull was seeking him throughout Germany, his mood fluctuated between the incendiary and the apocalyptic. In one unguarded outburst he incited to violence. A new attack by Prierias lashed Luther to rage. In a printed reply he declared:

It seems to me that if the Romanists are so mad the only remedy remaining is for the emperor, the kings, and princes to gird themselves with force of arms to attack these pests of all the world and fight them, not with words, but with steel. If we punish thieves with the yoke, highwaymen with the sword, and heretics with fire, why do we not rather assault these monsters of perdition, these cardinals, these popes, and the whole swarm of the Roman Sodom, who corrupt youth and the Church of God? Why do we not rather assault them with arms and wash our hands in their blood?

Luther explained afterwards that he really did not mean what the words imply.

I wrote "*If* we burn heretics, why do we not rather attack the pope and his followers with the sword and wash our hands in their blood?" Since I do not approve of burning heretics nor of killing any Christian—this I well know does not accord with the gospel—I have shown what they deserve *if* heretics deserve fire. There is no need to attack you with the sword.

Despite this disclaimer Luther was never suffered to forget his incendiary blast. It was quoted against him in the Edict of the Diet of Worms.

The disavowal was genuine. His prevailing mood was expressed in a letter of October to a minister who was prompted to leave his post. Luther wrote:

Our warfare is not with flesh and blood, but against spiritual wickedness in the heavenly places, against the world rulers of this darkness. Let us then stand firm and heed the trumpet of the Lord. Satan is fighting, not against us, but against Christ in us. We fight the battles of the Lord. Be strong therefore. If God is for us, who can be against us?

You are dismayed because Eck is publishing a most severe bull against Luther, his books, and his followers. Whatever may happen, I am not moved, because nothing can happen save in accord with the will of him who sits upon the heaven directing all. Let not your hearts be troubled. Your Father knows your need before you ask him. Not a leaf from a tree falls to the ground without his knowledge. How much less can any of us fall unless it be his will.

If you have the spirit, do not leave your post, lest another receive your crown. It is but a little thing that we should die with the Lord, who in our flesh laid down his life for us. We shall rise with him and abide with him in eternity. See then that you do not despise your holy calling. He will come, he will not tarry, who will deliver us from every ill. Fare well in the Lord Jesus, who comforts and sustains mind and spirit. Amen.

CHAPTER NINE

# THE APPEAL TO CAESAR

T ONE point Luther was perfectly clear. Whoever helped or did not help him, he would make his testimony.

"For me the die is cast. I despise alike Roman fury and Roman favor. I will not be reconciled or communicate with them. Let them damn and burn my books. I for my part, unless I cannot find a fire, will publicly damn and burn the whole canon law."

Neither did Luther neglect his defense. He had appealed in vain to the pope and in vain to a council. There was one more recourse, the appeal to the emperor. During the month of August Luther addressed Charles V in these words:

It is not presumptuous that one who through evangelical truth has ascended the throne of Divine Majesty should approach the throne of an earthly prince, nor is it unseemly that an earthly prince, who is the image of the Heavenly, should stoop to raise up the poor from the dust. Consequently, unworthy and poor though I be, I prostrate myself before your Imperial Majesty. I have published books which have alienated many, but I have done so because driven by others, for I would prefer nothing more than to remain in obscurity. For three years I have sought peace in vain. I have now but one recourse. I appeal to Caesar. I have no desire to be defended if I am found to be impious or heretical. One thing I ask, that neither truth nor error be condemned unheard and un-refuted.

Luther asked of Caesar, however, more than that he should hear a man. He was also to vindicate a cause. The Church was desperately in need of reform, and the initiative would have to come, as Hutten contended, from the civil power. A mighty program of reformation was delineated by Luther in the *Address to the German Nobility.* The term "nobility" was broadly used to cover the ruling class in Germany, from the emperor down. But by what right, the modern reader may well inquire, might Luther call upon them to reform the Church? The question has more than an antiquarian interest, because some contend that in this tract Luther broke with his earlier view of the Church as a persecuted remnant and laid instead the basis for a church allied with and subservient to the state. Luther adduced three grounds for his appeal. The first was simply that the magistrate was the magistrate, or-dained of God to punish evildoers. All that Luther demanded of the magistrate as magistrate was that he should hale the clergy before the civil courts, protect citizens against ecclesi-astical extortion, and vindicate the state in the exercise of civil functions from clerical interference. This was the sense in which Luther often asserted that no one in a thousand years had so championed the civil state as he. The theocratic pre-tensions of the Church were to be repulsed.

The *Address to the German Nobility,* however, goes far beyond a mere circumscribing of the Church to her proper sphere. Luther was much less concerned for the emancipation of the state than for the purification of the Church. The strip-ping away of temporal power and inordinate wealth was de-signed to emancipate the Church from worldly cares that she might better perform her spiritual functions. The basis of the right of the magistrate to undertaken this reform is stated in Luther's second reason, namely, "The temporal authorities are baptized with the same baptism as we." This is the language of the Christian society, built upon the sociological sacrament administered to every babe born into the community. In such a society, Church and state are mutually responsible for the support and correction of each other.

In a third passage Luther gave the additional ground, that
the magistrates were fellow Christians sharing in the priesthood
of all believers, from which some modern historians have

An den Christlichenn
Adel teutscher Nation:
von des Christlichen
standes besserung:
D. Martinus
Luther.

Durch yhn selbs ge/
mehret vnd corrigirt.

Buittemberg.

TITLE PAGE OF THE "ADDRESS TO THE GERMAN NOBILITY"

inferred that Luther would concede to the magistrate the role
of Church reformer only if he were himself a convinced
Christian, and then only in an emergency. But no such qualification is stated in this tract. The priesthood of all believers

itself was made to rest upon the lower grade of faith implicit in the baptized infant. Luther's whole attitude to the reformatory role of the magistrate is essentially medieval. What sets it off from so many other attempts at the redress of grievances is its deeply religious tone. The complaints of Germany were combined with the reform of the Church, and the civil power itself was directed to rely less on the arm of flesh than upon the hand of the Lord.

The program began with religious premises. Three walls of Rome must tumble down like the walls of Jericho. The first was that the spiritual power is above the temporal. This claim Luther countered with the doctrine of the priesthood of all believers. "We are all alike Christians and have baptism, faith, the Spirit, and all things alike. If a priest is killed, a land is laid under an interdict. Why not in the case of a peasant? Whence comes this great distinction between those who are called Christians?" The second wall was that the pope alone might interpret Scripture. This assertion was met, not so much by the vindication of the rights of Humanist scholarship against papal incompetence, as by the claims of lay Christianity to understand the mind of Christ. "Balaam's ass was wiser than the prophet himself. If God then spoke by an ass against a prophet, why should he not be able even now to speak by a righteous man against the pope?" The third wall was that the pope alone could call a council. Here again the priesthood of all believers gave the right to anyone in an emergency, but peculiarly to the civil power because of its strategic position.

Then follow all the proposals for the reforms to be instituted by a council. The papacy should return to apostolic simplicity, with no more triple crown and no toe kissing. The pope should not receive the sacrament seated, proffered to him by a kneeling cardinal through a golden reed, but should stand up like any other "stinking sinner." The cardinals should be reduced in number. The temporal possessions and claims of the Church should be abandoned that the pope might devote himself only to spiritual concerns. The income of the Church should be curtailed—no more annates, fees, indulgences, golden years, reservations, crusading taxes, and all the rest of the tricks by which the "drunken Germans" were despoiled. Litigation in Church courts involving Germans should be tried in Germany under a German primate. This suggestion looked in the direction of a national church. For Bohemia it was definitely recommended.

The proposals with regard to monasticism and clerical marriage went beyond anything Luther had said previously. The mendicants should be relieved of hearing confession and preaching. The number of orders should be reduced, and there should be no irrevocable vows. The clergy should be permitted to marry because they need housekeepers, and to place man and woman together under such circumstances is like setting straw beside fire and expecting it not to burn.

Miscellaneous recommendations called for the reduction of Church festivals and a curb on pilgrimages. Saints should be left to canonize themselves. The state should inaugurate legal reform and undertake sumptuary legislation. This program was comprehensive and for the most part would evoke hearty applause in Germany.

Underlying it all was a deep indignation against the corruption of the Church. Again and again the pope was shamed by a comparison with Christ. This theme went back through Hus to Wyclif. An illustrated work in Bohemian on the disparity of Christ and the pope was in the library of Frederick the Wise. A similar work was later issued in Wittenberg with annotations by Melanchthon and woodcuts by Cranach. The idea was already present in the *Address to the German Nobility*, where reference was made to Christ on foot, the pope in a palanquin with a retinue of three or four thousand mule drivers; Christ washing the disciples' feet, the pope having his feet kissed; Christ enjoining keeping faith even with an enemy, the pope declaring that no faith is to be kept with him who has no faith, and that promises to heretics are not binding. Still worse, constraint against them is employed. "But heretics should be vanquished with books, not with burnings. O Christ my lord, look down. Let the day of thy judgment break and destroy the devil's nest at Rome!"

*On the left Christ is washing the disciples' feet. On the right Antichrist, the pope, is having his toes kissed by monarchs.*

## PUBLICATION OF THE BULL

In the meantime the bull *Exsurge Domine* was being executed at Rome. Luther's books were burned in the Piazza Navona. The bull was printed, notarized, and sealed for wider dissemination. The task of its publication in the north was committed to two men who were named papal nuncios and special inquisitors for the purpose. One of them was John Eck. The other, Jerome Aleander, was a distinguished Humanist, master of three languages—Latin, Greek, and Hebrew—a former rector of the University of Paris. He had some acquaintance with German affairs through his youth in the Low Countries. His irregularities in private morals gave no offense in the days of the unreformed papacy. The field was divided between the two men, partly along geographical lines. Eck was to take the east, Franconia and Bavaria. Aleander should cover the Low Countries and the Rhine. There was further division of function in that Aleander should address himself to the emperor and his court and to the high magnates, lay and clerical, whereas Eck should go rather to the bishops and the universities. The two men were enjoined to act in perfect accord. Aleander's instructions told him first of all to deliver the bull "To our beloved son Charles, Holy Roman Emperor and Catholic King of Spain." At that moment all parties were looking to Charles. He was young and had not yet declared himself. The pope expected him to follow the example of his grandmother, Isabella the Catholic. The Germans saw in him the heir of his grandfather, Maximilian the German. Aleander was advised in case Luther should demand a hearing before the court of the emperor to reply that the case was being handled solely by Rome. This is the first suggestion that Luther might ask to have his case referred to a secular tribunal. The secretary who composed this memorandum was singularly clairvoyant, because the instructions were drafted prior to Luther's appeal to Caesar. Eck received a secret commission, unknown to Aleander, permitting the inclusion in the condemnation of more names than Luther's, according to discretion.

Neither man relished his assignment, which each undertook at the risk of his life. Eck made his task vastly more difficult by adding names at his indiscretion, six of them: three from Wittenberg, including Carlstadt; and three from Nürnberg, including Spengler and Pirkheimer. He could not have chosen a more inopportune moment to attack the leaders of German Humanism, who were never more united. Aleander likewise in the Netherlands was confronted with many Luther sympathizers. There was Erasmus, who said, "The inclemency of this bull ill comports with the moderation of Leo." And again, "Papal bulls are weighty, but scholars attach more weight to books with good arguments drawn from the testimony of divine Scripture, which does not coerce but instructs." In Antwerp the Marrani, Spaniards and Portuguese of Jewish extraction, were printing Luther in Spanish. German merchants were disseminating his ideas. Albrecht Dürer was executing commissions in Antwerp while looking to Luther and Erasmus to purify the Church. In the Rhine valley there were rumors that Sickingen might vindicate Luther, as he had done Reuchlin, by force of arms.

Eck met with the most unexpected opposition. Duke George held back on the ground that his locality had not been specifically named. Frederick the Wise was expected to obstruct, but he did so in the most disconcerting way by reporting that he had learned from Aleander that Eck had no authorization to include anyone save Luther. Eck then was forced to produce his secret instructions. On one ground or another the very bishops held back, some of them for six months, before publishing the bull. The University of Vienna declined to act without the bishop, and the University of Wittenberg protested the impropriety of entrusting the publication of the bull to a party in the dispute. "The goat should not be permitted to be a gardner, nor the wolf a shepherd, nor John Eck a papal nuncio." Not only the University of Wittenberg but even the Duke of Bavaria expressed fear that publication of the bull would produce disorder. There was some reason for such concern. At Leipzig, Eck had to hide for his life in a cloister. At Erfurt, when he had the bull reprinted, the students dubbed it a "bulloon" and threw all the copies in the river to see whether they would float. At Torgau it was torn down and besmeared. The only easy successes were with the bishops of Brandenburg, Meissen, and Merseburg, who permitted the publication of the bull on September 21, 25, and 29 respectively. Eck, in honor of this triumph, erected a votive tablet in the church at Ingolstadt: "John Eck, *professor ordinarius* of theology and university chancellor, papal nuncio and apostolic protonotary, having published in accord with the command of Leo X the bull against Lutheran doctrine in Saxony and Meissen, erects this tablet in gratitude that he has returned home alive."

Aleander found his task complicated because the bull leaked to Germany before its publication, and in a form discrepant from his own. He was well received, however, at the imperial court at Antwerp, and His Majesty promised to stake his life on the protection of the Church and the honor of the pope and the Holy See. He was perfectly ready to execute the bull in his hereditary domains, and Aleander was able therefore to institute an auto-da-fé of Lutheran books at Louvain on October 8. When the fire was started, however, students threw in works of scholastic theology and a medieval handbook for preachers entitled *Sleep Well*. A similar burning took place at Liége on the seventeenth. The mendicants and the conservatives of the university faculty at Louvain were incited to make life intolerable for Erasmus. The Counter Reformation, aided by the imperial arm, was already begun.

But in the Rhineland it was different. The emperor there ruled only by virtue of his election. When at Cologne on November 12 Aleander tried to have a bonfire, though the archbishop had given his consent, the executioner refused to proceed without an express imperial mandate. The archbishop asserted his authority, and the books were burned. At Mainz the opposition was more violent. The executioner, before applying the torch, turned to the as-

FROM TITLE PAGE OF HUTTEN'S PROTEST "AGAINST THE BURNING OF LUTHER'S BOOKS AT MAINZ"

sembled onlookers and inquired whether these books had been legally condemned. When with one voice the throng boomed back "No!" the executioner stepped down and refused to act. Aleander appealed to Albert, the archbishop, and secured from him authorization to destroy a few books on the following day. The order was carried out on the twenty-ninth of November, not by the public executioner, but by a gravedigger, and with no witnesses save a few women who had brought their geese to market. Aleander was pelted with stones, and he declared that except for the intervention of the abbot he would not have come off with his life. His word might be doubted had we no other evidence, for he magnified his danger to enhance his achievements.

But in this instance there is independent corroboration. Ulrich von Hutten came out in verse with an invective both in Latin and in German:

> O God, Luther's books they burn.
> Thy godly truth is slain in turn.
> Pardon in advance is sold,
> And heaven marketed for gold.
> The German people is bled white
> And is not asked to be contrite.

> To Martin Luther wrong is done—
> O God, be thou our champion.
> My goods for him I will not spare,
> My life, my blood for him I dare.

On October 10 the bull reached Luther. The following day he commented to Spalatin:

This bull condemns Christ himself. It summons me not to an audience but to a recantation. I am going to act on the assumption that it is spurious, though I think it is genuine. Would that Charles were a man and would fight for Christ against these Satans. But I am not afraid. God's will be done. I do not know what the prince should do unless to dissemble. I am sending you a copy of the bull that you may see the Roman monster. The faith and the Church are at stake. I rejoice to suffer in so noble a cause. I am not worthy of so holy a trial. I feel much freer now that I am certain the pope is Antichrist. Erasmus writes that the imperial court is overrun with mendicants, and there is no hope from the emperor. I am on the way to Lichtenburg for a conference with Miltitz. Farewell and pray for me.

The game of obstruction had already begun. Frederick the Wise played the instructions of Aleander and the commission of Miltitz against John Eck. Miltitz had never been recalled by the pope and now said frankly that Eck had no business to publish the bull while friendly negotiations were still in progress. Frederick resolved to keep them going, and therefore arranged for a new interview between Luther and Miltitz, and of course the Archbishop of Trier was still in the picture as an arbiter. For that reason Luther impugned the genuineness of the bull on the ground that Rome would not make monkeys of two electors by taking the case out of their hands. "Therefore I will not believe in the authenticity of this bull until I see the original lead and wax, string, signature, and seal with my own eyes."

For a time Luther reckoned with the double possibility that the bull might be either true or false. In that sense he came out with a vehement assault, apparently at the instance of Spalatin, to whom he wrote:

It is hard to dissent from all the pontiffs and princes, but there is no other way to escape hell and the wrath of God. If you had not urged, I would leave everything to God and do no more than I have done. I have put out a reply to the bull in Latin, of which I am sending you a copy. The German version is in the press. When since the beginning of the world did Satan ever so rage against God? I am overcome by the magnitude of the horrible blasphemies of this bull. I am almost persuaded by many and weighty arguments that the last day is at the threshold. The Kingdom of Antichrist begins to fall. I see an insuppressible insurrection coming out of this bull, which the Roman *curia* deserves.

### AGAINST THE EXECRABLE BULL OF ANTICHRIST

The reply to which he referred was entitled *Against the Execrable Bull of Antichrist*. Luther wrote:

I have heard that a bull against me has gone through the whole earth before it came to me, because being a daughter of darkness it feared the light of my face. For this reason and also because it condemns manifestly Christian articles I had my doubts whether it really came from Rome and was not rather the progeny of that man of lies, dissimulation, errors, and heresy, that monster John Eck. The suspicion was further increased when it was said that Eck was the apostle of the bull. Indeed the style and the spittle all point to Eck. True, it is not impossible that where Eck is the apostle there one should find the kingdom of Antichrist. Nevertheless in the meantime I will act as if I thought Leo not responsible, not that I may honor the Roman name, but because I do not consider myself worthy to suffer such high things for the truth of God. For who before God would be happier than Luther if he were condemned from so great and high a source for such manifest truth? But the cause seeks a worthier martyr. I with my sins merit other things. But whoever wrote this bull, he is Antichrist. I protest before God, our Lord Jesus, his sacred angels, and the whole world that with my whole heart I dissent from the damnation of this bull, that I curse and execrate it as sacrilege and blasphemy of Christ, God's Son and our Lord. This be my recantation, O bull, thou daughter of bulls.

Having given my testimony I proceed to take up the bull. Peter said that you should give a reason for the faith that is in you, but this bull condemns me from its own word without any proof from Scripture, whereas I back up all my assertions from the Bible. I ask thee, ignorant Antichrist, dost thou think that with thy naked words thou canst prevail against the armor of Scripture? Hast thou learned this from Cologne and Louvain? If this is all it takes, just to say, "I dissent, I deny," what fool, what ass, what mole, what log could not condemn? Does not thy meretricious brow blush that with thine inane smoke thou withstandest the lightning of the divine Word? Why do we not believe the Turks? Why do we not admit the Jews? Why do we not honor the heretics if damning is all that it takes? But Luther, who is used to *bellum,* is not afraid of *bullam.* I can distinguish between inane paper and the omnipotent Word of God.

They show their ignorance and bad conscience by inventing the adverb "respectively." My articles are called "respectively some heretical, some erroneous, some scandalous," which is as much as to say, "We don't know which are which." O meticulous ignorance! I wish to be instructed, not respectively, but absolutely and certainly. I demand that they show absolutely, not respectively, distinctly and not confusedly, certainly and not probably, clearly and not obscurely, point by point and not in a lump, just what is heretical. Let them show where I am a heretic, or dry up their spittle. They say that some articles are heretical, some erroneous, some scandalous, some offensive. The implication is that those which are heretical are not erroneous, those which are erroneous are not scandalous, and those which are scandalous are not offensive. What then is this, to say that something is not heretical, not scandalous, not false, but yet is offensive? So then, you impious and insensate papist, write soberly if you want to write. Whether this bull is by Eck or by the pope, it is the sum of all impiety, blasphemy, ignorance, impudence, hypocrisy, lying—in a word, it is Satan and his Antichrist.

Where are you now, most excellent Charles the Emperor, kings, and Christian princes? You were baptized into the name of Christ, and can you suffer these Tartar voices of Antichrist? Where are you, bishops? Where, doctors? Where are you who confess Christ? Woe to all who live in these times. The wrath of God is coming upon the papists, the enemies of the cross of Christ, that all men should resist them. You then, Leo X, you cardinals and the rest of you at Rome, I tell you to your faces: "If this bull has come out in your name, then I will use the power which has been given me in baptism whereby I became a son of God and co-heir with Christ, established upon the rock against which the gates of hell cannot prevail. I call upon you to renounce your diabolical blasphemy and audacious impiety, and, if you will not, we shall all hold your seat as possessed and oppressed by Satan, the damned seat of Antichrist, in the name of Jesus Christ, whom you persecute." But my zeal carries me away. I am not yet persuaded that the bull is by the pope but rather by that apostle of impiety, John Eck.

Then follows a discussion of the articles. The tract concludes:

If anyone despise my fraternal warning, I am free from his blood in the last judgment. It is better that I should die a thousand times than that I should retract one syllable of the condemned articles. And as they excommunicated me for the sacrilege of heresy, so I excommunicate them in the name of the sacred truth of God. Christ will judge whose excommunication will stand. Amen.

### THE FREEDOM OF THE CHRISTIAN MAN

Two weeks after the appearance of this tract another came out so amazingly different as to make one wonder whether it could be by the same man, or if by the same author, how he could pretend to any semblance of sincerity. It was entitled *Freedom of the Christian Man* and commenced with a deferential address to Leo X. This little work was the fruit of the interview with Miltitz, who reverted to his old principle of mediation by asking Luther to address to the pope a disclaimer of personal abusiveness and a statement of faith. Luther could respond in all integrity. He was not fighting a man but a system. Within a fortnight he could blast the papacy as Antichrist yet address the pope with deference.

Most blessed father, in all the controversies of the past three years I have ever been mindful of you, and although your adulators have driven me to appeal to a council in defiance of the futile decrees of your predecessors, Pius and Julius, I have never suffered myself because of their stupid tyranny to hold your Beatitude in despite. To be sure, I have spoken sharply against impious doctrine, but did not Christ call his adversaries a generation of vipers, blind guides, and hypocrites? And did not Paul refer to his opponents as dogs, concision, and sons of the Devil? Who could have been more biting than the prophets? I contend with no one about his life, but only concerning the Word of Truth. I look upon you less as Leo the Lion than as Daniel in the lion's den of Babylon. You may have three or four learned and excellent cardinals, but what are they among so many? The Roman *curia* deserves not you but Satan himself. What under heaven is more pestilent, hateful, and corrupt? It is more impious than the Turk. But do not think, Father Leo, that when I scathe this seat of pestilence I am inveighing against your person. Beware of the sirens who would make you not simply a man but half a god. You are a servant of *warning to Leo 8* servants. Do not listen to those who say that none can be Christians without your authority, who make you the lord of heaven, hell, and purgatory. They err who put you above a council and the universal Church. They err who make you the sole interpreter of Scripture. I am sending you a tract as an auspice of peace, that you may see the sort of thing with which I could and would more fruitfully occupy myself if your adulators would leave me alone.

Then followed Luther's canticle of the freedom of the Christian man. If Luther supposed that this letter and tract would mollify the pope, he was exceedingly naïve. The deferential letter itself denied the primacy of the pope over councils, and the treatise asserted the priesthood of all believers. The pretense that the attack was directed, not against the pope, but against the *curia* is the device commonly employed by constitutionally-minded revolutionaries who do not like to admit to themselves that they are rebelling against the head of a government. The English Puritans similarly for some time claimed that they were not fighting Charles I but only the "Malignants" by whom he was surrounded. As conflicts continue, such fictions soon become too transparent to be useful. Luther was early driven to abandon the distinction, for the bull had been issued in the name of the pope and had never been disclaimed from the Vatican. It demanded recantation. That Luther would never accord. On the twenty-ninth of November he came out with the *Assertion of All the Articles Wrongly Condemned in the Roman Bull*. The tone may be inferred from the two following:

No. 18. The proposition condemned was that "indulgences are the pious defrauding of the faithful." Luther commented:

I was wrong, I admit it, when I said that indulgences were "the pious defrauding of the faithful." I recant and I say, "Indulgences are the most impious frauds and imposters of the most rascally pontiffs, by which they deceive the souls and destroy the goods of the faithful.

No. 29. The proposition condemned was "that certain articles of John Hus condemned at the Council of Constance are most Christian, true, and evangelical, which the universal Church cannot condemn." Luther commented:

I was wrong. I retract the statement that certain articles of John Hus are evangelical. I say now, "Not some but all the articles of John Hus were condemned by Antichrist and his apostles in the synagogue of Satan." And to your face, most holy Vicar of God, I say freely that all the condemned articles of John Hus are evangelical and Christian, and yours are downright impious and diabolical.

This came out on the day Luther's books were burned at Cologne. There were rumors that the next bonfire would be at Leipzig. The sixty days of grace would soon expire. The count was usually reckoned from the day the citation was actually received. The bull had reached Luther on the tenth of October. On the tenth of December, Melanchthon on Luther's behalf issued an invitation to the faculty and students of the university to assemble at ten o'clock at the Elster gate, where, in reprisal for the burning of Luther's pious and evangelical books, the impious papal constitutions, the canon law, and works of scholastic theol-

LUTHER BURNING THE
PAPAL BULL

ogy would be given to the flames. Luther himself threw in the papal bull for good measure. The professors went home, but the students sang the *Te Deum* and paraded about the town in a wagon with another bull affixed to a pole, and an indulgence on the point of a sword. The works of Eck and other opponents of Luther were cremated.

Luther publicly justified what he had done.

Since they have burned my books, I burn theirs. The canon law was included because it makes the pope a god on earth. So far I have merely fooled with this business of the pope. All my articles condemned by Antichrist are Christian. Seldom has the pope overcome anyone with Scripture and with reason.

Frederick the Wise undertook to excuse Luther's course to the emperor. To one of the counselors he wrote:

After I left Cologne, Luther's books were burned, and again at Mainz. I regret this because Dr. Martin has already protested his readiness to do everything consistent with the name of Christian, and I have constantly insisted that he should not be condemned unheard, nor should his books be burned. If now he has given tit for tat, I hope that His Imperial Majesty will graciously overlook it.

Frederick had never before gone so far as this. He boasted that in his whole life he had not exchanged more than twenty words with Luther. He claimed to pass no judgment on his teachings but to demand only that he be given an impartial hearing. Frederick could still say that he was not defending Luther's views but merely excusing his act. The ground was not theology but law. Luther's books had been illegally burned. He ought not, indeed, to have retaliated, but the emperor should wink at the affront in view of the provocation. Frederick was saying that a German, subject to a miscarriage of justice, should be excused for burning not only a papal bull but the entire canon law, the great legal code which even more than the civil law in the Middle Ages had provided the legal basis for European civilization.

## CHAPTER TEN

# HERE I STAND

REDERICK was well advised to turn to the emperor. The case at Rome was settled, and a formal ban was inevitable. The question was whether any additional penalty would be inflicted by the state. That question the state itself would have to decide. Obviously Luther could do no more than preach, teach, and pray, and wait for others to determine the disposition to be made of his case.

Six months were required for the answer. That does not seem a long time in comparison with the four years of dallying on the part of the Church. Yet one might have supposed that since the emperor was imbued with the orthodoxy of Spain he would brook no delay. The emperor was not in the position,

*Emperor was Charles*

however, to do as he pleased. The pageantry of his coronation did not excuse him from the necessity of appending his signature to the imperial constitution, and two clauses of that constitution have been supposed by some to have been inserted by Frederick the Wise, in order to safeguard Luther. One stipulated that no German of any rank should be taken for trial outside Germany, and the other that none should be outlawed without cause and without a hearing. That these provisions were really meant to protect the rights of a monk accused of heresy is extremely dubious, and in no extant document did Frederick or Luther ever appeal to them. At the same time the emperor was a constitutional monarch; and whatever his own convictions, he would not find it expedient to govern Germany by arbitrary fiat.

He confronted a divided public opinion. Some were for Luther, some against, and some in between. Those who were for him were numerous, powerful, and vocal. Aleander, the papal nuncio in Germany, reported that nine tenths of the Germans cried, "Luther," and the other one tenth, "Death to the pope." This was unquestionably an exaggeration. Yet Luther's following was not contemptible. His supporters were powerful. Franz von Sickingen from his fortress on the Ebernburg controlled the Rhine valley and might well prevent the emperor, who came to Germany without Spanish troops, from taking action. Luther's supporters were also vocal, and notably Ulrich von Hutten, who, scorning submission to Rome in order to obviate excommunication, fulminated from the Ebernburg against the *curia* and curdled the blood of Aleander with successive manifestoes. The bull *Exsurge* was reprinted with stinging annotations, and in a tract Hutten portayed himself as the "Bull Killer." He appealed to the emperor to shake off the rabble of priests. Threats of violence were addressed to Albert of Mainz. Aleander, the papal nuncio, was urged to heed the groans of the German people and to accord a fair trial, which should not be denied to a parricide. "Do you suppose," demanded Hutten, "that through an edict extracted by guile from the emperor you will be able to separate Germany from liberty, faith, religion, and truth? Do you think you can intimidate us by burning books? This question will not be settled by the pen but by the sword."

The most influential of Luther's supporters was Frederick the Wise. He had gone so far as to excuse the burning of the papal bull. At the Diet of Worms he permitted Fritz, his court fool, to mimic the cardinals. Frederick had refused to be wooed by the golden rose, the indulgences for the Castle Church at Wittenberg, and a benefice for his natural son. The most clear-cut confession of Luther's cause on his part comes to us only at third hand. Aleander claimed to have heard from Joachim of Brandenburg that Frederick had said to him, "Our

TITLE PAGE OF HUTTEN'S
"SATIRE ON THE BULL
AGAINST LUTHER"

faith has long lacked this light which Martin has brought to it." The remark must be discounted because both narrators were eager to smear Frederick with adherence to Luther. The elector himself repeatedly insisted that he was not espousing Dr. Martin's opinions but merely demanding a fair hearing. If the friar was properly heard and condemned, Frederick would be the first to do his duty against him as a Christian prince. Yet Frederick's notion of a fair hearing meant that Luther should be convicted out of the Scriptures. Frederick was often murky as to the issues; but when clear, he was dogged.

On the opposite side were the papalists, men like Eck who took their cue from Rome. The *curia* reiterated pleas to root out the tare, expel the scabby sheep, cut away the putrid member, and throw overboard the rocker of the bark of St. Peter. The representative of Rome throughout the trial was Aleander, whose objective was to have the case settled arbitrarily by the emperor without consulting the German estates, which were known to be divided. Above all else Luther should not receive a hearing before a secular tribunal. He had already been condemned by the Church, and the laity should simply implement the Church's decision and not re-examine the grounds of condemnation.

Then there was the middle party, headed personally by Erasmus, who, despite his statement that the breach was irreparable, did not desist from efforts at mediation and even fathered a memorandum proposing the appointment by the emperor and the kings of England and Hungary of an impartial tribunal. The Erasmians as a party sensed less than their leader the depth of the cleavage between Luther and the Church and between Luther and themselves.

With opinion thus divided delays in settling Luther's case were inevitable. The Lutheran party deliberately resorted to filibustering. Curiously some of the greatest obstructionists were at the Vatican because the pope had seen his worst fears realized in the election of Charles as emperor, and was now disposed to curb his power by supporting France. But whenever a move was made in that direction, Charles, for all his orthodoxy, intimated that Luther could be used as a weapon.

Even the greatest activists on the scene were less active than might have been expected. Hutten was restrained by hope, because he believed that history would inevitably repeat itself and in due time any German emperor would clash with the temporal pretensions of the pope. Beguiled by these expectations he deferred his priests' war until a fellow Humanist taunted him with emitting only froth. But at the same time Aleander was intimidated by Hutten's fulminations; and when the pope sent a bull of excommunication against both Luther and Hutten, Aleander withheld the publication and sent the bull back to Rome to have the name of Hutten first expunged. Such communications of themselves took months, and thus by reason of Aleander's timidity Luther came actually to be outlawed by the empire before he had been formally excommunicated by the Church.

## A HEARING PROMISED AND RECALLED

Where, how, and by whom his case should be handled was the problem which faced Charles. A decision on the point was reached on the fourth of November, 1520, when Charles after his coronation at Aachen went to confer with "Uncle Frederick," marooned by the gout at Cologne. All knew that important decisions were pending. The Lutherans placarded the city with the appeal to Caesar. For the papalists Aleander hastened to interview Frederick the Wise and urged him to commit the case to the pope. Frederick instead called in Erasmus, the leader of the moderates, and asked his judgment. Erasmus pursed his lips. Frederick strained forward for the weighty answer. "Two crimes Luther has committed," came the verdict. "He has attacked the crown of the pope and the bellies of the monks." Frederick laughed.

Thus fortified Frederick conferred with the emperor and secured a promise that Luther should not be condemned without a hearing. On what grounds Charles was persuaded we do not know, nor what sort of hearing he had in mind. The University of Wittenberg promptly pointed to a hearing before the forthcoming diet of the German nation soon to be assembled at the city of Worms. Frederick transmitted the proposal to the emperor's counselors and received from His Majesty a reply dated November 28 and addressed to his "beloved Uncle Frederick: We are desirous that you should bring the above-mentioned Luther to the diet to be held at Worms, that there he may be thoroughly investigated by competent persons, that no injustice be done nor anything contrary to law." He does not say what law, nor by whom the investigation should be conducted, nor whether Luther would be at liberty to defend his views. Luther should come, that was all. The appeal to Caesar had been heard. This invitation on the twenty-eighth of November marked an amazing reversal of policy. The Defender of the Faith, who had been burning the books, now invited the author of those very books to some sort of hearing. Had the emperor been won over to the policy

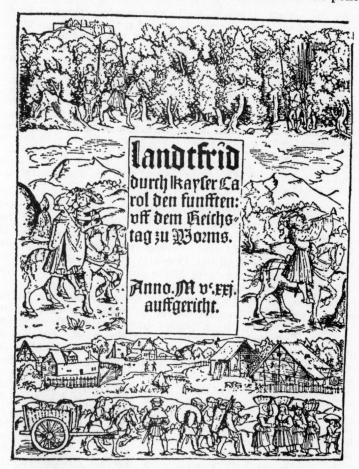

THE DIET OF WORMS AND THE PUBLIC PEACE

of Erasmus? Had some disquieting political news disposed him for a moment to bait the pope and cultivate the Germans? Was he fearful of popular insurrection? His motives elude us. This only we know, that the invitation was issued.

That was in November, but Luther did not actually appear at the diet until April of the next year. In the interim the invitation was rescinded and reissued. All the strife of the parties centered on this point: Should Luther be permitted to appear before a secular tribunal to be examined as to the faith? "Never," was the resolve of Aleander.

As for myself, I would gladly confront this Satan, but the authority of the Holy See should not be prejudiced by subjection to the judgment of the laity. One who has been condemned by the pope, the cardinals, and prelates should be heard only in prison. The laity, including the emperor, are not in a position to review the case. The only competent judge is the pope. How can the Church be called the ship of Peter if Peter is not at the helm? How can she be the ark of Noah if Noah is not the captain? If Luther wants to be heard, he can have a safe conduct to Rome. Or His Majesty might send him to the inquisitors in Spain. He can perfectly well recant where he is and then come to the diet to be forgiven. He asks for a place which is not suspect. What place to him is not suspect, unless it be Germany? What judges would he accept unless Hutten and the poets? Has the Catholic Church been dead for a thousand years to be revived only by Martin? Has the whole world gone wrong and Martin only has the eyes to see?

The emperor was impressed. On the seventeenth of December he rescinded the invitation to bring Luther to the diet. The reason assigned was that the sixty days had expired and in consequence if Luther were to come to Worms the city would find itself under an interdict. One may doubt whether this was the real reason. The motives of the emperor for recalling the invitation are as elusive as his motives for issuing it, for Luther was not yet formally under the ban; and even if he were, a papal dispensation could be secured. Charles may have been persuaded by Aleander, irritated by Luther's burning of the bull, depressed by news from Spain, and desirous of placating the *curia*. Whatever his reasons, he might have spared himself the onus of a public reversal had he but waited, because Frederick the Wise declined the invitation on the ground that the case appeared to be prejudged by the burning of Luther's books, for which he was sure the emperor was not responsible. Frederick might well entertain a doubt because on the very day of the burning at Mainz the emperor had issued the invitation to Luther. Frederick was determined to drive Charles to a clarification of his position and to an assumption of full responsibility.

ALEANDER

For that reason the elector inquired of Luther whether he would be willing to come in case he was invited directly by the emperor himself. He answered:

> You ask me what I shall do if I am called by the emperor. I will go even if I am too sick to stand on my feet. If Caesar calls me, God calls me. If violence is used, as well it may be, I commend my cause to God. He lives and reigns who saved the three youths from the fiery furnace of the king of Babylon, and if He will not save me, my head is worth nothing compared with Christ. This is no time to think of safety. I must take care that the gospel is not brought into contempt by our fear to confess and seal our teaching with our blood.

His mood is more fully revealed in letters to Staupitz.

> This is not the time to cringe, but to cry aloud when our Lord Jesus Christ is damned, reviled, and blasphemed. If you exhort me to humility, I exhort you to pride. The matter is very serious. We see Christ suffer. If hitherto we ought to have been silent and humble, I ask you whether now, when the blessed Saviour is mocked, we should not fight for him. My father, the danger is greater than many think. Now applies the word of the gospel, "He who confesses me before men, him will I confess in the presence of my father, and he who denies me before men, him will I deny." I write this candidly to you because I am afraid you hesitate between Christ and the pope, though they are diametrically contrary. Let us pray that the Lord Jesus will destroy the son of perdition with the breath of his mouth. If you will not follow, permit me to go. I am greatly saddened by your submissiveness. You seem to me to be a very different Staupitz from the one who used to preach grace and

LUTHER WITH A DOVE ABOVE HIS HEAD

> the cross. . . . Father, do you remember when we were at Augsburg you said to me, "Remember, brother, you started this in the name of the Lord Jesus." I have never forgotten that, and I say it now to you. I burned the pope's books at first with fear and trembling, but now I am lighter in heart than I have ever been in my life. They are so much more pestilent than I supposed.

### THE EMPEROR ASSUMES RESPONSIBILITY

Aleander, unaware of the new approaches to Luther, thought the occasion propitious to present an edict which the emperor should issue without consulting the diet. The emperor answered that he could not act alone. The Archbishop of Mainz had not yet arrived; and when he came, he opposed the edict, even though a month earlier he had himself authorized the burning of Luther's books. The Elector of Saxony also had not yet arrived. His entry coincided with the Feast of the Three Kings, and he rode into Worms like one of the Wise Men bearing gifts for the young emperor, from whom he secured another reversal of policy. Charles promised to assume responsibility for Luther's case. Luther being informed replied to Frederick, "I am heartily glad that His Majesty will take to himself this affair, which is not mine but that of all Christianity and the whole German nation."

But Charles by this promise evidently did not mean that Luther was to have a public hearing before the diet. Instead a committee was appointed to handle the case, and Aleander was permitted to address it. He bungled his advantage at the very beginning by undertaking to demonstrate that Luther was an abominable heretic, whereas in all consistency he ought to have pleaded that a lay committee had no jurisdiction. Instead he sought to demonstrate from a medieval manuscript that the papacy was at least as old as Charlemagne. All of this would have been pertinent enough at the Leipzig debate, but the time for such discussion had gone by. In the meantime the pope had spoken; and the diet was being invited, not to ratify, but simply to implement the papal verdict. The committee listened and said they would have to wait.

The delays served to feed the mood of popular violence in the city. The reports which we have from opposing sides indicate that religious war lay in the offing. Aleander, in the mood of a martyr, reported:

Martin is pictured with a halo and a dove above his head. The people kiss these pictures. Such a quantity have been sold that I was not able to obtain one. A cartoon has appeared showing Luther with a book in his hand, accompanied by Hutten in armor with a sword under the caption, "Champions of Christian Liberty." Another sheet portrays Luther in front and Hutten behind carrying a chest on which are two chalices with the inscription, "The Ark of the True Faith." Erasmus, in front, is playing the harp as David. In the background is John Hus, whom Luther has recently proclaimed his saint. In another part of the picture the pope and the cardinals are being bound by the soldiers of the guard. I cannot go out on the streets but the Germans put their hands to their swords and gnash their teeth at me. I hope the pope will give me a plenary indulgence and look after my brothers and sisters if anything happens to me.

The disturbances are described from the other side in a letter of a Humanist at Worms to Hutten:

A Spaniard tore up your edition of the bull and trampled it in the mud. A chaplain of the emperor and two Spaniards caught a man with sixty copies of *The Babylonian Captivity*. The people came to the rescue, and the assailants had to take refuge in the castle. A mounted Spaniard pursued one of our men, who barely escaped through a door. The Spaniard reined up so suddenly that he fell off his horse and could not rise until a German lifted him. Every day two or three Spaniards gallop on their mules through the market place, and the people have to make way for them. This is our freedom.

Overt violence was continually incited by the dissemination of defamatory pamphlets. Aleander claimed that a wagon would not hold the scurrilous tracts with which Worms was deluged, such as a parody on the Apostles' Creed:

I believe in the pope, binder and looser in heaven, earth, and hell, and in Simony, his only son our lord, who was conceived by the canon law and born of the Romish church. Under his power truth suffered, was crucified, dead and buried, and through the ban descended to hell, rose again through the gospel and Paul and was brought to Charles, sitting at his right hand, who in future is to rule over spiritual and worldly things. I believe in the canon law, in the Romish church, in the destruction of faith and of the communion of saints, in indulgences both for the remission of guilt and penalty in purgatory, in the resurrection of the flesh in an Epicurean life, because given to us by the Holy Father, the pope. Amen.

The emperor was irritated. When on February 6 Luther's appeal was handed to him, he tore it up and trampled on it. But he was quick to recover his composure and summoned a plenary session of the diet on the thirteenth of February. The plan was to present a new version of the edict, to be issued in the name of the emperor but with the consent of the diet. Aleander was given an opportunity to prepare their minds in a three-hour speech. Once again he allowed the opportunity to slip through his fingers. He was now in a position to correct the mistake he had made in addressing the committee. Two days previously the papal bull excommunicating Luther had come into his hands. He had only to produce it to allay the objection that the diet was being asked to outlaw a man not yet banned by the Church. This was the time when Aleander held back because the bull named not only Luther but Hutten. The document was not produced. The diet proceeded to examine a case of heresy, and Aleander himself rather than Luther was responsible for turning a secular assembly into a church council.

Aleander unquestionably made a very good case against Luther, a very much better case than did the bull, which simply incorporated the earlier condemnation of *Exsurge Domine*, with no fresh examination of the more subversive tracts of the summer of 1520. Aleander had memorized whole sections of these words and set out again to prove Luther was

a heretic who brought up John Hus from hell and endorsed not some but all of his articles. In consequence he must endorse also Wyclif's denial of the real presence [which he did not], and Wyclif's claim that no Christian can bind another by law. This point Luther claimed to have asserted in his *Freedom of the Christian Man* [which he did not]. He rejects monastic vows. He rejects ceremonies. He appeals to councils and rejects the authority of councils. Like all heretics he appeals to Scripture and yet rejects Scripture when it does not support him. He would throw out the Epistle of James because it contains the proof text for extreme unction [which certainly was not Luther's reason]. He is a heretic and an obstinate heretic. He asks for a hearing, but how can a hearing be given to one who will not listen to an angel from heaven? He is also a revolutionary. He claims that the Germans should wash their hands in the blood of the papists. [The reference is obviously to Luther's unbridled outburst against Prierias.]

No more damaging case could have been made against Luther before the diet, which was now asked to endorse the imperial edict proclaiming Luther a Bohemian heretic and a revolutionary who would soon be formally excommunicated by the pope. (The bull, of course, had been held back.) Unless absolved, he should be imprisoned and his books eradicated. Non-co-operators with the edict would be guilty of lese majesty. The presentation of this edict precipitated a storm. The electors of Saxony and Brandenburg had to be separated on the floor of the diet by Cardinal Lang. The Elector Palatinate, ordinarily taciturn, bellowed like a bull. The estates demanded time, and on the nineteenth answered that Luther's teaching was already so firmly rooted among the people that a condemnation without a hearing would occasion grave danger of insurrection. He should be brought to the diet under safe conduct, to be examined by learned men. He should be brought to answer, not to argue. If he would renounce what he had said against the faith, other points could be discussed. If he refused, then the diet would support the edict.

### INVITATION TO LUTHER RENEWED

The emperor thereupon reverted to his earlier agreement that Luther should come. The edict was subjected to dentistry. The penalties for lese majesty were dropped. The edict should be issued in the name of the estates rather than of the emperor alone, and Luther should be brought to the diet for examination. The emperor then composed a new invitation for Luther. It was dated the sixth, although not sent until the eleventh, because in the meantime another attempt was made to induce Frederick to assume responsibility for bringing the accused.

But again he passed the onus directly back to the emperor, who at last sent the missive addressed to "Our noble, dear, and esteemed Martin Luther." "Zounds!" exclaimed Aleander when he saw it, "that's no way to address a heretic." The letter continued: "Both we and the diet have decided to ask you to come under safe conduct to answer with regard to your books and teaching. You shall have twenty-one days in which to arrive." There is no clear statement that discussion would be precluded. The invitation was delivered at the hands, not of the common postman, but of the imperial herald, Caspar Sturm.

Would Luther come? There was real doubt. To Spalatin he wrote:

I will reply to the emperor that if I am being invited simply to recant I will not come. If to recant is all that is wanted, I can do that perfectly well right here. But if he is inviting me to my death, then I will come. I hope none but the papists will stain their hands in my blood. Antichrist reigns. The Lord's will be done.

To another he wrote:

This shall be my recantation at Worms: "Previously I said the pope is the vicar of Christ. I recant. Now I say the pope is the adversary of Christ and the apostle of the Devil."

Evidently Luther had decided to go.

On the way he learned of an edict for the sequestration of his books. Its publication had been delayed, perhaps through fear that if he saw it he would infer that the case was settled and would not come. But his comment was, "Unless I am held back by force, or Caesar revokes his invitation, I will enter Worms under the banner of Christ against the gates of hell." He had no illusions as to the probable outcome. After an ovation at Erfurt he commented, "I have had my Palm Sunday. I wonder whether this pomp is merely a temptation or whether it is also the sign of impending passion."

While his coming was awaited, another lampoon was published in Worms, entitled the *Litany of the Germans:*

Christ hear the Germans; Christ hear the Germans. From evil counselors deliver Charles, O Lord. From poison on the way to Worms deliver Martin Luther, preserve Ulrich von Hutten, O Lord. Suffer not thyself, Lord, to be crucified afresh. Purge Aleander, O Lord. The nuncios working against Luther at Worms, smite from heaven. O Lord Christ, hear the Germans.

The Catholic moderates, however, desired that the case might be disposed of out of court. The leader of this party was Glapion, the emperor's confessor. Whether he was a sincere Erasmian or a son of duplicity is debatable, but he certainly began his negotiations before there could be any suspicion that he was trying to divert Luther from Worms until

after the expiration of the safe conduct. Glapion had previously approached Frederick the Wise with a very engaging
argument. Luther's earlier works, he claimed, had warmed his
heart. He thoroughly agreed with the attack on indulgences
and saw in *The Freedom of the Christian Man* a wonderful
Christian spirit. But when he had read *The Babylonian
Captivity,* he was simply aghast. He could not believe that
Luther would acknowledge the book. It was not in his usual
style. If he had written it, he must have done so in a fit of
passion. In that case he should be ready to have it interpreted
in the sense of the Church. If he would comply, he would
have many supporters. The matter should be settled in private,
else the Devil would stir up contention, war, and insurrection.
No good could come of public controversy, and only the Devil
would profit from Luther's appearance at Worms.

The appeal was most ingratiating because it was so true.
Had Luther been willing to abandon the attack on the sacraments, he might have rallied a united German nation for the
reduction of papal power and extortion. The diet might have
wrung from the pope the sort of concessions already granted
to the strong national states of France, Spain, and England.
Schism might have been avoided, and religious war could have
been averted. To a man like Frederick the Wise this must have
been a most appealing proposal, but he was resolved to make
no overtures which would give the emperor an opportunity to
evade his responsibility.

Glapion then turned to another quarter. Why not work
through Sickingen and Hutten? First, engage Hutten with a
pension from the emperor; then let Luther be invited to Sick-
engen's castle at the Ebernburg for a conference. Glapion had
the courage to go in person and beard Hutten and Sickingen
in their eagle's nest. He was so sympathetic toward Luther
and made the emperor appear so favorable that Hutten accepted the pension (subsequently to be declined), and Sickingen sent his chaplain, Martin Bucer, to intercept Luther
on the way to Worms and to extend the invitation. But Luther
had set his face to go up to Jerusalem and would not be
turned aside. He would enter Worms though there were as
many devils as tiles on the roofs. Hutten was moved. "It is as
clear as day," he wrote Pirkheimer, "that he was directed by
divine guidance. He disregarded all human considerations and
threw himself utterly upon God." And to Luther, "Here is the
difference between us. I look to men. You, who are already
more perfect, trust everything to God."

### LUTHER BEFORE THE DIET

On the sixteenth of April, Luther entered Worms in a Saxon
two-wheeled cart with a few companions. The imperial herald

preceded, wearing the eagle upon his cloak. Although it was the dinner hour, two thousand turned out to conduct Luther to his lodging. On the following day at four o'clock Luther was waited upon by the herald and the imperial marshal, who conducted him furtively, to avoid the crowds, to a meeting of the emperor, the electors, and a portion of the estates. The monk stood before the monarch, who exclaimed, "That fellow will never make a heretic of me."

The scene lends itself to dramatic portrayal. Here was Charles, heir of a long line of Catholic sovereigns—of Maximilian the romantic, of Ferdinand the Catholic, of Isabella the orthodox—scion of the house of Hapsburg, lord of Austria, Burgundy, the Low Countries, Spain, and Naples, Holy Roman Emperor, ruling over a vaster domain that any save Charlemagne, symbol of the medieval unities, incarnation of a glorious if vanishing heritage; and here before him a simple monk, a miner's son, with nothing to sustain him save his own faith in the Word of God. Here the past and the future were met. Some would see at this point the beginning of modern times. The contrast is real enough. Luther himself was sensible of it in a measure. He was well aware that he had not been reared as the son of Pharaoh's daughter, but what overpowered him was not so much that he stood in the presence of the emperor as this, that he and the emperor alike were called upon to answer before Almighty God.

Luther was examined by an official of the Archbishop of Trier, Eck by name, not of course the Eck of the Leipzig debate. Luther was confronted with a pile of his books and asked whether they were his. The very question reopened the overture of Glapion. Luther might now repudiate *The Babylonian Captivity* and invite discussion of the financial and political pretensions of the papacy. This was his opportunity to rally a united Germany. In a voice barely audible he answered, "The books are all mine, and I have written more."

The door was closed, but Eck opened it again. "Do you defend them all, or do you care to reject a part?"

Luther reflected aloud, "This touches God and his Word. This affects the salvation of souls. Of this Christ said, 'He who denies me before men, him will I deny before my father.' To say too little or too much would be dangerous. I beg you, give me time to think it over."

The emperor and the diet deliberated. Eck brought the answer. He expressed amazement that a theological professor should not be ready at once to defend his position, particularly since he had come for that very purpose. He deserved no consideration. Nevertheless, the emperor in his clemency would grant him until the morrow.

Eck's amazement has been so shared by some modern historians as to prompt the suggestion that Luther's request was preconcerted, a part of the stalling tactic of Frederick the Wise. But anyone who recalls Luther's tremors at his first mass will scarcely so interpret this hesitation. Just as then he wished to flee from the altar, so now he was too terrified before God to give answer to the emperor. At the same time we must admit that Luther's tremor before the Divine Majesty served actually to bring him before a plenary session of the diet. On the following day, the eighteenth, a larger hall was chosen and was so crowded that scarcely any save the emperor could sit. The terror of the Holy conspired to give Luther a hearing before the German nation.

**Doctor Martini Luthers offentliche verber zu worms im Reichstag vor Kai. Ma. Red vnd wider red/am 17 tag Aprilis/im Tausent Sünffhundert vnd ainundzwaintzigisten Jar.**

LUTHER'S FIRST HEARING AT WORMS

He had been summoned for four o'clock on the afternoon of the morrow, but the press of business delayed his appearance until six. This time his voice was ringing. Eck reiterated the question of the previous day. Luther responded: "Most serene emperor, most illustrious princes, most clement lords, if I have not given some of you your proper titles I beg you to forgive me. I am not a courtier, but a monk. You asked me yesterday whether I would repudiate them. They are all mine, but as for the second question, they are not all of one sort."

This was a skillful move. By differentiating his works Luther won for himself the opportunity of making a speech instead of answering simply yes or no.

He went on: "Some deal with faith and life so simply and evangelically that my very enemies are compelled to regard them as worthy of Christian reading. Even the bull itself does not treat all my books as of one kind. If I should renounce these, I would be the only man on earth to damn the truth confessed alike by friends and foes. A second class of my works inveighs against the desolation of the Christian world by the evil lives and teaching of the papists. Who can deny this when the universal complaints testify that by the laws of the popes the consciences of men are racked?"

"No!" broke in the emperor.

Luther, unruffled, went on to speak of the "incredible tyranny" by which this German nation was devoured. "Should I recant at this point, I would open the door to more tyranny and impiety, and it will be all the worse should it appear that I had done so at the instance of the Holy Roman Empire." This was a skillful plea to German nationalism, which had a strong following in the diet. Even Duke George the Catholic took the fore in presenting grievances.

"A third class," continued Luther, "contains attacks on private individuals. I confess I have been more caustic than comports with my profession, but I am being judged, not on my life, but for the teaching of Christ, and I cannot renounce these works either, without increasing tyranny and impiety. When Christ stood before Annas, he said, 'Produce witnesses.' If our Lord, who could not err, made this demand, why may not a worm like me ask to be convicted of error from the prophets and the Gospels? If I am shown my error, I will be the first to throw my books into the fire. I have been reminded of the dissensions which my teaching engenders. I can answer only in the words of the Lord, 'I came not to bring peace but a sword.' If our God is so severe, let us beware lest we release a deluge of wars, lest the reign of this noble youth, Charles, be inauspicious. Take warning from the examples of Pharaoh, the king of Babylon, and the kings of Israel. God it is who confounds the wise. I must walk in the fear of the Lord. I say this not to chide but because I cannot escape my duty to my Germans. I commend myself to Your Majesty. May you not suffer my adversaries to make you ill disposed to me without cause. I have spoken."

Eck replied: "Martin, you have not suffiienctly distinguished your works. The earlier were bad and the latter worse. Your plea to be heard from Scripture is the one always made by heretics. You do nothing but renew the errors of Wyclif and Hus. How will the Jews, how will the Turks, exult to hear Christians discussing whether they have been wrong all these

years! Martin, how can you assume that you are the only one
to understand the sense of Scripture? Would you put your
judgment above that of so many famous men and claim that
you know more than they all? You have no right to call into
question the most holy orthodox faith, instituted by Christ the
perfect lawgiver, proclaimed throughout the world by the
apostles, sealed by the red blood of the martyrs, confirmed by
the sacred councils, defined by the Church in which all our
fathers believed until death and gave to us as an inheritance,
and which now we are forbidden by the pope and the emperor
to discuss lest there be no end of debate. I ask you, Martin—
answer candidly and without horns—do you or do you not
repudiate your books and the errors which they contain?"
Luther replied, "Since then Your Majesty and your lordships
desire a simple reply, I will answer without horns and without
teeth. Unless I am convicted by Scripture and plain reason—
I do not accept the authority of popes and councils, for they
have contradicted each other—my conscience is captive to
the Word of God. I cannot and I will not recant anything, for
to go against conscience is neither right nor safe. God help me.
Amen."

The earliest printed version added the words: "Here I stand,
I cannot do otherwise." The words, though not recorded on the
spot, may nevertheless be genuine, because the listeners at the
moment may have been too moved to write.

Luther had spoken in German. He was asked to repeat in
Latin. He was sweating. A friend called out, "If you can't do
it, Doctor, you have done enough." Luther made again his
affirmation in Latin, threw up his arms in the gesture of a
victorious knight, and slipped out of the darkened hall, amid
the hisses of the Spaniards, and went to his lodging. Frederick
the Wise went also to his lodging and remarked, "Dr. Martin
spoke wonderfully before the emperor, the princes, and the
estates in Latin and in German, but he is too daring for me."
On the following day Aleander heard the report that all six
of the electors were ready to pronounce Luther a heretic. That
would include Frederick the Wise. Spalatin says that Frederick was indeed much troubled to know whether Luther had
or had not been convicted from the Scriptures.

### THE EDICT OF WORMS

The emperor called in the electors and a number of the
princes to ask their opinions. They requested time. "Very
well," said the emperor, "I will give you my opinion," and he
read them a paper which he had written out himself in French.
This was no speech composed by a secretary. The young Hapsburg was confessing his faith:

I am descended from a long line of Christian emperors of this noble German nation, and of the Catholic kings of Spain, the archdukes of Austria, and the dukes of Burgundy. They were all faithful to the death to the Church of Rome, and they defended the Catholic faith and the honor of God. I have resolved to follow in their steps. A single friar who goes counter to all Christianity for a thousand years must be wrong. Therefore I am resolved to stake my lands, my friends, my body, my blood, my life, and my soul. Not only I, but you of this noble German nation, would be forever disgraced if by our negligence not only heresy but the very suspicion of heresy were to survive. After having heard yesterday the obstinate defense of Luther, I regret that I have so long delayed in proceeding against him and his false teaching. I will have no more to do with him. He may return under his safe conduct, but without preaching or making any tumult. I will proceed against him as a notorious heretic, and ask you to declare yourselves as you promised me.

Many of the emperor's hearers took on the hue of death. On the following day the electors declared themselves fully in accord with the emperor, but out of six only four signed. The dissenters were Ludwig of the Palatinate and Frederick of Saxony. He had come into the clear.

LUTHER'S SECOND HEARING AT WORMS

*In handwriting:* Intitulentur libri—*"Let them read the titles,"* *the words called out by Luther's lawyer; and* Hie stehe ich/ich kan nicht anders/Got helffe mir. Amen.—*"Here I stand. I cannot do otherwise. God help me. Amen."*

The emperor felt now that he had sufficient backing to proceed with the edict, but during the night there was posted on the door of the town hall and elsewhere in Worms a placard stamped with the *Bundschuh*. This was the symbol of the peasants' revolt, the sandal clog of the workingman in contrast to the high boot of the noble. For a century Germany had been distraught by peasant unrest. This poster strongly implied that if Luther were condemned, the peasants would rise. Where the poster came from could only be guessed. Hutten surmised that it had been placarded by the papalists in order to discredit the Lutherans, but Aleander was equally innocent of the source. Whoever did it, Albert of Mainz was in a panic. At dawn he rushed to the lodging of the emperor, who laughed at him. But Albert would not be put off, and enlisted his brother Joachim, the most ardent opponent of Luther. At the instance of these two the estates petitioned the emperor to permit Luther to be examined again. The emperor replied that he would have nothing to do with it himself, but that they might have three days.

Then began the attempt to break Luther down through a committee. The ordeal, though less dramatic, was more crucial than the public appearance. He who is able to give a ringing No before a public assembly may find it harder, if he is at all sensitive, to resist the kindly remonstrances of men concerned to prevent the disruption of Germany and the distintegration of the Church. The committee was headed by Richard of Greiffenklau, the Archbishop of Trier, the custodian of the seamless robe of Christ, whom Frederick the Wise had so long been proposing as the arbiter. With him were associated some of Luther's friends and some of his foes, among them Duke George.

In a slightly different form the attempt of Glapion to secure a partial revocation was renewed. Luther's attack on the indulgence sellers was again declared to have been warranted, and his denunciation of Roman corruption was heart-warming. He had written well about good works and the Ten Commandments, but *The Freedom of the Christian Man* would prompt the masses to reject all authority. One observes that this time the attack centered not on the demolition of the sacramental system in *The Babylonian Captivity* but on the alleged threat to public tranquillity in the tract on Christian liberty. Luther replied that he intended nothing of the sort and would counsel obedience even to evil magistrates. Trier besought him not to rend the seamless robe of Christendom. He answered with the counsel of Gamaliel, to wait and see whether his teaching was of God or of man. Luther was reminded that if he went down, Melanchthon would be pulled after him. At this his eye welled with tears; but when asked to name a judge whom he would accept, he stiffened and replied that he would name a child of eight or nine years. "The pope," he declared, "is no judge of matters pertaining to God's Word and faith, but a Christian man must examine and judge for himself." The committee reported failure to the emperor.

On the sixth of May, His Majesty presented to a diminishing diet the final draft of the Edict of Worms, prepared by Aleander. Luther was charged with attacking the seven sacraments after the manner of the damned Bohemians.

He has sullied marriage, disparaged confession, and denied the body and blood of our Lord. He makes the sacraments depend on the faith of the recipient. He is pagan in his denial of free will. This devil in the habit of a monk has brought together ancient errors into one stinking puddle and has invented new ones. He denies the power of the keys and encourages the laity to wash their hands in the blood of the clergy. His teaching makes for rebellion, division, war, murder, robbery, arson, and the collapse of Christendom. He lives the life of a beast. He has burned the decretals. He despises alike the ban and the sword. He does more harm to the civil than to the ecclesiastical power. We have labored with him, but he recognizes only the authority of Scripture, which he interprets in his own sense. We have given him twenty-one days, dating from April the 15th. We have now gathered the estates. Luther is to be regarded as a convicted heretic [although the bull of excommunication still had not been published]. When the time is up, no one is to harbor him. His followers also are to be condemned. His books are to be eradicated from the memory of man.

Aleander brought the edict to the emperor for his signature. He took up the pen. "Then," says Aleander, "I haven't the ghost of a notion why, he laid it down and said he must submit the edict to the diet." The emperor knew why. The members were going home. Frederick the Wise had left. Ludwig of the Palatinate had left. Those who remained were a rump ready to condemn Luther. Although the edict was dated as of the sixth of May, it was not issued until the twenty-sixth. By that time the diet was sufficiently reduced to consent. The emperor then signed. Aleander recorded:

His Majesty signed both the Latin and the German with his own blessed hand, and smiling said, "You will be content now." "Yes," I answered, "and even greater will be the contentment of His Holiness and of all Christendom." We praise God for giving us such a religious emperor. May God preserve him in all his holy ways, who has already acquired perpetual glory, and with God eternal reward. I was going to recite a paean from Ovid when I recalled that this was a religious occasion. Therefore blessed be the Holy Trinity for his immense mercy.

The Edict of Worms, passed by a secular tribunal entrusted with a case of heresy at the instance of Lutherans and against the opposition of the papalists, was at once repudiated by the

Lutherans as having been passed by only a rump, and was sponsored by the papalists because it was a confirmation of the Catholic faith. The Church of Rome, which had so strenuously sought to prevent turning the Diet of Worms into an ecclesiastical council, became in the light of the outcome the great vindicator of the pronouncement of a secular tribunal on heresy.

CHAPTER ELEVEN

# MY PATMOS

 ONTEMPORARIES deemed Luther's trial at Worms a re-enactment of the passion of Christ. Albrecht Dürer on the seventeenth of May recorded in his diary this prayer: "O Lord, who desirest before thou comest to judgment that as thy Son Jesus Christ had to die at the hands of the priests and rise from the dead and ascend to heaven, even so should thy disciple Martin Luther be made comfortable to him." The secularized twentieth century is more shocked by such a comparison than the sixteenth, when men walked in a perpetual Passion play. Some anonymous pamphleteer did not hesitate to narrate the proceedings at Worms in the very language of the Gospels, identifying Albert with Caiaphas, Lang with Annas, Frederick with Peter, and Charles with Pilate. Our sole account of the burning of Luther's books at Worms is from this document and reads:

Then the governor [Charles in the role of Pilate] delivered to them the books of Luther to be burned. The priests took them; and when the princes and the people had left, the diet made a great pyre in front of the high priest's palace, where they burned the books, placing on the top a picture of Luther with this inscription, "This is Martin Luther, the Doctor of the Gospel." The title was read by many Romanists because the place where Luther's books were burned was not far from the bishop's court. Now this title was written in French, German, and in Latin.

Then the high priests and the Romanists said to the governor, "Write not, 'A Doctor of evangelical truth,' but that he said, 'I am a Doctor of evangelical truth.' "

But the governor answered, "What I have written I have written."

And with him two other doctors were burned, Hutten and Carlstadt, one on the right and one on the left. But the picture of Luther would not burn until the soldiers had folded it and put it inside a vessel of pitch, where it was reduced to ashes. As a count beheld these things which were done, he marveled and said, "Truly he is a Christian." And all the throng present, seeing these things which had come to pass, returned beating their breasts.

The following day the chief priests and the Pharisees, together with the Romanists, went to the governor and said, "We recall that this seducer said he wished later to write greater things. Make an order, therefore, throughout the whole earth that his books be not sold, lest the latest error be worse than the first."

But the governor said, "You have your own guard. Go publish bulls, as you know how, through your false excommunication." They then went away and put forth horrible mandates in the name of the Roman pontiff and of the emperor, but to this day they have not been obeyed.

This picture of Charles as Pilate yielding only reluctantly to the churchmen does not of course fit the facts. In his private domains the Counter Reformation, already begun, was pursued in earnest. Aleander returned to the Netherlands, and the burning of books went on merrily. As a certain friar was supervising a bonfire, a bystander said to him, "You would see better if the ashes of Luther's books got into your eyes." He was a bold man who dared to say so much. Erasmus, at Louvain, began to realize that the choice for him would soon lie between the stake or exile. Ruefully confessing that he was not cut out for martyrdom, he transferred his residence to Basel.

Albrecht Dürer in the Netherlands received the word that Luther's passion was complete. He reflected in his diary:

I know not whether he lives or is murdered, but in any case he has suffered for the Christian truth. If we lose this man, who has written more clearly than any other in centuries, may God grant his spirit to another. His books should be held in great honor, and not burned as the emperor commands, but rather the books of his enemies. O God, if Luther is dead, who will henceforth explain to us the gospel? What might he not have written for us in the next ten or twenty years?

### AT THE WARTBURG

Luther was not dead. His friends began to receive letters "From the Wilderness," "From the Isle of Patmos." Frederick the Wise had decided to hide him, and gave instructions to court officials to make the arrangements without divulging the details, even to himself, that he might truthfully feign innocence. Spalatin, however, might know. Luther and one com-

panion were apprised of the
plan. Luther was not very
happy over it. He had set his
face to return to Wittenberg,
come what might. With a few
companions in a wagon he
was entering the woods on
the outskirts of the village of
Eisenach when armed horsemen fell upon the party and
with much cursing and show
of violence dragged Luther to
the ground. The one companion, privy to the ruse, played

THE WARTBURG

his part and roundly berated the abductors. They placed Luther upon a horse and led him for a whole day by circuitous
roads through the woods until at dusk loomed up against the
sky the massive contours of Wartburg Castle. At eleven
o'clock in the night the party reined up before the gates.

This ancient fortress was already the symbol of a bygone
day, when German knighthood was in flower and sanctity un-
questioned as the highest end of man. Here monarchs and
minstrels, knights and fools, had had their assemblage, and
here St. Elizabeth had left the relics of her holiness. But
Luther was of no mind for historic reveries. As he laid him
down in the chamber of the almost untenanted bastion, and
the owls and bats wheeled about in the darkness, it seemed to
him that the Devil was pelting nuts at the ceiling and rolling
casks down the stairs. More insidious than such pranks of the
Prince of Darkness was the unallayed question, "Are you
alone wise? Have so many centuries gone wrong? What if you
are in error and are taking so many others with you to eternal
damnation?" In the morning he threw open the casement
window and looked out on the fair Thuringian hills. In the
distance he could see a cloud of smoke rising from the pits of
the charcoal burners. A gust of wind lifted and dissipated the
cloud. Even so were his doubts dispelled and his faith restored.

But only for a moment. The mood of Elijah at Horeb was
upon him. The priests of Baal indeed were slain, but Jezebel
sought the prophet's life, and he cried, "It is enough! Now, O
Lord, take away my life!" Luther passed from one self-incrimi-
nation to another. If he had not been in error, then had he
been sufficiently firm in the defense of truth? "My conscience
troubles me because at Worms I yielded to the importunity of
my friends and did not play the part of Elijah. They would
hear other things from me if I were before them again." And
when he contemplated the sequel, he could not well feel encouraged. "What an abominable spectacle is the kingdom

LUTHER AS JUNKER GEORGE
AT THE WARTBURG

of the Roman Antichrist," he wrote to Melanchthon. "Spalatin writes of the most cruel edicts against me."

Yet all the outward peril was as nothing to the inner struggles. "I can tell you in this idle solitude there are a thousand battles with Satan. It is much easier to fight against the incarnate Devil—that is, against men—than against spiritual wickedness in the heavenly places. Often I fall and am lifted again by God's right hand." Solitude and idleness increased his distress. To Spalatin he wrote, "Now is the time to pray with our might against Satan. He is plotting an attack on Germany, and I fear God will permit him because I am so indolent in prayer. I am mightily displeasing to myself, perhaps because I am alone." He wasn't quite alone. There were the warden and two serving boys, but they were hardly the sort to whom he could unburden himself as to Staupitz of old. He had been warned not to seek out company and not to become confidential lest he betray himself. The monk's cowl was laid aside. He dressed as a knight and grew a long beard. The warden did his best to provide a diversion, and included Luther in a hunting party. But he was revolted. "There is some point," he reflected, "in tracking down bears, wolves, boars, and foxes, but why should one pursue a harmless creature like a rabbit?" One ran up his leg to escape the dogs, but they bit through the cloth and killed it. "Just as the pope and the Devil treat us," commented the inveterate theologian.

He was idle, so he said. At any rate he was removed from the fracas. "I did not want to come here," he wrote. "I wanted to be in the fray." And again, "I had rather burn on live coals than rot here."

To loneliness and lack of public activity were added physical ills which were not new but were greatly accentuated by the circumstances. While still at Worms he had been overtaken by acute attacks of constipation, due perhaps to nervous depletion after the crucial days. The restricted diet and the sedentary ways at the Wartburg made the case worse. He was minded to risk his life by forsaking his concealment in order to procure medical assistance at Erfurt. Complaints continued from May until October, when Spalatin was able to send in laxatives.

The other malady was insomnia. It began in 1520 through attempts to make up arrears in saying the canonical hours. All through his controversy with Rome he was still a monk, obligated to say matins, tierce, nones, vespers, and complin. But when he became a professor at the university, a preacher in the village church, and the director of eleven monasteries, he was simply too busy to keep up. He would stack his prayers for a week, two weeks, even three weeks, and then would take off a Sunday or, on one occasion, three whole days without food or drink until he was "prayed up." After such an orgy in 1520 his head reeled. For five days he could get no sleep, and lay on his bed as one dead, until the doctor gave him a sedative. During convalescence the prayer book revolted him, and he fell in arrears a quarter of a year. Then he gave up. This was one of the stages in his weaning from monasticism. The permanent residue of the experience was insomnia.

Luther found one cure for depressions at the Wartburg, and that was work. "That I may not be idle in my Patmos," he said, in dedicating a tract to Sickingen, "I have written a book of Revelation." He wrote not one, but closer to a dozen. To a friend at Strassburg he explained:

It would not be safe to send you my books, but I have asked Spalatin to see to it. I have brought out a reply to Catharinus and another to Latomus, and in German a work on confession, expositions of Psalms 67 and 36, a commentary on the Magnificat, and a translation of Melanchthon's reply to the University of Paris. I have under way a volume of sermons on the lessons from the epistles and Gospels. I am attacking the Cardinal of Mainz and expounding the ten lepers.

On top of all this he translated the entire New Testament into his mother tongue. This was his stint for the year. One wonders whether his depressions were anything more than the rhythm of work and fatigue.

### THE REFORMATION AT WITTENBERG: MONASTICISM

Nor was he actually removed from the fray. The reformation at Wittenberg moved with disconcerting velocity, and he was kept abreast of it in so far as tardy communication and the conditions of his concealment permitted. His opinion was continually solicited, and his answers affected the developments, even though he was not in a position to take the initiative. Leadership fell to Melanchthon, professor of Greek at the university; to Carlstadt, professor and archdeacon at the Castle Church; and to Gabriel Zwilling, a monk of Luther's own order, the Augustinians. Under the lead of these men the reformation for the first time assumed a form distinctly recognizable to the common man.

Nothing which Luther had done hitherto made any difference to the ways of ordinary folk, except of course the attack on indulgences, but that had not as yet proved especially effective. While at the Wartburg, Luther learned that Cardinal Albert of Mainz was continuing the old traffic at Halle. On the first of December, 1521, Luther informed His Grace that he was quite mistaken if he thought Luther dead.

You may think me out of the fray, but I will do what Christian love demands, without regard to the gates of hell, let alone unlearned popes, cardinals, and bishops. I beg you, show yourself not a wolf but a bishop. It has been made plain enough that indulgences are rubbish and lies. See what conflagration has come from a despised spark, so that now the pope himself is singed. The same God is still alive, and he can resist the Cardinal of Mainz though he be upheld by four emperors. This is the God who breaks the cedars of Lebanon and humbles the hardened Pharaohs. You need not think Luther is dead. I will show the difference between a bishop and a wolf. I demand an immediate answer. If you do not reply within two weeks, I will publish a tract against you.

The cardinal replied that the abuses had already been suppressed. He confessed himself to be a stinking sinner, ready to receive correction.

That was something. Yet Luther was not able to say while at the Wartburg that indulgences had been discontinued in his own parish of Wittenberg. Then during his absence in 1521 and 1522 one innovation followed another with disconcerting rapidity. Priests married, monks married, nuns married. Nuns and monks even married each other. The tonsured permitted their hair to grow. The wine in the mass was given to the laity, and they were suffered to take the elements into their own hands. Priests celebrated the sacrament without vestments, in plain clothes. Portions of the mass were recited in the German tongue. Masses for the dead were discontinued. Vigils ceased, vespers were altered, images were smashed. Meat was eaten on fast days. Endowments were withdrawn by patrons. The enrollment in universities declined because students were no longer supported by ecclesiastical stipends. All this could not escape the eye of Hans and Gretel. Doctrine might go over their heads, but liturgy was a part of their daily religious life. They realized now that the reformation meant something, and this began to worry Luther. The glorious liberty of the sons of God was in danger of becoming a matter of clothes, diet, and haircuts. But he applauded the changes at the start.

First came the marriage of priests. Luther had said in *The Babylonian Captivity* that the laws of men cannot annul the commands of God; and since God has ordained marriage, the union of a priest and his wife is a true and indissoluble union. In the *Address to the Nobility* he declared that a priest must have a housekeeper, and that to put man and woman thus together is like bringing fire to straw and expecting nothing to happen. Marriage should be free to priests, though the

# Wie gar gfarlich sey.So
### Ain Priester kain Ee weyb hat.Wye Vn christlich.vnd schedlich aim gmainen Nutz Die menschen seynd.Welche hindern die pfaffen Am Ee= lichen stand.Durch
### Johan Eberlin Von Güntzburg.Anno.

**MARRIAGE OF BISHOPS, MONKS, AND NUNS**

whole canon law go to pieces. Let there be an end to unchaste chastity. Luther's advice was being put into practice. Three priests married in 1521 and were arrested by Albert of Mainz. Luther sent him a warm protest. Albert consulted the University of Wittenberg. Carlstadt answered with a work on celibacy, in which he went so far as to assert not only that a priest might marry but that he must, and should also be the father of a family. For obligatory celibacy he would substitute obligatory matrimony and paternity. And he got married himself. The girl was described as of a noble family, neither pretty nor rich, appearing to be about fifteen years of age. Carlstadt sent an announcement to the Elector.

Most noble prince, I observe that in Scripture no estate is so highly lauded as marriage. I observe also that marriage is allowed to the clergy, and for lack of it many poor priests have suffered sorely in the dungeons of the Devil. Therefore if Almighty God permits, I am going to marry Anna Mochau on St. Sebastian's Eve, and I hope Your Grace approves.

Luther did. "I am very pleased over Carlstadt's marriage," he wrote. "I know the girl."

Yet he had no mind to do the like himself because he was not only a priest but also a monk. At first he was aghast when Carlstadt attacked also monastic celibacy. "Good heavens!" wrote Luther, "will our Wittenbergers give wives to monks? They won't give one to me!" But under the fiery preaching of Gabriel Zwilling the Augustinian monks began to leave the cloister. On November 30, fifteen withdrew. The prior reported to the Elector:

It is being preached that no monk can be saved in a cowl, that cloisters are in the grip of the Devil, that monks should be expelled and cloisters demolished. Whether such teaching is grounded in the gospel I greatly doubt.

But now should such monks be forced to go back? And if not, should they be allowed to marry? Melanchthon consulted Luther. "I wish I could talk this over with you," he replied.

The case of a monk seems to me to be different from that of a priest. The monk has voluntarily taken vows. You argue that a monastic vow is not binding because it is incapable of fulfillment. By that token you would abrogate all the divine precepts. You say that a vow entails servitude. Not necessarily. St. Bernard lived happily under his vows. The real question is not whether vows can be kept, but whether they have been enjoined by God.

To find the answer Luther set himself to search the Scriptures. He was not long in making up his mind, and soon sent to Wittenberg some theses about vows. When they were read to the circle of the Wittenberg clergy and professors, Bugenhagen, priest at the Castle Church, pronounced the judgment, "These propositions will upset public institutions as Luther's doctrine up to this point would not have done." The theses were shortly followed by a treatise *On Monastic Vows*. In a preface addressed to "my dearest father" Luther professed now to discern the hand of Providence in making him a monk against his parents' will in order that he might be able to testify from experience against monasticism. The monk's vow is unfounded in Scripture and in conflict with charity and liberty. "Marriage is good, virginity is better, but liberty is best." Monastic vows rest on the false assumption that there is a special calling, *a vocation,* to which superior Christians are invited to observe the counsels of perfection while ordinary Christians fulfill only the commands; but there simply is no special religious vocation, declared Luther, since the call of God comes to each man at the common tasks. "This is the work," said Jonas, "which emptied the cloisters." Luther's own order in Wittenberg, the Augustinians, at a meeting in January, instead of disciplining the apostate monks, ruled that thereafter any member should be free to stay or leave as he might please.

THE MASS

Next came the reform of the liturgy, which touched the common man more intimately because it altered his daily devotions. He was being invited to drink the wine at the sacrament, to take the elements into his own hands, to commune without previous confession, to hear the words of institution in his own tongue, and to participate extensively in sacred song.

Luther laid the theoretical groundwork for the most significant changes. His principle was that the mass is not a sacrifice but a thanksgiving to God and a communion with believers. It is not a sacrifice in the sense of placating God, because he does not need to be placated; and it is not an oblation in the sense of something offered, because man cannot offer to God, but only receive. What then should be done with such expressions in the mass as "this holy sacrifice," "this oblation," "these offerings"? In *The Babylonian Captivity,* Luther had interpreted them figuratively, but at the Wartburg he came to the more drastic conception: "The words of the canon are plain; the words of Scripture are plain. Let the canon yield to the gospel." The liturgy then would have to be revised.

A particular form of the mass rested exclusively upon its sacrificial character. This was the private mass for the benefit of departed spirits, for whom the priest offered a sacrifice; and since they could not possibly be present, he communed alone. This form of the mass was called private because privately endowed. It was also privately conducted. Luther objected first to the principle of sacrifice and second to the absence of the congregation. In *The Babylonian Captivity* he had been willing to tolerate such masses as private devotions on the part of the priest, provided of course that they were conducted in a devotional spirit and not rattled through to complete the quota for the day. At the Wartburg he reached a more pronounced position. To Melanchthon he wrote on the first of August, "I will never again celebrate a private mass in eternity." Luther concluded a tract on the abolition of private masses with an appeal to Frederick the Wise to emulate the crusade of Frederick Barbarossa for the liberation of the Holy Sepulchre. Let Frederick liberate the gospel at Wittenberg by abolishing all the masses which he had privately endowed. Incidentally, a staff of twenty-five priests was employed for the saying of such masses at the Castle Church.

On the old question raised by the Hussites, whether the wine as well as the bread should be given to the laity, Luther and the Wittenbergers were agreed in desiring to restore the apostolic practice. As to fasting and confession prior to communion Luther was indifferent. There was variance as to whether the priest should hold aloft the elements. Carlstadt viewed the act as the presentation of a sacrifice to be rejected, whereas Luther saw only a mark of reverence to be retained.

### THE OUTBREAK OF VIOLENCE

The agreement was certainly sufficient to warrant action, and Melanchthon made a beginning on September 29 by administering communion in both kinds to a few students in the parish church. In the Augustinian cloister Zwilling delivered impassioned pleas to the brothers to refuse to celebrate unless the mass was reformed. The prior responded that he would rather have no mass than to have it mutilated. Consequently the mass ceased in the Augustinian cloister on October 23. In the Castle Church on All Saints' Day, November 1, the very day for the exhibition of the relics and the dispensing of indulgences, Justus Jonas branded indulgences as rubbish and clamored for the abolition of vigils and private masses. In future he would refuse to celebrate unless communicants were present. Popular violence commenced. Students and townsmen so intimidated the old believers that the faithful Augustinians feared for their own safety and for that of their cloister. The elector was disturbed. As a prince he was responsible for the public peace. As a Christian he was concerned for the true faith. He wished to be enlightened as to the meaning of Scripture, and appointed a committee. But the committee could not agree. No group in Wittenberg could agree, neither the university, nor the Augustinians, nor the chapter at the Castle Church. "What a mess we are in," said Spalatin, "with everybody doing something else."

The old order argued that God would not have suffered his

Church so long to be deceived. Changes should wait at least until unanimity had been achieved, and the clergy should not be molested. Frederick the Wise pointed out, moreover, to the innovators that masses were endowed; and if the masses ceased, the endowments would cease. He could not see how a priest could expect to get married, stop saying mass, and still draw his stipend. The alteration of the mass concerned all Christendom, he argued; and if a little town like Wittenberg could not make up its mind, the rest of the world would not be impressed. Above all, let there be no division and tumult. The Evangelicals replied by pointing to the example of Christ and the apostles, who, though but a handful, were not deterred from reform by the fear of tumult. As for the ancestors who endowed the masses, if they could return to life and receive better instruction, they would be glad to have their money used to further the faith in a better way. The old believers rebutted, "You need not think because you are a handful that therefore you are in the position of Christ and the apostles."

Luther's sympathies for the moment were with the handful, and he was distressed because events were moving too slowly. He had sent Spalatin the manuscripts of his tracts entitled *On Monastic Vows, On the Abolition of Private Masses,* and *A Blast Against the Archbishop of Mainz.* None of them appeared. Luther resolved to make a trip incognito to Wittenberg to find the reason why.

CHAPTER TWELVE

# THE RETURN OF THE EXILE

 ITH BEARD SUFFICIENT to deceive his mother the exile from the Wartburg appeared on the streets of Wittenberg on the fourth of December, 1521. He was immensely pleased with all that his associates had lately introduced by way of reform, but irate because his recent tracts had not been published. If Spalatin had withheld them from the printer, let him note that worse would replace them. Spalatin thereupon released the treatises on vows and private masses but still retained the blast against Albert, which never did appear. Luther let it be known in Wittenberg that he was contemplating a blast also against Frederick if he did not disperse his collection

of relics and contribute to the poor fund all the gold and silver in which they were encased. At this moment Luther was distinctly for speeding up the reformation.

But not by violence. The day before he arrived in Wittenberg there had been a riot. Students and townsfolk, with knives under their cloaks, invaded the parish church, snatched the mass books from the altar, and drove out the priests. Stones were thrown against those saying private devotions to the Virgin Mary. On the morrow, the very day of Luther's arrival, the Franciscans were intimidated. This was not the worst of it. Luther might perhaps have excused this tumult as a student prank, but on the sortie from and back to the Wartburg he sensed among the people a revolutionary temper. He hastened, therefore, to bring out a warning against recourse to violence. "Remember," he warned, "that Antichrist, as Daniel said, is to be broken without the hand of man. Violence will only make him stronger. Preach, pray, but do not fight. Not that all constraint is ruled out, but it must be exercised by the constituted authorities."

But in the meantime at Wittenberg the constituted authority was inhibitive. Elector Frederick issued an order on December 19 in which he said that discussion might continue, but there could be no changes in the mass until unanimity was reached. Carlstadt thereupon undertook to defy the elector and announced that when his turn came to say mass at New Year's he would give communion in both kinds to the whole town. The elector interposed, but Carlstadt forestalled him by trading his turn for Christmas and by issuing the public invitation only the night before. The populace was stirred, and Christmas Eve was celebrated by rioting. The mob invaded the parish church, smashed the lamps, intimidated the priests, sang through the church, "My maid has lost her shoe," and then from the courtyard caterwauled against the choir. Finally they went to the Castle Church and as the priest was giving the benediction wished him pestilence and hell-fire.

### TURMOIL

On Christmas Day 2,000 people assembled in the Castle Church—"the whole town," said a chronicler. And it very nearly was, for the total population was only 2,500. Carlstadt officiated without vestments in a plain black robe. In his sermon he told the people that in preparation for the sacrament they had no need of fasting and confession. If they felt that they must first be absolved, then they lacked faith in the sacrament itself. Faith alone is needed, faith and heartfelt longing and deep contrition. "She how Christ makes you a sharer in his blessedness if you believe. See how he has cleansed and hallowed you through his promise. Still better, see that Christ stands before you. He takes from you all your struggle and doubt, that you may know that through his word you are blessed."

Then Carlstadt recited the mass in Latin, in very abbreviated form, omitting all the passages on sacrifice. At the consecration and distribution of the elements, both the bread and the wine, he passed from Latin into German. For the first time in their lives the 2,000 assembled people heard in their own tongue the words, "This is the cup of my blood of the new and eternal testament, spirit and secret of the faith, shed for you to the remission of sins." One of the communicants so trembled that he dropped the bread. Carlstadt told him to pick

A CARTOON AGAINST THE IMAGE BREAKERS

*With a very graphic illustration of the saying on the mote and the beam in the background.*

it up; but he who had had the courage to come forward and take the sacred morsel into his own hand from the plate, when he saw it desecrated on the floor was so overcome by all the terror of sacrilege to the body of God that he could not bring himself to touch it again.

Under Carlstadt's leading the town council at Wittenberg issued the first city ordinance of the reformation. Mass was to be conducted about as Carlstadt had done it. Luther's ideas on social reform were implemented. Begging was forbidden. Those genuinely poor should be maintained from a common fund. Prostitutes should be banned. And then came quite a new point: images should be removed from the churches.

The question of images, pictures, and statues of the saints and the Virgin, and crucifixes, had been greatly agitated during the preceding weeks. Zwilling had led an iconoclastic riot, overturning altars and smashing images and pictures of the saints. The author of the idea was Carlstadt. He took his stand squarely upon Scripture: "Thou shalt not make unto thee any graven image, or any likeness of any thing that is in heaven above, or that is in the earth beneath, or that is in the water under the earth." Scripture was reinforced by his own experience. He had been so deeply attached to images as to be diverted by them from true worship. "God is a spirit" and must be worshiped only in spirit. Christ is a spirit, but the image of Christ is wood, silver, or gold. One who contemplates a crucifix is reminded only of the physical suffering of Christ rather than of his spiritual tribulations.

Coupled with this attack on art in religion went an attack also on music in religion. "Relegate organs, trumpets, and flutes to the theater," said Carlstadt.

Better one heart-felt prayer than a thousand cantatas of the Psalms. The lascivious notes of the organ awaken thoughts of the world. When we should be meditating on the suffering of Christ, we are reminded of Pyramus and Thisbe. Or, if there is to be singing, let it be no more than a solo.

While Wittenberg was thus convulsed by iconoclasm, three laymen arrived from Zwickau near the Bohemian border, claiming to be prophets of the Lord and to have had intimate conversations with the Almighty. They had no need of the Bible but relied on the Spirit. If the Bible were important, God would have dropped it directly from heaven. They repudiated infant baptism and proclaimed the speedy erection of the kingdom of the godly through the slaughter of the ungodly, whether at the hands of the Turks or of the godly themselves. Melanchthon listened to them agape. He wrote to the Elector:

I can scarcely tell you how deeply I am moved. But who shall judge them, other than Martin, I do not know. Since the gospel is at stake, arrangements should be made for them to meet with him. They wish it. I would not have written to you if the matter were not so important. We must beware lest we resist the Spirit of God, and also lest we be possessed of the Devil.

But such a disputation with Martin appeared dangerous for him and disturbing for Wittenberg. She had already enough on her plate, was the opinion of Spalatin.

Luther in his letters rejected the prophets on religious grounds, because they talked too glibly.

Those who are expert in spiritual things have gone through the valley of the shadow. When these men talk of sweetness and of being transported to the third heaven, do not believe them. Divine Majesty does not speak directly to men. God is a consuming fire, and the dreams and visions of the saints are terrible. . . . Prove the spirits; and if you are not able to do so, then take the advice of Gamaliel and wait.

In another letter he added:

I am sure we can restrain these firebrands without the sword. I hope the Prince will not imbrue his hands in their blood. I see no reason why on their account I should come home.

Frederick the Wise was harassed by one eruption after another. Next came a blow from the right. The noise of the doings at Wittenberg reached Duke George over the border, and the confessional cleavage coalesced with the ancient rivalry between the two houses of Saxony. Luther was soon able to complete his trinity of opposition as the pope, Duke George, and the Devil. At the moment the duke was the most active of the three. He was at the Diet of Nürnberg and persuaded the estates to send both to Frederick the Wise and to the Bishop of Meissen, who had ecclesiastical jurisdiction over the Wittenberg region, the following instructions:

We have heard that priests celebrate mass in lay habit, omitting essential portions. They consecrate the holy sacrament in German. The recipients are not required to have made prior confession. They take the elements into their own hands and in both kinds. The blood of our Lord is served not in a chalice but in a mug. The sacrament is given to children. Priests are dragged from the altars by force. Priests and monks marry, and the common people are incited to frivolity and offense.

In response to this communication the Bishop of Meissen requested of Frederick the Wise permission to conduct a visitation throughout his domains, and Frederick consented, although making no promises to discipline offenders. Then on February 13 Frederick issued instructions of his own to the university and to the chapter at the Castle Church.

We have gone too fast. The common man has been incited to frivolity, and no one has been edified. We should have consideration for the weak. Images should be left until further notice. The question of begging should be canvassed. No essential portion of the mass should be omitted. Moot points should be discussed. Carlstadt should not preach any more.

This document can scarcely be described as a complete abrogation of the reforms. Frederick simply called a halt and invited further consideration, but he did emphatically abrogate the city ordinance of January. If there were to be reforms, he was determined they should not be by towns but by territories, as in the later German pattern. Carlstadt submitted and agreed not to preach. Zwilling left Wittenberg.

### THE INVITATION TO COME BACK

But the town council resolved to defy the elector by inviting Martin Luther to come home. An invitation was sent to him in the name of "The Council and the entire City of Wittenberg." If the elector nullified their ordinance, then they would bring back the author of the whole movement. Probably they expected Luther to exert a moderating influence. Carlstadt and Zwilling were smoldering firebrands. Melanchthon was in a dither, thought of leaving to escape the radicals, and frankly said, "The dam has broken, and I cannot stem the waters." The council knew nowhere to look for leadership save to the Wartburg, and without consulting or even informing the elector invited Luther to return.

He was not unwilling to come, for he had said as early as December that he had no intention of remaining in hiding longer than Easter. He would stay until he had finished a volume of sermons and the translation of the New Testament. Then he proposed to turn to the translation of the Old Testament and to settle somewhere in the neighborhood of Wittenberg in order that he might engage the collaboration of colleagues better versed than he in Hebrew.

At the time these scholarly concerns motivated him rather than any desire to take the wheel at Wittenberg. But when a direct invitation came from the town and congregation, that was to him a call from God.

Luther had the courtesy to notify the elector of his intention. Frederick replied that he realized he had perhaps not done enough. But what should he do? He did not wish to go counter to the will of God, nor to provoke disorder. The Diet of Nürnberg and the Bishop of Meissen threatened intervention. If Luther should return and the pope and the emperor should step in to harm him,

FREDERICK THE WISE

the elector would take it amiss. But if the elector should resist, there would be great disturbance in the land. So far as his person was concerned, the elector was prepared to suffer, but he would like to know for what. If he knew that the cross was from God, he would bear it; but at Wittenberg no one knew who was the cook and who the waiter. A new meeting of the diet would take place soon. In the meantime let Luther lie low. Time might change things greatly.

Luther answered:

I wrote for your sake, not for mine. I was disturbed that the gospel was brought into disrepute at Wittenberg. If I were not sure that the gospel is on our side, I would have given up. All the sorrow I have had is nothing compared to this. I would gladly have paid for this with my life, for we can answer neither to God nor to the world for what has happened. The Devil is at work in this. As for myself, my gospel is not from men. Concessions bring only contempt. I cannot yield an inch to the Devil. I have done enough for Your Grace by staying in hiding for a year. I did not do it through cowardice. The Devil knows I would have gone into Worms though there were as many devils as tiles on the roof, and I would ride into Leipzig now, though it rained Duke Georges for nine days.

I would have you know that I come to Wittenberg with a higher protection than that of Your Grace. I do not ask you to protect me. I will protect you more than you will protect me. If I thought you would protect me, I would not come. This is not a case for the sword but for God, and since you are weak in the faith you cannot protect me. You ask what you should do, and think you have done too little. I say you have done too much, and you should do nothing but leave it to God. You are excused if I am captured or killed. As a prince you should obey the emperor and offer no resistance. No one should use force except the one who is ordained to use it. Otherwise there is rebellion against God. But I hope you will not act as my accuser. If you leave the door open, that is enough. If they try to make you do more than that, I will then tell you what to do. If Your Grace had eyes, you would see the glory of God.

### THE RETURN TO WITTENBERG

The return to Wittenberg was incomparably brave. Never before had Luther stood in such peril. At the interview with Cajetan and at Worms he had not been under the ban of Church and empire, and Frederick had been ready to provide asylum. But this time Luther was made to know that he could count on no protection in case of extradition by the diet or the emperor. At Worms there had been a second line of defense in Sickingen, Hutten, and the knights. This wall was fast crumbling. Sickingen had had the indiscretion after Worms to embark on an adventure designed to arrest the doom of German knighthood at the expense of the territorial princes and bishops. The attack was focused on the prince bishop, Richard of Greiffenklau, elector and archbishop of Trier. A number of knights who had earlier proffered help to Luther joined Sickingen, but his campaign was doomed at the outset, because victims of his former depredations rallied to Trier and corralled Sickingen in one of his own castles, where he died of wounds. Hutten had been unable to accompany him on this campaign because he was ill of syphilis at the Ebernburg. But in intervals of health he had engaged in a foray of his own, a priests' war he called it, consisting mainly in the sacking of cloisters. When Sickingen failed, he fled to Switzerland to sizzle out his meteoric career on an island of Lake Zurich. The knights who had shared in Sickingen's exploit suffered the confiscation of their estates. Had Luther relied upon them, they would have proved a broken reed. But he had long since resolved to trust only to the Lord of Hosts, who does not always deliver his children from the mouth of the lion.

A detail of Luther's homeward journey is recorded by a Swiss chronicler who apologetically introduced into a cryptic history of the times a leisurely description of an experience of his own when with a companion on the way to Wittenberg he pulled up late one night out of the storm at the portal of the Black Bear Inn of a Thuringian village. The host brought the bedraggled travelers into a room where sat a knight with a bushy black beard clad in a scarlet cloak and woolen tights, his hands resting on the hilt of a sword as he engaged in reading. The knight rose and hospitably invited the muddy wayfarers to sit and share with him a glass. They noticed that his book was in Hebrew. They asked him whether he knew if Luther were in Wittenberg. "I know quite positively that he is not," said he, "but he will be." Then he inquired what the Swiss thought of Luther. The host, observing that the pair were well disposed to the reformer, confided to one that the knight was Luther himself. The Swiss could not believe his ears, thought he must have mistaken the name for Hutten. On parting the next morning they let the knight know that they took him for Hutten. "No, he is Luther," interposed the host. The knight laughed. "You take me for Hutten. He takes me for Luther. Maybe I am the Devil." Within a week they were to meet him again in Wittenberg.

Luther's first concern there was to restore confidence and order. With stalwart presence and mellifluous voice he mounted the pulpit to preach patience, charity, and consideration for the weak. He reminded his hearers that no man can die for another, no man can believe for another, no man can answer for another. Therefore every man should be fully persuaded in his own mind. No one can be intimidated into belief. The violence of those who demolish altars, smash images, and drag priests by the hair was to Luther a greater blow than any ever dealt him by the papacy. He was beginning to realize that perhaps after all he was closer to Rome than to his own sectaries. He was deeply cut because the predictions of his assailants that he would be the occasion of "division, war, and insurrection" were being all too abundantly fulfilled. He pleaded:

Give men time. I took three years of constant study, reflection, and discussion to arrive where I now am, and can the common man, untutored in such matters, be expected to move the same distance in three months? Do not suppose that abuses are eliminated by destroying the object which is abused. Men can go wrong with wine and women. Shall we then prohibit wine and abolish women? The sun, the moon, and stars have been worshiped. Shall we then pluck them out of the sky? Such haste and violence betray a lack of confidence in God. See how much he has been able to accomplish through me, though I did no more than pray and preach. The Word did it all. Had I wished I might have started a conflagration at Worms. But while I sat still and drank beer with Philip and Amsdorf, God dealt the papacy a mighty blow.

In response to these appeals Zwilling agreed to give up celebrating the Lord's Supper with feathers in his beret, and Luther cordially recommended him to a pastorate at Altenburg, one of the villages of Electoral Saxony. Carlstadt took over a congregation in the neighboring Orlamünde. Wittenberg was in hand.

Luther then turned to deal with the elector, who desired from him a statement to be submitted to the Diet at Nürnberg, exculpating the prince from any complicity in the return from the Wartburg. Luther gladly complied but in the course of the letter remarked that things are settled differently in heaven than in Nürnberg. Frederick suggested that the words "on earth" be substituted for "in Nürnberg." Luther again complied.

CHAPTER THIRTEEN

# NO OTHER FOUNDATION

---

 XTERNALLY speaking, Luther had reached the turning point of his career. The leader of the opposition was called to be the head of the government, albeit in a very restricted area. The demolisher was summoned to build. The change of course was not absolute because he had been constructive all along, and to the end he never ceased to flay the papacy. Nevertheless the change was vast between the role of railing against "the execrable bull of Antichrist" and that of providing a new pattern of Church, state, and society, a new constitution for the Church, a new liturgy, and a new Scripture in the vernacular.

In the accomplishment of this task there were two considerations. The first had to do with principles which Luther sought to realize in the concrete, and the second with the people who constituted the field in which these ideas were to be realized. Luther's views were for the most part already mature by the time of his return to Wittenberg. Controversy was to sharpen the emphases. Practical experience dictated the lines of advance or retrenchment, while long years in the pulpit and classroom afforded occasion for copious illustration.

Luther's principles in religion and ethics alike must constantly be borne in mind if he is not at times to appear unintelligible and even petty. The primary consideration with him was always the pre-eminence of religion. Into a society where the lesser breed were given to gaming, roistering, and wenching—the Diet of Worms was called a veritable Venusberg—at a time when the choicer sort were glorying in the accomplishments of man, strode this Luther, entranced by the song of angels, stunned by the wrath of God, speechless before the wonder of creation, lyrical over the divine mercy, a man aflame with God. For such a person there was no question which mattered much save this: How do I stand before God? Luther would never shirk a mundane task such as exhorting the elector to repair the city wall to keep the peasants' pigs from rooting in the villagers' gardens, but he was never supremely concerned about pigs, gardens, walls, cities, princes, or any and all of the blessings and nuisances of this mortal life. The ultimate problem was always God and man's relationship to God. For this reason political and social forms were to him a matter of comparative indifference. Whatever would foster the understanding, dissemination, and practice of God's Word should be encouraged, and whatever impeded must be opposed. This is why it is futile to inquire whether Luther was a democrat, aristocrat, autocrat, or anything else. Religion was for him the chief end of man, and all else peripheral.

And the religion which he had in mind was of course the Christian religion. Everyone in his age would have said that, if for no other reason than out of national or European pride. But Luther so spoke because he had experienced a sheer impasse in any other approach to God than through his own self-disclosure in Jesus Christ. "No other foundation is laid than has been laid in Jesus Christ our Lord."

### NATURE, HISTORY, AND PHILOSOPHY

Nature cannot reveal God. Nature is indeed very wonderful, and every particle of creation reveals the handiwork of God, if one has the eyes to see. But that is precisely the difficulty. If one already believes in the beneficence of God, then one is overcome with amazement and joy at the trembling of the dawn when night is not yet day and day is not night but light imperceptibly dispels darkness. How amazing are the clouds sustained without pillars and the firmament of heaven upheld without columns! How fair are the birds of heaven and the

lilies of the field! "If thou couldst understand a single grain
of wheat, thou wouldst die for wonder." God is in all this.
He is in every creature, inwardly and outwardly, through and
through, over and under, behind and before, so that nothing
can be more inward and hidden in any creature than God.
"In him we live, and move, and have our being." Without
him is naught. God fills all the world, but by the world he is
not contained. "Whither shall I flee from thy presence? If I
ascend up into heaven, thou art there: if I make my bed in hell,
behold, thou art there." But who sees all this? Only faith and
spirit. The trouble with Erasmus is that he is not stupefied with
wonder at the child in the womb. He does not contemplate
marriage with reverent amazement, nor praise and thank God
for the marvel of a flower or the bursting of a peach stone by
the swelling seed. He beholds these wonders like a cow staring
at a new door. The deficiency of faith is made evident by a
lack of wonder, for nature is a revelation only to those to
whom God has already been revealed.

It is no better with history, which also cannot reveal God, for
the whole of history appears at first glance to be nothing but a
commentary on the text, "He hath put down the mighty from
their seats, and exalted them of low degree." God suffers the
mighty empires to strut for a time upon the stage—Assyria,
Babylon, Persia, Greece, and Rome. Then when each becomes
too overweening, God places the sword in the hand of another
and releases him to cast down the braggart, only in turn after
his swaggering to be brought low. Here again we meet with
an Augustinian theme, save that for Augustine history is an
illustration of man's lust for domination and of the justice
of God in abasing the arrogant. But Luther wonders whether
God is amusing himself with a puppet show.

Even more disconcerting is the recognition that all too often
God does not cast down the mighty and does not exalt those
of low degree. But he leaves them in their squalor, unrequited
and unavenged. Throughout history it is the saints who are
despised and rejected, maltreated, abused, and trodden under
the feet of man. Joseph, for example, for no adequate reason
was seized by his brethren, cast into the well, sold to the
Ishmaelites, and carried as a slave into Egypt. And there precisely because he was honorable he was besmirched with the
accusation of adultery and thrown into prison. And the Virgin
Mary, after being informed by the angel Gabriel that she was
to be the mother of the Most High, had to suffer the suspicion
of her own husband. Joseph's situation is understandable, for
they had not yet come together, and she had been three months
absent with her cousin Elisabeth. He could not well put a good
construction upon her condition until the angel instructed him
in a dream. But why did God wait to disabuse him until after
Mary had been put to shame?

Some of the afflictions which fall upon the just were, in Luther's view, the work of the Devil, and here he was following the familiar Augustinian dualism of the eternal conflict between the City of God and the earthly city through which Satan operates. Luther could in this way take comfort in tumult because the Devil is bound to assail the faith, and tumult is the proof that faith is present and under attack. But it is not always the Devil who is responsible. God is a God who works through contraries. The Virgin had to be put to shame before she could come into glory. Joseph had to be humiliated by false accusation before he could become the prime minister and savior of Egypt. In such moments God appears hidden. Joseph must have had a fearful struggle. He would say, "Oh, if I could only get back to my father," and then he would grip himself and say, "Hold fast. If only I could find the way out of this dungeon. Hold fast. What if I die in disgrace in this prison? Hold fast." Such alternations of anguish and consolation assailed him until he was able to discern the hand of God.

There is no escaping from the horrors of darkness because God is such a God "that before he can be God he must first appear to be the Devil. We cannot reach heaven until we first descend into hell. We cannot be God's children unless first we are the Devil's children. Again before the world can be seen to be a lie it must first appear to be the truth."

It must seem so. Yet God has not really deserted us, but he is hidden, and by direct searching we cannot find him out. Why God wishes to hide himself from us we do not know; but this we know: our nature cannot attain unto his majesty. "David did not speak with the absolute God, whom we must fear if we would not perish, because human nature and the absolute God are implacable enemies. And it cannot but be that human nature should be oppressed by such majesty. Therefore David does not talk with the absolute God but with God clothed and mantled in the Word."

Neither can philosophy reveal God. In making this assertion Luther was in part echoing the language of the late scholastics, on whose works he had been reared. The Occamists had wrecked the synthesis of Thomas Aquinas whereby nature and reason lead through unbroken stages to grace and revelation. Instead between nature and grace, between reason and revelation, these theologies introduced a great gulf. So much so indeed that philosophy and theology were compelled to resort to two different kinds of logic and even two different varieties of arithmetic. The classic illustration was the doctrine of the Trinity, which asserts that three persons are one God. According to human arithmetic this is preposterous, and yet according to divine arithmetic it must be believed. Luther at this point outdid his teachers and asserted that whereas by the standard of human reason two and five equal seven, yet if God should declare them to be eight, one must believe against reason and against feeling. All this Luther could say with his teachers, but such conundrums gave him little concern.

The inadequacy of philosophy was to him the more apparent and the more depressing at those points where his master, St. Augustine, had accentuated the cleavage between the natural man and the redeemed man, and had thereby widened at the same time the breach between natural and revealed religion. Augustine freely conceded that in some respects man still resembled God, in whose image he was created. The fall of Adam did not obliterate all the vestiges, but their meaning is unintelligible to one who is not acquainted with the original pattern. The late scholastics heightened the point that as cow tracks in a meadow bespeak a cow only to one who has previously seen a cow, so the trinitarian structure of man, with intellect, memory, and will, bespeaks the trinitarian structure of God only to one to whom the doctrine has already been revealed. Luther took over this whole manner of thinking and applied it in a much more drastic and poignant way, because for him the problems were not so much metaphysical as religious. The crucial point was not as to the structure of God but as to the character of God. His structure remains an insoluble mystery into which we were wiser not to pry, but we must ask, Is he good? Is he just? Is he good to *me?* Augustine's heart was no longer restless after he had received the yoke that is easy. But Luther never ceased to revolve these old tormenting queries.

### CHRIST THE SOLE REVEALER

For his answer he was driven to seek God where he has chosen to make himself known, namely in the flesh of Jesus Christ our Lord, who is the sole revealer of God.

The prophet Isaiah said, "The people that walked in darkness have seen a great light." Don't you think that this is an inexpressible light which enables us to see the heart of God and the depth of the Godhead? And that we may also see the thoughts of the Devil and what sin is and how to be freed from it and what death is and how to be delivered. And what man is, and the world, and how to conduct oneself in it. No one before was sure what God is or whether there are devils, what sin and death are, let alone how to be delivered. This is all the work of Christ, and in this passage he is called Mighty and Wonderful.

He is the sole redeemer of man from the thralldom of sin and the gates of death. He alone is the hope of any enduring society upon earth. Where men do not know Bethlehem's babe they rave and rage and strive. The angels proclaimed peace on earth, and so shall it be to those who know and receive this Babe. For what is it like where Jesus Christ is not? What is the world if not a perfect hell with nothing but lying, cheating, gluttony, guzzling, lechery, brawling, and murder. That is the very Devil himself. There is no kindliness nor honor. No one is sure of another. One must be as distrustful of friends as of enemies, and sometimes more. This is the kingdom of the world where the Devil reigns and rules. But the angels show in their song that those who know and accept the Child Jesus not only give honor to God but treat their fellow men as if they were gods, with peaceable demeanor, glad to help and counsel any man. They are free from envy and wrangling, for the Christian way is quiet and friendly in peace and brotherly love where each gladly does the best he can for another.

All then would seem to be simple. "Believe on the Lord Jesus Christ, and thou shalt be saved," but faith in Christ is far from simple and easy because he is an astounding king, who, instead of defending his people, deserts them. Whom he would save he must first make a despairing sinner. Whom he would make wise he must first turn into a fool. Whom he would make alive he must first kill. Whom he would bring to honor he must first bring to dishonor. He is a strånge king who is nearest when he is far and farthest when he is near.

The attempt of Erasmus to make Christianity simple and easy was to Luther utterly vain because Christ must so deeply offend. Man's corruption must be assailed before ever his eyes can be opened. One of Luther's students recorded:

On Christmas eve of 1538 Dr. Martin Luther was·very jocund. All his words and songs and thoughts were of the incarnation of our Lord. Then with a sigh he said, "Oh, we poor men that we should be so cold and indifferent to this great joy which has been given us. This indeed is the greatest gift, which far exceeds all else that God has created. And we believe so feebly even ·though the angels proclaim and preach and sing, and their song is fair and sums up the whole Christian religion, for 'glory to God in the highest' is the very heart of worship. This they wish for us and bring to us in Christ. For the world, since Adam's fall, knows neither God nor his creatures. Oh, what fine, fair, happy thoughts would man have had were he not fallen! How he would have meditated upon God in all creatures, that he should see in the smallest and meanest flower God's omnipotent wisdom and goodness. Every tree and branch would have been more esteemed than if it were gold or silver. And properly considered every green tree is lovelier than gold and silver. Surely the contemplation of the whole creation, and especially of the simplest· grasses of the fields and the adornment of the earth, proves that our Lord God is an artist like unto none. Adam and his children would have gloried in all this, but now since the pitiable fall the Creator is dishonored and reviled. That is why the dear angels summon fallen men once more to faith in Christ and to love that they may give to God alone the honor and may dwell in this life in peace with God and one another."

The reason why faith is so hard and reason so inadequate is a problem far deeper than logic. Luther often railed at reason, and he has been portrayed in consequence as a complete irrationalist in religion. This is quite to mistake his meaning. Reason in the sense of logic he employed to the uttermost limits. At Worms and often elsewhere he asked to be instructed from Scripture and reason. In this sense reason meant logical deduction from known premises; and when Luther railed against the harlot reason, he meant something else. Common sense is perhaps a better translation. He had in mind the way in which man ordinarily behaves, feels, and thinks. It is not what God says that is a foreign tongue, but what God does that is utterly incomprehensible.

When I am told that God became man, I can follow the idea, but I just do not understand what it means. For what man, if left to his natural promptings, if he were God, would humble himself to lie in the feedbox of a donkey or to hang upon a cross? God laid upon Christ the iniquities of us all.

This is that ineffable and infinite mercy of God which the slender capacity of man's heart cannot comprehend and much less utter— that unfathomable depth and burning zeal of God's love toward us. And truly the magnitude of God's mercy engenders in us not only a hardness to believe but also incredulity itself. For I hear not only that the omnipotent God, the creator and maker of all things, is good and merciful, but also that the Supreme Majesty was so concerned for me, a lost sinner, a son of wrath and of everlasting death, that he spared not his own Son but delivered him to the most ignominious death, that, hanging between two thieves, he might be made a curse and sin for me, a cursed sinner, that I might be made just, blessed, a son and heir of God. Who can sufficiently declare this exceeding great goodness of God? Therefore the holy Scripture speaks of far other than philosophical or political matters, namely of the unspeakable and utterly divine gifts, which far surpass the capacity both of men and of angels.

In God alone can man ever find peace. God can be known only through Christ, but how lay hold on Christ when his ways are likewise so incredible? The answer is not by sight but by faith which walks gaily into the darkness. Yet once again, how shall one come by this faith? It is a gift of God. By no act of will can it be induced.

## THE WORD AND THE SACRAMENTS

No, but man is not left entirely without recourse. He can expose himself to those channels of self-disclosure which God has ordained. They are all summed up in the *Word*. It is not to be equated with Scripture nor with the sacraments, yet it operates through them and not apart from them. The *Word* is not the Bible as a written book because "the gospel is really not that which is contained in books and composed in letters, but rather an oral preaching and a living word, a voice which resounds throughout the whole world and is publicly proclaimed." This Word must be heard. This Word must be pondered. "Not through thought, wisdom, and will does the faith of Christ arise in us, but through an incomprehensible and hidden operation of the Spirit, which is given by faith in Christ only at the hearing of the Word and without any other work of ours." More, too, than mere reading is required. "No one is taught through much reading and thinking. There is a much higher school where one learns God's Word. One must go into the wilderness. Then Christ comes and one becomes able to judge the world."

Likewise faith is given to those who avail themselves of those outward rites which again God has ordained as organs of revelation, the sacraments.

For although he is everywhere and in all creatures and I may find him in stone, fire, water, or rope, since he is assuredly there, yet he does not wish me to seek him apart from the Word, that I should throw myself into fire or water or hang myself with a rope. He is everywhere, but he does not desire that you should seek everywhere but only where the Word is. There if you seek him you will truly find, namely in the Word. These people do not know and see who say that it doesn't make sense that Christ should be in bread and wine. Of course Christ is with me in prison and the martyr's death, else where should I be? He is truly present there with the Word, yet not in the same sense as in the sacrament, because he has attached his body and blood to the Word and in bread and wine is bodily to be received.

These were Luther's religious principles: that religion is paramount, that Christianity is the sole true religion to be apprehended by faith channeled through Scripture, preaching, and sacrament.

The practical deductions from such a view are obvious. All institutions must accord to religion the right of way. The study of Scripture must be cultivated in church and school. In church the pulpit and the altar must each sustain the other.

Still further consequences of a less tangible sort were implicit. If religion is so central, then all human relations must be conditioned by it. Alliances, friendships, and matings will be secure only if grounded in a common faith. Contemporaries were sometimes appalled that Luther would disrupt human relations or churchly unities over a single point of doctrine. To which he replied that he might as well be told it was unreasonable to sever friendship over the single point of strangling his wife or child. To deny God in one point is to attack God in all.

Again the exclusiveness which Luther assigned to Christianity was bound to entail a sentence of rejection upon other religions such as Judaism. He might or he might not be charitable to the worshipers of false gods, but their error he could never condone. Neither could he feel leniently disposed toward those who disparaged or in his judgment misinterpreted the Scripture and the sacraments.

### THE MENACE TO MORALS

In the field of morals many felt that his preoccupation with religion was dangerous. Particularly his insistence that upright conduct constitutes no claim upon God was believed to undercut the most potent motive for good behavior. The same retort was given to Luther as to Paul. If we are saved not by merit but by mercy, "let us then sin that grace may abound." Both Paul and Luther answered, "God forbid." And anyone who had followed Luther closely would have known that he was far from indifferent to morality. Nevertheless the charge was not altogether perverse. Luther did say things at times which emphatically sounded subversive to morals. The classic example is the notorious *pecca fortiter*, "Sin for all you are worth. God can forgive only a lusty sinner." To make this the epitome of Luther's ethic is grossly unfair because it was a piece of uproarious chaffing of the anemic Melanchthon, who was in a dither over scruples of conscience. Luther's counsel was essentially the same as that given to him by Staupitz, who told him that before coming so frequently to the confessional he should go out and commit a real sin like parricide. Staupitz was certainly not advising Luther to murder his father, and Luther well knew that his jest would not induce the impeccable Melanchthon to jettison the Ten Commandments. Luther was saying merely that it might do him good for once to spoil his record.

This is a point which Luther did make at times, that one sin is needed as medicine to cure another. An unblemished record engenders the worst of all sins, pride. Hence a failure now and then is conducive to humility. But the only sins which Luther actually recommended as record spoilers were a little overeating, overdrinking, and oversleeping. Such controlled excesses might be utilized as the antidote to arrogance.

He did say something else with an unethical ring, however, namely, that good works without faith "are idle, damnable sins." Erasmus was horrified to hear integrity and decency so stigmatized. But Luther never meant to say that from the social point of view decency is no better than indecency. What he meant was that the decency of the man who behaves himself simply for fear of damaging his reputation is in the eyes of God an idle, damnable sin, and far worse than the indecency of the contrite offender. Luther's statement is nothing more than a characteristically parodoxical version of the parable of the penitent publican.

But perhaps the deepest menace of Luther to morals lay in his rescue of morals. He would suffer no attenuation of the appalling demands of the New Testament. Christ said, "Give away your cloak, take no thought for the morrow, when struck turn the other cheek, sell all and give to the poor, forsake father and mother, wife and child." The Catholic Church of the Middle Ages had several devices for attenuating the inexorable. One was to make a distinction between Christians and to assign only to heroic souls the more arduous injunctions of the gospel. The counsels of perfection were consigned to monasticism. Luther closed this door by abolishing monasticism. Another distinction was between the continuous and the customary. Strenuous Christians should love God and the neighbor uninterruptedly, but ordinary Christians only ordinarily. Luther was scornful of all such casuistry; and when reminded that without it the precepts of the gospel are impossible, he would retort, "Of course they are. God commands the impossible." But then comes again the old question, If the goal cannot be reached, why make the effort?

Here one must be clear as to precisely how much Luther meant by calling the goal unattainable. He very clearly meant that the noblest human achievement will fall short in the eyes of God. All men are sinners. But they are not for that reason all rascals. A certain level of morality is not out of reach. Even the Jews, the Turks, and the heathen are able to keep the natural law embodied in the Ten Commandments.

"Thou shalt not steal" should be placed by the miller on his sack, the baker on his bread, the shoemaker on his last, the tailor on his cloth, and the carpenter on his ax.

Temptations of course cannot be avoided, but because we cannot prevent the birds from flying over our heads, there is no need that we should let them nest in our hair.

There is then a wide basis for genuine moral conduct even apart from Christianity.

But once more the danger to ethics arises because all this is not enough. God demands not only acts but attitudes. He is like the mother who asks her daughter to cook or to milk the cow. The daughter may comply gaily or grudgingly. Not only does God require that we refrain from adultery, but he exacts purity of thought and restraint within marriage. These are the standards to which we cannot attain. "A horse can be controlled with a golden bit, but who can control himself at those points where he is vitally touched?" Even our very quest for God is a disguised form of self-seeking. The pursuit of perfection is all the more hopeless because the goal is recessive. Every act of goodness opens the door for another; and if we do not enter in, we have failed. Hence all righteousness of the moment is sin with respect to that which must be added in the following instant. Even more disconcerting is the discovery that we are guilty of sins of which we are not aware. Luther had learned in the confessional the difficulty of remembering or recognizing his shortcomings. The very recognition that we are sinners is an act of faith. "By faith alone it must be believed that we are sinners, and indeed more often than not we seem to know nothing against ourselves. Wherefore we must stand by God's judgment and believe his words by which he calls us unrighteous."

### THE GROUND OF GOODNESS

Once again Luther's critics arise to inquire whether if man in the end has no standing with God he should make the effort to be good. Luther's answer is that morality must be grounded somewhere else than in self-help and the quest for reward. The paradox is that God must destroy in us all illusions of righteousness before he can make us righteous. First

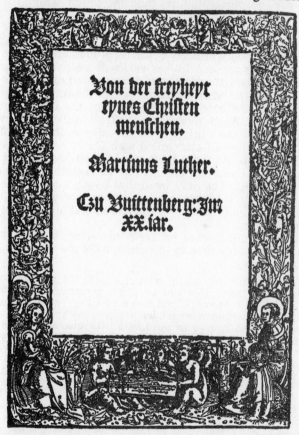

**Von der freyheyt eynes Christen menschen.**

**Martinus Luther.**

**Czu Buittenberg: Jm XX.iar.**

TITLE PAGE OF "ON THE FREEDOM OF THE CHRISTIAN MAN"

we must relinquish all claim to goodness. The way to eliminate feelings of guilt is to admit guilt. Then there is some hope for us. "We are sinners and at the same time righteous"—which is to say that however bad we are, there is a power at work in us which can and will make something out of us.

This is wonderful news to believe that salvation lies outside ourselves. I am justified and acceptable to God, although there are. in
me sin, unrighteousness, and horror of death. Yet I must look elsewhere and see no sin. This is wonderful, not to see what I see, not
to feel what I feel. Before my eyes I see a gulden, or a sword, or a
fire, and I must say, "There is no gulden, no sword, no fire." The
forgiveness of sins is like this.

And the effect of it is that the forgiven, unpretentious sinner
has vastly more potentialities than the proud saint.

The righteousness of the sinner is no fiction. It must and it
will produce good works, but they can never be good if done
for their own sake. They must spring from the fount of the
new man. "Good works do not make a man good, but a good
man does good works." Luther variously described the ground
of goodness. Sometimes he would say that all morality is gratitude. It is the irrepressible expression of thankfulness for food
and raiment, for earth and sky, and for the inestimable gift
of redemption. Again morality is the fruit of the spirit dwelling
in the heart of the Christian. Or morality is the behavior becoming the nature of one united with Christ as the bride with
the bridegroom. As there is no need to tell lovers what to do
and say, so is there no need for any rules to those who are in
love with Christ. The only word that covers all this is faith. It
removes all the inhibitions arising from worry and sets man
in such a relationship to God and Christ that all else will come
of itself.

Nowhere does Luther set forth his views in more rugged
and glowing words than in the canticle *On the Freedom of the
Christian Man*.

The soul which with a firm faith cleaves to the promises of God
is united with them, absorbed by them, penetrated, saturated, in-
ebriated by their power. If the touch of Christ was healing, how
much more does that most tender touch in the spirit, that absorption in the Word convey to the soul all the qualities of the Word
so that it becomes trustworthy, peaceable, free, full of every good,
a true child of God. From this we see very easily why faith can do
so much and no good work is like unto it, for no good work comes
from God's Word like faith. No good work can be within the soul,
but the Word and faith reign there. What the Word is that the soul
is, as iron becomes fire-red through union with the flame. Plainly
then faith is enough for the Christian man. He has no need for
works to be made just. Then is he free from the law.

But he is not therefore to be lazy or loose. Good works do not
make a man good, but a good man does good works. A bishop is not
a bishop because he consecrates a church, but he consecrates a
church because he is a bishop. Unless a man is already a believer
and a Christian, his works have no value at all. They are foolish,
idle, damnable sins, because when good works are brought forward
as ground for justification, they are no longer good. Understand
that we do not reject good works, but praise them highly. The
apostle Paul said, "Let this mind be in you which was also in

Christ Jesus, who being on an equality with God emptied himself, taking the form of a servant, and becoming obedient unto death." Paul means that when Christ was fully in the form of God, abounding in all things, so that he had no need of any work or any suffering to be saved, he was not puffed up, did not arrogate to himself power, but rather in suffering, working, enduring, and dying made himself like other men, as if he needed all things and were not in the form of God. All this he did to serve us. When God in his sheer mercy and without any merit of mine has given me such unspeakable riches, shall I not then freely, joyously, wholeheartedly, unprompted do everything that I know will please him? I will give myself as a sort of Christ to my neighbor as Christ gave himself for me.

This is the word which ought to be placarded as the epitome of Luther's ethic, that a Christian must be a Christ to his neighbor. Luther goes on to explain what this entails.

I must even take to myself the sins of others as Christ took mine to himself. Thus we see that the Christian man lives not to himself but to Christ and his neighbor through love. By faith he rises above himself to God and from God goes below himself in love and remains always in God and in love.

Where will one find a nobler restoration of ethics, and where will one find anything more devasting to ethics? The Christian man is so to identify himself with his neighbor as to take to himself sins that he has not personally committed. The parents assume the sins of the children, the citizens the sins of the state. Luther's scorn was directed against making the chief end of man to keep the record clean. The Christian, like Christ, must in some sense become sin with and for the sinner, and like Christ share in the alienation of those who through sin are separated from God.

## CHAPTER FOURTEEN

# REBUILDING THE WALLS

HE REBUILDING of the walls of Jerusalem by Ezra and Nehemiah is quaintly illustrated in Luther's German Bible by a woodcut in which the theme is from the Old Testament and the scenery from Saxony. The rebuilders of the walls are the Jews returned from Babylon. The stones, mortar, logs, saws, wheelbarrows, inclined planes, and derricks are precisely those employed to repair the walls of Wittenberg.

Very similar was Luther's application of Christian principles to the reconstruction of society. The pre-eminence of religion, the sole sufficiency of Christianity, the obligation of the Christian to be a Christ to the neighbor—these were the principles. The applications were conservative. Luther came not to destroy, but to fulfill, and against all misconception of his teaching sought to make plain that the traditional Christian ethic remained intact. *The Sermon on Good Works* is built, not around Beatitudes, but around the Ten Commandments, the core of the law of Moses equated with the law of nature. Like those before him Luther extended the command to honor father and mother to include reverence for all in authority, such as bishops, teachers, and magistrates. His domestic ethic was Pauline and patriachal, the economic ethic Thomistic and mainly agrarian, the political ethic Augustinian and small town.

REBUILDING THE WALLS OF JERUSALEM

### THE CALLINGS

In one respect Luther was more conservative than Catholicism because he abolished monasticism and thus eliminated a selected area for the practice of the higher righteousness. In consequence the gospel could be exemplified only in the midst of secular callings, except that Luther refused to call them secular. As he had extended the priesthood of all believers, so likewise he extended the concept of divine calling, vocation, to all worthy occupations.

Our expression "vocational guidance" comes directly from Luther. God has called men to labor because he labors. He works at common occupations. God is a tailor who makes for the deer a coat that will last for a thousand years. He is a shoemaker who provides boots that the deer will not outlive. God is the best cook, because the heat of the sun supplies all the heat there is for cooking. God is a butler who sets forth a feast for the sparrows and spends on them annually more than the total revenue of the king of France. Christ worked as a carpenter. "I can just imagine," said Luther from the pulpit, "the people of Nazareth at the judgment day. They will come up to the Master and say, 'Lord, didn't you build my house? How did you come to this honor?' " The Virgin Mary worked, and the most amazing example of her humility is that after she had received the astonishing news that she was to be the mother of the Redeemer, she did not vaunt herself but went back and milked the cows, scoured the kettles, and swept the house like any housemaid. Peter worked as a fisherman and was proud of his skill, though not too proud to take a suggestion from the Master when he told him to cast on the other side. Luther commented:

I would have said, "Now look here, Master. You are a preacher, and I am not undertaking to tell you how to preach. And I am a fisherman, and you need not tell me how to fish." But Peter was humble, and the Lord therefore made him a fisher of men.

The shepherds worked. They had a mean job watching their flocks by night, but after seeing the babe they went back.

Surely that must be wrong. We should correct the passage to read, "They went and shaved their heads, fasted, told their rosaries, and put on cowls." Instead we read, "The shepherds returned." Where to? To their sheep. The sheep would have been in a sorry way if they had not.

As God, Christ, the Virgin, the prince of the apostles, and the shepherds labored, even so must we labor in our callings. God has no hands and feet of his own. He must continue his labors through human instruments. The lowlier the task the better. The milkmaid and the carter of manure are doing a work more pleasing to God than the psalm singing of a Carthusian. Luther never tired of defending those callings which for one reason or another were disparaged. The mother was considered lower than the virgin. Luther replied that the mother exhibits the pattern of the love of God, which overcomes sins just as her love overcomes dirty diapers.

Workers with brawn are prone to despise workers with brain,

such as city secretaries and schoolteachers. The soldier boasts that it is hard work to ride in armor and endure heat, frost, dust, and thirst. But I'd like to see a horseman who could sit the whole day and look into a book. It is no great trick to hang two legs over a horse. They say writing is just pushing a feather, but I notice that they hang swords on their hips and feathers in high honor on their hats. Writing occupies not just the fist or the foot while the rest of the body can be singing or jesting, but the whole man. As for

A FATHER OF A HOUSEHOLD AT WORK

schoolteaching, it is so strenuous that no one ought to be bound to it for more than ten years.

Luther preferred to center his social thinking around the callings and to deal with men where they were in their stations, but he could not well treat all occupations in a purely personal way without regard to wider contexts. Luther recognized three broad areas of human relations, all of them good because instituted by God at the creation prior to the fall of man. These three are the ecclesiastical, the political, and the domestic, including the economic, which Luther conceived primarily in terms of raising a family. Among these only the ecclesiastical engaged his theoretical thinking in any detail. The state was for him ordinarily simply the magistrate, though he did envisage the state as an association for mutual benefit, and in view of the fall of man as that institution which is peculiarly invested with the exercise of coercive power. In the realm of economics he considered less abstract laws of supply and demand than the personal relations of buyer and seller, debtor and creditor. His views with regard to marriage and the family will be considered later.

### ECONOMICS

In the economic sphere Luther was as conservative in the same sense as in the theological. In both he charged the Church of his day with innovation and summoned his contemporaries to return to the New Testament and to the early Middle Ages. The new Europe after the barbarian invasions had been agrarian, and the Church had bestowed the highest esteem on agriculture, next on handicraft, and last of all on commerce. This too was Luther's scale of values. He was not

hospitable to the changes introduced by the Crusades, which recovered the Mediterranean for Christian trade and thus gave an immense stimulus to commerce. The altered situation greatly affected the propriety of lending at interest. When a loan was of food stuffs in a famine of the early Middle Ages, any replacement in excess of the goods consumed appeared to be extortion. But in a commercial venture for profit the case was different. St. Thomas saw this and sanctioned a sharing in profit by the lender provided there was also a sharing in loss. A con-

FROM TITLE PAGE OF
LUTHER'S TRACT "ON USURY"

tract of mutual risk was acceptable but not a contract of fixed return which would give to Shylock his ducats even though the ships of Antonio were on the rocks. In the age of the Renaissance, however, adventurers preferred a higher stake and bankers a more assured though lower return. The Church was ready to accommodate them both because she herself was so intimately involved in the whole process of the rise of capitalism, with banking, bookkeeping, credit, and loans. The Fuggers were not begrudged the services of the theologian John Eck to defend for a subsidy all the casuistic devices for evading the medieval and Thomistic restrictions on interest.

Luther on the other hand became the champion of the precapitalist economy. How agrarian was his thinking is vividly exemplified in a cartoon on the title page of his tract on usury, in which a peasant is shown in the act of returning not only the goose which he had borrowed but also the eggs. Luther took his stand on the Deuteronomic prohibition of usury and the Aristotelian theory of the sterility of money. One gulden, said Luther, cannot produce another. The only way to make money is to work. Monastic idleness is a stench. If Adam had never fallen, he would still have worked at tilling and hunting. Begging should be abolished. Those who cannot protect themselves should be maintained by the community and the rest should work. There is but one exception. The aged with available funds may loan at interest not in excess of 5 per cent or less, depending on the success of the enterprise. That is, Luther retained the contract of mutual risk. Otherwise loans for him came under the head of charity; and Luther, despite his contempt for the Franciscan vow of poverty, was himself Franciscan in the prodigality of his giving.

Obviously Luther was opposed to the spirit of capitalism, and naïvely attributed the rise of prices to the rapacity of the capitalists. At the same time he contributed himself unwittingly to the developments which he deplored. The abolition of monasticism and the expropriation of ecclesiastical goods, the branding of poverty as either a sin or at least a misfortune if not a disgrace, and the exaltation of work as the imitation of God stimulated distinctly the spirit of economic enterprise.

## POLITICS

With regard to the state one must bear in mind that Luther was not primarily interested in politics, but in his position he could not avoid politics. Concrete situations pressed upon him, and he offered prompt comments. Emperor Charles forbade his New Testament—intolerable! Elector Frederick protected his cause and his person—admissible! The papacy deposed heretical rulers—usurpation! The Church fomented crusades —abomination! The sectaries rejected all government—the very devil! When Luther came to construct a theory of government, he relied, as in theology, on Paul and Augustine.

The point of departure for all Christian political thinking has been the thirteenth chapter of Romans, where obedience is enjoined to the higher powers because they are ordained of God and bear not the sword in vain that as ministers of God they may execute wrath upon evildoers. Luther was perfectly clear that coercion can never be eliminated because society can never be Christianized.

The world and the masses are and always will be unchristian, although they are baptized and nominally Christian. Hence a man who would venture to govern an entire community or the world with the gospel would be like a shepherd who should place in one fold wolves, lions, eagles, and sheep. The sheep would keep the peace, but they would not last long. The world cannot be ruled with a rosary.

The sword to which Luther referred meant for him the exercise of restraint in preserving the peace both within and without the state. The police power in his day was not differentiated from war, and the soldier had a dual function.

In the use of the sword the ruler and his men act as the instruments of God. "Those who sit in the office of magistrate sit in the place of God, and their judgment is as if God judged from heaven." "If the emperor calls me," said Luther when invited to Worms, "God calls me." This would seem to settle the question that a Christian can serve as magistrate, but not necessarily, because God can make use of the worst sinners as his instruments, just as he employed the Assyrian as the rod of his anger. And in any case Christianity is not necessary for a sound political administration because politics belongs to the sphere of nature. Luther combined a denial of man's perfectibility with a sober faith in man's essential decency. It is perfectly true that men if unrestrained will devour each other like fishes, but equally is it true that all men recognize by the light of reason that murder, theft, and adultery are wrong. The propriety of gradations within society appeared to Luther equally obvious. "I do not need the Holy Spirit to tell me that the Archbishop of Mainz sits higher than the Bishop of Brandenburg." Reason in its own sphere is quite adequate to tell a man how to tend cows, build houses, and govern states. It is even "reported that there is no better government on earth than under the Turks, who have neither civil nor canon law but only the Koran." The natural man can be trusted to recognize and administer justice provided he operates within the framework of law and government and does not seek to vindicate himself. In that case he cannot be trusted. "If the magistrate allows any private feeling to enter in, then he is the very devil. He has a right to seek redress in an orderly way, but not to avenge himself by using the keys of his office."

But if under such conditions the non-Christian may perfectly well administer the state, why should a Christian be a statesman? And if the state is ordained because of sin, why not let sinners run it while the saints as a whole adopt the code of monks and renounce all exercise of the sword? To these questions Luther replied that if the Christian is involved for himself alone, he should suffer himself to be despoiled, but he has no right to make the same renunciation for his neighbor. This sounds as if Luther were saying that the ethical code of the Christian community should be set by the weaker members. The Christian who for himself would renounce protection must ensure justice to others. If the Christian abstains, the government may not be strong enough to afford the necessary protection. Not for himself then, but out of love for the neighbor the Christian accepts and upholds the office of the sword.

Is he not then involved in a double ethic? The charge has been leveled against Luther that he relegated the Christian ethic to private life and turned over the state to the Devil. This is a gross misunderstanding of his position. His distinction was not between private and public, but between individual and corporate. The point was that a man cannot act so blithely when responsible for wife, child, pupils, parishioners, and subjects as if involved only for himself. One has no right to forego rights if they are other people's rights. The line was not between the state and all other institutions, because Luther placed the family on the side of the state and classed the father with the magistrate as equally bound to exercise severity, however much the methods might differ. One can say that Luther consigned the literal observance of the Sermon on the Mount to individual relations. He would not have the private man defend himself. Perhaps by a miracle one could do so in a disinterested spirit, but the course is very hazardous. Further must it be recognized that the distinction between individual and corporate does not exhaust Luther's categories. The minister also might not use the sword, not for himself or anybody else because of a different office. The magistrate uses the sword, the father uses the fist, the minister uses the tongue. In other words, there are varying codes of behavior according to the callings. In all this, Luther was drawing from and simplifying St. Augustine, who in his ethic of war had posited four categories: that of the magistrate, who determines the justice of the cause and declares hostilities; that of the private citizen, who wields the sword only at the magistrate's behest; that of the minister, who abstains from the sword because of his service at the altar; and that of the monk, who abstains because dedicated to the counsels of perfection. Luther accepted these categories with the omission of the monk.

But for all the codes there must be only one disposition. The unifying factor is the attitude of Christian love. This is the sense in which the Sermon on the Mount applies in all relations, even in war, because the killing of the body in the eyes of Augustine and Luther was not incompatible with love. Slaying and robbing in war are to be compared to the amputation of a limb to save a life. Since the exercise of the sword is necessary for the maintenance of peace, war may be regarded as a small misfortune designed to prevent a greater. But then Luther would shift the problem from man to God.

When a magistrate condemns to death a man who has done him no harm, he is not his enemy. He does this at God's behest. There should be no anger or bitterness in the man's heart, but only the wrath and sword of God. Also in war, where in defense one has to hew, stab, and burn, there is sheer wrath and vengeance, but it does not come from the heart of man but from the judgment and command of God.

Luther's problem was thus ultimately theological. He believed that God had drowned the whole human race in a flood, and wiped out Sodom with fire, and had extinguished lands, peoples, and empires. God's behavior forces one to conclude that he is almighty and frightful. But this is the hidden God, and faith holds that at last his severities will appear as mercies. "Therefore the civil sword out of great mercy must be unmerciful and out of sheer goodness must exercise wrath and severity." The dualism does not lie in any outward sphere but in the heart of God and man. Hence the office of the magistrate must be fraught with sadness. "The godly judge is distressed by the condemnation of the guilty and is truly sorry for the death which justice brings upon them." "The executioner will say, 'Dear God, I kill a man unwillingly, for in thy sight I am no more godly than he.' "

### CHURCH AND STATE

With regard to the relations of Church and state, the matter is complicated because Luther introduced two other entities not to be equated with either. He called them the Kingdom of Christ and the Kingdom of the World. Neither actually exists on earth. They are rather contrary principles, like Augustine's City of God and City of the Earth. The Kingdom of Christ is the way men behave when actuated by the spirit of Christ, in which case they have no need for laws and swords. Such a society, however, is nowhere in evidence, not even in the Church itself, which contains the tares along with the wheat. And the Kingdom of the World is the way men behave when not restrained by law and government. But as a matter of fact they are so restrained. Church and state, then, are not to be identified with the Kingdom of Christ and the Kingdom of the World, but Church and state are both rent by the tugging of the demonic and the divine.

The demarcation of the spheres of Church and state corresponds in a rough way to dualisms running through the nature of God and man. God is wrath and mercy. The state is the instrument of his wrath, the Church of his mercy. Man is divided into outward and inward. Crime is outward and belongs to the state. Sin is inward and belongs to the Church. Goods are outward and fall to the state. Faith is inward and falls to the Church, because:

faith is a free work to which no one can be forced. Heresy is a spiritual matter and cannot be prevented by constraint. Force may avail either to strengthen alike faith and heresy, or to break down integrity and turn a heretic into a hypocrite who confesses with his lips what he does not believe in his heart. Better to let men err than to drive them to lie.

The most important distinction for Luther's political thought was between the lower and the higher capacities of man, corresponding to nature and reason on the one hand and to grace and revelation on the other. The natural man, when not involved for himself, has enough integrity and insight to administer the state in accord with justice, equity, and even magnanimity. These are the civil virtues. But the Church inculcates humility, patience, long-suffering, and charity—the Christian virtues—attainable even approximately only by those endowed with grace, and consequently not to be expected from the masses. That is why society cannot be ruled by the gospel. And that is why theocracy is out of the question. Then again there are different levels involved. The God of the state is the God of the Magnificat, who exalts the lowly and abases the proud. The God of the Church is the God of Gethsemane, who suffered at the hands of men without retaliation or reviling and refused the use of the sword on his behalf.

These distinctions all point in the direction of the separation of Church and state. But on the other hand Luther did not split God and did not split man. And if he did not contemplate a Christianized society, he was not resigned to a secularized culture. The Church must run the risk of dilution rather than leave the state to the cold light of reason, unwarmed by tenderness. Of course if the magistrate were not a Christian, separation would be the obvious recourse. But if he were a convinced church member, the Church should not disdain his help in making the benefits of religion accessible to the whole populace. The magistrate should be the nursing father of the Church. Such a parallelism is reminiscent of the dream of Dante, never actually realized in practice, because, where Church and state are allied, one always dominates, and the outcome is either theocracy or caesaropapism. Luther declined to separate Church and state, repudiated theocracy, and thereby left the door open for caesaropapism, however remote this was from his intent.

He has been accused of fostering political absolutism, of leaving the citizen without redress against tyranny, of surrendering conscience to the state, and of making the Church servile to the powers that be. These accusations rest upon a modicum of truth, because Luther did inculcate reverence for government and discountenanced rebellion. He was the more emphatic because he was accused by the papists of subversiveness to government. He countered with characteristic exaggeration which left him open on the other side to the charge of subservience. "The magistracy," said he, "has never been so praised since the days of the apostles as by me"—by which he meant that none had so stoutly withstood ecclesiastical encroachments. Christ himself, affirmed Luther, renounced any theocratic intentions by allowing himself to be born when a decree went out from Augustus Caesar. In most unqualified terms Luther repudiated rebellion because if the mob breaks loose, instead of one tyrant there will be a hundred. At this point he was endorsing the view of St. Thomas that tyranny is to be ended by insurrection only if the violence will presumably do less damage than the evil which it seeks to correct.

All of which is not to say that Luther left the oppressed without recourse. They had prayer, which Luther did not esteem lightly, and they had the right of appeal. Feudal society was graded, and every lord had his overlord. If the common man was wronged, he might address himself against the lord to the overlord, all the way up to the emperor. When, for example, Duke Ulrich of Württemberg murdered a Hutten and took his wife, the Hutten clan appealed to the empire, and the duke was expelled. The emperor in turn was subject to check by the electors. If one inquire as to the attitude of Luther to democracy, one must bear in mind that democracy is a complex concept. A widely extended franchise commended itself to none in his generation, except in Switzerland, but a responsiveness of government to the will and welfare of the people may have been better exemplified in the intimate patriarchalism of his feudal society than in the unwieldy modern democracies.

Neither was conscience surrendered to the state. The illegitimacy of rebellion did not exclude civil disobedience. This was not a right, but a duty on two counts: "In case the magistrate transgresses the first three of the Ten Commandments relating to religion, say to him, 'Dear Lord, I owe you obedience with life and goods. Command me within the limits of your power on earth, and I will obey. But to put away books [referring to Luther's New Testament] I will not obey, for in this you are a tyrant.' " Secondly, the prince is not to be obeyed if he requires service in a war manifestly unjust, as when Joachim of Brandenburg enlisted soldiers, ostensibly against the Turk but really against the Lutherans. They deserted with Luther's hearty approval. "Since God will have us leave father and mother for his sake, certainly he will have us leave lords for his sake."

Servility on the part of the Church to the magistrate was repugnant to Luther. The minister is commissioned to be the mentor of the magistrate.

We should wash the fur of the magistrate and clean out his

mouth whether he laughs or rages. Christ has instructed us preachers not to withhold the truth from the lords but to exhort and chide them in their injustice. Christ did not say to Pilate, "You have no power over me." He said that Pilate did have power, but he said, "You do not have this power from yourself. It is given to you from God." Therefore he upbraided Pilate. We do the same. We recognize the authority, but we must rebuke our Pilates in their crime and self-confidence. Then they say to us, "You are reviling the majesty of God," to which we answer, "We will suffer what you do to us, but to keep still and let it appear that you do right when you do wrong, that we cannot and will not do." We must confess the truth and rebuke the evil. There is a big difference between suffering injustice and keeping still. We should suffer. We should not keep still. The Christian must bear testimony for the truth and die for the truth. But how can he die for the truth if he has not first confessed the truth? Thus Christ showed that Pilate did exercise authority from God and at the same time rebuked him for doing wrong.

Here Luther was returning to the theme of the calling. The magistrate has his calling; the minister has his calling. Each must serve God according to his office. One calling is not better than another. One is not easier than another. There are temptations peculiar to each. The husband is tempted to lust, the merchant to greed, the magistrate to arrogance. And if the duty is faithfully performed, all the more will there be crosses.

If the burgomaster does his duty, there will scarcely be four who will like him. If the father disciplines his son, the lad will be ugly. It is true everywhere. The prince has nothing for his pains. One is tempted to say, "Let the Devil be burgomaster. Let Lucifer preach. I will go to the desert and serve God there." It is no light task to love your neighbor as yourself. The more I live, the more vexation I have. But I will not grumble. So long as I have my job I will say, "I did not start it for myself, and I will not end it. It is for God and those who want to hear the gospel, and I will not pass by on the other side."

But the spirit of work should not be grim. Let the birds here teach us a lesson.

If you say, "Hey, birdie, why are you so gay? You have no cook, no cellar," he will answer, "I do not sow, I do not reap, I do not gather into barns. But I have a cook, and his name is Heavenly Father. Fool, shame on you. You do not sing. You work all day and cannot sleep for worry. I sing as if I had a thousand throats."

The sum of it all is this, that at certain points Luther's attitudes on economic and political problems could be predicted in advance. He would tolerate no wanton disturbance of the ancient ways. Rebellion was to him intolerable; but since religion alone is the paramount concern of man, the forms of the external life are indifferent and may be left to be determined by circumstance.

## CHAPTER FIFTEEN

# THE MIDDLE WAY

ERSONS committed to his ideals were plainly necessary if Luther's program was to be implemented. At one time the hope did not appear unrealistic that all Europe could be enlisted for the reform. Luther naïvely supposed that the pope himself, when abuses were called to his attention, would promptly correct them. With the waning of this hope expectancy turned to the nobility of the German nation, including the emperor, but this dream also proved to be illusory; and when Luther returned to Wittenberg, he was under the ban of both the Church and the empire.

Yet even under those circumstances hope for a widespread reform did not appear altogether chimerical when a change occurred in the character of the papacy. The flippant popes of the Renaissance were succeeded by one of the austere popes of the Counter Reformation, a pope as much concerned as Luther for the correction of the moral and financial abuses. Such a pope was Hadrian VI, a Hollander reared in the tradition of the Brethren of the Common Life. If his brief pontificate did not suffice to cleanse the Augean stables of the papacy, it might have been enough to inaugurate a new policy with regard to Luther. But quite on the contrary the struggle was only intensified. This was, in Luther's eyes, precisely as it should be. All along he had declared that the contest was over the faith and not over the life, and that if the morals were amended the teaching would still be unsound. The verdict of Erasmus remained true that the breach was irreparable because even if the reformed popes had conceded clerical marriage as the Church does to the Uniats, and communion in both kinds as on occasion to the Hussites, and a national church under Rome as in Spain and France, and even justification by faith properly guarded as at Trent—even so they could scarcely have suffered the reduction of the number of the sacraments, the emasculation of the mass, the doctrine of the priesthood of all believers, let alone the rejection of papal infallibility, even though as yet it had not been formally promulgated.

## HOSTILITY OF THE REFORMED PAPACY

And Luther did nothing to placate them. His work of reconstruction commenced with further demolition. Indulgences were still being proclaimed in Wittenberg. Luther addressed

FREDERICK AND LUTHER

to the elector a demand that they be discontinued in so far as they rested on his patronage. Frederick was not hard to persuade, probably because indulgences had become so unpopular that the very preacher who announced them on All Saints' Day of 1522 declared them to be rubbish, and the crowds greeted the relics with booing. Frederick did not repeat the attempt on All Saints' Day of 1523.

When asked whether in that case he desired the annual exhibition of relics, he replied in the negative. Their whole purpose had been to advertise the indulgences. Yet he could not quite bring himself to destroy or dissipate the collection amassed during a lifetime. A few of the choicest relics should be placed upon the altar and the rest stored in the sacristy to be shown on request to foreign visitors. The elector who had traveled to the Orient and negotiated with monarchs and ecclesiastical dignitaries for one more holy bone renounced his cherished avocation and relinquished the most lucrative revenue of the Castle Church and the university.

Luther's next attack centered on the endowed masses in the Castle Church, where twenty-five priests were employed to celebrate for the souls of the departed members of the House of Saxony. These private sacrifices had come to be in Luther's eyes idolatry, sacrilege, and blasphemy. Part of his indignation was aroused by the immorality of the priests, for he estimated that out of the twenty-five not over three were not fornicators. But this was not the primary ground for his attack. He always insisted that he differed from previous reformers in that they attacked the life and he the doctrine. Certainly Frederick should as patron suppress this scandal, but that might have been done by dismissing the offenders and securing better recruits. Luther in that case would not have been satisfied. The mass must go. Frederick obviously would have to be persuaded. Preferably the clergy also should concur. But Luther was ready to move, either in accord with both or without either. The essential was always the reform, whether instituted by the prince without the clergy or by the clergy without the prince. Universal acquiescence was desirable but not imperative. The plea of weakness might become a cloak for wickedness. "Not all the priests of Baal under Josiah believed their rites to be impious, but Josiah paid no attention to that. It is one thing to tolerate the weak in nonessentials, but to tolerate in matters clearly impious is itself impious." The mob smashed the windows of the deanery. When the recalcitrants were down to three, Luther reproached them with a sectarian spirit in holding out against the unity of the universal Church—as if Wittenberg were Christendom. This obviously sounds incredibly naïve, but Luther was not thinking either of numbers or of centuries, but of the Church founded upon the Word of God as he understood it. The town council was more abrupt. They informed the priests that the celebration of the mass was an offense worthy of death. The clergy at length unanimously declared themselves convinced. By the beginning of 1525 the mass was at an end in Wittenberg. One cannot say precisely that it had been suppressed by force, but certainly the pressure was acute, though not inordinately hurried. The mass had continued for two and one half years after Luther's return from the Wartburg.

Such changes aroused in the papists intense antagonism, and Pope Hadrian addressed to Frederick the Wise a veritable manifesto of the Counter Reformation.

Beloved in Christ, we have endured enough and more than enough. Our predecessors exhorted you to desist from corrupting the Christian faith through Martin Luther, but the trumpet has sounded in vain. We have been moved by mercy and paternal affection to give you a fatherly admonition. The Saxons have ever been defenders of the faith. But now who has bewitched you? Who has wasted the vineyard of the Lord? Who but a wild boar? We have you to thank that the churches are without people, the people without priests, the priests without honor, and Christians without Christ. The veil of the temple is rent. Be not beguiled because

Martin Luther appeals to Scripture. So does every heretic, but Scripture is a book sealed with seven seals which cannot be so well opened by one carnal man as by all the holy saints. The fruits of this evil are evident. For this robber of churches incites the people to smash images and break crosses. He exhorts the laity to wash their hands in the blood of the priests. He has rejected or corrupted the sacraments, repudiated the expunging of sins through fasts, and rejects the daily celebration of the mass. He has committed the decretals of the holy Fathers to the flames. Does this sound to you like Christ or Antichrist? Separate yourself from Martin Luther and put a muzzle on his blasphemous tongue. If you will do this, we will rejoice with all the angels of heaven over one sinner that is saved. But if you refuse, then in the name of Almighty God and Jesus Christ our Lord, whom we represent on earth, we tell you that you will not escape punishment on earth and eternal fire hereafter. Pope Hadrian and Emperor Charles are in accord. Repent therefore before you feel the two swords.

Frederick replied:

Holy Father, I have never and do not now act other than as a Christian man and an obedient son of the holy Christian Church. I trust that God Almighty will give me his grace that for the few years I have left I may strengthen his holy word, service, peace, and faith.

But the fate of Luther and his reform rested not with the pope, the emperor, or the elector alone, but with the German diet meeting at Nürnberg. Like the Diet of Worms it was

DUKE GEORGE

divided. The Catholic party was rallied by the papal legate, who freely conceded abuses but blamed them all on the deceased Leo and called for obedience to his noble successor. Leadership among the laity fell in the absence of the emperor to his brother Ferdinand of Austria, who in his brief week of attendance tried to enforce the edict of Worms on his own authority and was promptly repulsed by the diet. Thereupon a coterie of Catholic princes formed the nucleus of the subsequent league. There was Joachim of Brandenburg, eager by zeal against Lutheranism to appease the emperor for having voted against his election. There was Cardinal Lang, spokesman of the Hapsburgs. The Bavarians were consistently Catholic, and the Palatinate was swinging over. This of course was not the definitive alignment.

Frederick the Wise with his bland obstructionism certainly did not speak the common mind of Catholic laity. There were other princes who gladly heeded the admonitions of the pope. Chief among them was Duke George, whose zeal against heresy was enough to set the Rhine on fire. Luther had felt a twinge of uneasiness over his blasts against the duke and made a gesture of reconciliation but was repulsed. George said:

I write not in hate but to bring you to yourself. As a layman I am unable to put on the armor of Saul and dispute Scripture with you, but I can see that you have offended against your neighbor. You have reviled not only me but the emperor. You have made Wittenberg an asylum for escaped monks and nuns. The fruit of your gospel is blasphemy of God and the sacrament, and rebellion against government. When has there been more corrupting of cloisters? When more breach of marriages than since you began to preach? No, Luther, keep your gospel. I will stay by the gospel of Christ with body and soul, goods and honor. But God is merciful. He will forgive you if you return, and I will then try to obtain for you a pardon from the emperor.

Henry VIII was another Catholic prince to have a tilt with Luther, and he was hardly mollified by the reply which referred to Martin Luther as "minister at Wittenberg by the grace of God" and to "Henry, King of England by the disgrace of God." Even though Luther made a subsequent gesture of reconciliation, Henry continued to regard him as a preacher of "unsatiate liberty." Plainly the "papists," whether clerical or lay, were Sanballats who would impede the building of the walls.

### RECOIL OF THE MODERATE CATHOLICS: ERASMUS

The Catholic moderates might conceivably react differently —the Erasmians, the Humanists who had constituted the middle party at Worms. And indeed their stand might have been different had not the pressures been so intense as to leave no room for neutrality. Reluctantly the mediators were driven to enter one camp or the other. They went in both directions. Some very outstanding persons returned to Rome, among them Pirkheimer of Nürnberg. The deepest offense to Luther lay in the stand taken by Erasmus of Rotterdam. His position had not essentially changed. He still felt that Luther had done much good, and that he was no heretic. This Erasmus openly said in a colloquy published as late as 1524. But he deplored the disintegration of Christendom. His dream of European concord had been shattered by the outbreak of war between

France and the empire before the close of the Diet of Worms. Coincidently the ecclesiastical division had rent the seamless robe of Christ. Erasmus preferred the role of mediator, but he was unremittingly pushed by prominent persons whom he esteemed—kings, cardinals, and his old friend Pope Hadrian— to declare himself. At last he yielded and consented to state at what point he differed from Luther. It was not indulgences. It was not the mass. It was the doctrine of man. Erasmus brought out a tract entitled *On the Freedom of the Will*.

Luther thanked him for centering the discussion at this point. "You alone have gone to the heart of the problem instead of debating the papacy, indulgences, purgatory, and similar trifles. You alone have gone to the core, and I thank you for it." Luther's fundamental break with the Catholic Church was over the nature and destiny of man, and much more over the destiny than the nature. That was why he and Erasmus did not come altogether to grips. Erasmus was interested primarily in morals, whereas Luther's question was whether doing right, even if it is possible, can affect man's fate. Erasmus succeeded in diverting Luther from the course by asking whether the ethical precepts of the Gospels have any point if they cannot be fulfilled. Luther countered with characteristic controversial recklessness that man is like a donkey ridden now by God and now by the Devil, a statement which certainly seems to imply that man has no freedom whatever to decide for good or ill. This certainly was not Luther's habitual thought. He was perfectly ready to say that even the natural man can practice the civil virtues as a responsible husband, an affectionate father, a decent citizen, and an upright magistrate. Man is capable of the integrity and valor displayed by the Romans of old or the Turks of today. Most of the precepts of the gospel can be outwardly kept. But in the eyes of God "there is none righteous, no, not one." Motives are never pure. The noblest acts are vitiated by arrogance, self-love, the desire of the eye and the lust of power. From the religious point of view man is a sinner. He has therefore no claim upon God. If man is not irretrievably lost, it can only be because God deigns to favor him beyond his desert.

The problem then shifts from man to God. Erasmus was concerned for morality in God as well as in man. Is it not unjust that God should create man incapable of fulfilling the conditions for salvation and then at whim save or damn for what cannot be helped? "Of course this is a stumbling block," answered Luther.

Common sense and natural reason are highly offended that God by his mere will deserts, hardens, and damns, as if he delighted in sins and in such eternal torments, he who is said to be of such mercy and goodness. Such a concept of God appears wicked, cruel, and intolerable, and by it many men have been revolted in all ages. I myself was once offended to the very depth of the abyss of desperation, so that I wished I had never been created. There is no use trying to get away from this by ingenious distinctions. Natural reason, however much it is offended, must admit the consequences of the omniscience and omnipotence of God.

But this was precisely what the natural reason of Erasmus would not concede. He perceived that the conflict lay between the power and goodness of God. He would rather limit the power than forfeit the goodness; Luther the reverse. At any rate Erasmus would not assert more than he had to. Difficulties he recognized—that some men, for example, are born morons, and God is responsible for their condition—but why project these riddles of life into eternity and transfix paradoxes into dogmas? "They are not my paradoxes," retorted Luther. "They are God's paradoxes." Erasmus inquired how Luther could know this, and he countered by citing the statement of the apostle Paul that the fates of Jacob and Esau were settled before they emerged from the womb. Erasmus rejoined that other passages of Scripture bear a different sense, and the matter is therefore not clear. If it were, why should debates over it have continued for centuries? Scripture needs to be interpreted, and the claim of the Lutherans to have the Spirit by which to interpret is not confirmed by the fruits of the Spirit in their behavior.

Luther's answer to Erasmus was to impute to him a spirit of skepticism, levity, and impiety. Tranquil discussion of man's destiny of itself betrays insensitivity to God's majesty. The craving of Erasmus to confine himself to the clear and simple spelled for Luther the abandonment of Christianity, for the reason that Christianity cannot be simple and obvious to the natural man.

Show me a single mortal in the whole universe, no matter how just and saintly, to whose mind it would have ever occurred that this should be the way of salvation to believe in him who was both God and man, who died for our sins, who rose and sits at the right hand of the Father. What philosopher ever saw this? Who among the prophets? The cross is a scandal to the Jews and a folly to the Gentiles. . . . If it is difficult to believe in God's mercy and goodness when he damns those who do not deserve it, we must recall that if God's justice could be recognized as just by human comprehension, it would not be divine. Since God is true and one, he is utterly incomprehensible and inaccessible to human reason. Therefore his justice also must be incomprehensible. "O the depth of the riches both of the wisdom and knowledge of God! how unsearchable are his judgements!"

They are hidden to the light of nature and revealed only to the light of glory. "Erasmus, who does not go beyond the light of nature," said Luther, "may like Moses die in the plains of Moab without entering into the promised land of those higher studies which pertain to piety."

Erasmus characterized his own position in these words: "The wise navigator will steer between Scylla and Charybdis. I have sought to be a spectator of this tragedy." Such a role was not permitted to him, and between the confessional millstones his type was crushed. Where again does one find precisely his blend of the cultivated Catholic scholar: tolerant, liberal, dedicated to the revival of the classical Christian heritage in the unity of Christendom? The leadership of Protestantism was to pass to the Neo-Scholastics and of the Catholics to the Jesuits.

Luther for all his bluster was not untouched by the reproach that his acrimony ill comported with the spirit of the apostles. He had angered Henry VIII, infuriated Duke George, estranged Erasmus. Had he perhaps hurt also old Dr. Staupitz, who had not written for some time? Luther inquired, and Staupitz answered:

> My love for you is unchanged, passing the love of women . . . , but you seem to me to condemn many external things which do not affect justification. Why is the cowl a stench in your nostrils when many in it have lived holy lives? There is nothing without abuse. My dear friend, I beseech you to remember the weak. Do not denounce points of indifference which can be held in sincerity, though in matters of faith be never silent. We owe much to you, Martin. You have taken us from the pigsty to the pasture of life. If only you and I could talk for an hour and open the secrets of our hearts! I hope you will have good fruit at Wittenberg. My prayers are with you.

Shortly after the receipt of this letter Luther received the news that Dr. Staupitz was dead. So it was then in the Catholic camp; the pope implacable, Henry VIII railing, Duke George raging, Erasmus refuting, Staupitz dead.

### DEFECTION OF THE PURITANS: CARLSTADT

Obviously, then, the walls could be rebuilt only by those who had definitely broken with Rome. And then came the next blow, vastly more stunning than the first. Those who had broken with Rome were not themselves united. Partly through defections from Lutheranism and partly through the independent rise of variant forms of Evangelicalism the pattern of diversity was displayed. Luther was stung. The initial disorders at Wittenberg had already dealt him a more severe stroke than any he had ever received from the papacy, and he had already begun to perceive that he was closer to Rome than to the radicals. At any rate he was in between. "I take," said he, "the middle road." He found himself now in the position formerly occupied by the Erasmians at Worms. When they were driven to the wall, the Lutherans emerged as the middle group between the papists to the right and the sectaries to the left.

One of the most curious aspects of the whole shift is that in many respects the radicals were the heirs of Erasmus, who saw the great abuse in Catholicism, not as did Luther in the exaltation of man, but in the externalization of religion. The degree to which the sectaries stressed the inward and spiritual led to drastic consequences for the theory and life of the Church. The spirit was set in opposition to the letters of Scripture, as already by the Zwickau prophets. The spirit was considered able to dispense with all external aids, whether of art or music, as Carlstadt had just been saying, or even of the sacraments as the outward channels of invisible grace. The experience of the spirit was made the necessary qualification for Church membership. Infant baptism was consequently rejected, if not indeed all baptism, on the ground that outward water "profiteth nothing." The idea of a national or territorial church was discarded because the total population of any given district never meets so exacting a test. The Church of the spirit is of necessity a sect which may seek to preserve its integrity by segregation from society, or may attempt to dominate the world through the reign of the saints. Here is the concept of all the Protestant theocracies. Within the religious community leadership falls to the spirit-filled, be they clerical or lay, and the outcome may well be the abolition of a professional ministry.

Another Erasmian idea, not altogether consonant with the first, is that of the restitution of primitive Christianity. The details selected for restoration were commonly those in accord with the religion of the spirit, but the very attempt to restore lent itself readily to a new externalism and legalism.

This whole pattern of ideas was alien to Luther. He could not separate spirit and flesh because man is a whole. Therefore art, music, and sacrament are the appropriate expressions of religion. The attempt to build the Church on a selective basis did intrigue him, and his fury against the sectaries was in large measure intensified by the conflict within himself. But the notion of a Protestant theocracy was to him as abhorrent as the papal monarchy. The effort to restore the minutiae of New Testament practice wore for him the air of a new legalism and externality against which he employed the very slogans of the radicals and became himself the champion of the spirit against the letter.

The first attempt to give concretion to many of the elements in this pattern occurred in Luther's own circle and might be regarded as defection from his ranks. The environs of Wittenberg provided the terrain, and the leaders are Andrew Carlstadt again and Thomas Müntzer. This was unfortunate because, although both were sensitive and gifted, neither was balanced and stable. If Luther had met such ideas first in Zwingli and the sober Anabaptists, he might not have been so devoid of understanding and so implacable in opposition.

Carlstadt's most serious radicalism developed after he had retired to the parish of Orlamünde. There he added to his prior attacks on images and church music a further denial of the real presence of Christ in the sacrament of the altar. The objection in all three instances was to the use of the physical as a means of communion with the divine. God is a spirit, and he cannot be in bread and wine. Christ said only, "This do in remembrance of me." Hence the bread and wine are merely reminders, not even symbols, let alone channels. Carlstadt interpreted the words of Christ, "This is my body, this is my blood," to mean. "This is the body which will be broken. This is the blood which will be shed." Luther countered that if this passage was in the least ambiguous there was another text which reads, "The cup . . . , is it not the communion of the blood of Christ? The bread . . . , is it not the communion of the body of Christ?" (I Cor. 10:16.) "This is the thunderclap from which there is no escape. If five years ago I could have been convinced of Carlstadt's position, I should have been grateful for such a mighty weapon against the papacy, but the Scripture was too strong for me." One wonders whether Scripture was really determinative. The roles of Luther and Carlstadt were reversed when they passed from the question of images to the Lord's Supper. Carlstadt was the literalist on the words of Moses, "Thou shalt not make unto thee any graven image," and Luther on the words of Christ, "This is my body." The real question was whether the physical is an aid or an impediment to religion. Carlstadt's Biblicism was in evidence mainly in restraining him from rejecting the Lord's Supper entirely, as did the Quakers. He retained the rite because Christ said, "This do in remembrance of me."

He rejected likewise infant baptism. The Zwickau prophets had done this before him, and the Anabaptists were to make this the cardinal tenet of their sect. The essential point was the necessity of an adult experience of religious conviction. There was with Carlstadt the added point that outward physical water is of no efficacy and is often destructive, as when the hosts of Pharaoh were swallowed in the Red Sea. One wonders again why he did not reject all baptism. His emphasis on Sabbatarianism was designed to give men relief from mundane tasks that they might have quiet times for the cultivation of the inner life.

His greatest eccentricities in Luther's eyes arose from his efforts to achieve a lay ministry. Luther had proclaimed the priesthood of all believers. The corollary might be, as with the Quakers, that there should be no professional minister at all. So far Carlstadt would not go, but he wished as a minister to be set off in no way from his fellows. The parishioners were not to call him *Herr Doktor* or *Herr Pfarrer,* but simply "good neighbor" or "Brother Andreas." He gave up any distinctive garb and wore only a plain gray coat, declined to be supported by the congregation, undertaking instead to earn his living at the plow.

Luther was completely without feeling for this whole program. He cared nothing indeed for the falderal of academic degrees, but he cared mightily for a trained ministry and perceived that if Carlstadt's plan prevailed the outcome would assuredly be not that the peasant would know as much as the preacher, but that the preacher would know no more than the peasant. He twitted Carlstadt for reeling off Hebrew quotations in a peasant's smock. As for the plain cloak and the "Brother Andreas," these appeared, if not as an affectation, then as a neomonastic attempt to win the favor of heaven by spectacular renunciations. As to the earning of one's bread at the plow, Luther was willing enough to support himself by manual labor if expelled from his ministry, but voluntarily to withdraw from a parish to a farm savored to him of an evasion of responsibility. "What would I not give to get away from a cantankerous congregation and look into the friendly eyes of animals?"

Other points in Carlstadt's program—such as Sabbatarianism, obligatory clerical matrimony, and the rejection of images —appeared to Luther as a new legalism. Carlstadt, he claimed, reversed the relation of inward and outward. By making absolute rules for days, dress, and status he was attaching altogether too much importance to the exterior. Here the spirit should decide. Plainly there were other notes in Carlstadt's religion than the stress on the spiritual. He was consumed by a passion for holiness and a concern for the renunciation of privilege with a degree of social leveling. At these points Luther would accord a wider latitude. And he might have been willing to grant latitude also to Carlstadt had it not been for the insurgence of a much more sinister figure.

### THE REVOLUTIONARY SAINTS: MÜNTZER

Thomas Müntzer came from Zwickau and revived some of the ideas of the prophets from that town, but with much greater allure because of his learning, ability, and intense enthusiasm. Müntzer gave a much more radical turn than

Carlstadt to the cleavage of spirit and flesh by rejecting not only infant baptism, but all baptism, and by applying this

THOMAS MÜNTZER

dualism to the spirit versus the letter of Scripture. Those who rely on the letter, said he, are the scribes against whom Christ inveighed. Scripture as a mere book is but paper and ink. "Bible, Babel, bubble!" he cried. Behind this virulence was a religious concern. Müntzer had not been troubled like Luther as to how to get right with God, but as to whether there is any God to get right with. The Scripture as a mere written record did not reassure him because he observed that it is convincing only to the convinced. The Turks are acquainted with the Bible but remain completely alienated. The men who wrote the Bible had no Bible at the time when they wrote. Whence, then, did they derive their assurance? The only answer can be that God spoke to them directly, and so must he speak to us if we are so much as to understand the Bible. Müntzer held, with the Catholic Church, that the Bible is inadequate without a divinely inspired interpreter, but that interpreter is not the Church nor the pope but the prophet, the new Elijah, the new Daniel, to whom is given the key of David to open the book sealed with seven seals.

Müntzer was readily able to find support for his view of the spirit in the Scripture itself, where it is said that "the letter killeth, but the spirit giveth life" (II Cor. 3:6). Luther replied that of course the letter without the spirit is dead, but the two are no more to be divorced than the soul is to be separated from the body. The real menace of Müntzer in Luther's eyes was that he destroyed the uniqueness of Christian revelation in the past by his elevation of revelation in the present. Luther for himself had had absolutely no experience of any contemporary revelation, and in times of despondency the advice to rely upon the spirit was for him a counsel of despair, since within he could find only utter blackness.

In such moments he must have assurance in tangible form in a written record of the stupendous act of God in Christ. Luther freely avowed his weakness and his need of historic revelation. Therefore he would not listen to Müntzer though "he had swallowed the Holy Ghost, feathers and all." At this point lies much of the difference not only between Müntzer and Luther, but between modern liberal Protestantism and the religion of the founders.

Had Müntzer drawn no practical consequences from his view, Luther would have been less outraged, but Müntzer proceeded to use the gift of the Spirit as a basis for the formation of a church. He is the progenitor of the Protestant theocracies, based not as in Judaism primarily on blood and soil, nor as in Catholicism on sacramentalism, but rather on inward experience of the infusion of the Spirit. Those who are thus reborn can recognize each other and can join in a covenant of the elect, whose mission it is to erect God's kingdom. Such a role for the Church was to Luther completely repugnant. Müntzer did not expect the elect to enter into their inheritance without a struggle. They would have to slaughter the ungodly. At this point Luther was horrified because the sword is given to the magistrate, not to the minister, let alone to the saints. In the struggle Müntzer well recognized that many of the godly would fall, and he was constantly harping on suffering and cross bearing as a mark of the elect. Luther was taunted as "Dr. Easychair and Dr. Pussyfoot," basking in the favor of the princes. His reply was that the outward cross is neither to be sought nor evaded. The constant cross is suffering within. Once again the tables were turned, and Luther appeared as the champion of the inward.

## BANISHMENT OF THE AGITATORS

In 1523 Müntzer succeeded in having himself elected as minister in the Saxon town of Alstedt. As many as two thousand outsiders flocked to his preaching. He was able to report thirty units ready to slaughter the ungodly. The only overt act, however, was the burning of a chapel dedicated to the Virgin Mary. This was in March, 1524.

Luther thereupon addressed the princes of Saxony:

These Alstedters revile the Bible and rave about the spirit, but where do they show the fruits of the spirit, love, joy, peace, and patience? Do not interfere with them so long as they confine themselves to the office of the Word. Let the spirits fight it out, but when the sword is drawn you must step in, be it they or we who take it. You must banish the offender from the land. Our office is simply preaching and suffering. Christ and the apostles did not smash images and churches, but won hearts with God's Word. The Old Testament slaughter of the ungodly is not to be imitated. If these Alstedters want to wipe out the ungodly, they will have to bathe in blood. But you are ordained of God to keep the peace, and you must not sleep.

The young prince John Frederick, nephew and heir apparent to Frederick the Wise, was already being associated with his uncle and his father in the administration of Saxony. To a subordinate he wrote in August, 1524:

I am having a terrible time with the Satan of Alstedt. Kindliness and letters do not suffice. The sword which is ordained of God to punish the evil must be used with energy. Carlstadt also is stirring up something, and the Devil wants to be Lord.

Here Carlstadt and Müntzer are linked together. For Carlstadt this was both unjust and unfortunate. He had written to Müntzer that he would have nothing to do with his covenant, nor with bloodshed. But the iconoclastic riots in Orlamünde and Alstedt appeared to be of one stripe. Carlstadt was summoned to Jena for an interview with Luther and convinced him of the injustice of the charge of rebellion. When, however, Luther himself visited Orlamünde and observed the revolutionary temper of the congregation, he came to question the sincerity of the disclaimer and acquiesced in the banishment of Carlstadt, who was compelled to quit Saxony, leaving his pregnant wife and their child to join him later. He departed claiming in the very words of Luther after Worms that he had been condemned "unheard and unconvicted," and that he had been expelled by his former colleague who was twice a papist and a cousin of Antichrist.

Müntzer, having been summoned to preach at Weimar in the presence of Frederick the Wise and his brother Duke John, had the temerity to seek to enlist them for his program. He took his text from Daniel's interpretation of the dream of King Nebuchadnezzar and began by saying that the Church was an undefiled virgin until corrupted by the scribes who murder the Spirit and assert that God no longer reveals himself as of old. He declared further:

But God does disclose himself in the inner word in the abyss of the soul. The man who has not received the living witness of God knows really nothing about God, though he may have swallowed 100,000 Bibles. God comes in dreams to his beloved as he did to the patriarchs, prophets, and apostles. He comes especially in affliction. That is why Brother Easychair rejects him. God pours out his Spirit upon all flesh, and now the Spirit reveals to the elect a mighty and irresistible reformation to come. This is the fulfillment of the prediction of Daniel about the fifth monarchy. You princes of Saxony, you need a new Daniel to disclose unto you this revelation and to show you your role. Think not that the power of God will be realized if your swords rust in the scabbard. Christ said that he came not to bring peace but a sword, and Deuteronomy says "You are a holy people. Spare not the idolators, break down their altars, smash their images and burn them in the fire." The sword is given to you to wipe out the ungodly. If you decline, it will be taken from you. Those who resist should be slaughtered without mercy as Elijah smote the priests of Baal. Priests and monks who mock the gospel should be killed. The godless have no right to live. May you like Nebuchadnezzar appoint a Daniel to inform you of the leadings of the Spirit.

The Saxon princes were of no mind to appoint Müntzer to such a post. Instead they referred the case to a committee. Müntzer did not wait for the report but by night escaped over the walls of Alstedt and fled from Saxony. Latitude had been vindicated at the expense of liberty. The regime of Carlstadt would have been rigoristic and the reign of Müntzer's saints intolerant of the godless. Yet the fact could not be gainsaid that the agitators had been expelled by the sword of the magistrate. Luther ruefully pondered the gibe that instead of being a martyr he was making martyrs.

CHAPTER SIXTEEN

# BEHEMOTH, LEVIATHAN, AND THE GREAT WATERS

 COPE FOR rebuilding was further reduced by the rise independently of rival forms of Evangelicalism, namely Zwinglianism and Anabaptism. These were Luther's Behemoth and Leviathan. Then came the conjunction of the religious ferment with a vast social revolt when the waters were unloosed in the Peasants' War. The outcome was at once a restriction of Luther's sphere of operations and a waning of his trust in humankind.

The new movements were largely independent but not wholly unrelated to the recent disturbances in Wittenberg. Carlstadt expelled from Saxony went to the south German cities. Luther shortly thereafter received letters from the ministers of Strassburg. "We are not yet persuaded by Carlstadt, but many of his arguments are weighty. We are disturbed because you have driven out your old colleague with such inhumanity. At Basel and Zurich are many who agree with him." "From the Lord's Supper, the symbol of love, arise such hatreds."

Basel was the residence of Erasmus, who both repudiated and abetted the inferences drawn from his premises by impetuous disciples. He would not concede, because the flesh of Christ in the sacrament profits nothing, that therefore the flesh is not present. At the same time he confided to a friend that were it not for the authority of the Church he would agree with the innovators.

## RIVALS: ZWINGLI AND THE ANABAPTISTS

Zurich was the seat of a new variety of the Reformation which was to be set over against that of Wittenberg and characterized as the Reformed. The leader was Ulrich Zwingli. He had received a Humanist training and as a Catholic priest divided his parsonage into a parish house on the ground floor and a library of the classics on the second. On the appearance of Erasmus' New Testament he committed the epistles to memory in Greek, and affirmed in consequence that Luther had been able to teach him nothing about the understanding of Paul. But what Zwingli selected for emphasis in Paul was the text, "The letter killeth, but the spirit giveth life," which he coupled with a Johannine verse, "The flesh profiteth nothing." Flesh was taken by Zwingli in the Platonic sense of body, whereas Luther understood it in the Hebraic sense of the evil heart which may or may not be physical. Zwingli made a characteristic deduction from his disparagement of the body that art and music are inappropriate as the handmaids of religion—and this, although he was himself a musician accomplished on six instruments. The next step was easy: to deny the real presence in the sacrament, which was reduced to a memorial of the death of Christ as the Passover was a commemoration of the escape of Israel from Egypt. When Luther appealed to the words, "This is my body," Zwingli countered that in the Aramaic tongue spoken by Jesus the copulative verb was omitted, so that what he said was simply, "This—my body." (In the Greek of the Lukan version the companion verse reads, "This cup the new testament.") And in this phrase one may with perfect right supply not "is" but "signifies." Luther sensed at once the affinity of Zwingli's view with that of Carlstadt, on whom he was not dependent, and with that of Erasmus, in whom he was steeped. The familiar reproach against Erasmus was hurled at Zwingli that he did not take religion seriously. "How does he know?" retorted Zwingli. "Can he read the secrets of our hearts?"

A similarity to Müntzer also impressed Luther because Zwingli was politically minded and not averse to the use of the sword even for religion. Zwingli was always a Swiss patriot, and in translating the Twenty-third Psalm rendered the second verse "He maketh me to lie down in an Alpine meadow." And there he could find no still waters. The evangelical issue threatened to disrupt his beloved confederation. For the Catholics turned to the traditional enemy, the House of Hapsburg. Ferdinand of Austria was instrumental in the calling of the assembly of Baden to discuss Zwingli's theory of the sacrament. This was his Diet of Worms, and the sequel convinced him that the gospel could be saved in Switzerland and the confederation conserved only if the Catholic League with Austria were countered by an evangelical league with the German Lutherans, ready if need be to use the sword. But the very notion of a military alliance for the defense of the gospel savored for Luther of Thomas Müntzer.

Then arose in Zwingli's circle a party at the opposite pole of the political question. These were the Anabaptists. Their point of departure was another aspect of the Erasmian program, dear also to Zwingli. This was the restoration of primitive Christianity, which they took to mean the adoption of the Sermon on the Mount as a literal code for all Christians, who should renounce oaths, the use of the sword whether in war or civil government, private possessions, bodily adornment, reveling and drunkenness. Pacifism, religious communism, simplicity, and temperance marked their communities. The Church should consist only of the twice-born, committed to the covenant of discipline. Here again we meet the concept of the elect, discernible by the two tests of spiritual experience and moral achievement. The Church should rest not on baptism administered in infancy, but on regeneration, symbolized by baptism in mature years. Every member should be a priest, a minister, and a missionary prepared to embark on evangelistic tours. Such a Church, though seeking to convert the world, could never embrace the unconverted community. And if the state comprised all the inhabitants, then Church and state would have to be separated. In any case religion should be free from constraint. Zwingli was aghast to see the medieval unity shattered and in panic invoked the arm of the state. In 1525 the Anabaptists in Zurich were subjected to the death penalty. Luther was not yet ready for such savage expedients. But he too was appalled by what to him appeared to be a reversion to the monastic attempt to win salvation by a higher righteousness. The leaving of families for missionary expeditions was in his eyes a sheer desertion of domestic responsibilities, and the repudiation of the sword prompted him to new vindications of the divine calling alike of the magistrate and of the soldier.

## RELIGION AND SOCIAL UNREST

Then came the fusion of a great social upheaval with the ferment of the Reformation in which Luther's principles were to his mind perverted and the radicalism of the sectaries contributed to a state of anarchy. Nothing did so much as the Peasants' War to make Luther recoil against a too drastic departure from the pattern of the Middle Ages.

The Peasants' War did not arise out of any immediate connection with the religious issues of the sixteenth century because agrarian unrest had been brewing for fully a century. Uprisings had occurred all over Europe, but especially in south Germany, where particularly the peasants suffered from changes which ultimately should have ministered to their security and prosperity. Feudal anarchy was being superseded through the consolidation of power. In Spain, England, and France this had taken place on a national scale, but in Germany only on a territorial basis; and in each political unit the princes were endeavoring to integrate the administration with the help of a bureaucracy of salaried court officials. The expenses were met by increased levies on the land. The peasant paid the bill. The law was being unified by displacing the diverse local codes in favor of Roman law, whereby the peasant again suffered, since the Roman law knew only private property and therefore imperiled the commons—the woods, streams, and meadows shared by the community in old Germanic tradition. The Roman law knew also only free men, freedmen, and slaves; and did not have a category which quite fitted the medieval serf.

Another change, associated with the revival of commerce in cities after the crusades, was the substitution of exchange in coin for exchange in kind. The increased demand for the precious metals enhanced their value; and the peasants, who were at first benefited by the payment of a fixed sum of money rather than a percentage in kind, found themselves hurt by deflation. Those who could not meet the imposts sank from freeholders to renters, and from renters to serfs. The solution which at first suggested itself to the peasants was simply resistance to the changes operative in their society, and a return to the good old ways. They did not in the beginning demand the abolition of serfdom but only the prevention of any further extension of peonage. They clamored rather for free woods, waters, and meadows as in the former days, for the reduction of imposts and the reinstatement of the ancient Germanic law and local custom. The methods to be used for the attainment of these ends were at first conservative. On the occasion of a special grievance the peasants would assemble in thousands in quite unpremeditated fashion and would present their petitions to the rulers with a request for arbitration. Not infrequently the petition was met in a patriarchal way and the burdens in some measure eased, yet never sufficiently to forestall recurrence.

On the other hand the peasant class was not uniformly impoverished; and the initiative for the redress of grievances came not from the downtrodden, but rather from the more prosperous and enterprising, possessed themselves of lands and a respectable competence. Inevitably their demands began to go beyond economic amelioration to political programs designed to insure for them an influence commensurate with and even exceeding their economic importance. The demands likewise changed as the movement worked north into the region around the big bend of the Rhine where peasants were also townsmen, since artisans were farmers. In this section urban aspirations were added to the agrarian. Farther down the Rhine the struggle became almost wholly urban, and the characteristic program called for a more democratic complexion in the town councils, a less restrictive membership in the guilds, the subjection of the clergy to civil burdens, and uncurtailed rights for citizens to engage in brewing.

Many of the tendencies coalesced in a movent in Alsace just prior to the Reformation. This uprising used the symbol characteristic of the great Peasants' War of 1525, the *Bundschuh*. The name came from the leather shoe of the peasant. The long thong with which it was laced was called a *Bund*. The word had a double meaning because a *Bund* was also an association, a covenant. Müntzer had used this word for his covenant of the elect. Before him the peasants had adopted the term for a compact of revolution. The aims of this *Bundschuh* centered not so much on economics as on politics. The ax should be laid to the root of the tree and all government abolished save that of the pope and the emperor. These were the two traditional swords of Christendom, the joint rulers of a universal society. To them the little men had always turned for protection against overlords, bishops, metropolitans, knights, and princes. The *Bundschuh* proposed to complete the process by wiping out all the intermediate grades and leaving only the two great lords, Caesar and Peter.

Prior to the Peasants' War of 1525 this movement was often anticlerical but not anti-Catholic. Bishops and abbots were resented as exploiters, but "Down with the bishop" did not mean "Down with the pope" or "Down with the Church." The banners of the *Bundschuh* often carried, besides the shoe, some religious symbol, such as a picture of Mary, a crucifix, or a papal tiara. The accompanying woodcut shows the crucifix resting upon a black shoe. On the right a group of peasants are swearing allegiance. Above them other peasants are tilling the soil, and Abraham is sacrificing Isaac as a sign of the cost to be paid by the members of the *Bund*.

### LUTHER AND THE PEASANTS

A movement so religiously minded could not but be affected by the Reformation. Luther's freedom of the Christian man was purely religious but could very readily be given a social turn. The priesthood of believers did not mean for him equalitarianism, but Carlstadt took it so. Luther certainly had blasted usury and in 1524 came out with another tract on the subject, in which he scored also the subterfuge of annuities, a device whereby capital was loaned in perpetuity for an annual return. His attitude on monasticism likewise admirably suited peasant covetousness for the spoliation of cloisters. The peasants with good reason felt themselves strongly drawn to Luther.

A cartoon displayed Luther surrounded by peasants as he expounded the Word of God to the ecclesiastics, and when the great upheaval came in 1524-25 a Catholic retorted by portraying Luther in armor seated before a fire greasing a *Bundschuh*. The Catholic princes never ceased to hold Luther responsible for the uprising, and the Catholic historian Janssen has in modern times endeavored to prove that Luther was actually the author of the movement which he so vehemently repudiated. Such an explanation hardly takes into account the century of agrarian unrest by which the Reformation had been preceded.

SWEARING ALLEGIANCE
TO THE BUND

One intangible contributory factor was utterly foreign to Luther's way of thinking, and that was astrology. Melanchthon dabbled in it but Luther never. Astrological speculation may well explain why so many peasant uprisings coincided in the fall of 1524 and the spring of 1525. It was in the year 1524 that all the planets were in the constellation of the Fish. This had been foreseen twenty years previously, and great disturbances had been predicted for that year. As the time approached, the foreboding was intense. In the year 1523 as many as fifty-one tracts appeared on the subject. Woodcuts like the one below displayed the Fish in the heavens and upheavals upon earth. The peasants with their banners and flails watch on one side; the emperor, the pope, and the ecclesiastics on the other. Some in 1524 held back in the hope that the emperor would call a diet and redress the grievances. The diet was not called, and the great Fish unloosed the waters.

With all this the Reformation had nothing to do. At the same time a complete dissociation of the reform from the

Practica vber die grossen vnd ma: nigfeltigen Conunction der Planeten/die im jar M. D. XXiiij. erscheinen/vñ vnge zweiffelt vil wunderparlicher ding geperen werden.

PROPHECY OF CONVULSION IN 1524

Peasants' War is not defensible. The attempt to enforce the Edict of Worms through the arrest of Lutheran ministers was not infrequently the immediate occasion for the assembly of peasant bands to demand their release, and Luther was regarded as a friend. When some of the peasants were asked to name persons whom they would accept as arbiters, the first name on the list was that of Martin Luther. No formal court was ever established, and no legal judgment was ever rendered. But Luther did pronounce a verdict on the demands of the peasants as couched in the most popular of their manifestoes,

*The Twelve Articles.* These opened with phrases reminiscent of Luther himself. "To the Christian reader, peace and the grace of God through Christ. . . . The gospel is not a cause of rebellion and disturbance." Rather those who refuse such reasonable demands are themselves the disturbers. "If it be the will of God to hear the peasants, who will resist His Majesty? Did he not hear the children of Israel and deliver them out of the hand of Pharaoh?" The first articles have to do with the Church. The congregation should have the right to appoint and remove the minister, who is obligated to "preach the Holy Gospel without human addition," which sounds very much like Luther. Ministers are to be supported on a modest scale by the congregations out of the so-called great tithe on produce. The surplus should go to relieve the poor and to obviate emergency taxation in war. The so-called little tithe on cattle should be abolished, "for the Lord God created cattle for the free use of man." The main articles embodied the old agrarian program of common fields, forests, waters. The farmer should be free to hunt, to fish, and to protect his lands against game. Under supervision he might take wood for fire and for building. Death dues which impoverish the widow and orphan by requisitioning the best cloak or the best cow, were to be abolished. Rents should be revised in accord with the productivity of the land. New laws should not displace the old, and the community meadows should not pass into private hands. The only article which exceeded the old demands was the one calling for the total abolition of serfdom. Land should be held on lease with stipulated conditions. If any labor in excess of the agreement was exacted by the lord, he should pay for it on a wage basis. *The Twelve Articles* conceded that any demand not consonant with the Word of God should be null. The whole program was conservative, in line with the old feudal economy. There was notably no attack on government.

The evangelical ring of the articles pleased Luther, but in addressing the peasants he disparaged most of their demands. As to the right of the congregation to choose its own minister, that depends upon whether they pay him. Even if they do and the princes will not tolerate them, they should rather emigrate than rebel. The abolition of tithes is highway robbery, and the abrogation of serfdom is making Christian liberty into a thing of the flesh. Having thus criticized the program, Luther then turned to the means employed for its realization. Under no circumstances must the common man seize the sword on his own behalf. If each man were to take justice into his own hands, then there would be "neither authority, government, nor order nor land, but only murder and bloodshed." But all this was not intended to justify the unspeakable wrongs perpetrated by the rulers. To the princes Luther addressed an appeal in which he justified many more of the peasant demands than he had done when speaking to them. The will of the congregation should be regarded in the choice of a minister. The demands of the peasants for redress of their grievances were fair and just. The princes had none but themselves to thank for these disorders, since they had done nothing but disport themselves in grandeur while robbing and flaying their subjects. The true solution was the old way of arbitration.

But that way neither side was disposed to take, and the prediction of Luther was all too abundantly fulfilled, that nothing would ensue but murder and bloodshed. Luther had long since declared that he would never support the private citizen in arms, however just the cause, since such means inevitably entailed wrong to the innocent. He could not envisage an orderly revolution. And how there could have been one in the sixteenth century is difficult to conceive, since the facilities were inadequate for the forging of a united front by either persuasion or force. A minority could not then seize the machinery of the state and by technological warfare impose its will upon the community, nor were modern means of propaganda available.

The Peasants' War lacked the cohesion of the Puritan revolution because there was no clear-cut program and no coherent leadership. Some groups wanted a peasant dictatorship, some a classless society, some a return to feudalism, some the abolition of all rulers save the pope and the emperor. The chiefs were sometimes peasants, sometimes secretaries, sometimes even knights. The separate bands were not co-ordinated. There was not even unity of religion because Catholics and Protestants were on both sides. In Alsace, where the program called for the elimination of the pope, the struggle took on the complexion of a religious war; and the duke and his brother the cardinal hunted the peasants as "unbelieving, divisive, undisciplined Lutherans, ravaging like Huns and Vandals." There can be no question that the hordes were undisciplined, interested mainly in pillaging castles and cloisters, raiding game, and depleting fish ponds.

The drawing below of the plundering of a cloister is typical of the Peasants' War. Observe the group in the upper left with a net in the fish pond. Some are carrying off provisions. The bloodshed is inconsiderable. One man only has lost a hand. At various points peasants are guzzling and vomiting, justifying the stricture that the struggle was not so much a peasants' war as a wine war.

Another glimpse of their behavior is afforded by a letter of an abbess who says that her cloister was raided till not an egg or a pat of butter was left. Through their windows the nuns could see the populace abused and the smoke rising from burning castles. When the war ended, 70 cloisters had been demolished in Thuringia, and in Franconia 270 castles and 52 cloisters. When the Palatinate succumbed to the peasants, the disorder was so great that their own leaders had to invite the former authorities to return to assist in the restoration of order. But the authorities preferred to wait until the peasants had first been beaten.

PEASANTS PLUNDERING A CLOISTER

Could it have been otherwise? Was there any person who could have conceived and carried through a constructive plan for adjusting the peasant to the new political and economic order? The most strategic person would have been an emperor, but no emperor would essay the role. There was only one other who was sufficiently known and trusted throughout Germany to have done it. That man was Martin Luther, and he refused. For him as a minister to take the sword and lead the peasants would have been to forsake his office as he conceived it. He had not demolished the papal theocracy to set up in its place a new theocracy of saints or peasants. The magistrate should keep the peace. The magistrate should wield the sword. Not for Luther the role of a Ziska at the head of the Hussite hordes, or of a Cromwell leading the Ironsides.

### MÜNTZER FOMENTS REBELLION

Yet Luther would never have condemned the peasants quite so savagely had it not been that someone else essayed the very role which he abhorred. In Saxony there would have been no Peasants' War without Thomas Müntzer. Banished, he had gone to Bohemia, then had returned and insinuated himself into a Saxon village, won control over the government, and now at last in the peasants discovered the *Bund* of the elect who should slaughter the ungodly and erect the kingdom of the saints. The point was not the redress of economic grievance, which in Saxony was not acute since serfdom had long since been abolished. Müntzer was interested in economic amelioration only for the sake of religion, and he did have the insight to see what no one else in his generation observed, that faith itself does not thrive on physical exhaustion. He exclaimed:

PEASANTS ABOUT TO TAKE OVER A CLOISTER

Luther says that the poor people have enough in their faith. Doesn't he see that usury and taxes impede the reception of the faith? He claims that the Word of God is sufficient. Doesn't he realize that men whose every moment is consumed in the making of a living have no time to learn to read the Word of God? The princes bleed the people with usury and count as their own the fish in the stream, the bird of the air, and the grass of the field, and Dr. Liar says, "Amen!" What courage has he, Dr. Pussyfoot, the new pope of Wittenberg, Dr. Easychair, the basking sycophant? He says there should be no rebellion because the sword has been committed by God to the ruler, but the power of the sword belongs to the whole community. In the good old days the people stood by when judgment was rendered lest the ruler pervert justice, and the rulers have perverted justice. They shall be cast down from their seats. The fowls of the heavens are gathering to devour their carcasses.

In such a mood Müntzer came to Mülhausen, and there he was responsible for fomenting a peasants' war. In front of the pulpit he unfurled a long, silk banner, emblazoned with a rainbow and the motto, "The Word of the Lord Abideth Forever." "Now is the time," he cried. "If you be only three wholly committed unto God, you need not fear one hundred thousand. On! On! On! Spare not. Pity not the godless when they cry. Remember the command of God to Moses to destroy utterly and show no mercy. The whole countryside is in commotion. Strike! Clang! Clang! On! On!"

The countryside was indeed in commotion. The peasants had been thoroughly aroused. And Frederick the Wise was weary and at the point of death. To his brother John he wrote: "Perhaps the peasants have been given just occasion for their uprising through the impeding of the Word of God. In many ways the poor folk have been wronged by the rulers, and now God is visiting his wrath upon us. If it be his will, the common man will come to rule; and if it be not his will, the end will soon be otherwise. Let us then pray to God to forgive our sins, and commit the case to him. He will work it out according to his good pleasure and glory." Brother John yielded to the peasants the right of the government to collect tithes. To Frederick he wrote "As princes we are ruined."

Luther tried to dike the deluge by going down into the midst of the peasants and remonstrating. They met him with derision and violence. Then he penned the tract, *Against the Murderous and Thieving Hordes of Peasants*. To his mind hell had been emptied because all the devils had gone into the peasants, and the archdevil was in Thomas Müntzer, "who does nothing else but stir up robbery, murder, and bloodshed." A Christian ruler like Frederick the Wise should, indeed, search his heart and humbly pray for help against the Devil, since our "warfare is not with flesh and blood but with spiritual wickedness." The prince, moreover, should exceed his duty in offering terms to the mad peasants. If they decline, then he must quickly grasp the sword. Luther had no use for the plan of Frederick the Wise to sit still and leave the outcome to the Lord. Philip of Hesse was more to his taste, who said: "If I hadn't been quick on my toes, the whole movement in my district would have been out of hand in four days."

Luther said:

If the peasant is in open rebellion, then he is outside the law of God, for rebellion is not simply murder, but it is like a great fire which attacks and lays waste a whole land. Thus, rebellion brings with it a land full of murders and bloodshed, makes widows and orphans, and turns everything upside down like a great disaster.

Therefore, let everyone who can, smite, slay, and stab, secretly or openly, remembering that nothing can be more poisonous, hurtful, or devilish than a rebel. It is just as when one must kill a mad dog; if you don't strike him, he will strike you, and the whole land with you.

TITLE PAGE OF LUTHER'S TRACT "AGAINST THE MURDEROUS AND THIEVING HORDES OF PEASANTS"

Some of the princes were only too ready to smite, stab, and slay; and Thomas Müntzer was only too prompt to provoke them. Duke George and Landgrave Philip, among others, were quick enough on their toes. Müntzer and the peasants were drawn up near Frankenhausen. They sent word to the princes that they sought nothing but the righteousness of God and desired to avoid bloodshed. The princes replied, "Deliver

SURRENDER OF THE UPPER SWABIAN PEASANTS. UPPER LEFT:

*arrival of the army.* CENTER: *slaughter of peasants.*
BOTTOM: *surrender.*

up Thomas Müntzer. The rest shall be spared." The offer was
tempting, but Müntzer loosed his eloquence: "Fear not.
Gideon with a handful discomfited the Midianites, and David
slew Goliath." Just at that moment a rainbow appeared in the
sky, the very symbol on Müntzer's banner. He pointed to
it as a sign. The peasants rallied. But the princes took advantage of a truce to surround them. Only six hundred were
taken prisoner. Five thousand were butchered. Müntzer
escaped, but was caught, tortured, and beheaded. The princes
then cleaned up the countryside.

### THE DEBACLE AND THE EFFECT ON THE REFORMATION

Other bands fared no better. The forces of the Swabian
League were led by a general who when outnumbered would
have recourse to diplomacy, duplicity, strategy, and at last
combat. He managed to isolate the bands and destroy them
one at a time. The peasants were tricked and finally outnumbered. It was claimed that 100,000 were liquidated. On
the day when Bishop Conrad rode in triumph into Würzburg,
the event was celebrated with the execution of 64 citizens and
peasants. Then the bishop made a tour of his diocese, accompanied by his executioner, who took care of 272 persons.
Excessive fines were imposed, yet the peasants as a class were
not exterminated; the nobles could not afford to wipe out
the tillers of the soil. Neither was their prosperity destroyed,
for they were able to pay the fines, but their hope for a share
in the political life of Germany was at an end. For three
centuries they became hornless oxen.

Unhappily Luther's savage tract was late in leaving the press
and appeared just at the time when the peasants were being
butchered. He tried to counteract the effect by another
pamphlet in which he still said that the ears of the rebels
must be unbuttoned with bullets, but he had no mind to decry
mercy to captives. All the devils, he declared, instead of leaving the peasants and returning to hell, had now entered the
victors, who were simply venting their vengeance.

But this tract was not noticed, and that one sentence of
Luther's, "smite, slay, and stab," brought him obloquy never
to be forgotten. He was reproached by the peasants as a traitor
to their cause, though he never ceased to be held responsible
by the Catholic princes for the entire conflagration. The peasants in consequence tended to find their religious home in
Anabaptism, thought this point must not be overdone. The
ultimate agrarian complexion of the Anabaptist movement is
not by any means wholly the result of the Peasants' War but
much more of the persecution which could more readily purge
the cities than the farms. Neither did the peasants secede en
masse, and to the end of his life Luther's congregation con-

sisted largely of the farmers around about Wittenberg. Nevertheless, Luther's stand was contributory to the alienation of the peasants.

At the same time the Catholic princes held Luther responsible for the whole outbreak, and color was lent to the charge by the participation on the peasants' side of hundreds of

**THREE VIEWS OF LUTHER AND THE PEASANTS**
**1. FRIENDLY: LUTHER INSTRUCTS THE PEASANTS**

Lutheran ministers, whether voluntarily or under constraint. The rulers in Catholic lands thereafter used the utmost diligence to exclude evangelical preachers, and the persistent Catholicism of Bavaria and Austria dates not so much from the Counter Reformation as from the Peasants' War.

The deepest hurt was to Luther's own spirit. He became afraid, not of God, not of the Devil, not of himself, but of chaos. Fear was to make him at times hard and undiscriminating, ready to condone the suppression of the innocuous lest in them might be concealed incipient Thomas Müntzers.

The sphere, then, of Luther's activity was being constantly curtailed. The Catholics, whether clerical or lay, were obdurate. The Swiss, the south German Protestant cities, and the Anabaptists had developed divergent forms. Even Wittenberg had experienced insurgent movements and might not be free from new infiltrations of the sectaries. But in the areas remaining Luther was resolved to build.

Den buntſchuch ſchmieren.
Wie der luther den buntſchuch ſchmiert/ das er den
einfaltigen menſchen angenem bleib.

Es wolt mein Herr gern wol verſehen
Das vnß kein mangel möcht beſchehen

**2. HOSTILE (CATHOLIC): LUTHER IN ARMOR PREPARES TO PUT ON THE PEASANT'S BOOT**

**3. HOSTILE (PEASANT SIDE): PEASANT TAXES LUTHER AS DOUBLE-TONGUED**

## CHAPTER SEVENTEEN

# THE SCHOOL FOR CHARACTER

 AFFLED, rebuffed, curtailed, restricted, Luther did what he could. The most unpremeditated and dramatic witness to his principles was his own marriage. If he could not reform all Christendom, at any rate he could and he did establish the Protestant parsonage. He had no thought of doing anything of the sort; and when the monks began to marry during his stay at the Wartburg, he had exclaimed, "Good heavens! They won't give me a wife." After the event he said that if anyone had told him at Worms that in six years he would have a wife he would not have believed him.

But a practical situation arose out of his teaching which caused a change of mind. Not only monks but also nuns were leaving the cloisters. Some sisters in a neighboring village sought his counsel as to what they should do in view of their evangelical persuasion. He took it upon himself to arrange their escape. This was hardy because the abduction of nuns was a capital offense, and Duke George exacted the penalty. Frederick the Wise might not be so severe, but he did not relish open violation of the law. Luther clandestinely enlisted the aid of a respected burgher of Torgau, Leonard Kopp, sixty years of age, a merchant who from time to time delivered barrels of herring to the convent. On the Eve of the Resurrection in 1523 he bundled twelve nuns into his covered wagon as if they were empty barrels. Three returned to their own homes. The remaining nine arrived in Wittenberg. A student reported to a friend, "A wagon load of vestal virgins has just come to town, all more eager for marriage than for life. God grant them husbands lest worse befall."

Luther felt responsible to find for them all homes, husbands, or positions of some sort. An obvious solution was that he should dispose of one case by marrying himself. Someone suggested it. His comment on November 30, 1524, was that he had no such intention, not because he was a sexless stone, nor because he was hostile to marriage, but because he expected daily the death of a heretic. Five months later Spalatin had apparently renewed the suggestion. He answered:

As for what you write about my marrying, do not be surprised that I do not wed, even if I am so famous a lover. You should be more surprised when I write so much about marriage and in this way have so much to do with women that I do not turn into a woman, let alone marry one. Although if you want my example you have it abundantly, for I have had three wives at once and have loved them so hard as to lose two to other husbands. The third I hold barely with my left hand, and she is perhaps about to be snatched from me. You are really the timid lover who do not dare to marry even one.

The jocular reference to the three wives was of course to the three last nuns waiting to be placed.

### KATHERINE VON BORA

In the end all were provided for save one, Katherine von Bora. Two years after the escape she was still in domestic service, where incidentally she received excellent training, but she was awaiting a better solution and had been intended for a young patrician of Nürnburg, studying at Wittenberg. On his return home his family presumably objected. Katherine was disconsolate and asked Luther to find out how things stood. The outcome was that the Nürnberger married someone else. Then Luther made another selection and picked for Katherine a certain Dr. Glatz, whom she would accept on no terms. But her position was delicate. She knew well that the whole affair had been a trial to Luther, doubly so that it fell in the midst of the Peasants' War, and her case had been the most protracted. In those days of early marriages a girl of twenty-six might begin to think of herself as verging on the upper limits of eligibility. In her embarrassment she bespoke the good offices of a visitor in Wittenberg, Dr. Amsdorf of Magdeburg. Would he please tell Luther that she could not abide Glatz but she was not unreasonable? She would take Amsdorf himself or Luther. These two were named presumably because they were out of the question, since beyond the customary age for marriage. Luther was forty-two.

He did not respond seriously to the suggestion until he went home to visit his parents. What he related, probably as a huge joke, was taken by his father as a realistic proposal. His desire was that his son should pass on the name. The suggestion began to commend itself to Luther for quite another reason. If he was to be burned at the stake within a year, he was hardly the person to start a family. But by marriage he could at once give a status to Katherine and a testimony to his faith. In May of 1525 he intimated that he would marry Katie before he died. And early in June, when Albert of Mainz contemplated secularizing his bishopric after the example of his cousin in Brandenburg, Luther wrote, "If my marrying will strengthen him, I am ready. I believe in marriage, and I intend to get married before I die, even though it should be only a betrothal like Joseph's." This was no love match. "I am not infatuated," said Luther, "though I cherish my wife." On another occasion he declared, "I would not exchange Katie for France or for Venice, because God has given her to me and other women have worse faults." He summed up by giving three reasons for his marriage: to please his father, to spite the pope and the Devil, and to seal his witness before martyrdom.

When once the resolve was taken, marriage followed speedily to scotch rumor and protest. "All my best friends," said Luther, "exclaimed, 'For heaven's sake, not this one.'" A jurist predicted that "the world and the Devil would laugh and Luthers' work would be undone." Curiously at that very juncture Spalatin asked Luther what he thought of long engagements. He replied, "Don't put off till tomorrow! By delay Hannibal lost Rome. By delay Esau forfeited his birthright. Christ said, 'Ye shall seek me, and ye shall not find.' Thus Scripture, experience, and all creation testify that the gifts of God must be taken on the wing." That was on the tenth of June. On the thirteenth Luther was publicly betrothed to Katherine and, in the eyes of the law, was thereby already a

A WEDDING PARTY IN FRONT OF THE CHURCH

*This is not the betrothal, which established the legal bond, but the public declaration. The party first paraded through the streets to the sound of the pipers.*

married man. The public ceremony which followed was only
an announcement party.

This was the social event. It was set for the twenty-seventh,
and Luther sent out letters of invitation: To Spalatin, "You
must come to my wedding. I have made the angels laugh and
the devils weep." To another, "Undoubtedly the rumor of my
marriage has reached you. I can hardly believe it myself, but
the witnesses are too strong. The wedding will be next Thursday in the presence of my father and mother. I hope you can
bring some game and come yourself." To Amsdorf, who had
mediated for Katie, "The rumor of my marriage is correct.
I cannot deny my father the hope of progeny, and I had to
confirm my teaching at a time when many are so timid. I hope
you will come." To a Nürnberger, "My tract has greatly
offended the peasants. I'd be sorry if it had not. While I was
thinking of other things, God has sudenly brought me to
marriage with Katherine. I invite you and absolve you from
any thought of a present." To Leonard Kopp, who organized
the escape of the nuns, "I am going to get married. God likes
to work miracles and to make a fool of the world. You must
come to the wedding." Curiously there is a second invitation
to Kopp. The editor of the letters in the Weimar edition questions the authenticity. It reads, "I am to be married on Thursday. My lord Katie and I invite you to send a barrel of the
best Torgau beer, and if it is not good you will have to drink
it all yourself."

On the appointed day at ten o'clock in the morning Luther
led Katherine to the sound of bells through the streets of Wittenberg to the parish church, where at the portal in the sight
of all the people the religious ceremony was observed. Then
came a banquet in the Augustinian cloister, and after dinner
a dance at the town hall. In the evening there was another
banquet. At eleven all the guests took their departure on pain
of being sent home by the magistrates.

### DOMESTICITY

Marriage brought many changes to Luther's way of living.
"Before I was married the bed was not made for a whole year
and became foul with sweat. But I worked so hard and was so
weary I tumbled in without noticing it." Katie cleaned house.
There were other adjustments to be made. "There is a lot to
get used to in the first year of marriage," reflected Luther.
"One wakes up in the morning and finds a pair of pigtails on
the pillow which were not there before." He soon discovered
that a husband must take the wishes of his wife into account.
The fears and tears of Katie restrained him from attending
Spalatin's wedding, in view of the danger of violence from
peasants on the way. If Martin referred jocularly to his wife

as "my rib," he called her quite as often "my lord." Sometimes he even punned upon the name Katie and turned it in German into *Kette,* meaning "chain."

KATHERINE VON BORA AND MARTIN LUTHER
IN THE YEAR OF THEIR MARRIAGE

Marriage also brought new financial responsibilities, because neither of them started with a cent. Katherine's mother died when she was a baby. Her father consigned her to a convent and married again. He did nothing for her now. Luther had only his books and his clothes. He was not entitled to the revenues of the cloister, since he had abandoned the cowl. He took never a penny from his books, and his university stipend was not enough for matrimony. In 1526 he installed a lathe and learned woodworking that in case of need he might be able to support his family. But one may doubt whether he ever took this thought very seriously. He was minded to give himself exclusively to the service of the Word, and he trusted that the heavenly Father would provide. The angel Gabriel must have been kept rather busy making suggestions to men of substance in Luther's entourage. The elector made over the Augustinian cloister to Luther and his bride, doubled his salary, and frequently sent game, clothes, and wine. And the Archbishop of Mainz, Albert of Brandenburg, presented Katie with twenty gold gulden which her husband was disposed to decline.

If marriage brought new responsibilities for Luther, vastly more was this the case for Katie. Keeping house for so improvident a husband was no light task. His giving was so prodigal that Lucas Cranach, the artist and banker, refused to honor his draft. Luther's comment was, "I do not believe I can be accused of niggardliness." He was irritatingly blithe. "I do not worry about debts," he said, "because when Katie pays one, another comes." She watched him, and she needed to watch him. In one letter he says to a friend, "I am sending you a vase as a wedding present. P.S. Katie's hid it." At one point he was of real help. He took care of the garden, which produced lettuce, cabbage, peas, beans, melons, and cucumbers. Katie looked after an orchard beyond the village, which supplied them with apples, grapes, pears, nuts, and peaches. She had also a fish pond from which she netted trout, carp, pike, and perch. She looked after the barnyard with hens, ducks, pigs, and cows, and did the slaughtering herself. Luther gives a glimpse into her activities in a letter of 1535: "My lord Katie greets you. She plants our fields, pastures and sells cows, *et cetera* [how much does that *et cetera* cover?]. In between she has started to read the Bible. I have promised her 50 gulden [where did he expect to get them?] if she finishes by Easter. She is hard at it and is at the end of the fifth book of Moses." In later years he acquired a farm at Zulsdorf, which Katie managed, spending there some weeks out of the year. Luther wrote her on such occasions: "To the rich lady of Zulsdorf, Mrs. Dr. Katherine Luther, who lives in the flesh at Wittenberg but in the spirit at Zulsdorf," and again, "To my beloved wife, Katherine, Mrs. Dr. Luther, mistress of the pig market, lady of Zulsdorf, and whatsoever other titles may befit thy Grace."

Looking after him was the more of a task because he was so often sick. He suffered at one time or another from gout, insomnia, catarrh, hemorrhoids, constipation, stone, dizziness, and ringing in the ears like all the bells of Halle, Leipzig, Erfurt, and Wittenberg. Katie was a master of herbs, poultices, and massage. Her son Paul, who became a doctor, said his mother was half one. She kept Luther from wine and gave him beer, which served as a sedative for insomnia and a solvent for the stone. And she brewed the beer herself. When he was away from home, how he appreciated her ministrations! After a year of marriage he wrote to a friend, "My Katie is in all things so obliging and pleasing to me that I would not exchange my poverty for the riches of Croesus." He paid her the highest tribute when he called St. Paul's epistle to the Galatians "my Katherine von Bora." He began to be a trifle worried over his devotion: "I give more credit to Katherine than to Christ, who has done so much more for me."

## CHILDREN AND TABLE TALK

Katie had soon more than Luther to think about. On October 21, 1525, Luther confided to a friend, "My Katherine is fulfilling Genesis 1:28." On May 26, 1526, he wrote to another, "There is about to be born a child of a monk and a nun. Such a child must have a great lord for godfather. Therefore I am inviting you. I cannot be precise as to the time." On the eighth of June went out the news, "My dear Katie brought into the world yesterday by God's grace at two o'clock a little son, Hans Luther. I must stop. Sick Katie calls me." When the baby was bound in swaddling clothes, Luther said, "Kick, little fellow. That is what the pope did to me, but I got loose." The next entry in Hans's *curriculum vitae* was this: "Hans is cutting his teeth and beginning to make a joyous nuisance of himself. These are the joys of marriage of which the pope is not worthy." On the arrival of a daughter Luther wrote to a prospective godmother, "Dear lady, God has produced from me and my wife Katie a little heathen. We hope you will be willing to become her spiritual mother and help make her a Christian." There were six children in all. Their names and birthdays are as follows: Hans, June 7, 1526; Elizabeth, December 10, 1527; Magdalena, December 17, 1529; Martin, November 9, 1531; Paul, January 28, 1533; Margaretha, December 17, 1534.

And besides the children there were all those whom the Luthers took in. On the very night of their wedding, when the guests had departed by eleven o'clock, another guest unbeknown to the magistrate appeared. It was Carlstadt, fleeing from the Peasants' War and asking for shelter; and Luther, who had done so much to put him out of Saxony, took him into his own home on his wedding night. Carlstadt of course did not stay indefinitely, but others arrived. And since the cloister was large and suited for a hospital, the sick also were taken in. Furthermore the Luthers brought up four orphaned children from among relatives, in addition to their own six. To eke out the finances they had recourse to a device familiar in professional families of opening a pension for student boarders. The household would number as many as twenty-five.

Katie of course could not do all the labor for such an establishment. There were maidservants and manservants, but she had to superintend everything. Perhaps the hardest part of her position, however, was that she was invariably overshadowed by her famous husband. She expected it and did not resent it. She always called him Doctor, and used the polite form *Ihr* rather than the familiar *Du*. Yet at times she must have been a trifle disquieted because he was on every occasion the center of the conversation. It was not altogether his fault. The student boarders regarded mealtime as an opportunity to continue their education, and sat at table with notebooks to scribble down every nugget and every clod from his voluble mouth. Katie thought he should have charged them for it.

THE LUTHER HOUSEHOLD AT TABLE

*There is an unpardonable omission. Katie is not there.*

Luther was himself irritated at times, though he never put a stop to it. At one point he was responsible for stepping in front of the lights. He talked a great deal about his bouts with Satan until to have experienced none placed one in a lower category. Katie was not to be outdone. One day she arose from the table, retired to her room, fainted, and afterwards reported that she had experienced *multa perniciosa,* and she announced it in Latin. From then on Katie qualified.

Luther's *Table Talk* would deserve a notice if for no other reason than its sheer volume. There are 6,596 entries, and it is among the better known of his works because his students after his death culled, classified, and produced a handy volume adorned with a woodcut of Luther at the table with his family. The classification obscures the lush profusion and unpredictable variety of the original. Luther ranged from the ineffable majesty of God the Omnipotent to the frogs in the Elbe. Pigs, popes, pregnancies, politics, and proverbs jostle one another. Some random samples may convey a faint impression:

The monks are the fleas on God Almighty's fur coat.

When asked why he was so violent, Luther replied, "A twig can be cut with a bread knife, but an oak calls for an ax."

God uses lust to impel men to marriage, ambition to office, avarice to earning, and fear to faith.

The only portion of the human anatomy which the pope has had to leave uncontrolled is the hind end.

Printing is God's latest and best work to spread the true religion throughout the world.

I am a pillar of the pope. After I am gone he will fare worse.

Birds lack faith. They fly away when I enter the orchard, though

I mean them no ill. Even so do we lack faith in God.

There are rumors that the world will end in 1532. I hope it won't be long. The last decade seems like a new century.

A cartoon has appeared of me as a monster with seven heads. I must be invincible because they cannot overcome me when I have only one.

A dog is a most faithful animal and would be more highly prized if less common.

A melancholic claimed to be a rooster and strutted about crowing. The doctor said he, too, was a rooster and for several days crowed with him. Then he said, "I am not a rooster any more, and you are changed too." It worked.

Germany is the pope's pig. That is why we have to give him so much bacon and sausages.

What lies there are about relics! One claims to have a feather from the wing of the angel Gabriel, and the Bishop of Mainz has a flame from Moses' burning bush. And how does it happen that eighteen apostles are buried in Germany when Christ had only twelve?

I cannot think what we shall find to do in heaven, mused Luther. "No change, no work, no eating, no drinking, nothing to do. I suppose there will be plenty to see." "Yes," said Melanchthon, " 'Lord, show us the Father, and it sufficeth us.' " "Why, of course," responded Luther, "that sight will give us quite enough to do."

The ark of Noah was 300 ell long, 50 wide, and 30 high. If it were not in Scripture, I would not believe it. I would have died if I had been in the ark. It was dark, three times the size of my house, and full of animals.

They are trying to make me into a fixed star. I am an irregular planet.

An officer in the Turkish war told his men that if they died in battle they would sup with Christ in Paradise. The officer fled. When asked why he did not wish to sup with Christ, he said he was fasting that day.

In 1538 on May the 26th there was a big rain. Luther said, "Praise God. He is giving us one hundred thousand gulden worth. It is raining corn, wheat, barley, wine, cabbage, onions, grass, and milk. All our goods we get for nothing. And God sends his only begotten Son, and we crucify him."

"I am the son of a peasant," said Luther, "and the grandson and the great-grandson. My father wanted to make me into a burgomaster. He went to Mansfeld and became a miner. I became a baccalaureate and a master. Then I became a monk and put off the brown beret. My father didn't like it, and then I got into the pope's hair and married an apostate nun. Who could have read that in the stars?"

The above selections speak well enough for themselves, but a word of comment is in order with regard to Luther's vulgarity, because he is often represented as inordinately coarse, and the *Table Talk* is cited by way of example. There is no denying that he was not fastidious, nor was his generation. Life itself stank. One could not walk around Wittenberg without encountering the odors of the pigsty, offal, and the slaugh-

terhouse. And even the most genteel were not reticent about
the facts of daily experience. Katie, when asked about the
congregation on a day when Luther was unable to attend,
replied, "The church was so full it stank." "Yes," said Luther,
"they had manure on their boots." Erasmus did not hesitate
to compose a colloquy in which the butcher and the fishmonger
celebrated the offensiveness of each other's wares. Luther delighted less in muck than many of the literary men of his age;
but if he did indulge, he excelled in this as in every other area
of speech. The volume of coarseness, however, in his total
output is slight. Detractors have sifted from the pitchblende

**LUTHER AS A SEVEN-HEADED MONSTER**

*One head is a fanatic with wasps in his hair.*

of his ninety tomes a few pages of radioactive vulgarity. But there are whole volumes which contain nothing more offensive than a quotation from the apostle Paul, who "suffered the loss of all things," and counted them but dung, that he might win Christ.

A word may be said at this point also about Luther's drinking. He imbibed and took some pride in his capacity. He had a mug around which were three rings. The first he said represented the Ten Commandments, the second the Apostles' Creed, and the third the Lord's Prayer. Luther was highly amused that he was able to drain the glass of wine through the Lord's Prayer, whereas his friend Agricola could not get beyond the Ten Commandments. But Luther is not recorded ever to have exceeded a state of hilarity.

### VIEWS OF MARRIAGE

But to return to marriage. The Luther who got married in order to testify to his faith actually founded a home and did more than any other person to determine the tone of German domestic relations for the next four centuries. We may conveniently at this point consider his views on marriage. Here as elsewhere he walked in the steps of Paul and Augustine. His position with regard to marriage was tinctured throughout by patriarchalism. According to Luther the man is the head of the wife because he was created first. She is to give him not only love but also honor and obedience. He is to rule her with gentleness, but he is to rule. She has her sphere, and she can do more with the children with one finger than he with two fists. But she is to confine herself to her sphere. If Luther did not say that children, church, and kitchen are the province of women, he did say that women have been created with large hips in order that they should stay at home and sit on them. Children are subject to parents and especially to the father, who exercises in the household the same sort of authority as does the magistrate in the state. Disrespect for parents is a breach of the Ten Commandments. On one occasion Luther refused to forgive his son for three days, although the boy begged his pardon and Katie and others interceded. The point was that the boy in disobeying his father had offended the majesty of God. If only Luther could have left God out of it now and then, he would have been more humane. Yet it might be remembered that in his judgment the apple should always lie alongside of the rod.

The whole institution of marriage was set by Luther within the framework of family relationships. There was no room left for the exercise of unbridled individualism. Matings should be made by families; and whereas parents should not force children to repulsive unions, children in turn should not, be-

cause of infatuations, resist reasonable choices on the part
of their elders. This whole picture was carried directly over
from the Middle Ages, in which Catholic sacramentalism and
agrarian society tended to make of marriage an institution for
the perpetuation of families and the preservation of properties.
The romantic revolution of the Courts of Love in France was
at first extramatrimonial, and the combination of romance
and marriage was effected only during the Renaissance.

To these currents Luther was entirely a stranger. His ideal
was Rebecca, who accepted the mate selected for her by the
family. Jacob was reprehensible in his eyes because after receiving Leah, who bore him children, he worked yet seven
other years out of infatuation for the pretty face of Rachel.
Luther was glad, however, of this failing because it proved
that he was saved by faith and not by works. But if in this
respect Luther followed the medieval view, on other counts
he broke with it, and notably in the rejection of virginity as
an ideal. By this move the way was open for the romanticizing
and refinement of marriage. But its immediate effect was
rather the contrary. In Luther's early polemic, marriage was
reduced to the most elemental physical level because in order
to repulse ecclesiastical interference Luther insisted that sexual
intercourse is as necessary and inevitable as eating and drinking. Those not gifted with chastity must find gratification.
To refuse them is to prefer fornication to wedlock. In inter-
preting these words, however, one must be careful. Luther
did not really mean that external chastity is impossible, but
merely that without sexual satisfaction many will be tormented
by desire, and for that reason marriage is a purer state than
monasticism. The controversial tracts, however, up to 1525
are certainly unguarded in creating the impression that the
sole object of marriage is to serve as a remedy for sin.

But after his own wedding the emphasis shifted, and he
began to portray marriage as a school for character. In this
sense it displaces the monastery, which had been regarded
by the Church as the training ground of virtue and the surest
way to heaven. Luther in rejecting all earning of salvation
did not exclude exercise in fortitude, patience, charity, and
humility. Family life is exacting. The head of the house has the
lifelong worry over daily bread. The wife has the bearing of
children. During pregnancy she suffers from dizziness, head-
ache, nausea, toothache, and swelling of the legs. In travail
her husband may comfort her by saying, "Think, dear Greta,
that you are a woman and your work is pleasing to God.
Rejoice in his will. Bring forth the child. Should you die,
it is for a noble work and in obedience to God. If you were
not a woman, you should wish to be one, that you might
suffer and die in so precious and noble a work of God."
The rearing of children is a trial for both parents. To one of

his youngsters Luther said, "Child, what have you done that I should love you so? You have disturbed the whole household with your bawling." And when a baby cried for an hour and the parents were at the end of their resources, he remarked, "This is the sort of thing that has caused the Church fathers to vilify marriage. But God before the last day has brought back marriage and the magistracy to their proper esteem." The mother of course has the brunt of it. But the father may have to hang out the diapers, to the neighbors' amusement. "Let them laugh. God and the angels smile in heaven."

There are vexations between the married couple. "Good God," ejaculated Luther, "what a lot of trouble there is in marriage! Adam has made a mess of our nature. Think of all the squabbles Adam and Eve must have had in the course of their nine hundred years. Eve would say, 'You ate the apple,' and Adam would retort, 'You gave it to me.' "

Luther once at the table was expatiating with gusto in response to student questions. When he paused, Katie broke in, "Doctor, why don't you stop talking and eat?"

"I wish," snapped Luther, "that women would repeat the Lord's Prayer before opening their mouths." The students tried to get him on the track again, but he was derailed for that meal.

On occasion Katie could have well returned the compliment. Once she was praying out loud for rain, and Luther broke in, "Yes, why not, Lord? We have persecuted thy Word and killed thy saints. We have deserved well of thee."

Part of the difficulty was that the rhythm of work and rest did not coincide for Luther and his wife. After a day with children, animals, and servants, she wanted to talk with an equal; and he, after preaching four times, lecturing and conversing with students at meals, wanted to drop into a chair and sink into a book. Then Katie would start in, "Herr Doktor, is the prime minister of Prussia the Duke's brother?"

"All my life is patience," said Luther. "I have to have patience with the pope, the heretics, my family, and Katie." But he recognized that it was good for him.

Nor should it be for a moment supposed that he excluded love from marriage. Of course the Christian should love his wife, said Luther. He is bound to love his neighbor as himself. His wife is his nearest neighbor. Therefore she should be his dearest friend. And Luther signed himself to Katie, *Dir lieb und treu*. The greatest grace of God is when love persists in marriage. "The first love is drunken. When the intoxication wears off, then comes the real marriage love." The couple should study to be pleasing to each other. In the old days this sound advice was given to the bride: "My dear, make your husband glad to cross his threshold at night"; and to the groom, "Make your wife sorry to have you leave." "The dearest life is to live with a godly, willing, obedient wife in peace and unity." "Union of the flesh does nothing. There must also be union of manners and mind." "Katie, you have a husband that loves you. Let someone else be empress."

When Katie was ill, Luther exclaimed, "Oh, Katie, do not die and leave me."

When he was ill and thought he was about to die, he turned to his wife. "My dearest Katie, if it be God's will accept it. You are mine. You will rest assured of that, and hold to God's word. I did want to write another book on baptism, but God's will be done. May he care for you and Hans."

Katie answered, "My dear Doctor, if it is God's will I would rather have you with our Lord than here. But I am not thinking just of myself and Hans. There are so many people that need you. But don't worry about us. God will take care of us."

## CONSOLATIONS OF HOME

Luther thoroughly enjoyed his home. Once his colleague Jonas remarked that he saw the blessing of God in fruit and for that reason had hung a cherry bough above his table. Luther said, "Why don't you think of your children? They are in front of you all the time, and you will learn from them more than from a cherry bough." But there was no sentimentality in what Luther expected him to learn. "O dear God, how Adam must have loved Cain, and yet he turned out to be the murderer of his brother." When Luther looked at his family in 1538, he remarked, "Christ said we must become as little children to enter the kingdom of heaven. Dear God, this is too much. Have we got to become such idiots?" One wonders whether the children were ever minded to wonder who was the idiot when Luther cut up Hans's pants to mend his own. Yet what child would not cheerfully forgive a father who wrote to him a letter like this? On August 22, 1530, Luther wrote to Hans, then four years old:

My dearest son:
I am glad to know that you learn well and pray hard. Keep on, my lad, and when I come home, I'll bring you a whole fair.
I know a lovely garden where many children in golden frocks gather rosy apples under the trees, as well as pears, cherries, and plums. They sing, skip, and are gay. And they have fine ponies with golden bridles and silver saddles. I asked the gardener who were these children, and he said, "They are the children who like to pray and learn and be good." And I said, "Good man, I too have a son, and his name is Hans Luther. Couldn't he come into the garden, too, and eat the rosy apples and the pears and ride a fine pony and play with these children?" And the man said, "If he likes to pray and learn and be good, he too may come into the garden,

and Lippus and Jost [the sons of Melanchthon and Jonas] as well; and when they all come together, they shall have golden whistles and drums and fine silver crossbows." But it was early, and the children had not yet had their breakfasts, so I couldn't wait for the dance. I said to the man, "I will go at once and write all this to my dear son Hans that he may work hard, pray well, and be good, so that he too may come into this garden. But he has an Aunt Lena he'll have to bring too." "That will be all right," said he. "Go and write this to him."

So, my darling son, study and pray hard and tell Lippus and Jost to do this too, so that you may all come together into the garden. May the dear God take care of you. Give my best to Auntie Lena and give her a kiss for me.

> Your loving father,
> MARTIN LUTHER

Luther reveled in household festivities and may well have composed for Hans and Lenchen the Christmas pageant *Vom Himmel Hoch* with its delightful, childlike quality. Equally charming is this brief carol:

> Our little Lord, we give thee praise
> That thou has deigned to take our ways.
> Born of a maid a man to be,
> And all the angels sing to thee.
>
> The eternal Father's Son he lay
> Cradled in a crib of hay.
> The everlasting God appears
> In our frail flesh and blood and tears.
>
> What the globe could not enwrap
> Nestled lies in Mary's lap.
> Just a baby, very wee,
> Yet Lord of all the world is he.

When Magdalena was fourteen years old, she lay upon her deathbed. Luther prayed, "O God, I love her so, but thy will be done." And turning to her, "*Magdalenchen*, my little girl, you would like to stay with your father here and you would be glad to go to your Father in heaven?"

And she said, "Yes, dear father, as God wills."

And Luther reproached himself because God had blessed him as no bishop had been blessed in a thousand years, and yet he could not find it in his heart to give God thanks. Katie stood off, overcome by grief; and Luther held the child in his arms as she passed on. When she was laid away, he said, "*Du liebes Lenchen*, you will rise and shine like the stars and the sun. How strange it is to know that she is at peace and all is well, and yet to be so sorrowful!"

## CHAPTER EIGHTEEN

# THE CHURCH TERRITORIAL

 OWEVER much Luther's activity may have been curtailed by defections, he did found a church. Feverish missionary activity was to win most of northern Germany within a decade for the Reform. This success was achieved through a wave of propaganda unequaled hitherto and in its precise form never repeated. The primary tools were the tract and the cartoon. The number of pamphlets issued in Germany in the four years 1521 through 1524 exceeds the quantity for any other four years of German history until the present. This is not to say, of course, that there was more reading than after the introduction of the newspaper and periodical, but only that the tracts were more numerous. In all this Luther himself took the lead, and his own pamphlets in the vernacular run into the hundreds; but a vast cohort assisted him, and the printers who brought out these highly controversial materials were an intrepid breed who risked their establishments and their lives. The cohesiveness and adroitness of this underground is strikingly exemplified in the case of a press which issued, without any identifying marks, an attack on the Bishop of Constance for tolerating and taxing priests' bastards. Two hundred other works can be traced by the paper and the type to this press, and yet its identity has never yet been disclosed. The Catholics of course retaliated in kind, though by no means in equal volume.

## DISSEMINATION OF THE REFORM

A brief glance at the content of this pamphleteering is revealing alike for the methods and the selection of themes for popular dissemination. All the external abuses of the Roman Church were easy to lampoon. The familiar theme of the contrast between Christ and the pope was exploited. Christ in a skit is made to say, "I have not where to lay my head." The pope comments, "Sicily is mine. Corsica is mine. Assisi is mine. Perugia is mine." Christ: "He who believes and is baptized will be saved." Pope: "He who contributes and receives indulgences will be absolved." Christ: "Feed my sheep." Pope: "I shear mine." Christ: "Put up your sword." Pope: "Pope Julius killed sixteen hundred in one day." In a cartoon the pope in armor on a war horse accompanied by a devil drops his lance on seeing Christ on a donkey carrying a large cross.

Monasticism, images, and magic received many gibes. "Three finches in a birdhouse praise God more joyfully than one hundred monks in a cloister." A pamphleteer describes an image of the Virgin with the head hollowed out and needle holes in the eyes, through which water could be squirted to make her weep. A Catholic mother in Swabia had sent to her son studying at Wittenberg a little wax lamb marked *Agnus Dei* to protect him against mishap. His reply to her was printed in 1523.

*Liebe Mutter:*
You should not be upset over Dr. Martin Luther's teaching, nor worried about me. It is safer here than in Swabia. I am grateful to you for sending me the little wax *Agnus Dei*, to protect me against being shot, cut, and from falling, but honestly it won't do me any good. I cannot set my faith on it because God's Word teaches me to trust only in Jesus Christ. I am sending it back. We'll try it out on this letter and see whether it is protected from tampering. I don't thank you one bit less, but I pray God you won't believe any more in sacred salt and holy water and all this devil's tomfoolery. I hope you won't give the wax lamb to my brother. And dearest mother, I hope father will let me stay longer in Wittenberg. Read Dr. Martin Luther's New Testament. It is on sale at Leipzig. I am going to buy a brown hat at Wittenberg. Love to my dear father and brother and sisters.

The tracts did not forget to extol Luther. In one of the pamphlets a peasant, meeting a resplendent figure, inquires whether he is God. "No," comes the answer, "I am a fisher of men, Peter by name, and I have just come from Wittenberg, where in God's good pleasure my fellow apostle Martin Luther has arisen to tell the people the truth that I never was the bishop of Rome, nor was I ever a bloodsucker of the poor, for I had neither silver nor gold."

The Devil was called in to assist both sides. A Catholic cartoon shows him whispering into the ear of his confidant, Martin Luther. On the other hand a Reformation cut depicts Luther at his desk when the Devil breaks in with a letter which reads:

We Lucifer, lord of eternal darkness and ruler of all the kingdoms of the world, declare to you, Martin Luther, our wrath and

THREE POLEMICAL CARTOONS
1. CHRIST DISARMS THE POPE

2. LUTHER AND LUCIFER IN LEAGUE

displeasure. We have learned from our legates, Cardinals Campeggio and Lang, the damage you have done in that you have revived the Bible which at our behest has been little used for the last four hundred years. You have persuaded monks and nuns to leave the cloisters in which formerly they served us well, and you are your-

**3.** THE DEVIL DELIVERS A DECLARATION OF WAR TO LUTHER

self an apostate from our service. Therefore we will persecute you with burning, drowning, and beheading. This is a formal declaration of war, and you will receive no other notice. Sealed with our hellish seal in the City of Damnation on the last day of September, 1524.

The drama reinforced the tract. A play disclosed a conspiracy to overthrow the kingdom of Christ through the erection of the papacy with such success that Satan invited the pope and his satellites to a banquet. When they were sated with roast princes and sausages made from the blood of the poor, a messenger broke in with the news that justification by faith was being preached at Wittenberg. Hell was thrown into confusion, and Christ took over.

These examples illustrate the attack on Romish abuses. Luther's positive teaching was less graphic and more difficult to popularize; but Hans Sachs, the shoemaker poet of Nürn-

berg, succeeded not badly in rhyming couplets on Luther as
"The Wittenberg Nightingale":

> Luther teaches that we all
> Are involved in Adam's fall.
> If man beholds himself within,
> He feels the bite and curse of sin.
> When dread, despair, and terror seize,
> Contrite he falls upon his knees.
> Then breaks for him the light of day.
> Then the gospel may have sway.
> Then sees he Christ of God the Son,
> Who for us all things has done.
> The law fulfilled, the debt is paid,
> Death overcome, the curse allayed,
> Hell destroyed, the devil bound,
> Grace for us with God has found.
> Christ, the Lamb, removes all sin.
> By faith alone in Christ we win.

By such simple summaries Luther's teaching was taken to
the common man in every walk of life. When Luther was reproached for making his appeal to the laity, one of the
pamphleteers replied:

You subtle fools, I tell you there are now at Nürnberg, Augsburg, Ulm, in Switzerland, and in Saxony wives, maidens, and
maids, students, handworkers, tailors, shoemakers, bakers, knights,
nobles, and princes such as the Elector of Saxony, who know more
about the Bible than all the schools of Paris and Cologne and all
the papists in the world.

### PRACTICAL CHURCH PROBLEMS

But this very dissemination of the gospel raised many
practical problems as to the organization of the Church.
Luther's views on that subject had never been clarified. The
true Church for him was always the Church of the redeemed,
known only to God, manifest here and there on earth, small,
persecuted and often hidden, at any rate scattered and united
only in the bond of the spirit. Such a view could scarcely issue
in anything other than a mystical fellowship devoid of any
concrete form. This was what Luther meant by the kingdom
of Christ. He did not pretend that it could be actualized, but
he was not prepared to leave the Church disembodied. The
next possibility was to gather together such ardent souls as
could be assembled in a particular locality, and Luther came
close to forming such an association in 1522 when he in-

structed those who desired communion in both kinds to receive it apart from the rest. After such communion became the common practice, he still desired to gather true believers into an inner fellowship, but not at the price of abandoning the church comprising the community. He would rather form a cell within the structure of the comprehensive body. The practical difficulties, however, in his judgment were insuperable, and by 1526 he declared his dream to be impossible. On that score he was mistaken, because the Anabaptists succeeded, but they did so by making a clean break with the church territorial. Luther's dilemma was that he wanted both a confessional church based on personal faith and experience, and a territorial church including all in a given locality. If he were forced to chose, he would take his stand with the masses, and this was the direction in which he moved.

To do so required some efforts in the direction of organization. By 1527 the whole of electoral Saxony could be regarded as evangelical. At many points the abandonment of the old ways had produced confusion. Notably was this the case at the point of ecclesiastical properties and finances. Cloisters had been abandoned. What then should become of their endowments and revenues? The donors in some instances had been dead for centuries, and the heirs were beyond identification. The lands were in danger of expropriation by powerful neighbors, and revenues in any case declined because the peasants were indisposed to surrender the produce after the object had been altered. Secondly, the liturgical reforms had engendered chaos, because Luther was so averse to uniformity. Each village and even each church had its own variety. Soon within the very same city the several churches exhibited diversity, and even a single church might vary in its practice. To those whose sense of religious security depended upon hallowed usage, such variety and unpredictability were genuinely disturbing. Luther began to feel that uniformity would have to be established, at least within the limits of each town.

Worst of all, differences in doctrine imperiled the public peace. Remnants of Catholicism survived, and Zwinglianism and Anabaptism were infiltrating. Such was the public temper that positive strife ensued. For this Luther saw no solution other than that one religion only should be publicly celebrated in a given locality. How to bring this to pass was by no means clear in his mind, because he was impelled by conflicting principles. He regarded the mass as idolatry and blasphemy, but he would compel no one to the faith. He was driven to the recognition of the rights of rival confessions. The outcome was the territorial church, in which the confession was that of the majority in a given locality, and the minority were free to migrate to favorable terrain. Whether this principle should apply only to the Catholics or also to the sectaries was another question.

But who should take the initiative in terminating the confusion? Hitherto Luther had been inclined to congregationalism and had stoutly objected to the dismissal of Zwilling from Altenburg by a patron against the wishes of the people. But independent local congregations were not in a position to cope with problems affecting several areas. These would have been handled by the bishops, but the bishops had not embraced the reform; and even if they had, Luther would not have accorded to them their ancient functions because he had come to be persuaded that in the New Testament every pastor was a bishop. Hence in more than jest he referred to his colleagues as "the bishop of Lochau or the bishop of Torgau." Some substitute, then, would have to be devised for the bishop. The answer was to create the office of superintendent, but how and by whom should he be chosen? If by the churches, who could call them together?

### THE GODLY PRINCE

To all these questions Luther saw no answer other than for the time being to call upon the prince. He should act not as a magistrate, but as a Christian brother advantageously situated to serve as an emergency bishop. All the church property should temporarily at least be vested in him that he might redirect the revenues for the support of ministers, teachers, and the poor. As to uniformity in liturgy and faith, if the will of the majority was to be determinative the situation called for a survey. Let Saxony be investigated. Visitations in the old days had been conducted by the bishops. Now let the elector appoint a commission for the purpose. This was done; and Visitors, including theologians with Luther at the head, and jurists to handle financial matters were appointed. Melanchthon composed the visitation articles to be presented in print to each of the clergy. Luther's preface stressed the provisional nature of the whole plan, but the elector referred to the commissioners as "My Visitors," and Melanchthon's instructions were less a questionnaire than a program to be instituted. Luther had unwittingly started down the road which was to lead to the territorial church under the authority of the prince.

The Visitors in two months investigated thirty-eight parishes inquiring into finances, behavior, forms of worship, and the faith. In the matter of finances they discovered great confusion and neglect. Parsonages were in a deplorable condition. One minister complained that four gulden worth of books had been ruined through a leaky roof. The Visitors decided to hold the parishioners responsible for repairs. Morals were not too shocking. The liturgy required standardization within limits. With regard to the faith, the determinative point was the evangelical complexion of all Saxony. The implementation of the reform therefore could not be regarded as an imposition of faith on a majority of the citizens. But there were dissenters, and in the interests of the public peace two religions could not be permitted to exist side by side. For that reason remnants of Catholicism must disappear. Priests who declined to accept the reform were dismissed. If young, they were left to fend for themselves. If old, they were pensioned. One minister on the arrival of the Visitors married his cook. He was asked why he had not done so earlier, and he replied that he expected her to die soon and he could then marry someone younger. He was adjudged to be popish and was deposed. A case was discovered in which a minister served two parishes, one in Catholic and one in evangelical territory, and ministered to each according to its respective rites. This arrangement was deemed unacceptable.

A sharp eye was kept on the sectaries, whether Zwinglian or Anabaptist. But Luther was not yet willing to treat the Anabaptists as the Zwinglians had already done in subjecting them to the death penalty. As late as June, 1528, Luther replied to an inquiry as follows:

You ask whether the magistrate may kill false prophets. I am slow in a judgment of blood even when it is deserved. In this matter I am terrified by the example of the papists and the Jews before Christ, for when there was a statute for the killing of false prophets and heretics, in time it came about that only the most saintly and innocent were killed. . . . I cannot admit that false teachers are to be put to death. *It is enough to banish.*

But even banishment required some adjustment of theory. Luther still held stoutly to his objection to any compulsion to faith. But this did not preclude restriction of the public profession of faith. The outward manifestations of religion, he held, may be subjected to regulation in the interests of orderliness and tranquillity. In all this Luther never dreamed that he was subordinating the Church to the state. The system later introduced in England which made the king the head of the Church was hardly to his taste. But Christian princes in his view were certainly responsible for fostering the true religion. Luther's concern was always that the faith be unimpeded. Anyone might help; no one might hinder. If the prince would render assistance, let it be accepted. If he interfered, then let him be disobeyed. This remained Luther's principle to the end of his life. Nevertheless the sharp line

of demarcation which he had delineated between the spheres
of the Church and the state in his tract *On Civil Government*
in 1523 was already in process of being blurred.

### THE PROTEST

This was all the more the case because the evangelical cause
was menaced in the political terrain, and inevitably the defense
fell to the lay leaders. From now on the electors, princes, and
delegates of the free cities rather than the theologians were
called upon to say, "Here I stand." Luther himself was not so
much the confessor as the mentor of confessors. It was his to
encourage, chide, guide, counsel, and warn against undue
concessions or unworthy means.

The fortunes of Lutheranism depended upon the decisions
of the German diets in conjunction with the emperor or his
deputy Ferdinand. A brief review is in order of the struggle
of Lutheranism for recognition and of the part played by
Luther in the events from the Diet of Worms through the Diet
of Augsburg.

After the Diet of Worms each succeeding gathering of the
German estates had been forced to occupy itself with the
Lutheran question. First came the Diet of Nürnberg in 1522.
It differed from the Diet of Worms in that the middle party
was gone and the implacables confronted the intransigents. A
Catholic group began to form in terms even of political alignment. Duke George of Saxony was the most militant and to
inflame his colleagues took it upon himself to copy with his
own hand the most offensive passages from Luther's successive
works. Joachim of Brandenburg, the Hapsburgs, and the
Bavarians constituted the core.

On the other side the free imperial cities were strong for
the reform. Augsburg and Strassburg, despite their bishops,
were infected with heresy. Nürnberg, where the diet was in
session, declared that though the pope had three more layers
on his tiara he could not induce them to abandon the Word.
Frederick the Wise pursued his usual discreet course, refrained
from suppressing the mass in the Castle Church at Wittenberg
until the diet was over, but declined equally to banish Luther.

Each side overestimated the other. Ferdinand reported to
the emperor that in Germany not one in a thousand was un-
tainted by Lutheranism. But Frederick's delegate reported that
he was in danger of being subjected to economic sanctions.
With the forces so evenly matched, even though there was
no middle party, compromise was the only possible solution.
And the Catholics were the readier to concede it because they
could not gainsay the word of Frederick's delegate that Luther
had actually become a bulwark against disorder, that without
him his followers were quite unmanageable, and that his re-

turn to Wittenberg against the wishes of his prince had been quite imperative to allay chaos.

The diet at its session of March 6, 1523, contented itself with the ambiguous formula that until the meeting of a general council Luther and his followers should refrain from publishing and that nothing should be preached other than the holy gospel in accord with the interpretation of the writing approved by the Christian Church. When the assembly reconvened the following year, again at Nürnberg, the accession of a new pope, Clement VII, a Medici quite as secular as Leo X, made under the circumstances no difference. The formula adopted on April 18, 1524, was: "The gospel should be preached in accord with the interpretation of the universal Church. Each prince in his own territory should enforce the Edict of Worms in so far as he might be able." Here in germ was the principle of *cuius regio eius religio,* that each region should have its own religion.

Everyone knew that this was only a respite, and the Peasants' War of 1525 intensified the conflict because the Catholic princes hanged Lutheran ministers in batches. In consequence a new brand of Lutheranism began to emerge, political in complexion. The genius of the movement was a recent convert, Philip of Hesse. He was young, impetuous, and always active. He it was who had been on his toes in the Peasants' War when the Saxon princes were for leaving the outcome to God. Philip was guided by three principles: he would compel none to the faith; he would fight rather than suffer compulsion for himself; and he would make an alliance with those of another faith. He was now eager to demonstrate his attachment to the gospel. When the diet of the empire reassembled at Speyer in 1526, Philip marched in with two hundred horsemen and Lutheran preachers, who, being denied the pulpits, stood upon balconies of the inns and addressed throngs of four thousand. Philip made evident his faith by serving an ox on Friday. A representative from Strassburg wished that he had chosen a more significant testimony than staging a barbecue on a fast day. Such flagrant flouting of ancient usage would never have been tolerated by the emperor had he been free. But having defeated France in 1525, he was subsequently embroiled with the pope and unable to attend the diet. The outcome was another temporizing measure. Each member was left on the religious question to act "as he would have to answer to God and the emperor." This was practically a recognition of the territorial principle.

This respite lasted for three years, during which time most of northern Germany became Lutheran, and in the south the cities of Strassburg, Augsburg, Ulm, and Nürnberg. Constance embraced the reform, severed connections with the Hapsburgs, and joined the Swiss. Basel came over to the reform in 1529.

This was the year of the Second Diet of Speyer. The significance of this gathering is that it solidified the confessions and divided Germany into two camps. On the eve of the diet such was by no means the case. The Evangelicals were divided alike on faith and tactics. Philip of Hesse, duped into believing that the Catholics meditated an attack, had negotiated with France and Bohemia, the traditional enemies of the House of Hapsburg, to the horror of the Saxon princes who had no mind to dismember the empire. The Catholics were divided on policy. The emperor was for the gloved hand, his brother Ferdinand for the mailed fist. The Diet of Speyer brought clarification, because Ferdinand chose to suppress the instructions of his brother Charles, who again was absent, and demanded the extirpation of heresy. His attempt, even though but moderately successful, solidified the Evangelicals. The time appeared propitious for their suppression, because France, the pope, and the Turk were at the moment either in hand or less menacing. But the diet was not too amenable to Ferdinand's wishes, and the decree was far less severe than it might have been. The Edict of Worms was reaffirmed only for Catholic territories. Provisionally until the meeting of the general council Lutheranism was to be tolerated in those regions where it could not be suppressed without tumult. In Lutheran lands the principle of religious liberty for Catholics must be observed, whereas in Catholic lands the same liberty would not be extended to the Lutherans. Against this invidious arrangement the Evangelicals protested, whence the origin of the name Protestant. They contended that the majority of one diet could not rescind the unanimous action of the previous assembly. They questioned whether this was the intent of the emperor, and on that score they were correct. They affirmed that they could not have two religions side by side in their territories without menace to the public peace, and if their plea was not heard, then "they must protest and testify publicly before God that they could consent to nothing contrary to his Word."

Their stand has been variously misrepresented. In the Protestant camp the emphasis has been all too much on the first word, "protest," rather than on the second, "testify." Above all else they were confessing their faith. On the Catholic side the misrepresentation has been flagrant. The historian Janssen said that they were protesting against religious liberty. In a sense of course they were. Neither side was tolerant, but the objection was to the inequality of the arrangement which demanded liberty for Catholics and denied it to Protestants. In this protest the Zwinglians and Lutherans were joined.

## PROTESTANT ALLIANCE: THE MARBURG COLLOQUY

Philip of Hesse believed that the time had come to go futher. The rescript of this diet also was only provisional. The

Protestants then should protect themselves by a common confession and a common confederation. His hope was to unite the Lutherans, the Swiss, and the Strassburgers, who took an intermediate position on the Lord's Supper. But Luther was of no mind for a political confederation. "We cannot in conscience," said he, "approve such a league inasmuch as bloodshed or other disaster may be the outcome, and we may find ourselves so involved that we cannot withdraw even though we would. Better be ten times dead than that our consciences should be burdened with the insufferable weight of such disaster and that our gospel should be the cause of bloodshed, when we ought rather to be as sheep for the slaughter and not avenge or defend ourselves."

The common confession was another matter, and Luther with some misgivings accepted an invitation to assemble with a group of German and Swiss theologians in Philip's picturesque castle on a hillock overlooking the slender Lahn and the towers of Marburg. A notable company assembled. Luther and Melanchthon represented Saxony, Zwingli came from Zurich, Oekolampadius from Basel, Bucer from Strassburg, to name only the more outstanding. All earnestly desired a union. Zwingli rejoiced to look upon the faces of Luther and Melanchthon, and declared with tears in his eyes that there were none with whom he would be more happy to be in accord. Luther likewise exhorted to unity. The discussion commenced inauspiciously, however, when Luther drew a circle with chalk upon the table and wrote within it the words, "This is my body." Oekolampadius insisted that these words must be taken metaphorically, because the flesh profits nothing and the body of Christ has ascended into heaven. Luther inquired why the ascent should not also be metaphorical. Zwingli went to the heart of the matter when he affirmed that flesh and spirit are incompatible. Therefore the presence of Christ can only be spiritual. Luther replied that flesh and spirit can be conjoined, and the spiritual, which no one denied, does not exclude the physical. They appeared to have arrived at a deadlock, but actually they had made substantial gains because Zwingli advanced from his view that the Lord's Supper is only a memorial to the position that Christ is spiritually present. And Luther conceded that whatever the nature of the physical presence, it is of no benefit without faith. Hence any magical view is excluded.

This approximation of the two positions offered hope for agreement, and the Lutherans took the initiative in proposing a formula of concord. They confessed that hitherto they had misunderstood the Swiss. For themselves they declared "that Christ is truly present, that is, substantively, essentially, though not quantitatively, qualitatively, or locally." The Swiss rejected this statement as not clearly safeguarding the spiritual char-

acter of the Lord's Supper, because they could not understand
how something could be present but not locally present. Luther
told them that geometrical conceptions cannot be used to
describe the presence of God.

The common confession had failed. But then the Swiss proposed that despite the disagreement intercommunion be practiced, and to this "Luther momentarily agreed." This we know
on the testimony of Bucer, "until Melanchthon interposed out
of regard for Ferdinand and the emperor." This statement is
extremely significant. It means that Luther did not play the
role of utter implacability commonly ascribed to him, and was
disposed to join with the Swiss until Melanchthon made him
aware that to coalesce with the left would estrange the right.
Melanchthon still entertained a hope for the reform of all
Christendom and the preservation of the larger medieval unities through a reconciliation of the Lutherans and the Catholics. The alignment of Speyer did not seem to him definitive,
but he sensed that the price would be the repudiation of the
sectaries. Luther was far less sanguine as to the Catholics
and preferred a consolidated Protestantism, but he yielded to
Melanchthon, the one friend who was ever able to deflect him
from an intransigent course. Luther's judgment was ultimately
to be confirmed; and when Melanchthon had exhausted his
efforts at conciliation with the Catholics, the line dropped at
Marburg was resumed and issued in the Wittenberg Concord.

A united confession had failed. Intercommunion had failed.
But the confederation ought nevertheless to be possible, argued
Philip of Hesse. People can unite to defend the right of each
to believe what he will even though they are not altogether
of the same persuasion. His pleas were very plausible. They
were referred for consideration not only to the theologians but
also to the lay leaders of Saxony. If Luther is reproached for
his willingness to accept so much help from the state, we must
recall that the statesmen of that day were Christian believers
who were ready to stake everything upon their convictions,
and with much more to lose than Luther himself. It was the
chancellor of Saxony who composed the answer to Philip of
Hesse. The chancellor was not like Luther averse to any political alliance, nor like Philip indifferent to a confessional basis.
The arguments on both sides were reviewed. In favor of the
confederation it might be said that among the Zwinglians were
doubtless many good Christians who did not agree with Zwingli, and in any case a political alliance could be made even
with the heathen. To this the reply was that an alliance with
the heathen would be more defensible than an alliance with
apostates. The faith is supreme. Therefore the considerable
assistance which might be rendered by the Swiss must be renounced and the outcome left entirely in the hands of God.

This left the Swiss to take care of themselves. In the second

*[handwritten signatures]*

## THE SIGNATURES AT THE MARBURG COLLOQUY

*Joannes Oecolampadius, Huldrychus Zwinglius, Martinus Bucerius, Caspar Hedio, Martinus Luther, Justus Jonas, Philippus Melanchthon, Andreas Osiander, Stephanus Agricola, Joannes Brentius.*

Kappel War in 1531 Zwingli fell sword in hand on the field of battle. Luther considered his death a judgment upon him because as a minister he wielded the sword.

### THE AUGSBURG CONFESSION

The Lutherans were left also to take care of themselves. In 1530 Emperor Charles was at last free to come to Germany. Having humbled France and the pope, he approached Germany with a gracious invitation that each should declare himself on the score of religion, but with the intent not to spare severe measures should the milder fail. Luther was not permitted to attend the diet. For six months he was again "in the wilderness" as he had been at the Wartburg, this time in another castle called the Feste Coburg. He was not quite so lonely because he was attended by his secretary, from whose pen we have a little glimpse of the doctor in a report sent to his wife.

Dear and gracious Mrs. Luther:

Rest assured that your lord and we are hale and hearty by God's grace. You did well to send the doctor the portrait [of his daughter Magdalena], for it diverts him from his worries. He has nailed it on the wall opposite the table where we eat in the elector's apartment. At first he could not quite recognize her. "Dear me," said he, "Lenchen is too dark." But he likes the picture now, and more and more comes to see that it is Lenchen. She is strikingly like Hans in the mouth, eyes, and nose, and in fact in the whole face, and will come to look even more like him. I just had to write you this.

Do not be concerned about the doctor. He is in good trim, praise God. The news of his father's death shook him at first, but he was himself again after two days. When the letter came, he said, "My father is dead." He took his psalter, went to his room, and wept so that he was incapacitated for two days, but he has been all right since. May God be with Hans and Lenchen and the whole household.

As at the Wartburg, Luther devoted himself to biblical studies and likewise to admonitions and advice to those who were conducting the defense of the evangelical cause at Augsburg. His absence and their success were the manifest proof that the movement could survive without him. The great witness was borne this time not by the monk of Wittenberg or even by the ministers and theologians, but by the lay princes who stood to lose their dignities and their lives. When the Holy Roman Emperor, Charles the Fifth, approached the city of Augsburg, the dignitaries went out to receive him. As the notables knelt, bareheaded, for the benediction of Cardinal Campeggio, the Elector of Saxony stood bolt upright. On the following day came one of the most colorful processions in the history of medieval pageantry. In silk and damask, with gold brocade, in robes of crimson and the colors appropriate to each house, came the electors of the empire followed by the most exalted of their number, John of Saxony, carrying in accord with ancient usage the glittering naked sword of the emperor. Behind him marched Albert, the Archbishop of Mainz, the Bishop of Cologne, King Ferdinand of Austria, and his brother the emperor. They marched to the cathedral, where the emperor and all the throng knelt before the high altar. But Elector John of Saxony and the landgrave, Philip of Hesse, remained standing. On the morrow the emperor took the Lutheran princes aside. John and Philip were of course among them, and also the aged George, the margrave of Brandenburg. The emperor told them that their ministers must not preach in Augsburg. The princes refused. The emperor insisted that at any rate the ministers must not preach polemical sermons. The princes again refused. The emperor informed them that the following day would see the *Corpus Christi* procession, in which they would be expected to march. The princes once more refused. The emperor continued to insist, when the margrave stepped forward and said, "Before I let anyone take from me the Word of God and ask me to deny my God, I will kneel and let him strike off my head."

The emperor, despite all these rebuffs, was willing to let the Protestants state their case. The commission fell to Melanchthon. He was still hopeful for the emperor and for the moderates in the Catholic camp, led now by Albert, the Archbishop of Mainz, who had once sent Luther a wedding present. To be sure Eck and Campeggio were raving and disseminating lies and all manner of misrepresentation, but after all they were not the whole Catholic Church.

Melanchthon himself had a deep streak of the Erasmian. He wished neither to deny the faith of Martin Luther nor to be the man to remove the keystone and let fall the arch of Christendom. He sat in his room and wept. At the same time he explored every avenue of conciliation and even went so far as to say that the differences between the Lutherans and the Catholics were no more serious than the use of German in the mass.

Luther was exceedingly concerned and wrote to him that the difference between them was that Melanchthon was stout and Luther yielding in personal disputes, but the reverse was true on public controversies. Luther was thinking of the discussion at Marburg when he had been concessive, Melanchthon obdurate. Now Melanchthon was for recognizing even the pope, whereas Luther felt that there could be no peace with the pope unless he abolished the papacy. The real point was not between personal and public controversies, but in their respective judgments of the left and of the right. Melanchthon in his efforts to conciliate the Catholics was in danger of emasculating the reform.

But he did not. The Augsburg Confession was his work, and in the end it was as stalwart a confession as any made by the princes. Luther was immensely pleased with it and thought its moderate tone better than anything he could have achieved. In the first draft the Augsburg Confession spoke only in the name of electoral Saxony, but in the final draft it confessed the faith of a united Lutheranism. Even Philip of Hesse signed, despite his leanings to the Swiss. But the statement on the Lord's Supper was such that the Swiss declined and submitted a statement of their own. The Strassburgers also refused to sign, and they too brought in another confession. In all there were three Protestant statements of faith submitted at Augsburg. The Anabaptists of course received no hearing at all. Yet despite these divergences in the Evangelical ranks, the Augsburg Confession did much to consolidate Protestantism and to set it over against Catholicism. One might take the date June 25, 1530, the day when the Augsburg Confession was publicly read, as the death day of the Holy Roman Empire. From this day forward the two confessions stood over against each other, poised for conflict. Charles V allowed the Evangelicals until April, 1531, to make their submission. If at that time they declined, they would then feel the edge of the sword.

Against this threat Luther addressed an appeal for moderation to the leader of the conciliatory party in the Roman camp, his old opponent and friend, Albert the Archbishop of Mainz, in the following words:

> Inasmuch as there is now no hope of unanimity in the faith, I humbly beseech your Grace that you will endeavor to have the other side keep the peace, believing as they will and permitting us to believe this truth which has been confessed and found blameless. It is well known that no one, be he pope or emperor, should or can force others to believe, for God himself has never yet seen fit to drive anyone by force to believe. How then shall his miserable creatures presume to coerce men not only to faith but to that which they themselves must regard as lies? Would to God that your Grace or anyone else would be a new Gamaliel to commend this counsel of peace.

Luther's counsel was taken not on principle but by reason of necessity, for the emperor was not to find himself again in a position to intervene for another fifteen years.

CHAPTER NINETEEN

# THE CHURCH TUTORIAL

 ISITATION had established the outward form of the Church, but Luther well knew that the Church of the spirit cannot be engendered by the arm of the magistrate. The true Christian Church is the work of the Word communicated by every available means. Early Luther sensed the need for a new translation of the Scriptures from the original tongues into idiomatic German. There must be likewise a body of instructional material for the young. The liturgy

would have to be revised to eliminate popish abuses and to enlighten the people. Congregational singing should be cultivated alike to inspire and instruct. The Bible, the catechism, the liturgy, and the hymnbook thus constituted the needs, and all four were to be met by Luther himself.

### THE BIBLE TRANSLATION

For the translation of the Bible, Luther availed himself of the enforced leisure at the Wartburg to produce in three months a rendering of the complete New Testament. The Old Testament came later. The German Bible is Luther's noblest achievement, unfortunately untranslatable because every nation has its own direct version. For the Germans, Luther's rendering was incomparable. He leaped beyond the tradition of a thousand years. There had been translations before him of the Scripture into German, reaching back to the earliest transcription of the Gothic tongue by Ulfilas. There were even portions of the Bible translated not from the Latin Vulgate, but from the Hebrew and the Greek. But none had the majesty of diction, the sweep of vocabulary, the native earthiness, and the religious profundity of Luther. "I endeavored," said he, "to make Moses so German that no one would suspect he was a Jew."

The variety of German chosen as a basis was the court tongue of electoral Saxony, enriched from a number of dialects with which Luther had gained some familiarity in his travels. He went to incredible pains to find words. The initial translation did not satisfy him. His New Testament was first published in September, 1522, but he was revising it to the day of his death in 1546. The last printed page on which he ever looked was the proof of the latest revision. The Old Testament was commenced after his return from the Wartburg. The complete translation of the entire Bible did not appear until 1534. This, again, was subject to constant reworking in collaboration with a committee of colleagues.

Luther on occasion achieved the most felicitous rendering at the first throw. At other times he had to labor. In that case he would first make a literal translation in the word order of the original. Then he would take each word separately and gush forth a freshet of synonyms. From these he would select those which not only best suited the sense but also contributed to balance and rhythm. All of this would then be set aside in favor of a free rendering to catch the spirit. Finally the meticulous and the free would be brought together. Sometimes he was at a loss for terms and would set out in quest of words. In order to name the precious stones in the twenty-first chapter of Revelation he examined the court jewels of the elector of Saxony. For the coins of the Bible he consulted the numismatic collections in Wittenberg. When he came to describe the sacrifices of Leviticus and needed terms for the inward parts of goats and bullocks, he made repeated trips to the slaughterhouse and inquired of the butcher. The birds and beasts of the Old Testament proved a hard knot. To Spalatin he wrote:

I am all right on the birds of the night—owl, raven, horned owl, tawny owl, screech owl—and on the birds of prey—vulture, kite, hawk, and sparrow hawk. I can handle the stag, roebuck, and chamois, but what in the Devil am I to do with the taragelaphus, pygargus, oryx, and camelopard [names for animals in the Vulgate]?

Another problem was the translation of idioms. Here Luther insisted that the idiom of one language must be translated into the equivalent idiom of the other. He was scornful of the Vulgate translation, "Hail, Mary, full of grace." "What German would understand that if translated literally? He knows the meaning of a purse full of gold or a keg full of beer, but what is he to make of a girl full of grace? I would prefer to say simply, '*Liebe Maria*.' What word is more rich than that word, '*liebe*'?"

There is no doubt that it is a rich word, but its connotations are not precisely the same as "endowed with grace," and Luther did not use the word in his official version. Here is the problem of the translator. Should he use always an indigenous word which may have a particular local connotation? If the French call a centurion a gendarme, and the Germans make a procurator into a burgomaster, Palestine has moved west. And this

CRANACH'S "JACOB WRESTLING WITH THE ANGEL"

is what did happen to a degree in Luther's rendering. Judea was transplanted to Saxony, and the road from Jericho to Jerusalem ran through the Thuringian forest. By nuances and turns of expression Luther enhanced the graphic in terms of the local. When he read, "There is a river, the streams whereof shall make glad the city of God," he envisaged a medieval town begirt with walls and towers, surrounded by a moat through which course a living stream laving with laughter the massive piers.

What the word could not do at this point, the pictures supplied. The Luther Bibles were copiously illustrated, particularly for the earlier portion of the Old Testament and for the book of Revelation in the New Testament. The restriction of illustrations to these portions of the Bible had become a convention in Germany. The Gospels and the epistles were adorned only with initial letters. Why this should have been

LEMBERGER'S "JACOB WRESTLING WITH THE ANGEL"

the case is difficult to see. Certainly there was no objection to illustrating the Gospels; witness Dürer's "Life of Mary," or the woodcuts of the Passion, or Schongauer's nativities. Within the conventional limits Luther's Bible was richly illustrated. In the various editions to appear during his lifetime there were some five hundred woodcuts. They were not the choicest expressions of the art, but they did Germanize the Bible. Moses and David might almost be mistaken for Frederick the Wise and John Frederick.

An interesting development is to be observed in the illustrations from one artist to another in the successive editions of the Luther Bible, notably from Cranach to Lemberger. One senses something of the transition from the Renaissance to baroque. Compare their renderings of the wrestling of Jacob with the angel. Cranach has a balance of spaces, with decorative background. Lemberger displays strains in tension, with even the trees participating in the struggle.

Unfortunately the illustrations for the book of Revelation were made all too contemporary. The temptation was too strong to identify the pope with Antichrist. In the first edition of the New Testament in September, 1522, the scarlet woman sitting on the seven hills wears the papal tiara. So also does the great dragon. The beast out of the abyss has a monk's cowl. Fallen Babylon is plainly Rome. There is no mistaking the Belvedere, the Pantheon, and the Castelo de St. Angelo. Duke George was so enraged by these pictures that he sent a warm protest to Frederick the Wise. In consequence, in the issue of December, 1522, the tiaras in the woodcuts were chiseled down to innocuous crowns of a single layer, but other details were left unchanged and attracted so little notice that Emser, Luther's Catholic opponent, actually borrowed the blocks from Cranach to illustrate his own Bible. In the New Testament of 1530 Luther introduced an annotation explaining that the frogs issuing from the mouth of the dragon were his opponents, Faber, Eck, and Emser. In the completed edition of the whole Bible in 1534, after Frederick the Wise was dead, the woodcuts were done over and the papal tiaras restored.

## DOCTRINAL PROBLEMS IN TRANSLATION

The most difficult task in translating consisted not in making vivid the scenes but in capturing the moods and ideas. "Translating is not an art that everyone can practice. It requires a right pious, faithful, diligent, God-fearing, experienced, practical heart." Luther did not think to add that it requires an instructed head, but he had his ideas about the Bible which in some measure affected alike what he did and what he left undone. He did not attempt any minor harmonization of discrepancies, because trivial errors gave him no concern. If on occasion he could speak of every iota of Holy Writ as sacred, at other times he displayed blithe indifference to minor blemishes, such as an error in quotation from the Old Testament in the New Testament. The Bible for him was not strictly identical with the Word of God. God's Word is the work of redemption in Christ which became concrete in Scripture as God in Christ became incarnate in the flesh; and as Christ by the incarnation was not denuded of human characteristics, so the Scripture as the medium of the Word was not divested of human limitations. Hence Luther was not subject to the slightest temptation to accommodate a gospel citation from the prophets to the text of the Old Testament. No more was he concerned to harmonize the predictions of Peter's denial with the accounts of the denial itself.

But when doctrinal matters were involved, the case was different. Luther read the New Testament in the light of the Pauline message that the just shall live by faith and not by works of the law. That this doctrine is not enunciated with equal emphasis throughout the New Testament and appears to be denied in the book of James did not escape Luther, and in his preface to the New Testament of 1522 James was stigmatized as "an epistle of straw." Once Luther remarked that he would give his doctor's beret to anyone who could reconcile James and Paul. Yet he did not venture to reject James from the canon of Scripture, and on occasion earned his own beret by effecting a reconciliation. "Faith," he wrote, "is a living, restless thing. It cannot be inoperative. We are not saved by works; but if there be no works, there must be something amiss with faith." This was simply to put a Pauline construction

THE WHORE OF BABYLON IN THREE SUCCESSIVE
EDITIONS OF LUTHER'S BIBLE

**RIGHT:** *In the New Testament of September, 1522, she is shown wearing the papal tiara.*

LEFT: *The papal tiara elicited such a vigorous remonstrance from Duke George to Frederick the Wise that he interposed, and in the issue of December, 1522, the tiara was reduced to an innocuous single layer.*

BELOW: *In the Bible of 1534 after Frederick's death the cut was done over and the tiara restored.*

upon James. The conclusion was a hierachy of values within
the New Testament. First Luther would place the Gospel of
John, then the Pauline epistles and First Peter, after them the
three other Gospels, and in a subordinate place Hebrews,
James, Jude, and Revelation. He mistrusted Revelation because of its obscurity. "A revelation," said he, "should be revealing."

These presuppositions affected the translation but slightly.
Yet occasionally an overly Pauline turn is discernible. There is
the famous example where Luther rendered "justification by
faith" as "justification by faith alone." When taken to task for
this liberty, he replied that he was not translating words but
ideas, and that the extra word was necessary in German in
order to bring out the force of the original. Through all the
revisions of his lifetime he would never relinquish that word
"alone." In another instance he was more flexible. In 1522 he
had translated the Greek words meaning "by the works of the
law" with German words meaning "by the merit of works."
In 1527 he substituted a literal rendering. That must have
hurt. He was an honest workman, and successive revisions of
the New Testament were marked by a closer approximation to
the original. And yet there were places where Luther's peculiar
views, without any inaccuracy, lent a nuance to the rendering.
In the benediction, "The peace of God, which passeth all
understanding," Luther translated, "The peace which tran-
scends all reason." One cannot exactly quarrel with that. He
might better have said, "which surpasses all comprehension,"
but he was so convinced of the inadequacy of human reason
to scale the heavenly heights that he could not but see here a
confirmation of his supreme aversion.

If the New Testament was for Luther a Pauline book, the
Old Testament was a Christian book. Only the ceremonial law
of the Jews was abrogated. The moral law was still valid
because it was in accord with the law of nature. But more
significant than the ethic was the theology. The Old Testament
foreshadowed the drama of redemption. Adam exemplified the
depravity of man. Noah tasted the wrath of God, Abraham
was saved by faith, and David exhibited contrition. The pre-
existent Christ was working throughout the Old Testament,
speaking through the mouths of the prophets and the psalm-
ist. A striking witness to the Christological interpretation of
the Old Testament current in Luther's day is to be found in
the illustrations of his Bible. Among the hundreds of woodcuts
the only portrayal of the nativity of Jesus is located not in the
Gospels, where one would expect to find it, but on the title
page to Ezekiel. Reading the Old Testament in this fashion
Luther could not well escape Christianizing shades of meaning. The "lovingkindness of the Lord" became "grace"; the
"Deliverer of Israel" became "the Saviour"; and "life" was

rendered "eternal life." That was why Bach could treat the Sixteenth Psalm as an Easter hymn.

Luther's liberties were greatest with the Psalms because here he was so completely at home. They were the record of the spiritual struggles through which he was constantly passing. The favorite words of his *Anfechtungen* could not be excluded. Where the English version of Ps. 90 speaks of "secret sins" Luther has "unrecognized sins." He was thinking of his fruitless efforts in the cloister to recall every wrongdoing, that it might be confessed and pardoned. Where the English translates, "So teach us to number our days, that we may apply our hearts unto wisdom," Luther is blunt: "Teach us so to reflect on death that we may be wise."

Luther so lived his way into the Psalms that he improved them. In the original the transitions are sometimes abrupt and the meaning not always plain. Luther simplified and clarified. When he came to a passage which voiced his wrestlings in the night watches, he was free to paraphrase. Take his conclusion to the Seventy-third Psalm.

My heart is stricken and my bones fail, that I must be a fool and know nothing, that I must be as a beast before thee. Nevertheless I will ever cleave to thee. Thou holdest me by thy right hand and leadest me by thy counsel. Thou wilt crown me at last with honor. If only I have that, I will not ask for earth or heaven. When body and soul fail me, thou art ever God, my heart's comfort and my portion.

The Bible, just as it stood in Luther's rendering, was a great educational tool; but more was needed, obviously for children but also for adults, who were almost equally ignorant. The children should be taught at church, at school, and at home; and to that end pastors, teachers, and parents should receive prior training. Hence Luther's plea that Catholic schools be replaced by municipal schools with a system of compulsory education including religion. "The Scripture cannot be understood without the languages," argued Luther, "and the languages can be learned only in school. If parents cannot spare their children for a full day, let them send them for a part. I would wager that in half of Germany there are not over four thousand pupils in school. I would like to know where we are going to get pastors and teachers three years from now."

### CATECHISMS

The mere training of pastors, teachers, and parents would, however, not suffice. They must in turn be provided with a body of religious literature adapted to children. The Middle Ages supplied little by way of models because the catechisms had been for adults. The Humanists had made a beginning, as in the *Colloquies of Erasmus,* and the Bohemian Brethren had a question book for children; but the material was so scant that one can without exaggeration ascribe to the Reformation the creation of the first body of religious literature for the young. Luther was so exceedingly busy that he attempted to delegate this assignment to others, and they undertook it with zest. In the seven years between his return to Wittenberg and the appearance of his own catechisms his collaborators had produced materials comprising five goodly volumes in a modern reprint.

For the most part they were crude and boiled down to about this: "You are a bad child. You deserve to be punished forever in hell; but since God has punished his Son Jesus Christ in your place, you can be forgiven if you will honor, love, and obey God." That *if* bothered Luther, because it restored the merit of man as in the penitential system. Even Melanchthon moralized too much, for his manual was a compilation of the ethical portions of the New Testament with the maxims of the pagan sages. Some catechisms pitted the inner against the outer word of Scripture, and some even spiritualized the sacraments. In other words the radicals were appropriating the catechetical method. High time that Luther undertook the task himself!

He produced two catechisms in the year 1529: the Large Catechism for adults, with a long section on marriage, scarcely suitable for the young; and the Small Catechism for children. Both were built about five points: the Ten Commandments as a mirror of sin, the Apostles' Creed as a proclamation of forgiveness, the Lord's Prayer as an acceptance of mercy, and the two sacraments of baptism and the Lord's Supper as channels of grace.

In the Large Cathechism the exposition was comparatively full and the tone at times polemical. The command to worship only the Lord gave an opportunity to upbraid the Catholic cult of the saints, whereas the sections on the sacraments called for a refutation of the radicals. The Small Catechism for children is devoid of all polemic, an inimitable affirmation of faith. The section on the death of Christ stresses not the substitution of penalty but the triumph over all the forces of darkness.

I believe in Jesus Christ . . . who when I was lost and damned saved me from all sin and death and the power of the Devil, not with gold and silver but with his own precious, holy blood and his sinless suffering and death, that I might belong to him and live in his kingdom and serve him forever in goodness, sinlessness, and happiness, just as he is risen from the dead and lives and reigns forever. That is really so.

Luther said that he would be glad to have all his works perish except the reply to Eramus and the catechism.

Do not think the catechism is a little thing to be read hastily and cast aside. Although I am a doctor, I have to do just as a child and say word for word every morning and whenever I have time the Lord's Prayer and the Ten Commandments, the Creed and the Psalms. I have to do it every day, and yet I cannot stand as I would. But these smart folk in one reading want to be doctors of doctors. Therefore I beg these wise saints to be persuaded that they are not such great doctors as they think. To be occupied with God's Word helps against the world, the flesh, and the Devil, and all bad thoughts. This is the true holy water with which to exorcise the Devil.

Luther's intention was that the catechism should be used in church as a basis for sermons, but more particularly in the home. The father should check up on the children at least once a week and also on the servants. If the children would not learn, they should not eat; if the servants declined, they should be dismissed.

The catechisms were enlivened with quaint woodcuts of episodes from the Bible suitable to each point. "I believe in God the Father Almighty" naturally called for a view of the creation. "Hallowed be thy name" was illustrated by a preaching scene. "Remember the Sabbath day" showed a devout group inside a church while outside a man was gathering

OUR FATHER

HALLOWED BE THY NAME

wood. Luther was, however, no rigid sabbatarian, and incidentally he did not select these pictures. Excessively modest is the cut accompanying the sixth commandment, where David with his harp is seduced by the sight of Bathsheba having her feet washed. At the close of the catechetical hour Luther suggested the singing of a psalm or a hymn.

### LITURGY

Another of Luther's great contributions lay in the field of public worship, which he revised first in the interests of purity and then as a medium of instruction. While still at the Wartburg he had come to realize that some changes in the liturgy were imperative, and had applauded Carlstadt's initial endeavors. Yet Luther himself was very conservative in such matters and desired to alter the beloved mass as little as possible. The main point was that all pretension to human merit should be excluded. Luther undertook in 1523 to make the minimal revisions essential to evangelical doctrine. His *Formula Missae* was in Latin. The canon of the mass disappeared

REMEMBER THE SABBATH DAY     THOU SHALT NOT COVET THY
NEIGHBOR'S WIFE

because this was the portion in which the reference to sacrifice occurred. Luther restored the emphasis of the early Church upon the Lord's Supper as an act of thanksgiving to God and of fellowship through Christ with God and with each other. This first Lutheran mass was solely an act of worship in which true Christians engaged in praise and prayer, and were strengthened in the inner man.

But speedily Luther came to the recognition that an act of worship was not possible for many in the congregation without explanation. The Church embraced the community, and the congregation consisted of the townsfolk of Wittenberg and of the peasants from the villages round about. How much would these peasants understand of his revision of the Latin mass? They would of course recognize the change involved in giving to them the wine as well as the bread, and they would sense that something had altered when the inaudible portions were discontinued. But since it was still all in a foreign tongue they would hardly perceive that the idea of sacrifice was gone. The mass therefore would have to be in German. Others had felt this earlier than Luther, and Müntzer had prepared a German mass which Luther liked so long as he did not know it was Müntzer's. Gradually Luther came to the conclusion that he must undertake the revision himself. In 1526 he came out with the German mass.

Everything was in German save for the Greek refrain, "Kyrie eleison." The changes left intact the essential structure; and a Swiss visitor in 1536, accustomed to simpler services, felt that the Lutherans had retained many elements of popery: genuflections, vestments, veerings to the altar or the audience, lectern and pulpit on opposite sides. Even the elevation of the elements was retained until 1542. To Luther all such points were indifferent. He would not substitute a new formalism for an old and allowed very wide latitude and variation in liturgical matters. The main point was that in the German as in the Latin the canon of the mass was gone. In its place there was a simple exhortation to receive communion. But the whole tone of the service was altered in two respects: there was more of the scriptural and more of the instructional. With the canon removed the Gospel and Epistle assumed a more prominent position; the words of institution were given in German; the sermon occupied a larger place, and not infrequently the notices were as long as the sermon. The church thus became not only the house of prayer and praise but also a classroom.

### MUSIC

The most far-reaching changes in the liturgy were with regard to the music, and those at three points: the chants intoned by the priest, the chorals rendered by the choir, and the hymns sung by the congregation. Luther set himself to revise all three. He was competent, if not to execute, at least to direct and inspire, since he could play the lute and sing even though he did not regard himself as skilled in composition. Modern specialists are not agreed as to how many of the musical settings to his hymns may be his own. Ten are commonly ascribed to him. Certainly he knew how to compose simple melodies, to harmonize and arrange. Above all else he was able to inspire, because his enthusiasm for music was so great. He said:

Music is a fair and lovely gift of God which has often wakened and moved me to the joy of preaching. St. Augustine was troubled in conscience whenever he caught himself delighting in music, which he took to be sinful. He was a choice spirit, and were he living today would agree with us. I have no use for cranks who despise music, because it is a gift of God. Music drives away the

Devil and makes people gay; they forget thereby all wrath, unchastity, arrogance, and the like. Next after theology I give to music the highest place and the greatest honor. I would not exchange what little I know of music for something great. Experience proves that next to the Word of God only music deserves to be extolled as the mistress and governess of the feelings of the human heart. We know that to the devils music is distasteful and insufferable. My heart bubbles up and overflows in response to music, which has so often refreshed me and delivered me from dire plagues.

Perhaps the fact that Dürer was old and Luther young when each embraced the reform may explain in a measure why in German Lutheranism pictorial art declined in favor of the musical expression of the faith.

The first melodic portion of the liturgy to be reformed was the part intoned by the priest, including the Epistle and Gospel. Since Luther was so desirous that every word of Scripture should be distinctly heard and understood, one wonders why he did not discontinue the music entirely in favor of reading in a natural voice. The answer lies in the architectural structure, which was more conducive to the word sung than to the word spoken. But Luther did employ every device to bring out the meaning. Only one note should be used for one syllable, and the organ accompaniment should not obscure the words. Throughout the service the organ was used only antiphonally. The Gospel texts should not be conflated, and the seven words of Christ from the cross were not to be blended from all four Gospels. The Lutheran tradition explains why Bach should write a *St. Matthew's Passion*. The meaning should be further emphasized by dramatic coloring. The Gregorian chants for the Epistle and the Gospel were monotone save for the lowering of the voice at the end. Luther introduced different registers for the narrative of the evangelist, the words of Christ, and the words of the apostles. The mean register he set high because his own voice was tenor, but he explained that he was offering only suggestions and each celebrant should discover and adapt the musical setting to suit his own liturgical range. Again the modes should be varied: the sixth should be used for the Gospel because Christ was joyful, and the eighth for the Epistle because Paul was more somber. This terminology calls for a word of explanation. Today we have a number of keys and only two modes, the major and minor. The intervals in all keys are those of C, conserved by the use of accidentals in transposing. In the sixteenth century eight modes were in vogue with different intervals formed by starting on each note of the octave and ascending without accidentals. The attention which Luther in all these respects devoted to musical settings for the prose text of the Scripture in the vernacular prepared the way for the oratorios.

The degree to which he was assisted in his task appears in an account by his collaborator Walther, who wrote:

When Luther forty years ago wanted to prepare his German mass, he requested of the Elector of Saxony and Duke John that Conrad Rupff and I be summoned to Wittenberg, where he might discuss music and the nature of the eight Gregorian psalm modes. He prepared the music for the Epistles and Gospels, likewise for the words of institution of the true body and blood of Christ; he chanted these for me and asked me to express my opinion of his efforts. At that time he kept me in Wittenberg for three weeks; we discussed how the Epistles and Gospels might properly be set. I spent many a pleasant hour singing with him and often found that he seemingly could not weary of singing or even get enough of it; in addition he was always able to discuss music eloquently.

The second element to be revised was the choral for the choir. Here a rich background was available in the polyphonic religious music of the Netherlands which Luther admired above all other. The melody of the Gregorian chant was taken as a base, and about it three, four, or more voices rotated in counterpoint with elaborate embellishments. Luther himself in the preface to the musical work of 1538 gathered into a single passage all of his praises of music together with the most apt description ever penned of the Netherlandish polyphonic choral:

To all lovers of the liberal art of music Dr. Martin Luther wishes grace and peace from God the Father and our Lord Jesus Christ. With all my heart I would extol the precious gift of God in the noble art of music, but I scarcely know where to begin or end. There is nothing on earth which has not its tone. Even the air invisible sings when smitten with a staff. Among the beasts and the birds song is still more marvelous. David, himself a musician, testified with amazement and joy to the song of the birds. What then shall I say of the voice of man, to which naught else may be compared? The heathen philosophers have striven in vain to explain how the tongue of man can express the thoughts of the heart in speech and song, through

laughter and lamentation. Music is to be praised as second only to the Word of God because by her are all the emotions swayed. Nothing on earth is more mighty to make the sad gay and the gay sad, to hearten the downcast, mellow the overweening, temper the exuberant, or mollify the vengeful. The Holy Spirit himself pays tribute to music when he records that the evil spirit of Saul was exorcised as David played upon his harp. The fathers desired that music should always abide in the Church. That is why there are so many songs and psalms. This precious gift has been bestowed on men alone to remind them that they are created to praise and magnify the Lord. But when natural music is sharpened and polished by art, then one begins to see with amazement the great and perfect wisdom of God in his wonderful work of music, where one voice takes a simple part and around it sing three, four, or five other voices, leaping, springing round about, marvelously gracing the simple part, like a square dance in heaven with friendly bows, embracings, and hearty swinging of the partners. He who does not find this an inexpressible miracle of the Lord is truly a clod and is not worthy to be considered a man.

Not the least merit of music, according to Luther, is that it is not contentious. He was never controversial in song. The great polyphonic chorals of the Netherlands were Catholic, but Luther did not for that reason cease to love and draw from them. Again, when the dukes of Bavaria became so much his violent enemies that to receive a letter from him might endanger one in their territories, he ventured nevertheless to write to the Bavarian composer Senfl: "My love for music leads me also to hope that my letter will not endanger you in any way, for who even in Turkey would reproach one who loves the art and lauds the artist? At any rate I laud your Bavarian dukes even though they dislike me, and I honor them above all others because they cultivate and honor music." Erasmus sought to preserve the European unities in politics; Luther conserved them in music.

The polyphonic choral called for a choir. Luther was very assiduous in his efforts on behalf of trained choirs. George Rhaw, the cantor of Duke George and conductor of the twelve-part singing at the Leipzig debate, was brought to Wittenberg to serve alike as the cantor of the court choir and to the church. The choirs supported by the German princes are worthy of note because they provided ready to hand bodies of trained singers. Luther was greatly distressed when John Frederick economized by discontinuing the choir long maintained through the bounty of Frederick the Wise. By way of compensation choral societies were formed in the cities, and above all the children were trained thoroughly in the schools.

The last and greatest reform of all was in congregational song. In the Middle Ages the liturgy was almost entirely restricted to the celebrant and the choir. The congregation joined in a few responses in the vernacular. Luther so developed this element that he may be considered the father of congregational song. This was the point at which his doctrine of the priesthood of all believers received its most concrete realization. This was the point and the only point at which Lutheranism was thoroughly democratic. All the people sang. Portions of the liturgy were converted into hymns: the Creed and the *Sanctus*. The congregation sang not, "I believe," but, "We believe in one God." The congregation sang how the prophet Isaiah saw the Lord high and lifted up and heard the seraphim intone, Holy, Holy, Holy.

### HYMNBOOK

In addition in 1524 Luther brought out a hymnbook with twenty-three hymns of which he was the author and perhaps in part the composer. Twelve were free paraphrases from Latin hymnody. Six were versifications of the Psalms. His own

## QVINTA VOX. BASSVS.

### PRIMA PARS.

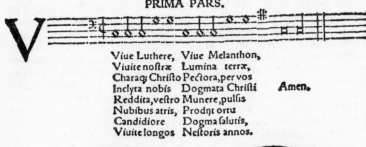

Viue Luthere, Viue Melanthon,
Viuite noſtræ Lumina terræ,
CharacꝪ Chriſto Pectora, per vos
Inclyta nobis Dogmata Chriſti
Reddita, veſtro Munere, pulſis
Nubibus atris, Prodꝫt ortu
Candidiore Dogma ſalutis,
Viuite longos Neſtoris annos.

Amen.

experiences of anguish and deliverance enabled him in such free renderings to invest the Psalms with a very personal feeling. "Out of the depths" became "In direst need." That great battle hymn of the Reformation, "A Mighty Fortress," appeared only in a later hymnbook. Here if anywhere we have both Luther's words and music, and here more than elsewhere we have the epitome of Luther's religious character. The hymn is based on the Vulgate version of the Forty-sixth Psalm, for Luther in his personal devotions continued to use the Latin on which he had been reared. Whereas in this psalm the Hebrew reads "God is our refuge." The Latin has "Our God is a refuge." Similarly Luther begins, "A mighty fortress is *our* God." Though the Forty-sixth Psalm is basic, it is handled with exceeding freedom and interwoven with many reminiscences of the Pauline epistles and the Apocalypse. Richly quarried, rugged words set to majestic tones marshal the embattled hosts of heaven. The hymn to the end strains under the overtones of cosmic conflict as the Lord God of Sabaoth smites the prince of darkness grim and vindicates the martyred saints.

Luther's people learned to sing. Practices were set during the week for the entire congregation, and in the home after the catechetical hour singing was commended to the family. A Jesuit testified that "the hymns of Luther killed more souls than his sermons." How the songs were carried to the people is disclosed in this excerpt from a chronicle of the city of Magdeburg:

On the day of St. John between Easter and Pentecost, an old man, a weaver, came through the city gate to the monument of Kaiser Otto and there offered hymns for sale while he sang them to the people. The burgomaster, coming from early mass and seeing the crowd, asked one of his servants what was going on. "There is an old scamp over there," he answered, "who is singing and selling the hymns of the heretic Luther." The burgomaster had him arrested and thrown into prison; but two hundred citizens interceded and he was released.

Among the hymns which he was singing through the streets of Magdeburg was Luther's *Aus tiefer Not*:

I cry to thee in direst need.
O God, I beg thee hear me.
To my distress I pray give heed.
O Father, draw thou near me.
If thou shouldst wish to look upon
The wrong and wickedness I've done,
How could I stand before thee?

With thee is naught but untold grace
Evermore forgiving.
We cannot stand before thy face,
Not by the best of living.
No man boasting may draw near.
All the living stand in fear.
Thy grace alone can save them.

Therefore in God I place my trust,
My own claim denying.
Believe in him alone I must,
On his sole grace relying.
He pledged to me his plighted word.
My comfort is in what I heard.
There will I hold forever.

## CHAPTER TWENTY

# THE CHURCH MINISTERIAL

ISTINGUISHED alike in the translation of the Bible, the composition of the catechism, the reform of the liturgy, and the creation of the hymnbook, Luther was equally great in the sermons preached from the pulpit, the lectures delivered in the class hall, and the prayers voiced in the upper room. His versatility is genuinely amazing. No one in his own generation was able to vie with him.

## PREACHING

The Reformation gave centrality to the sermon. The pulpit was higher than the altar, for Luther held that salvation is through the Word and without the Word the elements are devoid of sacramental quality, but the Word is sterile unless it is spoken. All of this is not to say that the Reformation invented preaching. In the century preceding Luther, for the single province of Westphalia ten thousand sermons are in print, and though they are extant only in Latin they were delivered in German. But the Reformation did exalt the sermon. All the educational devices described in the preceding chapter found their highest utilization in the pulpit. The reformers at Wittenberg undertook an extensive campaign of religious instruction through the sermon. There were three public services on Sunday: from five to six in the morning on the Pauline epistles, from nine to ten on the Gospels, and in the afternoon at a variable hour on a continuation of the theme of the morning or on the catechism. The church was not locked during the week, but on Mondays and Tuesdays there were sermons on the catechism, Wednesdays on the Gospel of Matthew, Thursdays and Fridays on the apostolic letters, and Saturday evening on John's Gospel. No one man carried this entire load. There was a staff of the clergy, but Luther's share was prodigious. Including family devotions he spoke often four times on Sundays and quarterly undertook a two-week series four days a week on the catechism. The sum of his extant sermons is 2,300. The highest count is for the year 1528, for which there are 195 sermons distributed over 145 days.

His pre-eminence in the pulpit derives in part from the earnestness with which he regarded the preaching office. The task of the minister is to expound the Word, in which alone are to be found healing for life's hurts and the balm of eternal blessedness. The preacher must die daily through concern lest he lead his flock astray. Sometimes from the pulpit Luther confessed that gladly like the priest and the Levite would he pass by on the other side. But Luther was constantly repeating to himself the advice which he gave to a discouraged preacher who complained that preaching was a burden, his sermons were always short, and he might better have stayed in his former profession. Luther said to him:

*Contrasts of the Evangelical service, where devout hearers listen with reverent attention and signs of contrition. The girl on the left is reading the Scriptures.*

*And the Catholic service, where the people lightheartedly tell their beads. The man behind the pillar is pointing in both directions.*

If Peter and Paul were here, they would scold you because you wish right off to be as accomplished as they. Crawling is something, even if one is unable to walk. Do your best. If you cannot preach an hour, then preach half an hour or a quarter of an hour. Do not try to imitate other people. Center on the shortest and simplest points, which are the very heart of the matter, and leave the rest to God. Look solely to his honor and not to applause. Pray that God will give you a mouth and to your audience ears. I can tell you preaching is not a work of man. Although I am old [he was forty-eight] and experienced, I am afraid every time I have to preach. You will most certainly find out three things: first, you will have prepared your sermon as diligently as you know how, and it will slip through your fingers like water; second, you may abandon your outline and God will give you grace. You will preach your very best. The audience will be pleased, but you won't.

And thirdly, when you have been unable in advance to pull anything together, you will preach acceptably both to your hearers and to yourself. So pray to God and leave all the rest to him.

Luther's sermons followed the course prescribed by the Christian year and the lessons assigned by long usage to each Sunday. In this area he did not innovate. Because he commonly spoke at the nine o'clock service, his sermons are mostly on the Gospels rather than upon his favorite Pauline epistles. But the text never mattered much to him. If he did not have before him the Pauline words, "The just shall live by faith," he could readily extract the same point from the example of the paralytic in the Gospels, whose sins were forgiven before his disease was cured. Year after year Luther preached on the same passages and on the same great events: Advent, Christmas, Epiphany, Lent, Easter, Pentecost. If one now reads through his sermons of thirty years on a single theme, one is amazed at the freshness with which each year he illumined some new aspect. When one has the feeling that there is nothing startling this time, then comes a flash. He is narrating the betrayal of Jesus. Judas returns the thirty pieces of silver with the words, "I have betrayed innocent blood," and the priest answers, "What is that to us?" Luther comments that there is no loneliness like the loneliness of a traitor since even his confederates give him no sympathy. The sermons cover every theme from the sublimity of God to the greed of a sow. The conclusions were often abrupt because the sermon was followed by the announcements, themselves frequently as long as the sermon because all the events of the coming week were explained with appropriate or inappropriate exhortations and castigations. A few samples from the sermons and announcements will have to suffice.

The first example shows how he would pass directly from the sermon to the announcements. The financial difficulties to which he refers had not been solved by the intervention of the prince, and each member of the congregation was therefore urged to give four pennies. Luther points out that personally he is not affected because he receives his stipend as a university professor from the prince. The following excerpts are of course exceedingly condensed.

The sermon on the 8th of November, 1528, was on the lord who forgave his servant: This lord, said Luther, is a type of the Kingdom of God. The servant was not forgiven because he had forgiven his fellow servant. On the contrary he received forgiveness before he had done anything whatever about his fellow servant. From this we see that there are two kinds of forgiveness. The first is that which we receive from God; the second is that which we exercise by bearing no ill will to any upon earth. But we must not overlook the two administrations, the civil and the spiritual, because the prince cannot and should not forgive. He has a different administration than Christ, who rules over crushed and broken hearts. The Kaiser rules over scoundrels who do not recognize their sins and mock and carry their heads high. That is why the emperor carries a sword, a sign of blood and not of peace. But Christ's kingdom is for the troubled conscience. He says, "I do not ask of you a penny, only this, that you do the same for your neighbor." And the lord in the parable does not tell the servant to found a monastery, but simply that he should have mercy on his fellow servants.

But now what shall I say to you Wittenbergers? It would be better that I preach to you the *Sachsenspiegel* [the imperial law], because you want to be Christians while still practicing usury, robbing and stealing. How do people who are so sunk in sins expect to receive forgiveness? The sword of the emperor really applies here, but my sermon is for crushed hearts who feel their sins and have no peace. Enough for this gospel.

I understand that this is the week for the church collection, and many of you do not want to give a thing. You ungrateful people should be ashamed of yourselves. You Wittenbergers have been relieved of schools and hospitals, which have been taken over by the common chest, and now you want to know why you are asked to give four pennies. They are for the ministers, schoolteachers, and sacristans. The first labor for your salvation, preach to you the precious treasure of the gospel, administer the sacraments, and visit you at great personal risk in the plague. The second train children to be good magistrates, judges, and ministers. The third care for the poor. So far the common chest has cared for these, and now that you are asked to give four miserable pennies you are up in arms. What does this mean if not that you do not want the gospel preached, the children taught, and the poor helped? I am not saying this for myself. I receive nothing from you. I am the prince's beggar. But I am sorry I ever freed you from the tyrants and the papists. You ungrateful beasts, you are not worthy of the treasure of the gospel. If you don't improve, I will stop preaching rather than cast pearls before swine.

And now another point: couples to be blessed by the curate before a wedding should come early. There are stated hours: in summer, mornings at eight and afternoons at three; in winter, mornings at nine and afternoons at two. If you come later, I will bless you myself, and you won't thank me for it. And the invited guests should prepare themselves in good time for the wedding and let not Miss Goose wait for Mrs. Duck.

On January 10th, 1529, the lesson was the wedding at Cana of Galilee. This passage, said Luther, is written in honor of marriage. There are three estates: marriage, virginity, and widowhood. They are all good. None is to be despised. The virgin is not to be esteemed above the widow, nor the widow above the wife, any more than the tailor is to be esteemed above the butcher. There is no estate to which the Devil is so opposed as to marriage. The clergy have not wanted to be bothered with work and worry. They have been afraid of a nagging wife, disobedient children, difficult relatives, or the dying of a pig or cow. They want to lie abed until the sun shines through the window. Our ancestors knew this and would say, "Dear child, be a priest or a nun and have a good time." I have heard married people say to monks, "You have it easy, but when we get up we do not know where to find our bread." Marriage is a heavy cross because so many couples quarrel. It is the grace of God when they agree. The Holy Spirit declares there are three wonders: when brothers agree, when neighbors love each other, and when a man and a wife are at one. When I see a pair like that, I am as glad as if I were in a garden of roses. It is rare.

### SERMON ON THE NATIVITY

Luther is at his best and most characteristic in his sermons on the Nativity. The entire recital appears utterly artless, but by way of preparation he had steeped himself in the interpretations of the story by Augustine, Bernard, Tauler, and Ludwig of Saxony, the author of a life of Christ. All that thus had preceded was infused by Luther with the profundities of his theology and vitalized by his graphic imagination. Here is an example:

How unobstrusively and simply do those events take place on earth that are so heralded in heaven! On earth it happened in this wise: There was a poor young wife, Mary of Nazareth, among the meanest dwellers of the town, so little esteemed that none noticed the great wonder that she carried. She was silent, did not vaunt herself, but served her husband, who had no man or maid. They simply left the house. Perhaps they had a donkey for Mary to ride upon, though the Gospels say nothing about it, and we may well believe that she went on foot. The journey was certainly more than a day from Nazareth in Galilee to Bethlehem, which lies on the farther side of Jerusalem. Joseph had thought, "When we get to Bethlehem, we shall be among relatives and can borrow everything." A fine idea that was! Bad enough that a young bride married only a year could not have had her baby at Nazareth in her own house instead of making all that journey of three days when heavy with child! How much worse that when she arrived there was no room for her! The inn was full. No one would release a room to this pregnant woman. She had to go to a cow stall and there bring forth the Maker of all creatures because nobody would give way. Shame on you, wretched Bethlehem! The inn ought to have been burned with brimstone, for even though Mary had been a beggar maid or unwed, anybody at such a time should have been glad to give her a hand. There are many of you in this congregation who think to yourselves: "If only I had been there! How quick I would have been to help the Baby! I would have washed his linen. How happy I would have been to go with the shepherds to see the Lord lying in the manger!" Yes, you would! You say that because you know how great Christ is, but if you had been there at that time you would have done no better than the people of Bethlehem. Childish and silly thoughts are these! Why don't you do it now?

You have Christ in your neighbor. You ought to serve him, for what you do to your neighbor in need you do to the Lord Christ himself. The birth was still more pitiable. No one regarded this young wife bringing forth her first-born. No one took her condition to heart. No one noticed that in a strange place she had not the very least thing needful in childbirth. There she was without preparation: no light, no fire, in the dead of night, in thick darkness. No one came to give the customary assistance. The guests swarming in the inn were carousing, and no one attended to this woman. I think myself if Joseph and Mary had realized that her time was so close she might perhaps have been left in Nazareth. And now think what she could use for swaddling clothes—some garment she could spare, perhaps her veil—certainly not Joseph's breeches, which are now on exhibition at Aachen.

"THE NATIVITY" FROM LUTHER'S BIBLE OF 1534

*On the left is Luther's seal. He desired that the cross be black for mortification, the rose white for the joy of faith, the field blue for the joy of heaven, and the ring gold for eternal blessedness.*

Think, women, there was no one there to bathe the Baby. No warm water, nor even cold. No fire, no light. The mother was herself midwife and the maid. The cold manger was the bed and the bathtub. Who showed the poor girl what to do? She had never had a baby before. I am amazed that the little one did not freeze. Do not make of Mary a stone. For the higher people are in the favor of God, the more tender are they.

Let us, then, meditate upon the Nativity just as we see it happening in our own babies. Behold Christ lying in the lap of his young mother. What can be sweeter than the Babe, what more lovely than the mother! What fairer than her youth! What more gracious than her virginity! Look at the Child, knowing nothing. Yet all that is belongs to him, that your conscience should not fear but take comfort in him. Doubt nothing. To me there is no greater consolation given to mankind than this, that Christ became man, a child, a babe, playing in the lap and at the breasts of his most gracious mother. Who is there whom this sight would not comfort?

Now is overcome the power of sin, death, hell, conscience, and guilt, if you come to this gurgling Babe and believe that he is come, not to judge you, but to save.

## EXPOSITION OF JONAH

As Luther's sermons were often didactic, so were his lectures commonly sermonic. He was always teaching, whether in the classroom or the pulpit; and he was always preaching, whether in the pulpit or the classroom. His lectures on Jonah are even more of a sermon than many preached in the Castle Church. Luther handled Jonah as he did every other biblical character—as a mirror of his own experience. Here is a digest of the exposition.

Jonah was sent to rebuke the mighty king of Assyria. That took courage. If we had been there, we should have thought it silly that one single man should attack such an empire. How silly it would seem for one of us to go on such a mission to the Turks. And how ridiculous often it has appeared that a single man should rebuke the pope. But God's work always appears as folly.

"And Jonah took ship for Tarshish." The godless think they can get away from God by going to a town where he is not recognized. Why did Jonah refuse? First because the assignment was very great. No prophet had ever been chosen to go to the heathen. Another reason was that he felt the enmity of Nineveh. He thought God was only the God of the Jews, and he would rather be dead than proclaim the grace of God to the heathen.

Then God sent a great wind. Why should he have involved the other passengers in Jonah's punishment? We are not the ones to lay down rules for God, and for that matter the other persons on the boat were not innocent. We have all transgressed. The storm must have been very sudden because the people felt that it must have an unusual cause. Natural reason taught the sailors that God is God. The light of reason is a great light, but it fails in that it is ready to believe that God is God, but not to believe that God is God *to you*. These people called on God. This proves that they believed he was God, that is to others, but they did not really believe he would help them, otherwise they would not have thrown Jonah overboard. They did their uttermost to save the ship like the papists who try to be saved by works.

Jonah was asleep in the hold. Men are like that when they have sinned. They feel no compunction. If God had forgotten his sin, Jonah would never have given it another thought. But when he was awakened and saw the state of the ship he recognized his guilt. His conscience became active. Then he felt the sting of death and the anger of God. Not only the ship but the whole world was too small for him. He admitted his fault and cleared all the others. This is what contrition does. It makes all the world innocent and yourself only a sinner. But Jonah was not yet ready to make a public acknowledgment. He let the sailors wrestle until God made it plain that they would all perish with him. No one would confess. They had to cast lots. Wounds cannot be healed until they are revealed, and sins cannot be forgiven until they are confessed. Some say that they sinned in casting lots, but I cannot see that lot-casting is forbidden in Scripture.

Then Jonah said, "I am a Hebrew. I fear the God who made heaven and earth." The weight of sin and conscience is made greater if confessed. Then faith begins to burn, albeit weakly. When God's wrath overtakes us there are always two things, sin and anxiety. Some allow the sin to stand and center on the anxiety. That won't do. Reason does this when faith and grace are not present.

Jonah confessed his sin to be all the greater when he said, "I am a Hebrew and a worshiper of the true God." This made him all the more inexcusable. And Jonah said, "Throw me into the sea." The sailors thought confession was enough, and they set to work again on the oars. Jonah had to plumb the shame which was a thousand times greater because it was against God. For such a one there is no corner into which he may creep, no, not even in hell. He did not foresee his deliverance. God takes all honor and all comfort away and leaves only shame and desolation.

Then came death, for the sting of death is sin. Jonah pronounced his own sentence, "Throw me into the sea." We must always remember that Jonah could not see to the end. He saw only death, death, death. The worst of it was that this death was due to God's anger. It would not be so bad to die as a martyr, but when death is a punishment it is truly horrible. Who does not tremble before death, even though he does not feel the wrath of God? But if there be also sin and conscience, who can endure shame before God and the world? What a struggle must have taken place in Jonah's heart. He must have sweat blood. He had to fight against sin, against his own conscience, the feeling of his heart, against death, and against God's anger all at once.

As if the sea were not enough, God prepared a great fish. As the monster opened its frightful jaws, the teeth were jagged like mountain peaks. The waves rushed in and swept Jonah into the belly. What a picture is this of *Anfechtung*. Just so the conscience wilts before the wrath of God, death, hell, and damnation. "And Jonah was three days and three nights in the belly of the whale." Those were the longest three days and three nights that ever happened under the sun. His lungs and liver pounded. He would hardly have looked around to see his habitation. He was thinking, "When, when, when will this end?"

How could anyone imagine that a man could be three days and three nights in the belly of a fish without light, without food, absolutely alone, and come out alive? Who would not take this for a fairy tale if it were not in Scripture?

But God is even in hell.

"And Jonah prayed unto the Lord from the belly of the whale." I do not believe he could compose such a fine psalm while he was down there, but this shows what he was thinking. He was not expecting his salvation. He thought he must die, yet he prayed, "I cried by reason of mine affliction unto the Lord." This shows that we must always pray to God. If you can just cry, your agony is over. Hell is not hell any more if you can cry to God. But no one can believe how hard this is. We can understand wailing, trembling, sighing, doubting, but to cry out, this is what we cannot do. Conscience, sin, and the wrath of God are about our necks. Nature cannot cry out. When Jonah reached the point that he could cry, he had won. Cry unto the Lord in your anguish, and it will be milder. Just cry and nothing else. He does not ask about your merit. Reason does not understand this, and always wants to bring in something to placate God. But there just is nothing to bring. Reason does not believe that all that is needed to quiet God's anger is a cry.

"All thy waves and thy billows are gone over me." Observe that Jonah calls them *thy* waves. If a wind-blown leaf can affright a host, what must not the sea have done to Jonah? And what will not the majesty of God at the judgment day do to all angels and all creatures? "My soul melted within me, and I thought of the Lord." This is to turn from the God of judgment to God the Father. But this does not lie in the power of man. "I will sacrifice unto thee with the voice of thanksgiving, I will pay that I had vowed." "And the Lord spake unto the fish, and it cast Jonah forth upon the dry land." The instrument of death is become the agency of life.

### PRAYER

Luther was above all else a man of prayer, and yet of his prayers we have less than of his sermons and conversations because he succeeded in keeping his students out of the secret chamber. There are the collects which he composed for the liturgy, the prayer for the sacristy, and a prayer reputed to have been overheard by his roommate at Worms. We are on safer ground in the following excerpts from his exposition of the Lord's Prayer:

Luther instructs his readers to say: O Heavenly Father, dear God, I am not worthy that I should lift up mine eyes or my hands to thee in prayer, but since thou hast commanded us to pray and hast taught us how through Jesus Christ our Lord, I will say, "Give us this day our daily bread." O dear Lord Father, give us thy blessing in this earthly life. Give us graciously thy peace and spare us from war. Grant to our Kaiser wisdom and understanding that he may govern his earthly kingdom in peace and blessedness. Give to all kings, princes, and lords good counsel that they may direct their lands in quietness and justice, and especially guard the ruler of our dear land. Protect him from malignant tongues, and instill into all subjects grace to serve in fidelity and obedience. Bestow on us good weather and the fruits of the earth. We commend unto thee house, grounds, wife, and child. Help that we may govern, nourish, and rear. Ward off the Corrupter and the evil angels who impede these things. Amen.

"Forgive us our trespasses, as we forgive those who trespass against us." Dear Lord and Father, enter not into judgment with us, since before thee is no man living justified. Reckon not unto us our transgressions and that we are so ungrateful of all thy unspeakable mercies of the spirit and of the body, and that we daily fail more than we know or are aware. Mark not how good or evil we be, but vouchsafe to us thy unmerited mercy through Jesus

Christ, thy dear Son. Forgive also all our enemies and all who
have hurt and done us wrong as we also forgive them from our
hearts, for they do themselves the greatest wrong in that they
kindle thee against them. But we are not helped by their loss and
would much rather that they be blessed. Amen. (And if anyone
here feels that he cannot forgive, let him pray for grace that he
may. But that is a point which belongs to preaching.)

CHAPTER TWENTY-ONE

# THE STRUGGLE FOR FAITH

---

 LWAYS more intimately personal than his
teaching and preaching was Luther's pas-
toral counseling. Neither in the classroom
nor in the pulpit was the personal ever
wholly absent. But when the physician was
engaged in the cure of souls, he drew almost
exclusively on that which he had himself
discovered to be good for like ailments. For
that reason any consideration of what he did for others by way
of allaying spiritual distress must take the form of the further
analysis of his own maladies and of the remedies which he
found to be of avail alike for himself and for others.

### LUTHER'S PERSISTENT STRUGGLE

At the outset the recognition is inescapable that he had
persistent maladies. This man who so undergirded others with
faith had for himself a perpetual battle for faith. Perhaps the
severest upheaval of his whole life came in the year 1527. The
recurrence of these depressions raises for us again the question
whether they may have had some physical basis, and the question really cannot be answered. The attempt to discover a cor-
relation between his many diseases and the despondencies has
proved unsuccessful, and one must not forget in this connection that his spiritual ailments were acute in the monastery
before the physical had begun. To discover a connection with
outward events is more plausible. Crises were precipitated by a
thunderstorm, by the saying of the first mass, and in 1527 by
the total impact of the radicals, coupled with the fact that

Luther was still sleeping in his own bed while his followers were dying for the faith. As he came out from under the state of shock which overtook him, he was wrestling with the self-reproach of being still alive. "I was not worthy," he was saying, "to shed my blood for Christ as many of my fellow confessors of the gospel have done. Yet this honor was denied to the beloved disciple, John the Evangelist, who wrote a much worse book against the papacy than ever I did." Although

MARTYRDOM OF HEINRICH OF ZUETPHEN

outward events affected him, the very nature of the dark night of the soul is that it may be occasioned by nothing tangible whatever. Physical debilitation was more often the effect than the cause.

The content of the depressions was always the same, the loss of faith that God is good and that he is good to *me*. After the frightful *Anfechtung* of 1527 Luther wrote, "For more than a week I was close to the gates of death and hell. I trembled in

# The Struggle For Faith

all my members. Christ was wholly lost. I was shaken by desperation and blasphemy of God." His agony in the later years was all the more intense because he was a physician of souls; and if the medicine which he had prescribed for himself and for them was actually poison, how frightful was his responsibility. The great problem for him was not to know where his depressions came from, but to know how to overcome them. In the course of repeated utterances on the subject he worked out a technique for himself and for his parishioners.

The first comfort which he offered was the reflection that intense upheavals of the spirit are necessary for valid solutions of genuine religious problems. The emotional reactions may be unduly acute, for the Devil always turns a louse into a camel. Nevertheless the way of man with God cannot be tranquil.

If I live longer, I would like to write a book about *Anfechtungen,* for without them no man can understand Scripture, faith, the fear or the love of God. He does not know the meaning of hope who was never subject to temptations.

David must have been plagued by a very fearful devil. He could not have had such profound insights if he had not experienced great assaults.

Luther verged on saying that an excessive emotional sensitivity is a mode of revelation. Those who are predisposed to fall into despondency as well as to rise into ecstasy may be able to view reality from an angle different from that of ordinary folk. Yet it is a true angle; and when the problem or the religious object has been once so viewed, others less sensitive will be able to look from a new vantage point and testify that the insight is valid.

### HIS DEPRESSIONS

Luther felt that his depressions were necessary. At the same time they were dreadful and by all means and in every way to be avoided and overcome. His whole life was a struggle against them, a fight for faith. This is the point at which he interests us so acutely, for we too are cast down and we too would know how to assuage our despondency. Luther had two methods: the one was a head-on attack, the other an approach by way of indirection. Sometimes he would engage in direct encounter with the Devil. This particular *mise en scène* may amuse the modern reader and incline him not to take Luther seriously; but it is noteworthy that what the Devil says to Luther is only what one says to oneself in moments of introspection, and, what is still more significant, only the minor difficulties were referred to the Devil. In all the major encounters, God himself was the assailant. The Devil was something of a relief. Luther relished, by comparison, the personification of his enemy in the form of a being whom he could bait without danger of blasphemy. He describes with gusto some of these bouts:

When I go to bed, the Devil is always waiting for me. When he begins to plague me, I give him this answer: "Devil, I must sleep. That's God's command, 'Work by day. Sleep by night.' So go away." If that doesn't work and he brings out a catalog of sins, I say, "Yes, old fellow, I know all about it. And I know some more you have overlooked. Here are a few extra. Put them down." If he still won't quit and presses me hard and accuses me as a sinner, I scorn him and say, "St. Satan, pray for me. Of course you have never done anything wrong in your life. You alone are holy. Go to God and get grace for yourself. If you want to get me all straightened out, I say, 'Physician, heal thyself.' "

Sometimes Luther had the temerity to undertake also the greater encounter with God himself. "I dispute much with God with great impatience," said he, "and I hold him to his promises." The Canaanite woman was a source of unending wonder and comfort to Luther because she had the audacity to argue with Christ. When she asked him to come and cure her daughter, he answered that he was not sent but to the lost sheep of the house of Israel, and that it was not meet to take the children's bread and give it to the dogs. She did not dispute his judgment. She agreed that she was a dog. She asked no more than that which befits a dog, to lick up the crumbs which fall from the children's table. She took Christ at his own words. He then treated her not as a dog but as a child of Israel.

All this is written for our comfort that we should see how deeply God hides his face and how we must not go by our feeling but only by his Word. All Christ's answers sounded like no, but he did not mean no. He had not said that she was not of the house of Israel. He had not said that she was a dog. He had not said no. Yet all his answers were more like no than yes. This shows how our heart feels in despondency. It sees nothing but a plain no. Therefore it must turn to the deep hidden yes under the no and hold with a firm faith to God's word.

### THE WAY OF INDIRECTION

At times, however, Luther advised against any attempt to wrestle one's way through. "Don't argue with the Devil," he said. "He has had five thousand years of experience. He has tried out all his tricks on Adam, Abraham, and David, and he knows exactly the weak spots." And he is persistent. If he does not get you down with the first assault, he will commence a siege of attrition until you give in from sheer exhaustion. Better banish the whole subject. Seek company and discuss some irrelevant matter as, for example, what is going on in Venice. Shun solitude. "Eve got into trouble when she walked in the garden alone. I have my worst temptations when I am

by myself." Seek out some Christian brother, some wise counselor. Undergird yourself with the fellowship of the church.
Then, too, seek convivial company, feminine company, dine,
dance, joke, and sing. Make yourself eat and drink even though
food may be very distasteful. Fasting is the very worst expedient. Once Luther gave three rules for dispelling despondency:
the first is faith in Christ; the second is to get downright angry;
the third is the love of a woman. Music was especially commended. The Devil hates it because he cannot endure gaiety.
Luther's physician relates that on one occasion he came with
some friends for a musical soiree only to find Luther in a
swoon; but when the others struck up the song, he was soon
one of the party. Home life was a comfort and a diversion. So
also was the presence of his wife when the Devil assaulted him
in the night watches. "Then I turn to my Katie and say, 'Forbid me to have such temptations, and recall me from such vain
vexations.' "

**DEVIL AND DEATH HARASS
A SOUL**

Manual labor was a relief. A
good way, counseled Luther,
to exorcise the Devil is to
harness the horse and spread
manure on the fields. In all
this advice to flee the fray
Luther was in a way prescrib-
ing faith as a cure for the
lack of faith. To give up the
argument is of itself an act of
faith akin to the *Gelassenheit*
of the mystics, an expression
of confidence in the restora-
tive power of God, who operates in the subconscious
while man occupies himself
with extraneous things.

This explains why Luther
liked to watch those who take life blithely, such as birds and
babies. When he saw his little Martin nursing, he remarked,
"Child, your enemies are the pope, the bishops, Duke George,
Ferdinand, and the Devil. And there you are sucking uncon-
cernedly."

When Anastasia, then four years old, was prattling of
Christ, angels, and heaven, Luther said, "My dear child, if
only we could hold fast to this faith."

"Why, papa," said she, "don't you believe it?"

Luther commented:

Christ has made the children our teachers. I am chagrined that
although I am ever so much a doctor, I still have to go to the same
school with Hans and Magdalena, for who among men can understand the full meaning of this word of God, "Our Father who art

in heaven"? Anyone who genuinely believes these words will often say, "I am the Lord of heaven and earth and all that is therein. The Angel Gabriel is my servant, Raphael is my guardian, and the angels in my every need are ministering spirits. My Father, who is in heaven, will give them charge over me lest I dash my foot against a stone." And while I am affirming this faith, my Father suffers me to be thrown into prison, drowned, or beheaded. Then faith falters and in weakness I cry, "Who knows whether it is true?"

### WRESTLING WITH THE ANGEL

Merely watching children could not answer that question. The encounter had to be resumed on the direct level. If Luther was disturbed about the state of the world and the state of the Church, he could gain reassurance only through the recognition that as a matter of plain fact the situation was not bad. Despite the many pessimistic judgments of his later years Luther could say, "I entertain no sorry picture of our Church, but rather that of the Church flourishing through pure and uncorrupted teaching and one increasing with excellent ministers from day to day."

At other times the depression was with regard to himself. One recalls his oscillation of feeling at the Wartburg as to whether he had been brash or craven. The answer in his own case could never be that he had any claim on God, and then the question forever recurred whether God would then be gracious. When one is assailed by this doubt, where shall one turn? Luther would say that one never knows where, but always somewhere. To inquire after the starting point of Luther's theology is futile. It begins where it can. Christ himself appears variable, sometimes as a good Shepherd and sometimes as the avenging Judge. If then Christ appeared hostile, Luther would turn to God and would recall the first commandment, "I am the Lord thy God." This very pronouncement is at the same time a promise, and God must be held to his promises.

In such a case we must say, "Let go everything in which I have trusted. Lord, thou alone givest help and comfort. Thou hast said that thou wouldst help me. I believe thy word. O my God and Lord, I have heard from thee a joyful and comforting word. I hold to it. I know thou wilt not lie to me. No matter how thou mayest appear, thou wilt keep what thou hast promised, that and nothing else."

On the other hand, if God hides himself in the storm clouds which brood over the brow of Sinai, then gather about the manger, look upon the infant Jesus as he leaps in the lap of his mother, and know that the hope of the world is here. Or again, if Christ and God alike are unapproachable, then look upon the firmament of the heavens and marvel at the work of

God, who sustains them without pillars. Or take the meanest flower and see in the smallest petal the handiwork of God.

All the external aids of religion are to be prized. Luther attached great importance to his baptism. When the Devil assailed him, he would answer, "I am baptized." In his conflicts with the Catholics and the radicals he reassured himself similarly by making appeal to his doctorate. This gave him authority and the right to speak.

Des lutters gestalt mag wol verderbenn
Sein cristlich gmuet wirt nymer sterben
D · XXIII · D

### THE ROCK OF SCRIPTURE

But always and above all else the one great objective aid for Luther was the Scriptures, because this is the written record of the revelation of God in Christ. "The true Christian pilgrimage is not to Rome, or Compostela, but to the prophets, the Psalms, and the Gospels." The Scriptures assumed for Luther an overwhelming importance, not primarily as a source book for antipapal polemic, but as the one ground of certainty. He had rejected the authority of popes and councils, and could not make a beginning from within as did the prophets of the inward word. The core of his quarrel with them was that in moments of despondency he could find nothing within but utter blackness. He was completely lost unless he could find something without on which to lay hold. And this he found in the Scriptures.

He approached them uncritically, from our point of view, but not with credulity. Nothing so amazed him in all the biblical record as the faith of the participants: that Mary credited the annunciation of the angel Gabriel; that Joseph gave credence to the dream which allayed his misgivings; that the shepherds believed the opening of the heavens and the angels' song; that the Wise Men were ready to go to Bethlehem at the word of the prophet. There were three miracles of the Nativity: that God became man, that a virgin conceived, and that Mary believed. And the greatest of these was the last. When the Wise Men relied upon their judgment and went straight to Jerusalem without consulting the star, God lifted it out of heaven and left them bewildered to make inquiry of Herod, who then called his wise men and they searched the Scriptures. And that is what we must do when we are bereft of the star.

But this is just the point where Luthers' lead begins to elude us. We can follow him well enough in the description of his distress. It is when he offers us this way out that we are cast down. Must we leave him now like some Vergil in Purgatory and seek in another the Beatrice who may be able to conduct us to Paradise? Perhaps a word of Luther may help us, after all, for he declared tnat the gospel is not so much a miracle as a marvel, *non miracula sed mirabilia*. There is no better way to feel the wonder than to take Luther as guide. Let him portray for us, with all his power and poignancy, the spiritual despondencies of the biblical characters and the way in which they were able to find the hand of the Lord.

We have already seen an example in the case of his treatment of Jonah. By way of further illustration let us take his portrayal of the sacrifice of Isaac by Abraham. Save for the initial assumption that God commanded the sacrifice and that the angel intervened in the end, all else is the record of an inner struggle which is not hard to translate into the story of an emerging insight or an unfolding revelation. Hear Luther as he expounds the tale:

Abraham was told by God that he must sacrifice the son of his old age by a miracle, the seed through whom he was to become the father of kings and of a great nation. Abraham turned pale. Not only would he lose his son, but God appeared to be a liar. He had said, "In Isaac shall be thy seed," but now he said, "Kill Isaac." Who would not hate a God so cruel and contradictory? How Abraham longed to talk it over with someone! Could he not tell Sarah? But he well knew that if he mentioned it to anyone he would be dissuaded and prevented from carrying out the behest. The spot designated for the sacrifice, Mount Moriah, was some distance away; "and Abraham rose up early in the morning, and saddled his ass, and took two of his young men with him, and Isaac his son, and clave the wood for the burnt-offering." Abraham did not leave the saddling of the ass to others. He himself laid on the beast the wood for the burnt offering. He was thinking all the time that these logs would consume his son, his hope of seed. With these very sticks that he was picking up the boy would be burned. In such a terrible case should he not take time to think it over? Could he not tell Sarah? With what inner tears he suffered! He girt the ass and was so absorbed he scarcely knew what he was doing.

He took two servants and Isaac his son. In that moment everything died in him: Sarah, his family, his home, Isaac. This is what it is to sit in sackcloth and ashes. If he had known that this was only a trial, he would not have been tried. Such is the nature of our trials that while they last we cannot see to the end. "Then on the third day Abraham lifted up his eyes, and saw the place afar off." What a battle he had endured in those three days! There Abraham left the servants and the ass, and he laid the wood upon Isaac and himself took the torch and the sacrificial knife. All the time he was thinking, "Isaac, if you knew, if your mother knew that you are to be sacrificed." "And they went both of them together." The whole world does not know what here took place. They two walked together. Who? The father and the dearest son —the one not knowing what was in store but ready to obey, the other certain that he must leave his son in ashes. Then said Isaac, "My father." And he said, "Yes, my son." And Isaac said, "Father, here is the fire and here the wood, but where is the lamb?" He called him father and was solicitous lest he had overlooked something, and Abraham said, "God will himself provide a lamb, my son."

When they were come to the mount, Abraham built the altar and laid on the wood, and then he was forced to tell Isaac. The boy was stupefied. He must have protested, "Have you forgotten: I am the son of Sarah by a miracle in her age, that I was promised and that through me you are to be the father of a great nation?" And Abraham must have answered that God would fulfill his promise even out of ashes. Then Abraham bound him and laid him upon the wood. The father raised his knife. The boy bared his throat. If God had slept an instant, the lad would have been dead. I could not have watched. I am not able in my thoughts to follow. The lad was as a sheep for the slaughter. Never in history was there such obedience, save only in Christ. But God was watching, and all the angels. The father raised his knife; the boy did not wince. The angel cried, "Abraham, Abraham!" See how divine majesty is at hand in the hour of death. We say, "In the midst of life we die." God answers, "Nay, in the midst of death we live."

Luther once read this story for family devotions. When he had finished, Katie said, "I do not believe it. God would not have treated his son like that."

"But, Katie," answered Luther, "he did."

Hear Luther also as he describes the passion of Christ. The narrative is placed on a most human level. We are reminded that the death of Christ was of all the most terrible because it was an execution. This means death at a known moment for one who is fully aware of what is involved. In old age the angel of death often muffles his wings and permits us to slip peacefully away. Jesus went to his death in full possession of his faculties. He suffered even more than did the malefactors. A robber was simply crucified, not at the same time reviled. To Christ were spoken words of raillery, "If you are the Son of God, come down." As if to say, "God is just. He would not suffer an innocent man to die upon a cross." Christ at this point was simply a man, and it was for him as it is for me when the Devil comes and says, "You are mine." After the reviling of Christ, the sun was darkened and the earth trembled. If a troubled conscience shudders at the rustling of a wind-blown leaf, how much more terrible must it have been when the sun was blotted out and the earth was shaken. Christ was driven to a cry of desperation. The words are recorded in the original tongue that we may sense the stark desolation: *Eli, Eli, lama sabachthani?* "My God, my God, why hast thou forsaken me?" But note this, the prayer of the forsaken began, *"My God."* The cry of despair was a confession of faith.

What wonder then that Luther, in the year of his deepest depression, composed these lines:

> A mighty bulwark is our God
> A doughty ward and weapon.
> He helps us clear from every rod
> By which we now are smitten.
> Still our ancient foe
> Girds him to strike a blow.
> Might and guile his gear.
> His armor striketh fear.
> On earth is not his equal.

By our own strength is nothing won.
　We court at once disaster.
There fights for us the Champion
　Whom God has named our Master.
Would you know his name?
Jesus Christ the same
Lord Sabaoth is he.
No other God can be.
　The field is his to hold it.

"A MIGHTY FORTRESS" IN LUTHER'S HAND

And though the fiends on every hand
　Were threatening to devour us,
We would not waver from our stand.
　They cannot overpower us.
This world's prince may rave.
However he behave,
He can do no ill.
God's truth abideth still.
　One little word shall fell him.

That word they never can dismay.
　However much they batter,
For God himself is in the fray
　And nothing else can matter.

Then let them take our life,
Goods, honor, children, wife.
We will let all go.
They shall not conquer so,
  For God will win the battle.

CHAPTER TWENTY-TWO

# THE MEASURE OF THE MAN

 HE LAST sixteen years of Luther's life, from the Augsburg Confession in 1530 to his death in 1546, are commonly treated more cursorily by biographers than the earlier period, if indeed they are not omitted altogether. There is a measure of justification for this comparative neglect because the last quarter of Luther's life was neither determinative for his ideas nor crucial for his achievements. His own verdict in 1531 was more than a grim jest, namely, "Should the papists by their devouring, biting, tearing help me to put off this sinful carcass and should the Lord not wish this time to deliver me as he has so often done before, then may he be praised and thanked. I have lived long enough. Not until I am gone will they feel Luther's full weight." He was right; his ideas were matured; his church was established; his associates could carry on, as indeed in the public sphere they were compelled to do because for the remainder of his life he was under the ban of Church and state.

### THE BIGAMY OF THE LANDGRAVE

This exile from the public scene chafed him the more because the conflicts and the labors of the dramatic years had impaired his health and made him prematurely an irascible old man, petulant, peevish, unrestrained, and at times positively coarse. This is no doubt another reason why biographers prefer to be brief in dealing with this period. There are several incidents over which one would rather draw the veil, but precisely because they are so often exploited to his discredit they are not to be left unrecorded. The most notorious was his attitude toward the bigamy of the landgrave, Philip of Hesse. This prince had been given in marriage with no regard to his own affections—that is, for purely political reasons—at the age of nineteen to the daughter of Duke George. Philip, unable to combine romance with marriage, found his satisfaction promiscuously on the outside. After his conversion his conscience so troubled him that he dared not present himself at the Lord's Table. He believed that if he could have one partner to whom he was genuinely attached he would be able to keep himself within the bounds of matrimony. There were several ways in which his difficulty could have been solved. If he had remained a Catholic, he might have been able to secure an annulment on the grounds of some defect in the marriage; but since he had become a Lutheran, he could expect no consideration from the pope. Nor would Luther permit recourse to the Catholic device. A second solution would have been divorce and remarriage. A great many Protestant bodies in the present day would countenance this method, particularly since Philip had been subjected in his youth to a loveless match. But Luther at this point interpreted the Gospels rigidly and held to the word of Christ as reported by Matthew that divorce is permissible only for adultery. But Luther did feel that there should be some remedy, and he discovered it by a reversion to the mores of the Old Testament patriarchs, who had practiced bigamy and even polygamy without any manisfestation of divine displeasure. Philip was given the assurance that he might in good conscience take a second wife. Since, however, to do so would be against the law of the land, he should keep the union a secret. This the new bride's mother declined to do; and then Luther counseled a lie on the ground that his advice had been given as in the confessional, and to guard the secrets of the confessional a lie is justified. But the secret was out, and the disavowal was ineffective. Luther's final comment was that if anyone thereafter should practice bigamy, let the Devil give him a bath in the abyss of hell.

The whole episode had disastrous political consequences for the Protestant movement because Philip, in order to secure pardon from the emperor, had to dissociate himself from a military alliance with the Protestants. The scene of Philip abjectly seeking grace from His Imperial Majesty has a certain irony because Charles deposited illegitimate children all over Europe, whom the pope legitimatized in order that they might occupy high offices of state. Luther's solution of the problem can be called only a pitiable subterfuge. He should first have directed his attack against the evil system of degrading marriage to the level of a political convenience, and he might well have adopted the later Protestant solution of divorce.

## ATTITUDE TO THE ANABAPTISTS

The second development of those later years was a hardening toward sectaries, notably the Anabaptists. Their growth constituted a very real problem to the territorial church, since despite the decree of death visited upon them at the Diet of Speyer in 1529 with the concurrence of the Evangelicals, the intrepidity and irreproachable lives of the martyrs had enlisted converts to the point of threatening to depopulate the established churches. Philip of Hesse observed more improvement of life among the sectaries than among the Lutherans, and a Lutheran minister who wrote against the Anabaptists testified that they went in among the poor, appeared very lowly, prayed much, read from the Gospel, talked especially about the outward life and good works, about helping the neighbor, giving and lending, holding goods in common, exercising authority over none, and living with all as brothers and sisters. Such were the people executed by Elector John in Saxony. But the blood of the martyrs proved again to be the seed of the church.

Luther was very much distraught over the whole matter. In 1527 he wrote with regard to the Anabaptists:

It is not right, and I am deeply troubled that the poor people are so pitifully put to death, burned, and cruelly slain. Let everyone believe what he likes. If he is wrong, he will have punishment enough in hell fire. Unless there is sedition, one should oppose them with Scripture and God's Word. With fire you won't get anywhere.

This obviously did not mean, however, that Luther considered one faith as good as another. Most emphatically he believed that the wrong faith would entail hell-fire; and although the

THE ANABAPTIST PREACHER

true faith cannot be created by coercion, it can be relieved of impediments. The magistrate certainly should not suffer the faith to be blasphemed. In 1530 Luther advanced the view that two offenses should be penalized even with death, namely sedition and blasphemy. The emphasis was thus shifted from incorrect belief to its public manifestation by word and deed. This was, however, no great gain for liberty, because Luther construed mere abstention from public office and military service as sedition and a rejection of an article of the Apostles' Creed as blasphemy.

In a memorandum of 1531, composed by Melanchthon and signed by Luther, a rejection of the ministerial office was described as insufferable blasphemy, and the disintegration of the Church as sedition against the ecclesiastical order. In a memorandum of 1536, again composed by Melanchthon and signed by Luther, the distinction between the peaceful and the revolutionary Anabaptists was obliterated. Philip of Hesse had asked several cities and universities for advice as to what he should do with some thirty Anabaptists whom he was holding under arrest. He had steadfastly refused to inflict the death penalty and had resorted to no more than banishment. But this was ineffective because the Anabaptists argued that the earth is the Lord's and refused to stay away. Of all the replies which Philip received those from the Lutherans were the most severe. Melanchthon this time argued that even the passive action of the Anabaptists in rejecting government, oaths, private property, and marriages outside of the faith was itself disruptive of the civil order and therefore seditious. The Anabaptist protest against the punishment of blasphemy was itself blasphemy. The discontinuance of infant baptism would produce a heathen society and separation from the Church, and the formation of sects was an offense against God.

Luther may not have been too happy about signing these memoranda. At any rate he appended postscripts to each. To the first he said, "I assent. Although it seems cruel to punish them with the sword, it is crueler that they condemn the ministry of the Word and have no well-grounded doctrine and suppress the true and in this way seek to subvert the civil order." Luther's addition to the second document was a plea that severity be tempered with mercy. In 1540 he is reported in his *Table Talk* to have returned to the position of Philip of Hesse that only seditious Anabaptists should be executed; the others should be merely banished. But Luther passed by many an opportunity to speak a word for those who with joy gave themselves as sheep for the slaughter. One would have thought that he might have been moved by the case of Fritz Erbe, who died at the Wartburg after sixteen years of incarceration. As to the effectiveness of such severity Luther might have pondered had he learned that the steadfastness of Erbe

had converted one half of the populace of Eisenach to Anabaptism.

For the understanding of Luther's position one must bear in
mind that Anabaptism was not in every instance socially innocuous. The year in which Luther signed the memorandum
counseling death even for the peaceful Anabaptists was the
year in which a group of them ceased to be peaceful. Goaded
by ten years of incessant persecution, bands of fanatics in
1534 received a revelation from the Lord that they should no
more be as sheep for the slaughter but rather as the angel with
the sickle to reap the harvest. By forcible measures they took
over the city of Münster in Westphalia and there inaugurated
the reign of the saints, of which Thomas Müntzer had
dreamed. Catholics and Protestants alike conjoined to suppress
the reign of the new Daniels and Elijahs. The whole episode
did incalculable damage to the reputation of the Anabaptists,
who before and after were peaceable folk. But this one instance of rebellion engendered the fear that sheep's clothing
concealed wolves who might better be dealt with before they
threw off the disguise. In Luther's case it should further be remembered that the leading Anabaptist in Thuringia was Melchior Rink, and he had been with Thomas Müntzer at the
battle of Frankenhausen. Yet when all of these attenuating
considerations are adduced, one cannot forget that Melanchthon's memorandum justified the eradication of the peaceful,
not because they were incipient and clandestine revolutionaries, but on the ground that even a peaceful renunciation of
the state itself constituted sedition.

The other point to remember alike in the case of Luther and
Melanchthon is that they were quite as much convinced as was
the church of the inquisition that the truth of God can be
known, and being known lays supreme obligations upon mankind to preserve it unsullied. The Anabaptists were regarded
as the corrupters of souls. Luther's leniency toward them is the
more to be remarked than his severity. He did insist to the
end that faith is not to be forced, that in private a man may
believe what he will, that only open revolt or public attack on
the orthodox teaching should be penalized—in his own words,
that only sedition and blasphemy rather than heresy should
be subject to constraint.

## ATTITUDE TO THE JEWS

Another dissenting group to attract Luther's concern was
the Jews. He had early believed that they are a stiff-necked
people to have rejected Christ, but contemporary Jews could
not be blamed for the sins of their fathers and might readily
be excused for their rejection of Christianity by reason of the
corruptions of the papacy. He said:

If I were a Jew, I would suffer the rack ten times before I would go over to the pope.

The papists have so demeaned themselves that a good Christian would rather be a Jew than one of them, and a Jew would rather be a sow than a Christian.

What good can we do the Jews when we constrain them, malign them, and hate them as dogs? When we deny them work and force them to usury, how can that help? We should use toward the Jews not the pope's but Christ's law of love. If some are stiff-necked, what does that matter? We are not all good Christians.

Luther was sanguine that his own reform, by eliminating the abuses of the papacy, would accomplish the conversion of the Jews. But the converts were few and unstable. When he endeavored to proselytize some rabbis, they undertook in return to make a Jew of him. The rumor that a Jew had been suborned by the papists to murder him was not received with complete incredulity. In Luther's latter days, when he was often sorely frayed, news came that in Moravia, Christians were being induced to Judaize. Then he came out with a vulgar blast in which he recommended that all the Jews be deported to Palestine. Failing that, they should be forbidden to practice usury, should be compelled to earn their living on the land, their synagogues should be burned, and their books including the Bible should be taken away from them.

One could wish that Luther had died before ever this tract was written. Yet one must be clear as to what he was recommending and why. His position was entirely religious and in no respect racial. The supreme sin for him was the persistent rejection of God's revelation of himself in Christ. The centuries of Jewish suffering were themselves a mark of the divine displeasure. The territorial principle should be applied to the Jews. They should be compelled to leave and go to a land of their own. This was a program of enforced Zionism. But if it were not feasible, then Luther would recommend that the Jews be compelled to live from the soil. He was unwittingly proposing a return to the condition of the early Middle Ages, when the Jews had been in agriculture. Forced off the land, they had gone into commerce and, having been expelled from commerce, into money lending. Luther wished to reverse the process and thereby inadvertently would accord the Jews a more secure position than they enjoyed in his day. The burning of the synagogues and the confiscation of the books was, however, a revival of the worst features of Pfefferkorn's program. One other word must be added: if similar tracts did not appear in England, France, and Spain in Luther's day, it was because the Jews had already been completely expelled from these countries. Germany, disorganized in this as in so many other respects, expelled the Jews from certain localities and tolerated them in others, such as Frankfurt and Worms. The irony of the situation was that Luther justified himself by appealing to the ire of Jehovah against those who go awhoring after other gods. Luther would not have listened to any impugning of the validity of this picture of God, but he might have recalled that Scripture itself discountenances human imitation of the divine vengeance.

### THE PAPISTS AND THE EMPEROR

The third group toward whom Luther became more bitter was the papists. His railing against the pope became perhaps the more vituperative because there was so little else that could be done. Another public appearance such as that at Worms, where an ampler confession could be made, was denied Luther, and the martyrdom which came to others also passed him by. He compensated by hurling vitriol. Toward the very end of his life he issued an illustrated tract with outrageously vulgar cartoons. In all of this he was utterly unrestrained.

The case was different in his attitude toward the emperor. Here Luther entertained his last great illusion. Even in 1531 he lauded Charles for his previous clemency and could not be persuaded that the emperor would yield to the goading of the papists. But should he do so and should he take up arms to suppress the gospel, then his subjects should do no more

**TERTIA VOX. ALTVS.**

PRIMA PARS.

IVAT, VIVAT, VIVAT. VIVAT IOANNES FRIDERICH,
ELECTOR ET DVX SAXONVM,
DEFENSOR VERI DOGMATIS,
PACISQVE CVSTOS PERVIGIL,
VIVAT PER OMNE SECVLVM.

THE LOWER MAGISTRATE:
JOHN FREDERICK, ELECTOR OF SAXONY

than refuse to serve under his banners, and for the rest should leave the outcome to the Lord, who delivered Lot from Sodom. Should God not intervene to preserve his own, yet would he be the Lord God, and under no circumstances should subjects take up arms against the powers ordained. The next year, however, Luther was brought to observe that the word used by the apostle Paul, namely "powers," is in the plural, and that although the common man may not take the sword which is committed only to the "power," yet one power may legitimately exercise a check even by the sword upon another. In other words, one department of the government may employ force to restrain the injustice of another. The Holy Roman Empire was a constitutional monarchy, and the emperor had sworn at his coronation that no German subject should be outlawed unheard and uncondemned. Although this clause had not been invoked to protect a monk accused of heresy, yet when princes and electors came to be involved the case was altered. If Charles were faithless to that oath, then he might be resisted even in arms by the lower magistrates. The formula thus suggested to Luther by the jurists was destined to have a very wide and extended vogue. The Lutherans employed it only until they gained legal recognition in 1555. Thereafter the Calvinists took up the slogan and equated the lower magistrates with the lesser nobility in France. Subsequently the Puritans in England made the same identification with Parliament. Later historians are so accustomed to regard Lutheranism as politically subservient and Calvinism as intransigent that they would do well to recall the origin of this doctrine on Lutheran soil.

But it was not the invention of Luther, even though he accepted its validity, never, however, without a measure of misgiving and such qualification as to make one uncertain whether his conditions were ever actually fulfilled. The emperor, he felt, might be forcibly resisted, not in case he should reintroduce the mass, but only in case he endeavored to force the Lutherans to attend the mass. This the emperor did only after Luther's death when Philip of Hesse was captured and required to be present at the celebration. Whether in that instance Luther would have felt the time had come for the legitimate use of the sword we shall never know. He was always ready to disobey, but exceedingly loath to raise a hand against the Lord's anointed.

Such were the public questions which engaged the later years, but in none of them could Luther do much more than write a memorandum. He must devote his labors to more restricted tasks, and that he did by preference. "A cow," said he, "does not get to heaven by giving milk, but that is what she is made for," and by the same token he would say that Martin Luther by his ministry could not settle the fate of Europe, but for the ministry he was made. To all the obligations of university and parish he gave himself unremittingly. To the end he was preaching, lecturing, counseling, and writing. However much the superb defiance of the earlier days might degenerate into the peevishness of one racked by disease, labor, and discouragement, yet a case of genuine need would always restore his sense of proportion and bring him into the breach. The closing events of his life are an example. He was in such a panic of disgust because the girls at Wittenberg were wearing low necks that he left home declaring that he would not return. His physician brought him back. Then came a request from the counts of Mansfeld for a mediator in a dispute. Melanchthon was too sick to go. Luther was too sick to live.

He went, reconciled the counts, and died on the way home.

LUTHER IN THE YEAR OF HIS DEATH

Luther's later years are, however, by no means to be written off as the sputterings of a dying flame. If in his polemical tracts he was at times savage and coarse, in the works which constitute the real marrow of his life's endeavor he grew constantly in maturity and artistic creativity. The biblical translation was improved to the very end. The sermons and the biblical commentaries reached superb heights. The delineation of the sacrifice of Isaac, already quoted, comes from the year 1545. Some of the passages cited throughout this book to illustrate Luther's religious and ethical principles are also from the later period.

### THE MEASURE OF THE MAN

When one comes to take the measure of the man, there are three areas which naturally suggest themselves. The first is his own Germany. He called himself the German prophet, saying that against the papist asses he must assume so presumptuous a title, and he addressed himself to his beloved Germans. The claim is frequent that no man did so much to fashion the character of the German people. Their indifference to politics and their passion for music were already present in him. Their language was so far fashioned by his hand that the extent of their indebtedness is difficult to recognize. If a German is asked whether a passage of Luther's Bible is not remarkable, he may answer that this is precisely the way in which any German would speak. But the reason is simply that every German has been reared on Luther's version. The influence of the man on his people was deepest in the home. In fact the home was the only sphere of life which the Reformation profoundly affected. Economics went the way of capitalism and politics the way of absolutism. But the home took on that quality of affectionate and godly patriarchalism which Luther had set as the pattern in his own household. The most profound impact of Luther on his people was in their religion. His sermons were read to the congregations, his liturgy was sung, his catechism was rehearsed by the father with the household, his Bible cheered the fainthearted and consoled the dying. If no Englishman occupies a similar place in the religious life of his people, it is because no Englishman had anything like Luther's range. The Bible translation in England was the work of Tyndale, the prayer book of Cranmer, the catechism of the Westminster divines. The sermonic style stemmed from Latimer; the hymnbook came from Watts. And not all of these lived in one century. Luther did the work of more than five men. And for sheer richness and exuberance of vocabulary and mastery of style he is to be compared only with Shakespeare.

The Germans naturally claim such a German for themselves. Yet when one begins to look over the centuries for those whom one would most naturally compare with this man, not a single one of his stature proves to be a German. In fact a German historian has said that in the course of three hundred years only one German ever really understood Luther, and that one was Johann Sebastian Bach. If one would discover parallels to Luther as the wrestler with the Lord, then one must turn to Paul the Jew, Augustine the Latin, Pascal the Frenchman, Kierkegaard the Dane, Unamuno the Spaniard, Dostoevski the Russian, Bunyan the Englishman, and Edwards the American.

And that is why in the second great area, that of the Church, Luther's influence extends so far beyond his own land. Lutheranism took possession of Scandinavia and has an extensive following in the United States, and apart from that his movement gave the impetus which sometimes launched and sometimes helped to establish the other varieties of Protestantism. They all stem in some measure from him. And what he did for his own people to a degree, he did also for others. His translation, for example, affected the English version. Tyndale's preface is take from Luther. His liturgical reforms likewise had an influence on the *Book of Common Prayer*. And even the Catholic Church owes much to him. Often it is said that had Luther never appeared, an Erasmian reform would have triumphed, or at any rate a reform after the Spanish model. All of this is of course conjectural, but it is obvious that the Catholic Church received a tremendous shock from the Lutheran Reformation and a terrific urge to reform after its own pattern.

The third area is of all the most important and the only one which to Luther mattered much, and that is the area of religion. Here it is that he must be judged. In his religion he was a Hebrew, not a Greek fancying gods and goddesses disporting themselves about some limpid pool or banqueting upon Olympus. The God of Luther, as of Moses, was the God who inhabits the storm clouds and rides on the wings of the wind. At his nod the earth trembles, and the people before him are as a drop in the bucket. He is a God of majesty and power, inscrutable, terrifying, devastating, and consuming in his anger. Yet the All Terrible is the All Merciful too. "Like as a father pitieth his children, so the Lord . . ." But how shall we know this? In Christ, only in Christ. In the Lord of life, born in the squalor of a cow stall and dying as a malefactor under the desertion and the derision of men, crying unto God and receiving for answer only the trembling of the earth and the blinding of the sun, even by God forsaken, and in that hour taking to himself and annihilating our iniquity, trampling down the hosts of hell and disclosing within the wrath of the All Terrible the love that will not let us go. No longer did Luther tremble at the rustling of a wind-blown leaf, and instead of calling upon St. Anne he declared himself able to laugh at thunder and jagged bolts from out the storm. This was what enabled him to utter such words as these: "Here I stand. I cannot do otherwise. God help me. Amen."

# BIBLIOGRAPHY

MARTIN LUTHER AND HIS TIMES

Albrecht, Otto. "Luthers Katechismen," *Schriften des Vereins für Reformationsgeschichte,* XXXIII (1915).

Althaus, Paul. "Die Bedeutung des Kreuzes im Denken Luthers," *Vierteljahrschrift der Luthergesellschaft,* VIII (1926), 97-107.

——. "Luthers Haltung im Bauernkrieg," *Jahrbuch der Luthergesellschaft,* VII (1925), 1-39.

Archivio di Firenze. "I manoscritte Torrigiani," *Archivio stor. italiano,* XXIV (1876).

Arnold, Franz Xaver. *Zur Frage des Naturrechts bei Martin Luther* (1937).

Bainton, Roland H. *Bibliography of the Continental Reformation* (1935).

——. "The Development and Consistency of Luther's Attitude Toward Religious Liberty," *Harvard Theological Review,* XXII (1929), 107-49.

——. "Dürer and Luther as the Man of Sorrows," *Art Bulletin,* XXIX (1947), 269-72.

——. "Eyn Wunderliche Weyssagung Osiander, Sachs, Luther," *Germanic Review,* XXI, 3(1946), 161-64.

——. "Luther's Struggle for Faith," *Gerhard Ritter Festschrift.* Also in *Church History,* XVII (1948), 3-16.

——. *The Martin Luther Christmas Book* (1948).

——. Review of Boehmer's *Road to Reformation, Church History,* XVI (1947), 167-76.

Balan, Petrus. *Monumenta Reformationis Lutheranae* (1884).

Barge, Hermann. *Andreas Bodenstein von Karlstadt,* I-II (1905).

Bauer, Karl. "Die Heidelberger Disputation Luthers," *Zeitschrift für Kirchengeschichte,* XXI (1901), 233-68, 299-329.

——. *Die Wittenberger Universitäts-theologie* (1928).

Benz, Ernst. *Wittenberg und Byzanz* (1940).

Berbig, Georg. "Die erste kursächsische Visitation in Ortsland Franken," *Archiv für Reformationsgeschichte,* III (1905-6), 336-402; IV (1906-7), 370-408.

Berger, Arnold E. *Reihe Reformation.* "Deutsche Literatur" series:
——. *Die Sturmtruppen* (1931).
——. *Satirische Feldzüge* (1933).
——. *Lied, Spruch, und Fabeldichtung* (1938).
——. *Die Schaubühne,* I & II (1935-36).

Betcke, Werner. *Luthers Sozialethik* (1934).

Beyer, Hermann Wolfgang. "Der Christ und die Bergpredigt," *Luther Jahrbuch* (1932), 33-60.

Bezold, Friedrich. "Luthers Rückkehr von der Wartburg," *Zeitschrift für Kirchengeschichte*, XX (1900), 186-233.

Blanke, Fritz. *Der verborgene Gott bei Luther* (1928).

Bluhm, H. S. "The Significance of Luther's Earliest Extant Sermon," *Harvard Theological Review*, XXXVII (1914), 175-81.

Blume, Friedrich. *Die evangelische Kirchenmusik* (1931-34).

Boehmer, Heinrich. *Der junge Luther;* 3rd ed. (Heinrich Bornkamm, ed., 1939).
    English trans. (from the German of 1929), *Road to Reformation* (1946).

——. "Luthers Ehe," *Luther Jahrbuch*, VII (1925), 40-76.

——. *Luthers Romfahrt* (1914).

Bönhoff. "Die sächsische Landeskirche und die Visitation des Jahres 1529," *Beiträge zur sächsischen Kirchengeschichte*, XXXVIII (1929), 8-48.

Boller, Fritz. *Luthers Berufung nach Worms* (dissertation, 1912).

Bornkamm, Heinrich. "Christus und das erste Gebot in der Anfechtung bei Luther," *Zeitschrift für systematische Theologie*, V (1928), 453-77.

——. *Das Wort Gottes bei Luther* (1933).

——. *Luthers geistige Welt* (1947).

Brandenburg, Erich. "Martin Luthers Anschauung von Staat und Gesellschaft," *Schriften des Vereins für Reformationsgeschichte*. LXII (1901).

Brandt, Otto H. *Die Fugger* (1928).

——. *Der grosse Bauernkrieg, zeitgenössische Berichte* (1925).

——. *Der deutsche Bauernkrieg* (1920).

——. *Thomas Müntzer, sein Leben und seine Schriften* (1933).

Brieger, Theodor. "Aleander und Luther 1521. Die . . . Aleander-Depeschen," *Quellen und Forschungen zur Reformationsgeschichte*, I (1884).

——. *Das Wesen des Ablasses* (1897).

——. "Indulgenzen," *Realencyklpädie*, 3rd ed.

Bring, Ragnar. *Dualismen hos Luther* (1929).

Buchwald, Georg. *D. Martin Luthers Leben und Lehre* (1947).

——. *Predigten D. Martin Luthers,* I & II (1925-26).

——. "Luther Kalendarium," *Schriften des Vereins für Reformationsgeschichte*, XLVII (1929).

Bühler, Paul Theodor. *Die Anfechtung bei Martin Luther* (1942).

Bullen, Henry Lewis. *The Nuremberg Chronicle* (1930).

Burgdorf, Martin. *Luther und die Wiedertäufer* (1928).

Buszin, Walter E. "Luther on Music," *The Musical Quarterly*, XXXII (1946), 80-97.

Carlson, Edgar M. *The Reinterpretation of Luther* (1948).

Clemen, Otto. *Beiträge zur Reformationsgeschichte*, I-III (1900-1903).

——. *Flugschriften aus den ersten Jahren der Reformation,* I-IV (1907-11).

Cohrs, Ferdinand. "Die evangelischen Katechismusversuche vor Luthers Enchiridion," *Monumenta Germaniae Paedagogica,* XX-XXIII, XXXIX (1900).

Denifle, Heinrich. *Luther und Lutherthum,* I-III (1904-9).

*Deutsche Reichstagsakten,* jüngere Reihe. I (1893), Kluckhorn, ed.; II-IV (1896-1908), Wrede, ed.; VII (1935), Kühn, ed.

Diem, Harold. *Luthers Lehre von den zwei Reichen* (1938).

Dittrich, Ottmar. *Luthers Ethik* (1930).

Dress, Walter. *Martin Luther, Versuchung und Sendung* (1937).

Drews, Paul. *Disputationen Dr. Martin Luthers in den Jahren 1535-1547* (1895).

——. "Entsprach das Staatskirchentum dem Ideale Luthers?" *Zeitschrift für Theologie und Kirche,* XVIII (1908).

——. *Willibald Pirckheimers Stellung zur Reformation* (1887).

Ebstein, Wilhelm. *Dr. Martin Luthers Krankheiten* (1908).

Eger, Karl. *Die Anschauungen Luthers vom Beruf* (1900).

Elert, Werner. *Morphologie des Lutherthums,* I & II (1931-32).

Farner, Alfred. *Huldreich Zwingli,* II (1946).

——. *Die Lehre von Kirche und Staat bei Zwingli* (1930).

Fendt, Leonard. "Der Lutherische Gottesdienst des 16. Jahrhunderts," *Aus der Welt christlicher Frömmigkeit,* V (1923).

Fife, Robert. *Young Luther* (1928).

Fischer, Robert H. *"Propter Christum" in Luther's Early Theology* (unpublished dissertation, Yale University, 1947).

Foerster, Erich. "Fragen nach Luthers Kirchenbegriff aus der Gedankenwelt seines Alters," *Festgabe Julius Kaftan* (1920).

Franz, Günther. *Der deutsche Bauernkrieg,* I & II (1933-35).

Friedensburg, Walter. "Die Reformation und der Speierer Reichstag," *Luther Jahrbuch,* VIII (1926), 120-95.

Friedmann, Robert. "Conception of the Anabaptists," *Church History,* IX (1940), 341-65.

Fullerton, Kemper. "Luther's Doctrine and Criticism of Scripture," *Bibliotheca Sacra,* LXIII (1906), 1-34, 284-99.

Gebhardt, Bruno. *Die Gravamina der deutschen Nation,* 2nd ed. (1895).

Gennrich, Paul Wilhelm. *Die Christologie Luthers im Abendmahlstreit 1524-29* (1929).

Gerke, Friedrich. "Die satanische Anfechtung in der *Ars moriendi* und bei Martin Luther," *Theologische Blätter,* XI (1932), 320-31.

Gieseler, Johann C. L. *Lehrbuch der Kirchengeschichte,* I-VIII (1824-57).

Gravier, Maurice. *Luther et l'opinion publique* (1942).

Grisar, Hartmann. *Luther* (English), I-VI (1913-17).

——. *Luther-Studien,* I-VI (1921-33), Nos. 2, 3, 5, and 6, "Luthers Kampfbilder."

Habler, Konrad. "Die Stellung der Fugger zum Kirchenstreite des 16. Jahrhunderts," *Historische Vierteljahrschrift*, I (1898), 473-510.

Hahn, Fritz. "Luthers Auslegungsgrundsätze und ihre theologische Voraussetzungen," *Zeitschrift für systematische Theologie*, XII (1934), 165-218.

——. "Zur Verchristlichung der Psalmen durch Luthers Übersetzung," *Theologische Studien und Kritiken*, CVI (1934-35), 173-203.

Hamel, Adolf. *Der junge Luther und Augustin*, I & II (1934-35).

Harnack, Theodosius, *Luthers Theologie*, I & II (1862-86).

Hasenzahl, Walter. "Die Gottverlassenheit des Christus," *Beiträge zur Förderung christlicher Theologie*, XXXIX (1937), 1.

Hausrath, Adolf. *Luthers Leben*, I & II (1913-14).

Held, Paul. "Ulrich von Hutten," *Schriften des Vereins für Reformationsgeschichte*, XLVI (1928).

Hermann, Rudolf. "Luthers These 'Gerecht und Sünder,'" *Zeitschrift für systematische Theologie*, VI (1928), 278-338, 497-537; VII (1930), 125-72.

Hermelink, Heinrich. "Der Toleranzgedanke im Reformationszeitalter," *Schriften des Vereins für Reformationsgeschichte*, XXVI (1908).

Hertsch, Erich. *Karlstadt und seine Bedeutung für das Lutherthum* (1932).

Hill, Richard S. "Not So Far Away in a Manger," *Music Library Association Notes*, III (1945), 12-36.

Hildebrandt, Franz. *Melanchthon: Alien or Ally?* (1946).

Hirsch, Emanuel. "Initium Theologiae Lutheri," *Festgabe Julius Kaftan* (1920).

Holborn, Hajo. *Ulrich von Hutten* (1929, English trans. 1937).

Holl, Karl. "Luther," *Gesammelte Aufsätze zur Kirchengeschichte*, I (1932).

Hovland, Clarence Warren. *Luther's Treatment of "Anfechtung" in his Biblical Exegesis from the Time of the Evangelical Experience to 1545* (unpublished dissertation, Yale University, 1950).

Hunzinger, August Wilhelm. *Das Furchtmotiv in der katholischen Busslehre* (1906).

Iwand, Hans Joachim. *Rechtfertigungslehre und Christusglaube* (1930).

Jacob, Günther. "Der Gewissensbegriff in der Theologie Luthers," *Beiträge zur historischen Theologie*, IV (1929).

Joachimsen, Paul. "Luther und die soziale Welt," *Martin Luthers Ausgewählte Werke*, VI (1923).

——. "Das Zeitalter der Reformation," *Propylaenweltgeschichte*, V (1930), 4-216.

——. *Sozialethik des Luthertums* (1927).

Kalkoff, Paul. *Ablass und Reliquienverehrung an der Schlosskirche zu Wittenberg* (1907).

———. *Aleander gegen Luther* (1908).

———. "Die Anfänge der Gegenreformation in den Niederlanden," *Schriften des Vereins für Reformationsgeschichte*, XXI (1903-4).

———. "Briefe, Depeschen und Berichte über Luther vom Wormser Reichstage 1521," *Schriften des Vereins für Reformationsgeschichte*, XV (1898), 2.

———. "Die Bulle *Exsurge*," *Zeitschrift für Kirchengeschichte*, XXXV (1914), 166-203.

———. "Die von Cajetan verfasste Ablassdekretale," *Archiv für Reformationsgeschichte*, IX (1911-12), 142-71.

———. *Die Depeschen des Nuntius Aleander* (1897).

———. *Die Entstehung des Wormser Edikts* (1913).

———. "Erasmus, Luther, und Friedrich der Weise," *Schriften des Vereins für Reformationsgeschichte*, XXXVII (1919).

———. "Forschungen zu Luthers römischen Prozess," *Bibliothek des Königlichen preussischen historischen Instituts in Rom*, II (1905).

———. *Luther und die Entscheidungsjahre der Reformation* (1917).

———. "Zu Luthers römischen Prozess," *Zeitschrift für Kirchengeschichte*, XXV (1904), 90-147, 272-90, 399-459, 503-603; XXXI (1910), 48-65, 368-414.

———. "Die Vermittlungspolitik des Erasmus," *Archiv für Reformationsgeschichte*, I (1903-4), 1-83.

———. *Der Wormser Reichstag von 1521* (1922).

Kattenbusch, Ferdinand. "Die Doppelsichtigkeit in Luthers Kirchenbegriff," *Theologische Studien und Kritiken*, C (1927-28), 197-347.

Kawerau, Gustav. "Thesen Luthers *De Excommunicatione*" and "Thesen Karlstadts," *Zeitschrift für Kirchengeschichte*, XI (1890), 477-83.

Kawerau, Waldener. "Die Reformation und die Ehe," *Schriften des Vereins für Reformationsgeschichte*, X (1892).

Kiessling, Elmer Carl. *The Early Sermons of Luther* (1935).

Kirn, Paul. *Friedrich der Weise und die Kirche* (1926).

Koehler, Walther. *Dokumente zum Ablassstreit von 1517* (1902).

———. "Entstehung des *Reformatio ecclesiarum Hassiae* von 1526," *Deutsche Zeitschrift für Kirchenrecht*, XVI (1906), 199-232.

———. *Die Geisteswelt Ulrich Zwinglis* (1920).

———. "Luther und das Lutherthum in ihrer weltgeschichtlichen Auswirkung," *Schriften des Vereins für Reformationsgeschichte*, LI (1933).

———. *Luther und die Kirchengeschichte* (1900).

———. *Luthers 95 Thesen* (1903).

———. "Das Marburge Religionsgespräch 1529," *Schriften des Vereins für Reformationsgeschichte*, XLVIII (1929).

———. *Die Quellen Luthers Schrift "An den christlichten Adel"* (1895).

———. *Reformation und Ketzerprozess* (1901).

——. "Sozialwissenschaftliche Bemerkung zur Lutherforschung," *Zeitschrift für die gesammte Staatswissenschaft*, LXXXV (1928), 2, 343-53.

——. "Wie Luther den Deutschen das Leben Jesu erzählt hat," *Schriften des Vereins für Reformationsgeschichte*, XXXV (1917).

——. "Zwingli und Luther," *Quellen and Forschungen zur Reformationsgeschichte*, VI (1924).

Köstlin, Julius. *Luthers Theologie*, I & II (1901).

Köstlin, Julius, and Kawerau, Georg. *Martin Luther*, I & II (1903).

Kohlschmidt, K. "Luther im Kloster," *Vierteljahrschrift der Luthergesellschaft*, XIII (1931), 4-18, 33-56.

Kolde, Theodor. "Ältester Bericht über die Zwickauer Propheten," *Zeitschrift für Kirchengeschichte*, V (1882), 323-33.

——. "Innere Bewegungen unter den deutschen Augustinern und Luthers Romreise," *Zeitschrift für Kirchengeschichte*, II (1878), 460-72.

——. "Luther und sein Ordensgeneral in Rom," *Zeitschrift für Kirchengeschichte*, II (1878), 472-80.

Kroker, Ernst. *Katherina von Bora* (1906).

Kühn, Johannes. "Zur Entstehung des Wormser Edikt," *Zeitschrift für Kirchengeschichte*, XXXV (1914), 372-92, 529-47.

——. "Die Geschichte des Speyrer Reichstage 1529," *Schriften des Vereins für Reformationsgeschichte*, XLVII (1929).

——. *Toleranz und Offenbarung* (1923).

Kurz, Alfred. *Die Heilsgewissheit bei Luther* (1933).

Lammers, Heinrich. "Luthers Anschauung vom Willen," *Neue deutsche Forschungen*, I (1935).

Lamparter, Helmut. "Luthers Stellung zum Türkenkrieg," *Forschungen zur Geschichte und Lehre des Protestantismus*, IX (1940), 4.

Lau, Franz. *"Äusserliche Ordnung" und "Weltlich Ding" in Luthers Theologie* (1932).

Lewin, Rheinhold. "Luthers Stellung zu den Juden," *Neue Studien zur Geschichte der Theologie und der Kirche*, X (1911).

Lilje, Hanns. "Luthers Geschichtsanschauung," *Furche-Studien*, II (1932).

Link, Wilhelm. "Das Ringen Luthers um die Freiheit der Theologie von der Philosophie," *Forschungen zur Geschichte und Lehre des Protestantismus*, IX (1940), iii.

Littell, Franklin Hamlin. *The Anabaptist View of the Church* (unpublished dissertation, Yale University, 1946).

Loescher, Valentin Ernst. *Vollständige Reformations-acta*, I-III (1720-29).

Loewenich, Walter. "Luthers *Theologia crucis*," *Forschungen zur Geschichte und Lehre des Protestantismus*, II (1929), 2.

Lohmann, Annemarie. "Zur geistigen Entwicklung Thomas Müntzers," *Beiträge zur Kulturgeschichte des Mittelalters und der Renaissance*, XLVII (1931).

Ludwig, Martin. "Religion und Sittlichkeit bei Luther bis. . . . 1520," *Quellen und Forschungen zur Reformationsgeschichte,* XIV (1931).

McGiffert, Arthur C. *Martin Luther* (1917).

MacKinnon, James. *Luther and the Reformation,* I-IV (1925-30).

Matthes, Kurt. "Das *Corpus Christianum* bei Luther," *Studien zur Geschichte der Wirtschaft und Geisteskultur,* V (1929).

———. "Luther und die Obrigkeit," *Aus der Welt christlicher Frömmigkeit,* XII (1937).

May, Jacob. *Der Kurfürst, Cardinal und Erzbischof Albrecht II von Mainz* (1865).

Meinecke, Friedrich. "Luther über christliches Gemeinwesen und christlichen Staat," *Historische Zeitschrift,* CXXI (1920), 1-22.

Meinhold, Peter. "Die Genesisvorlesungen Luthers und ihre Herausgeber," *Forschungen zur Kirchen- und Geistesgeschichte,* VIII (1936).

Merz, Georg. *Glaube und Politik.* 2nd ed. (1933).

Miegge, Giovanni. *Lutero* (1946).

Müller, Alphons Victor. *Luther und Tauler* (1918).

———. *Luthers Werdegang bis zum Turmerlebnis* (1920).

Müller, Hans Michael. *Erfahrung und Glaube bei Luther* (1929).

Müller, Karl. *Kirche, Gemeinde und Obrigkeit nach Luther* (1910).

———. "Luthers Äusserungen über das Recht des bewaffneten Widerstands," *Sitzungsberichte der Königlichen Bayerischen Akademie der Wissenschaften, philosophischhistorische Klasse,* VIII (1915).

———. *Luther und Karlstadt* (1907).

———. "Luthers römischer Prozess," *Zeitschrift für Kirchengeschichte,* XXIV (1903), 46-85.

Müller, Nikolaus. *Die Wittenberger Bewegung.* 2nd ed. (1911).

Murray, Robert Henry, *Erasmus and Luther* (1920).

Negwer, Joseph. "Konrad Wimpina," *Kirchengeschichtliche Abhandlungen,* VII (1909).

Nettl, Paul. *Luther and Music* (1948).

Nitsch, Friedrich. *Luther und Aristoteles* (1883).

Olsson, Herbert. *Grundproblemet i Luthers Socialethik* (1934).

Pallas, Karl. "Briefe und Akten zur Visitationsreise des Bischofs Johannes VII von Meissen im Kurfürstentum Sachsen 1522," *Archiv für Reformationsgeschichte,* V (1907-8), 217-312.

Panofsky, Erwin. *Albrecht Dürer,* I & II (1943).

Paquier, Jules. *L'Humanisme et la réforme: Jérome Aléandre* (1900).

Pascal, Roy. *The Social Basis of the German Reformation* (1933).

Pastor, Ludwig von. *History of the Popes,* VII & VIII.

Pauck, Wilhelm. "Historiography of the German Reformation During the Last Twenty Years," *Church History,* IX (1940), 305-40.

———. *Heritage of the Reformation* (1950).

Pauls, Theodor. *Luthers Auffassung von Staat und Volk* (1925).

Paulus, Nikolaus. *Geschichte des Ablasses,* I-III (1922-23).

———. *Johann Tetzel* (1899).

———. *Protestantismus und Toleranz im 16. Jahrhundert* (1911).

Pinomaa, Lenhart. "Der Zorn Gottes in der Theologie Luthers," *Annales Academiae Scientiarum Fennicae,* XLI, 1 (1938).

Planitz, Hans von. "Hans von Planitz Berichte aus dem Reichsregiment in Nürnberg 1521-25," *Schriften der Königlichen sächsichen Kommission für Geschichte* (1889).

Prenter, Regin. *Spiritus Creator* (1944).

Preuss, Hans. *Martin Luther der Künstler* (1931).

———. *Martin Luther der Prophet* (1933).

———. *Martin Luther der Deutsche* (1934).

———. *Martin Luther der Christenmensch* (1942).

———. *Die Vorstellungen von Antichrist in späteren Mittelalter* (1906).

Raynaldus (Rinaldi), Odoricus. *Annales Ecclesiastici,* XX (1691).

Reiter, Paul J. *Martin Luthers Umwelt, Charakter und Psychose,* I & II (1937-41).

Reu, Michael. *The Augsburg Confession* (1930).

———. *Luther's German Bible* (1934).

Reymann, Heinz. *Glaube und Wirtschaft bei Luther* (1934).

Rieker, Karl. *Die rechtliche Stellung der evangelischen Kirche Deutschlands* (1893).

Rietschel, Ernst. "Luthers Anschauung von der Unsichtbarkeit und Sichtbarkeit der Kirche," *Theologische Studien und Kritiken,* LXXIII (1900), 404-56.

———. "Das Problem der unsichtbar-sichtbaren Kirche bei Luther," *Schriften des Vereins für Reformationsgeschichte,* L (1932).

Rietschel, Georg. *Luther und die Ordination* (1889).

Ritter, Gerhard. *Luther, Gestalt und Tat* (1943).

———. "Renaissance und Reformation," *Neue Propylaenweltgeschichte* (1942).

Rockwell, William Walter. *Die Doppelehe des Landgrafen Philip von Hessen* (1904).

Rupp, Ernest Gordon. *Martin Luther: Hitler's Cause or Cure?* (1946).

Schade, Oskar. *Satiren und Pasquillen aus der Reformationszeit,* I-III (1856-58).

Scheel, Otto. *Martin Luther,* I (2nd ed. 1921) & II (3rd & 4th eds. 1930).

———. *Dokumente zu Luthers Entwicklung* (1929).

Schempp, Paul. "Luthers Stellung zur heiligen Schrift," *Forschungen zur Geschichte und Lehre des Protestantismus,* II & III (1929).

Schirrmacher, Friedrich W. *Briefe und Acten zu der Geschichte . . . des Reichstages zu Augsburg 1530* (1876).

Schmidt, Hans. "Luthers Übersetzung des 46. Psalms," *Luther Jahrbuch,* VIII (1926), 98-119.

Schneider, Charles. *Luther, poète et musicien* (1942).

Schou, Hans. *Religion and Morbid Mental States* (1926).

Schrade, Leo. "The Choral Music of the Lutheran 'Kantorei,'" *Valparaiso University Pamphlets*, Series No. 2 (1946).

Schramm, Albert. *Luther und die Bibel. Die Illustrationen der Lutherbibel* (1923).

Schubert, Hans von. "Die Anfänge der evangelischen Bekenntnis-bildung," *Schriften des Vereins für Reformationsgeschichte* (1928).

——. *Bekenntnisbildung und Religionspolitik 1529-30* (1910).

——. "Bündnis und Bekenntnis 1529-30," *Schriften des Vereins für Reformationsgeschichte*, XXVI (1908).

——. "Lazarus Spengler" (Hajo Holborn, ed.), *Quellen und Forschungen zur Reformationsgeschichte*, XVII (1934).

——. "Luthers Frühentwicklung," *Schriften des Vereins für Reformationsgeschichte*, XXXIV (1916).

——. "Der Reichstag von Augsburg," *Schriften des Vereins für Reformationsgeschichte*, XLVIII (1930).

——. *Reich und Reformation* (1910).

——. "Die Vorgeschichte der Berufung Luthers auf den Reichstag zu Worms 1521," *Sitzungsberichte der Heidelberger Akademie der Wissenschaften philosophischhistorische Klasse*, III (1912).

Schulte, Aloys. *Die Fugger in Rom* (1904).

——. "Die römische Verhandlungen über Luther 1520," *Quellen und Forschungen aus italienischen Archiven und Bibliotheken*, V-VI (1904), 32-52.

Schwiebert, E. G. "The Electoral Town of Wittenberg," *Medievalia et Humanistica*, III (1945), 99-116.

Seeberg, Erich. *Luthers Theologie:* vol. I, *Die Gottesanschauung* (1929); vol. II, *Christus* (1937).

Seeberg, Reinhold. "Luthers Anschauung von dem Geschlechtleben und der Ehe," *Luther Jahrbuch*, VII (1925), 77-122.

Seidemann, Johann Karl. "Luthers Grundbesitz," *Zeitschrift für die historische Theologie*, XXX (1860), 375-564.

Smith, Preserved. *Erasmus* (1923).

——. *The Life and Letters of Martin Luther* (1911).

Smith, Preserved, and Jacobs, C. M. *Luther's Correspondence*, I & II (1913-18).

Spitta, Friedrich, *Ein feste Burg* (1905).

Söderblom, Nathan. *Humor och melankoli* (1919).

Stange, Carl. "Karfreitagsgedanken Luthers," *Zeitschrift für systematische Theologie*, IX, 1 (1932), 55-92.

——. "Luthers Gedanken über Tod . . . ," *Zeitschrift für systematische Theologie*, X (1933), 490-513.

——. "Luthers Gedanken über die Todesfurcht," *Greifswalder Studien*, VII (1932).

——. "Luthers Theorie von gesellschaftlichen Leben," *Zeitschrift für systematische Theologie*, VII (1929), 57-124.

Stolze, Wilhelm. "Bauernkrieg und Reformation," *Schriften des Vereins für Reformationsgeschichte*, XLIV (1926).

Stomps, M. A. H. "Die Anthropologie Martin Luthers," *Philosophische Abhandlungen*, IV (1935).

Stracke, Ernst. "Luthers grosses Selbstzeugnis 1545," *Schriften des Vereins für Reformationsgeschichte*, XLIV (1926).

Strohl, Henri. "L'épanouissement de la pensée religieuse de Luther de 1515 à 1520," *Études . . . d'histoire et de philosophie religieuse . . . de l'Université de Strassbourg*, IX (1924).

Thiel, Rudolf. *Luther*, I & II (1936-37).

Thoma, Albrecht. *Katherina von Bora* (1900).

Tililä, Osmo. "Das Strafleiden Christi," *Annales Academiae Scientiarum Fennicae*, B, XLVIII, 1 (1941).

Tiling. "Der Kampf gegen die *Missa Privata* in Wittenberg," *Neue Kirchliche Zeitschrift*, XX (1909), 85-130.

Törnvall, Gustaf. *Andligt och världsligt regemente hos Luther* (1940). German trans., *Geistliches und weltliches Regiment bei Luther* (1947).

Ulmann, Heinrich. *Franz von Sickingen* (1872).

Vignaux, Paul. "Luther, Commentateur des Sentences," *Études de philosophie médiévale*, XXI (1935).

Völker, Karl. *Toleranz und Intoleranz im Zeitalter der Reformation* (1912).

Vogelsang, Erich. "Die Anfänge von Luthers Christologie," *Arbeiten zur Kirchengeschichte*, XV (1929).

——. "Der angefochtene Christus bei Luther," *Arbeiten zur Kirchengeschichte*, XXI (1932).

Von Rohr, John. *A Study of the Anfechtung of Martin Luther* (unpublished dissertation, Yale University, 1947).

Wagner, Elizabeth. "Luther und Friedrich der Weise auf den Wormser Reichstag von 1521," *Zeitschrift für Kirchengeschichte*, XLII (1923), 331-90.

Waldeck, Oscar. "Die Publizistik des Schmalkaldischen Krieges," *Archiv für Reformationsgeschichte*, VII (1909-10), 1-55.

Walser, Fritz. "Die politische Entwicklung Ulrich von Hutten," *Historische Zeitschrift Beiheft*, XIV (1929).

Walther, Wilhelm. *Für Luther wider Rom* (1906).

Wappler, Karl. *Inquisition und Ketzerprozesse in Zwickau zur Reformationszeit* (1908).

Wappler, Paul. "Die Stellung Kursachsens und des Landgrafen Philipp zur Täuferbewegung," *Reformationsgeschichtliche Studien und Texte*, XIII-XIV (1910).

——. "Die Täuferbewegung in Thüringen," *Beiträge zur neueren Geschichte Thüringens*, II (1913).

Watson, Philip S. *Let God Be God: An Interpretation of the Theology of Martin Luther* (1947).

Wendorf, Hermann. "Der Durchbruch der neuen Erkenntnis Luthers," *Historische Vierteljahrschrift*, XXVII (1932), 124-44, 285-327.

——. *Martin Luther* (1930).

Werdermann, Hermann. *Die deutsche evangelische Pfarrfrau.* 3rd ed. (1940).

——. *Luthers Wittenberger Gemeinde* (1929).

Wernle, Paul. *Der Evangelische Glaube:* vol. I, *Luther* (1918); vol. II, *Zwingli* (1919).

Wiedemann, Theodor. *Dr. Johann Eck* (1865).

Winter, F. "Die Kirchenvisitation von 1528 in Wittenberger Kreise," *Zeitschrift für die historische Theologie,* XXXIII (1863), 295-322.

Wiswedel, Wilhelm. *Bilder und Führergestalten aus dem Täufertum,* I & II (1928-30).

Wolf, Ernst. *Luthers Praedestinationsanfechtungen* (1925).

——. "Staupitz und Luther," *Quellen und Forschungen zur Reformationsgeschichte,* IX (1927).

——. "Johannes von Staupitz und die theologischen Anfänge Luthers," *Luther Jahrbuch,* XI (1929), 43-86.

——. "Über neuere Lutherliteratur," *Christentum und Wissenschaft* (1933).

Wünsch, Georg. *Die Bergpredigt bei Luther* (1920).

Zarncke, Lilly Der Begriff der Liebe in Luthers Äusserungen über die Ehe," *Theologische Blätter,* X, 2 (1931), 45-49.

——. "Der geistliche Sinn der Ehe bei Luther," *Theologische Studien und Kritiken,* CVI (1934), 20-39.

——. "Luthers Stellung zur Ehescheidung und Mehrehe," *Zeitschrift für systematische Theologie,* XII (1934), 98-117.

——. "Die naturhafte Eheanschauung des jungen Luther," *Archiv für Kulturgeschichte,* XXV (1934-35), 281-305.

## LUTHER'S CONTEMPORARIES

Beatus, Rhenanus. *Briefwechsel* (Horawitz and Hartfelder, eds., 1836).

Carlstadt, Andreas. *Von Abtuung der Bilder* (Lietzmann, ed., 1911).

——. *Von dem widerchristlichen Missbrauch des Herren Brod und Kelch.* Walch XX, 92-109.

——. *Von dem alten und neuen Testament.* Walch XX, 286-305.

——. *Karlstadts Erklärung.* Walch XX, 313-22.

——. *De coelibatu* (1521). (Yale Library.)

Dürer, Albrecht. *Dürers Briefe, Tagebücher und Reime* (Thausing, ed., 1872).

Erasmus, Desiderius. *Opera,* I-XI (LeClerc, ed., 1703-6).

——. *Ausgewählte Werke* (Hajo and Annemarie Holborn, eds., 1933).

——. *Erasmi Epistolae,* I-XI (Mr. and Mrs. P. S. Allen, eds., 1906-47).

——. *Erasmi Opuscula* (Wallace Ferguson, ed., 1933).

Hutten, Ulrich von. *Opera,* I-XII (Böcking, ed., 1859-62).

Kessler, Johann. *Johannes Kesslers Sabbata* (Egli, ed., 1902).

Menius, Justus. *Der Widerteuffer Lere und geheimnis* (1530).
Müntzer, Thomas; Boehmer, Heinrich; and Kirn, Paul. *Thomas Müntzers Briefwechsel* (1931).
Pirckheimer, Willibald. "Eccius Dedolatus," *Hutteni Opera,* IV.
Ratzeberger, Matthäus. *Die handschriftliche Geschichte Ratzebergers über Luther* (1850).
Sachs, Hans. *Hans Sachsens ausgewählte Werke,* I (1923).
Sanuto, Marino. *I Diarii di Marino Sanuto,* XXVIII (1890).
Schedel, Hartmann. *Das Buch der Chroniken* (1493).
Seckendorf, Veit Ludwig von. *Commentarius historicus et Apologeticus de Lutheranismo,* I & II (1692).
Spalatin, Georg. *Annales Reformationis* (Cyprian ed., 1718).
Spengler, Lazarus. *Schutzrede und christenliche Antwort* (1519).

ILLUSTRATIONS

Barbagallo, Corrado. *Storia Universale,* IV, "Evo Moderno" (1936).
Boehmer, Heinrich. *Der junge Luther* (Heinrich Bornkamm, ed., 1939).
Clemen, Otto. *Flugschriften aus den ernsten Jahren der Reformation,* I-III (1907-9).
Geisberg, Max. *Die Reformation im Einblatt Holzschnitt* (1929).
——. *Bilder-Katalog* (1930).
——. *Die deutsche Buchillustration,* I (1930).
Joachimsen, Paul. "Das Zeitalter der Reformation," *Propylaenweltgeschichte,* V (1930).
—— *Die neue Propylaenweltgeschichte* (1941).
Pflugk-Harttung, Julius von. *Im Morgenrot der Reformation*
Schramm, Albert. *Luther und die Bibel* (1923).
(1912).
Schreckenbach, Paul. *Martin Luther* (1921).

# REFERENCES

## KEY TO ABBREVIATIONS

*AD—Aleander Depeschen* (Kalkoff, ed.)
*Ann—Annales*
*ARG—Archiv für Reformationsgeschichte*
*Bd*—Buchwald, *Luthers Predigten*
*BDF—Briefe, Depeschen und Berichte* (see Kalkoff)
*Bibel*—Bible in *WA*
*BR—Briefwechsel* in *WA*
*CR—Corpus reformatorum*
*Dok* (K)—*Dokumente zum Ablassstreit von 1517* (Walther Koehler, ed., 1902)
*Dok* (S)—*Dokumente zu Luthers Entwicklung* (Otto Scheel, ed., 1929)
*EA—Erlangen Ausgabe*
*EE—Erasmi epistolae*
*Ep—Epistolae Ulrichi Huttenis*
*F—Forschungen*
*JLG—Jahrbuch der Luthergesellschaft*

*LJ—Luther Jahrbuch*
*QFRG—Quellen und Forschungen zur Reformationsgeschichte*
*ova—Opera varii argumenti* in *EA*
*RA—Deutsche Reichstagsakten*
*SVRG—Schriften des Vereins für Reformationsgeschichte*
*TR—Tischreden* in *WA*
*VLG—Vierteljahrschrift der Luthergesellschaft*
*W*—Walch ed. of Luther's works
*WA—Weimar Ausgabe*, ordinarily referred to simply by volume and page
*ZHT—Zeitschrift für die historische Theologie*
*ZKG—Zeitschrift für Kirchengeschichte*
*ZST—Zeitschrift für systematische Theologie*

For full titles see the bibliography.

**PAGE LINE**

### CHAP. I

17- 8 *TR*, 3566 A (1537)
17-12 *TR*, 1559 (1532)
17-16 *TR*, 5571 (1543)
18- 7 XXXVIII, 338
18-30 Scheel, 1, 290, n. 13
19-14 Boehmer, *JL*, p. 24
19-28 *TR*, 3841
20-35 *TR*, 3593, p. 439
21-41 Gerke, *Th.Bl.*, XI, 320
22-16 Bullen, p. XXV
22-31 *Dok* (S), Nos. 346, 358, 381
24- 4 Coulton, 1, 92
24-13 Coulton, III, 17
25- 1 *Dok* (S), No. 371
25-11 Scheel, 1, 95, n. 65

**PAGE LINE**

25-28 Buchwald, *LL*, p. 6
25-39 *Dok* (S), under *Eintritt*
27- 3 Scheel, 1, 261-62

### CHAP. II

27-16 *Dok* (S), No. 50
28-11 Scheel, II, 35-36
28-23 *Ibid.*, II, 62
28-25 *Dok* (S), No. 35
30- 6 *Ibid.*, Nos. 24, 477
30-47 *Ibid.*, under *Primitz*
31- 9 *Ibid.*, No. 201
32-10 *Ibid.*, Nos. 286, **303**, 343, 508, 536
34- 2 *Ibid.*, No. 418
34- 5 *Ibid.*, No. 176
34- 6 *Ibid.*, No. 346

PAGE LINE

34- 9 *Ibid.*, No. 180
34-11 *Ibid.*, No. 90
34-12 *Ibid.*, No. 470
34-17 XXXVIII, 143
34-30 Scheel, II, 209
35-33 X, 3, 244
36- 1 Paulus, *Ablass*, III, 431
36- 5 *TR*, 4829
36-34 Scheel, II, 523-26
37-15 Boehmer, *Romfahrt*
37-37 *Dok* (S), No. 479
38- 7 *TR*, 3478
38-12 *TR*, 6453
38-31 *Dok* (S), No. 527
38-39 Scheel, II, 334

CHAP. III

39-18 *TR*, Nos. 3642, 2210*b*,
       2880*a*
40- 6 *Dok* (S), No. 461
41- 2 *Ibid.*, No. 52
41- 3 *Ibid.*, No. 84
41-11 *Ibid.*, Nos. 199, 241
41-17 *Ibid.*, No. 487
41-30 XXIV, 94
41-31 XIX, 209
41-36 XXIV, 96
41-40 VI, 159-69
42- 3 Lev. 26:36
42-33 Jacobs ed., I, 76-78
43-30 *TR*, 6561 (German) =
       *BR*, 1340 (Latin)
43-38 *Dok* (S), No. 362
43-43 *Ibid.*, No. 18
43-44 *Ibid.*, No. 460
43-46 *Ibid.*, Nos. 346, 358
44- 1 *Ibid.*, No. 62
44- 4 *Ibid.*, No. 418
44-37 XVIII, 719
44-37 LIV, 185; XIV, 132; II,
       688; *TR*, 2654*a;*
       Scheel, II, 307-9; *Dok*
       (S), Nos. 273, 207
45- 1 *Dok* (S), Nos. 225, 256,
       262
46-16 *Dok* (S), Nos. 174, 230,
       444, 485
47-16 1, 557
47-24 Vogelsang, *ACh*, 24; X,
       3, 75; XXVII, 108-10
48-25 IV, 243
48-36 VII, 364
48-37 LVI, 381
48-39 LVI, 392

PAGE LINE

50- 3 LIV, 185
50-11 XXXII, 328
51-10 XXXV, 421-22

CHAP. IV

51-38 Boehmer, *JL*, p. 132
53- 7 *BR*, 28
53-48 Kalkoff, *Ablass*
54-18 *Dok* (K), No. 30, pp.
       94-95
54-19 Koestlin-Kawerau,   1,
       142
56-26 Gebhardt, *Gravamina*,
       p. 85
57-31 Schulte, *Fugger*, p. 117
59- 7 *Dok* (K), No. 31
60-10 *Ibid.*, No. 32 and p. 132,
       and Paulus, *Tetzel*
60-34 Raynald, *Annales*, XX,
       160
63-32 From Koehler, *Ls 95
       Thesen*

CHAP. V

65- 7 *BR*, 48
65-11 *TR*, 2635*b*
65-13 Gieseler, *KG*, III, 38,
       n. 1
65-34 *W*, XV, No. 144
66- 1 *BR*, 64
66- 5 *BR*, 72
66-10 *BR*, 75
66-11 I, 350-51
66-15 *BR*, No. 83, p. 186, n.
       22; Kalkoff, *F*, 47;
       Stracke, *Selbstzeug-
       nis*, 132
66-20 *BR*, 75
66-28 Beatus Rhenanus, *BR*,
       No. 75, p. 108
66-36 *BR*, 75; cf. Bauer
66-43 *Dok* (K), p. 132
67- 2 *BR*, 64
67-25 I, 526
67-32 I, 571
68- 2 *BR*, 92 and 1, 201
68-14 I, 635-45; Kawerau,
       *Thesen Ls*
68-32 *ova*, I, 341-46
68-48 I, 650, 647, 677, 657,
       685
69-10 Müller, *Ls röm. Prozess*
69-33 *RA*, II, 461
70- 8 *ova*, II, 349-50
70-16 *TR*, 2668*a*

PAGE LINE
70-18 *BR*, 97
70-36 *W*, XV, No. 174
71- 8 *Ibid.*, No. 166, and *BR*, 112
71-16 *ova*, II, 354-58
71-21 *BR*, 105
71-26 *Archivio stor. ital.*, XXIV (1876), 23
71-43 *ova*, II, 352-53, cf. Kolde, *ZKG*, II, 472-80
72- 2 Kalkoff, *F*, *59*
72-23 *BR*, 99
73- 8 *Dok* (S), No. 10
73-43 *BR*, 99-110; *Acta Aug. WA*, II
73-45 *BR*, 100
74- 5 *BR*, 99
74- 9 *W*, XV, 208
74-11 Koestlin-Kawerau, 211
74-18 *TR*, 225, 409
74-21 II, 17; *BR*, 1, 242
74-46 II, 27-33
74-48 *BR*, I, 242; II, 17
75- 3 *TR*, 5349, p. 78
75- 8 *BR*, 105
75-14 *BR*, 110
75-34 II, 18-22 = *ova*, 1, 386-92
76- 3 II, 39-40
76- 7 *BR*, 124
76-35 *W*, XV, No. 247
76-42 *BR*, 110 = I, 245
77- 4 *BR*, 114
77- 7 *TR*, 5349, p. 79
77-11 *BR*, 112
77-18 *BR*, 119
77-20 *BR*, 118
77-22 *BR*, 116
77-23 *TR*, 1203
77-27 *BR*, 121, p. 271
78-10 *BR*, I, 250
78-14 *BR*, 124

CHAP. VI
78-26 II, 447
78-36 *ova*, II, 423-32
80- 2 Kalkoff, *F*, 184-87
80-14 *W*, XV, No. 311
80-20 Smith, *Corr.*, No. 108
80-25 *BR*, 205, cf. 196; *TR*, 156; *TR*, 3413
80-29 *W*, XV, Nos. 249-53
80-34 *BR*, 152

PAGE LINE
80-35 *BR*, 196
80-38 *W*, XIV, p. 445
80-41 *BR*, 140
80-45 *RA*, I, 824; *BR*, No. 122, p. 274
80-47 *BR*, 204
81- 2 *BR*, 134, 136
81- 4 *BR*, 140
81-11 Smith, *Corr.*, I, 570
81-23 *W*, XV, Nos. 284, 297-99, 302, 306-8, 321-27
81-44 *BR*, 82, 249
82- 3 *TR*, 1245
83- 1 *BR*, 151
83- 6 *W*, XVIII, No. 32
83-18 II, 180-239
83-33 *W*, XV, 393
83-36 *BR*, 167
83-45 *BR*, 141
84- 6 *BR*, 161
86- 7 *W*, XV, Nos. 392, 396
86-10 *BR*, I, 442, n. 9
86-12 *W*, XV, No. 396
86-19 *Ibid.*, No. 392, cf. No. 396 and *BR*, I, 442, n. 9
86-31 *W*, XV, Nos. 390, 392
86-43 *W*, XV, Nos. 395, 393
87- 1 *BR*, I, pp. 477, 498
87- 4 *BR*, 187; *W*, XV, No. 396
87- 5 *Ibid.*, No. 392
87- 8 *BR*, I, 428-30
87-29 *W*, XV, p. 1201; Smith, *Corr.*, I, 262; Loescher, *Analecta*, III, 248
88- 7 II, 400
88-17 II, 313-14
88-23 II, 316
88-37 *Decret.*, pt. I, *dist.* 22, c.2; *dist.* 21, c.21
88-48 II, 265, 276, 279, 285; *BR*, I, p. 422; Koehler, *LKG*
89-11 II, 275
89-27 *Ibid.*, 279, 287
89-29 *W*, XV, No. 392, p. 1207
90-16 II, 280-308
90-20 II, 400; *BR*, I, 471
90-21 II, 649; *BR*, I, 391
90-23 II, 427

PAGE LINE

90-24 *BR*, No. 192, p. 472
90-27 II, 282
90-33 *W*, XV, p. 1318
90-36 II, 283
90-40 II, 311
90-43 II, 406
90-48 II, 324
91-11 *BR*, I, 422
92- 9 II, 404
92-14 *W*, XV, p. 1199
92-28 *Ibid.*, p. 1215
92-30 *BR*, I, 451
92-35 *BR*, 185, 186
92-38 II, 702
92-39 *BR*, 254

CHAP. VII

93-26 *BR*, 146
93-29 Farner, *Zwingli*, 315
93-31 *BR*, 213
95-13 *Eccius Dedolatus*
96-44 II, 449
97- 2 *BR*, 163 = *EE*, 932
97- 5 *BR*, 50
97- 8 *Op.*, IV, 474
97-19 *Op.*, I, 870
97-33 *Op.*, VI, 64 D-E
97-48 *Ausg. Werke*, 205-6
98- 9 Spengler, *Schutzrede*
98-35 *Op.*, IV, 459-60
99-13 *EE*, Nos. 939, 967, 1033, 1167
99-25 Benz
100-26 Panofsky, *Dürer*, I, 198-99
101-46 *Op.*, IV, 262-64
102- 2 *Op.*, I, 167
102-14 I, 378-79
103-21 *BR*, 360
103-34 Schade, II, 1-59
103-43 *BR*, 281
103-47 *BR*, 298
104- 2 *BR*, 287
104-17 *BR*, 310
104-20 *BR*, 323
104-31 *BR*, 282
104-43 *BR*, 368

CHAP. VIII

105-29 VI, 497-573
105-33 *EE*, 1203
106-48 VI, 563-64
107-38 *W*, XV, No. 238, p. 640; cf. *BR*, 110, p. 237

PAGE LINE

108-10 Koehler, *ZL*, 50-52
108-24 Bornkamm, *LgW*, Chap. V
109-11 X, 3, 1
109-16 VI, 521
109-40 III, 304; Seeberg, I, 133-41
111- 2 *ova*, IV, 172-85
111-12 VI, 181-95
111-20 Kolde, *ZKG*, II, 460-70
111-21 *BR*, 285
111-34 Kalkoff, *ZKG*, XXV, 589-91
111-37 *Ibid.*, 593
111-41 Sanuto, *Diarii*, XXVIII, col. 549
112-20 *BR*, 122
112-21 Kalkoff, *ZKG*, XXV, 115, n. 2; Schubert, *Spengler*, 220, n. 2
112-23 *ova*, IV, 310-14 = Ferguson, *E Op.*, 322
113- 8 *ova*, IV, 283
114- 4 *ova*, IV, 312 = Ferguson, *E Op.*, 325
114-32 *ova*, IV, 269, 290, 293
115-10 *ova*, V, 10-12
115-18 Ps. 91:21, 24
115-23 *BR*, 295
115-38 VI, 347
115-46 VII, 645-46
116-24 *BR*, 333, p. 189

CHAP. IX

116- 9 *BR*, 310
117-13 *BR*, 332
121- 4 Kalkoff, *ZKG*, XXV, 129-30
121-22 Balan, No. 3
121-30 *Ibid.*, No. 4
121-35 Schubert, *Spengler*, 241
121-43 *EE*, No. 1167, p. 409
122- 7 Kalkoff, *Anfänge*
122-15 Schubert, *Spengler*, 232, 241
122-18 Wiedemann, *Eck*, 156-65
122-23 Schubert, *Vorgeschichte*, 21
122-25 *W*, XV, No. 466
122-29 *BR*, 340, 348, 351, 352
122-32 *W*, XV, No. 340
122-38 Wiedemann, *Eck*, 165
123- 9 Kalkoff, *Anfänge*

PAGE LINE

123-38 Beatus Rhenanus, *BR*, No. 194; Pacquier, *Aléandre*, 172-73; cf. *AD*, 17; *RA*, II, 472
124- 4 *Hutteni Op.*, III, 455-59
124-19 *BR*, 341
124-33 *W*, XV, No. 442, sec. 39-42
125- 2 *BR*, 351
126-36 VI, 597-612
127-26 VII, 42-49
128- 3 *Ibid.*, 125
128-14 *Ibid.*, 135
128-35 *Ibid.*, 183
128-40 *Ibid.*, 184-85; *BR*, 361; *W*, XV, No. 486
128-46 VII, 161-82
129- 8 *W*, XV, No. 519

CHAP. X

130- 3 *RA*, II, 90-94
130-21 *AD*, 48
130-40 *Ep.* 229, cf. *Op.* IV, 309-31; *Ep.* 233-34
130-44 Kalkoff, *WR*, 213, n. 3
131- 1 *AD*, 182
131-20 *RA*, II, 471
131-24 Balan, Nos. 13, 32, 34, 52
131-38 Ferguson, *E Op.*, 334-35; cf. 336-37, 352-61
131-49 *AD*, p. 92
132- 4 *Ep*, 230
132- 6 *Ep*, 247
132-10 *W*, XV, No. 526 and Balan, p. 18
132-20 *BR*, 349; *WA*, VI, 477-80
132-27 Spalatin, *Ann.*, p. 29; Seckendorf, I, 126; *RA*, II, 464, n. 1
132-29 *EE*, 1166, p. 399
132-36 *W*, XV, 1585
132-43 *RA*, II, No. 61
134-16 Balan, No. 34, pp. 85-86
134-18 *AD*, p. 34
134-20 Balan, No. 35, p. 90
134-25 *RA*, II, No. 62
134-40 *Ibid.*, No. 63
135-13 *BR*, 365
135-45 *BR*, 376
136- 2 *AD*, p. 36
136-13 *BR*, 371, p. 254

136-27 *AD*, pp. 35-36
136-46 *AD*, pp. 30, 40, 55-57, 82
137-10 Hutten, *Ep.*, 247, p. 63; Kalkoff, *BDB*, p. 6
137-13 *AD*, p. 56
137-26 Schade, II, 177
137-28 *RA*, II, 476, n. 3
137-40 *AD*, p. 169
138-19 *RA*, II, 496-505
138-27 *RA*, II, No. 68
138-30 *AD*, p. 73
138-38 *RA*, II, No. 69
138-43 *Ibid.*, No. 72
139- 1 *Ibid.*, No. 74
139- 4 *AD*, p. 101
139- 8 *RA*, II, No. 73
139-18 *BR*, 389
139-22 *BR*, 391
139-29 *BR*, 395, 396
139-33 *BR*, 395
139-41 *Hutteni Op.*, II, 52-53; cf. *AD*, pp. 183, 198
140-15 *RA*, II, No. 66
140-38 *RA*, II, No. 78
140-40 Spalatin, *Ann.*, p. 38; *W*, XV, No. 554
140-43 *Op.*, II, 62, 55
141- 1 *W*, XV, No. 557
141- 7 *AD*, p. 170
141-33 *RA*, II, p. 851
141-47 *RA*, II, pp. 548-49, 574
142-10 *Ibid.*, Note 112; *RA*, II, No. 209, p. 885
143-14 *AD*, p. 152
143-43 *RA*, II, pp. 551-55
144-14 VII, 836-38
144-23 *RA*, II, p. 555
144-32 *AD*, p. 153; *RA*, p. 558
144-34 Spalatin, *Ann.*, 49-50
144-37 *RA*, II, p. 867
144-39 Spalatin, *Ann.*, 50-51
145-16 *RA*, II, pp. 595-96
145-20 *Ibid.*, II, p. 596, n. 3
146-11 *Op.*, II, 61
146-12 *AD*, 158
146-19 *AD*, 160; *RA*, II, No. 84
146-41 *RA*, II, No. 86; pp. 617, 621
146-45 *Ibid.*, No. 85, pp. 603, 610
146-47 *RA*, II, p. 631
147- 4 *BR*, 404, p. 325

PAGE LINE

147-26 *RA*, II, No. 92
147-45 *AD*, pp. 221-24

CHAP. XI

148- 9 Dürer, *Briefe*, 121
149-19 Clemen, *Beiträge*, III,
10-15; Bainton, *Dürer*
149-26 Kalkoff, *Anfänge*, II, 22
149-30 Kalkoff, Vermittlung,
*ARG*, I
149-40 Dürer, *Briefe*, 119-22
150-19 *BR*, 408; *TR*, 5353
150-25 VIII, 211
150-28 *TR*, 6816, p. 209
150-33 VIII, 412, 483; XXXVI,
476
150-37 VIII, 139
150-42 I Kings 19:4
150-48 *BR*, 429
151- 4 *BR*, 407
151-16 *BR*, 435
151-25 *BR*, 429
151-32 *BR*, 410, p. 338
151-37 *BR*, 427
151-40 *BR*, 409
151-41 *BR*, 413, p. 348
151-45 *BR*, 417
152- 2 *BR*, Nos. 413, 418-20,
429, 434
152-18 *TR*, Nos. 495, 1253,
5428, 6077
152-22 VIII, 139
152-33 *BR*, 435
153-21 *BR*, 442
153-24 *BR*, 448
154- 7 VI, 441
154-10 *BR*, 442, p. 408
155- 6 N. Müller, *WB*, No. 102
155-13 *CR*, I, No. 184
155-15 *BR*, 444
155-20 *BR*, 426
155-22 N. Müller, *WB*, No. 31
155-27 *Ibid.*, No. 28
155-37 *BR*, 424, 428
155-44 VIII, 317
156- 6 VIII, 330
156-12 VIII, 569
156-29 VIII, 441-42
156-37 VIII, 448
157- 4 *BR*, No. 424, p. 372
157-11 N. Müller, *WB*, 612
157-21 K. Müller, *LK*, 6
157-31 *Ibid.*, p. 24

PAGE LINE

157-34 N. Müller, *WB*, Nos.
25, 28
157-42 *CR*, I, No. 150
158-16 Frederick: *CR*, I, No.
145; N. Müller, *WB*,
No. 56; Old Believ-
ers: N. Müller, Nos.
25, 44; Evangelicals:
*CR*, I, No. 161; N.
Müller, *WB*, No. 43

CHAP. XII

158-12 *BR*, 443
159- 1 N. Müller, *WB*, 159
159- 9 K. Müller, *LK*, 27
159-12 *BR*, 438
159-16 Dan. 8:25
159-19 VIII, 676-87
160-17 Barge, *Carlstadt*, I, 357-
61; N. Müller, *WB*,
No. 73
160-24 N. Müller, *WB*, No. 75;
Barge, *Carlstadt*, I,
379-86
160-29 N. Müller, *WB*, No. 72
161- 7 Carlstadt, *Von Abtuung*
161-15 Barge, *Carlstadt*, I, 368-
69
161-25 *CR*, I, Nos. 170, 183; N.
Müller, *WB*, Nos. 63,
54, 68, p. 160; *BR*,
450
161-32 *CR*, I, No. 170
161-35 *CR*, I, No. 183, col. 536
161-44 *BR*, 450
162- 2 *BR*, 452
162-21 Pallas, *ARG*, V, 238-40
162-26 *Ibid.*, Nos. 3, 4
162-35 N. Müller, *WB*, No. 92
162-42 *Ibid.*, No. 97
162-45 *BR*, II, p. 462, n. 4
163- 7 Bezold, "Rückkehr,"
*ZKG*, XX, 223-26
163- 9 *BR*, 445
163-15 *BR*, 444
163-44 *BR*, 454
164-15 *BR*, 455
165-28 Kessler, *Sabbata*, 76-80
165-31 Beatus Rhenanus, *BR*,
303
165-38 X, 3, 47
166- 7 *Ibid.*, pp. 25, 18-19
166- 9 *BR*, 478
166-21 *BR*, No. 456, p. 461;
No. 457, p. 469

PAGE LINE

CHAP. XIII

167-10 *RA*, II, No. 153
167-18 *BR*, 1826
167-36 I Cor. 3:11
167-42 II, 586
167-44 XXXVIII, 53
168- 2 XIX, 496
168- 6 Acts 17:28
168-10 XXIII, 135-37; Ps. 139:7-8
168-11 XXVIII, 53
168-18 *TR*, 1160
168-27 VII, 587; XV, 370
168-31 XIX, 360
168-41 XLIV, 429
168-49 XXVII, 482-83
169- 8 XVIII, 626
169-19 XLIV, 429
169-25 XXXI, I, 249
169-30 XVIII, 685
169-35 XL, 2, 329-30
170- 3 XXXVII, 40
170-34 Isa. 9:2
170-42 XIX, 133
171-12 LII, 55-56
171-14 Acts 16:31
171-21 XIX, 154
171-50 *TR*, 4201
173- 4 *TR*, 5015
173-23 XL, 1, 455
173-40 XXVII, 154
173-45 V, 550
174- 2 IX, 610
174-18 XIX, 492
175-10 *BR*, 424
176- 8 *Dok* (S), 672, 755; *BR*, 428, p. 383
176-19 *Bd*, I, 99
176-22 *BR*, 1593
176-28 *Bd*, I, 88
176-30 *Ibid.*, I, 90
176-32 *Ibid.*, I, 249
176-34 LVI, 304, 361
176-39 IV, 324, 364
176-48 LVI, 231
177- 9 II, 496
178- 6 *Bd*, II, 25
179-13 VII, 53, 59-64

CHAP. XIV

181- 8 *TR*, 2223
181-11 *TR*, 2123*b*
181-14 *TR*, 5360
181-20 VII, 575

PAGE LINE

181-26 LII, 399-400
181-32 XXXII, 292-94
181-40 *Bd*, II, 518, 528; *WA*, VII, 244
181-45 *TR*, 437
182- 9 XXX, 2, 570-75
182-10 *TR*, 5252
184-14 XV, 321
185- 4 II, 252
185- 5 XVIII, 389
185-13 XXVIII, 525
185-14 *BR*, 365
185-28 XXIX, 355
185-29 XL, 1, 292
185-32 VI, 459
185-38 XLI, 747
186- 6 II, 254-61
186-24 *Ibid.*, II, 261
186-48 XIX, 625-26
187- 7 XLI, 746-47
187-11 XXVIII, 699
187-16 XVIII, 391
187-20 VI, 267
187-22 XVI, 474
188- 6 XI, 268-69
189- 2 *TR*, 433
189- 6 XXVII, 515-17
189- 8 VIII, 680
189-38 XI, 267
189-42 *TR*, 3263*b*
189-44 XIX, 657
190- 1 Pauls, 69; **LII, 189**; XXXVII, 319
190-18 XXVIII, 360-61; Matthes, 143
190-25 *Bd*, I, 147
190-35 *Bd*, I, 555-56
190-42 *Bd*, I, 572

CHAP. XV

192- 9 N. Müller, *WB*, No. 25, pp. 62-63
192-10 Kalkoff, *Ablass*, 85
192-22 *Ibid.*, 115-16
193- 5 *BR*, 558, 566
193-17 *BR*, 572, 586, 678, 748
193-21 *BR*, 648
193-25 *BR*, 799
193-36 Bainton, *Development*, 113-14
194-17 *W*, XV, No. 716
194-23 *Ibid.*, No. 717
194-30 Planitz, No. 121, p. 271
194-41 *Ibid.*, No. 153

PAGE LINE
195- 8 *Ibid.*, No. 29
195-24 *BR*, 956
195-29 X, 2, 227
195-30 *BR*, 914
195-31 Smith, *Corr.*, No. 737
196- 9 *Op.*, IX, 1215-48
197- 7 XVIII, 719
197-40 *Ibid.*, 758-59
197-47 *Ibid.*, 784-85
198- 3 *BR*, 626
198- 6 *Op.*, X, 1251, 1257-58
198-30 *BR*, 726
198-46 XV, 392
200-23 *W*, XX, Nos. 6, 7; XV, 391-96
201-28 XV, 394
203- 1 XVII, 1, 361-62
203-32 XV, 199-200
203-47 *Ibid.*, 210-11
204- 8 *BR*, 754
204-12 Boehmer-Kirn, No. 56
205- 5 Brandt, *Muentzer*, 148-63
205-15 *BR*, 785

CHAP. XVI

205-35 *BR*, 797
206- 1 *BR*, IV, p. 2, n. 4
206- 7 Koehler, *LZ*, 146-47
206-19 II Cor. 3:6
206-20 John 6:63
206-36 Koehler, *LZ*, 111
206-41 *Ibid.*, 466
206-47 Koehler, *Geisteswelt*, 14
207- 3 Koehler, *LZ*, 175, 328
213- 8 XVIII, 291-334
213-37 Franz, 242, 249-51
216- 2 Boehmer-Kirn, 118, 124; Brandt, *Muentzer*, 187-201
216-12 Boehmer-Kirn, 110
217- 5 XVIII, 358

CHAP. XVII

223-10 *BR*, 426
223-12 *TR*, 1654, 3177
223-25 *BR*, 600
223-30 Beatus Rhenanus, *BR*, p. 319
223-37 *BR*, 800
224-10 *BR*, 857
224-21 *BR*, 782
224-38 *BR*, 890, 900

PAGE LINE
224-45 *BR*, 860
225- 3 *BR*, 883
225- 4 *BR*, 900
225- 7 *TR*, 49
225- 9 *BR*, 900
225-14 Boehmer, *Ls Ehe*, 65
225-20 *BR*, 886
226- 6 *BR*, 892
226-10 *BR*, 897
226-14 *BR*, 900
226-18 *BR*, 896
226-21 *BR*, 894
226-26 *BR*, 898
226-38 Smith, *ML*, 168
226-42 *TR*, 1656, 3178*a*
226-46 *BR*, 946
227- 3 *BR*, 906
227-12 *BR*, 1065
227-21 Seidemann, *ZHT*, 1860, 475-564
227-23 *TR*, 3038*b*, p. 154
228- 2 *BR*, 1078
228- 4 *TR*, 1457
228- 6 *BR*, 1009
228-11 Kroker, 105
228-12 *TR*, 3390*b*
228-19 *BR*, 2267
228-24 *BR*, 3519
228-27 *BR*, 3509
228-31 *TR*, 2437
228-37 Thoma
228-40 *BR*, 1032
228-42 *TR*, 146
228-44 *TR*, 2458, 2397*b*
229- 1 *BR*, 932
229- 4 *BR*, 1013
229- 7 *BR*, 1017
229-10 *TR*, 2447
229-13 *BR*, 1067
229-17 *TR*, 3541
229-21 *TR*, 1101
230- 8 *TR*, 3298*b*
231-46 *TR*, Nos. 301, 397, 566, 613, 1038, 1106, 1637, 2258*b*, 2439, 2849*b*, 2889*a-b*, 3627, 3637*b*, 3901, 4351, 5378, 5742, 5847, 6238, 6250
232- 5 *TR*, 2563*a*
233-13 *TR*, 6725
233-28 XX, 149
233-32 *TR*, 55
233-37 *TR*, 6102

PAGE LINE

233-42 *TR*, 3566
234-10 XXX, 3, 236
234-15 XXIV, 518-21
234-40 XII, 106
234-42 XVII, 1, 24-25
234-48 X, 2, 296
235- 3 *TR*, 3141, 1004
235- 7 *TR*, 2867b
235-10 X, 2, 296
235-16 *TR*, 3675
235-23 *TR*, 2047
235-27 *TR*, 4859
235-34 *TR*, 1656
235-36 *TR*, 2173a
235-41 XXXVI, 360
235-43 *TR*, 236
235-45 *TR*, 3530
235-49 *TR*, 6320
236- 2 *TR*, 3508
236- 3 *TR*, 5524
236- 4 *TR*, 2350a-b
236- 6 *TR*, 2764b
236-16 *TR*, 2922a
236-22 *TR*, 3613
236-25 *TR*, 2963
236-29 *TR*, 4027
236-31 *TR*, 4531

CHAP. XVIII

237-15 *BR*, 1595
237-31 XXXV, 434-35
237-45 *TR*, 5494, pp. 190-91
238-23 Clemen, *Flugschriften*, IV, 278-80
239- 5 *Ibid.*, II, 133-34
239- 8 *Ibid.*, I, 69
239-11 *Ibid.*, II, 147
239-14 *Ibid.*, II, 142
239-32 *Ibid.*, I, 10-17
239-40 *Ibid.*, III, 201-3
241-10 *Ibid.*, III, 362-63
241-18 Berger, V, 260-61
242-18 Sachs, *Werke*, I, 8-24
242-28 Clemen, *Flugschriften*, II, 172; cf. Berger, II, 286
243- 2 *BR*, 465
243- 8 XIX, 75; Holl L, 360; Bainton, *Development*, 130-31
244-15 Cf. Clemen, *Flugschriften*, I, 53-54
244-41 Holl, I, 326-80
245-15 Berbig, *ARG*, III, 376

PAGE LINE

245-18 Winter, 301
245-32 *BR*, No. 1294, pp. 498-99
246-33 *RA*, III, p. 386; Planitz, No. 133
246-40 *RA*, III, No. 242
246-41 Planitz, Nos. 200, 206, 209; *RA*, III, p. 385
247- 2 Planitz, No. 121, p. 273
247- 7 *RA*, III, No. 84
247-15 *RA*, IV, No. 149
247-37 Friedensburg, 161-62
247-43 *Ibid.*, 188
248-26 *RA*, VII, pp. 1142-43
248-30 *Ibid.*, No. 72
248-35 *Ibid.*, No. 137, p. 1286
249-13 *BR*, 1496
249-48 Koehler, *Marburg*, 131
250- 9 *Ibid.*, 139
250-48 Reu, *AC*, No. 13
252-23 *BR*, 1595
252-35 Schirrmacher, 55
253-10 *CR*, II, 107, 115
253-30 *BR*, No. 1611, p. 412
253-42 *BR*, 1621
254-26 XXX, 2, 397-412

CHAP. XIX

255-22 *TR*, 2771a
255-47 *BR*, 492
256- 3 Reu, *Bible*, 160, 187
256-11 *BR*, 556
256-20 XXX, 2, 632-33
257- 9 Cf. Schmidt
258-29 Grisar, *L Studien*, III; Schramm; *WA, Bibel* II, 625
258-35 XXX, 2, 632–33
259-15 *EA*, LXXIII, 115
259-17 *TR*, 3292a
259-22 VIII, 361
261- 7 Cf. Fullerton
261-11 XXX, 2, 637
261-16 *Bibel*, VII, *ad loc.*
262-40 XXX, 2, 550
263-46 XXX, 1, 249
264-11 *Ibid.*, 126-27
264-30 *Ibid.*, 132
267-10 *TR*, 4441, 7034, 968; *Op. Lat.*, VII, 591, 554; *BR*, 1727
268-14 Buszin, *Music Q.*, 95–96
269-15 L, 368-73
269-17 *TR*, 1300, 2362

PAGE LINE
269-28 BR, 1727
271- 9 Bd, I, 539-40
271-12 Buszin, *Mus. Heritage,*
116
271-23 Koehler, "Lutherthum,"
*SVRG,* LI, 43
271-46 XXXV, 419-21; cf. 97-
109

CHAP. XX

273- 2 Cf. Kiessling
273- 7 TR, 272
273-10 Bd, I, 555
274- 3 TR, 2606a-b
274-23 LII, 774
275-41 Bd, I, No. 4
276-10 Bd, I, No. 28
278- 3 X, 1, 62-63; XLI, 480;
XVII, 2, 302; LII,
38; XVII, 2, 303; X,
1, 65-66; XXXII, 253-
55; IX, 439-46
280-18 XIX, 185-251
281- 7 XXXVIII, 360-62

CHAP. XXI

282- 9 Reiter, II, 578
283- 2 BR, 1126
283-13 TR, 1289, 1113; XXVII,
96
283-18 TR, 4777
283-21 TR, 199
284-13 TR, 1557
284-17 TR, 3558b
284-35 XVII, 2, 202
284-38 TR, 4329
284-41 TR, 590
284-42 BR, 1670
284-44 TR, 1089
284-46 TR, 4857
285- 1 TR, 122, p. 52
285- 3 BR, 1670
285- 4 TR, 1349
285- 6 TR, 833; cf. BR, 1670
285- 8 TR, 194
285-13 Ratzeberger, 58
285-17 TR, 1557
285-21 XLVI, 210
285-40 TR, 1631
285-43 TR, 660
286- 9 TR, 2047

PAGE LINE
286-19 Enders, XV, 172
286-22 BR, 429
286-30 XXVII, 64
286-41 XXI, 111
286-46 IX, 440-41
287- 1 BR, 1675
287- 2 XXIII, 133-34
287- 5 Bühler, 100-101
287- 8 Preuss, *ML Prophet,* 96-
97
288- 5 TR, 3588
288-18 XII, 459
288-20 XXVII, 482-84
288-21 XXXVII, 241
288-21 X, 1, 612-13
288-24 IX, 517-19
288-30 XVII, 2, 364-65
290- 8 XLIII, 200-220
290-12 TR, 1032, 1033, 2754b
290-20 Stamge
290-36 XVII, 1, 67-68
290-37 V, 607
292- 5 XXXV, 455-57

CHAP. XXII

292-20 XXX, 3, 279
293-49 Rockwell, *Doppelehe*
294- 5 RA, VII, 1299, 1264
294- 9 Wappler, *Kursachsen,* 21
294-16 Menius, *Wiedertäufer,*
307a
294-25 XXVI, 145-46
295-10 XXXI, 1, 208
295-14 CR, IV, 739-40
295-29 L, 6-14
295-39 CR, IV, 740
295-42 TR, 5232b
295-49 Wappler, *Kursachsen,*
41, 94
296-13 Menius, *Wiedertäufer,*
316b
297- 2 TR, 2912a
297- 5 XI, 314
297-10 XI, 336
297-24 LIII, 417-18
299-40 K. Müller, *Wiederstand,*
and Waldeck
299-46 Bd, 1, 468
300-11 BR, 4158
300-16 Smith, *ML,* 416-22

# SOURCES OF ILLUSTRATIONS

PAGE

Inside
Cover   Albert Schramm, *Luther und die Bibel,* Tafel 107, No. 190.
Title   Boehmer, p. 111.
16–17   Emil Reicke, *Der Lehrer in der deutschen Vergangenheit* (1901), Nos. 36, 41, and 48.
19      *Luther Kalender* (1909), p. 34.
21      Friedrich Gerke, "Die satanische Anfechtung in der Ars Moriendi und bei Luther," *Theologische Blätter,* II (1932), 321.
23      Hartmann Schedel, *Das Buch der Chroniken* (1493).
24      *Propylaenweltgeschichte,* V, 12.
26      J. A. Herbert, *Illuminated Manuscripts* (1911), p. 238.
28      Michael Reu, *Dr. Martin Luthers Leben* (1917), p. 42.
29      *Propylaenweltgeschichte,* V, 14.
32      Luther's Bible (Sept., 1522).
34–37   Albert Schramm, *Die Bilderschmuck der Frühdrucke,* X (1927), Tafel 57, Nos. 91–94.
40      *VJLG,* XV (1933), opp. p. 16.
46      Luther's Bible (1541). Albert Schramm, *Luther und die Bibel,* Tafel 277, p. 542.
52      F. Lippmann, ed., *Lucas Cranach* (1895), No. 34.
54–55   Alfred Woltmann, *Holbein* (1866), opp. p. 74.
57      Geisberg, *Bilder-Katalog,* No. 1293.
58      Geisberg, *Reformation,* Plate XIV, 7.
59      From a contemporary tract *On Aplas von Rom* (n.d.).
61      Schreckenbach, p. 64.
62      Barbagallo, IV, 349.
69      Boehmer, p. 135.
72      Boehmer, p. 195.
74      Thomas Wright, *History of Caricature* (1864), 258, No. 151.
74      Paul Drews, *Der evangelische Geistliche* (1905), 51, No. 39.
81      Schreckenbach, p. 145.
82      Boehmer, p. 179.
85      Hartmann Schedel, *Das Buch der Chroniken* (1493).
87      Boehmer, p. 229.
91      Schreckenbach, p. 138.
94      After Holbein. Cf. Bainton, *Castellio,* pp. xi, 44.
100     Hutten, *Gesprächbuchlein.*
101     Clemen, *Flugschriften,* III (1909), 239.
102     *Propylaenweltgeschichte,* V, 99.
113     Boehmer, p. 289.
118     Justus Hashagen, *Martin Luther* (1934), p. 41.
120     *Passional Christi und Antichristi* (reprint 1885).
123     Pflugk-Harttung, p. 523.
128     Boehmer, p. 304.
131     Hjalmar Holmquist, *Martin Luther* (1917), p. 136.
133     *Propylaenweltgeschichte,* V, 87.
134     Schreckenbach, p. 103.
135     Schreckenbach, p. 100.
142     Pflugk-Harttung, p. 437.
145     *Illustrirte Zeitung* (1917).

PAGE
150    Kunstverlag Bruno Hansmann, *Cassell,* No. 32335.
151    Geisberg, *Bilder-Katalog,* No. 302.
154    Boehmer, p. 277.
160    Geisberg, *Reformation,* XXVI, 27.
163    Geisberg, *Bilder-Katalog,* No. 634.
172    Geisberg, *Bilder-Katalog,* No. 671.
177    Schreckenbach, p. 90.
180    Luther's Bible (1534, facsimile 1934).
182    Paul Hohenemser, ed., *Flugschriftensammlung Gustav Freytag* (1925), p. 95.
183    Barbagallo, IV, 338.
192    Pflugk-Harttung, p. 396.
194    Geisberg, *Bilder-Katalog,* No. 420.
202    Gunther Franz, *Bauernkrieg,* p. 413.
210    Otto Brandt, *Der deutsche Bauernkrieg* (1929), p. 25.
211    Franz, *Bauernkrieg,* p. 101.
214    *Propylaenweltgeschichte,* V. 109.
215    Wilhelm Hansen, *Das deutsche Bauerntum* (1938), p. 70.
217    Otto H. Brandt, *Der grosse Bauernkrieg* (1925), opp. p. 184.
218–19    Franz, *Bauernkrieg,* p. 215.
221    Geisberg, *Reformation,* X, 7.
222    Above: Friedrich Bezold, *Geschichte der deutschen Reformation* (1890), p. 361. Below: Gerhard Ritter, *Propylaenweltgeschichte* (2nd ed.), p. 255.
225    Adolf Bartels, *Der Bauer in der deutschen Vergangenheit* (1900), No. 58.
227    Geisberg, *Bilder-Katalog,* Nos. 423 and 424.
230    Aurifaber, *Tischreden* (1568).
232    Geisberg, *Die deutsche Buchillustration* (1930), Tafel 139, No. 309.
240    Clemen, *Flugschriften,* I (1907), 69.
240    Geisberg, *Die deutsche Buchillustration,* III (1930), Tafel 142, No. 312.
241    Clemen, *Flugschriften,* III (1909), 362
251    *Propylaenweltgeschichte,* V, 140.
256    Luther's Bible (1534, facsimile 1934).
257    Albert Schramm, *Luther und die Bibel,* Tafel 222, No. 433.
259–60    Albert Schramm, *Luther und die Bibel,* Tafel 19, No. 28; Tafel 26, No. 35; Tafel 192, No. 336.
264–65    Above: Geisberg, *Die Reformation,* IX, 25. Below: *Luther Kalender* (1909), pp. 99, 101.
268    Hans Preuss, *Martin Luther der Künstler* (1931), opp. p. 104.
270    *Luther-Jahrbuch,* XV (1933), 107.
273    Geisberg, *Reformation,* XX, 28.
277    Albert Schramm, *Luther und die Bibel,* Tafel 129, No. 233.
282    Hjalmar Holmquist, *Martin Luther* (1917), p. 153.
285    *Lucas Cranach Ausstellung im deutschen Museum Berlin* (1937), p. 1933.
287    Schreckenbach, p. 71.
291    Charles Schneider, *Luther, poète et musicien* (1942), p. 71.
294    Luther's Bible (1534, facsimile 1934), adapted from the title page of Hosea.
298    *Luther Jahrbuch,* XV (1933), 106.
300    Schreckenbach, p. 152.

# INDEX

Aachen, 132, **277**
Abel, 109
Abraham, 27, 77, 209, **261, 284, 289–90**
Absolution, 106
Adam, 41, 112, 170, 171, 184, 235, 242, 261, 284
*Address to the Nobility*, 105, 117–20, 154
Advent, 274
Accolti, Cardinal, 112
*Against the Execrable Bull*, **125–26**
*Against the Peasants*, 216–17
*Agnus Dei*, 20, 239
Agricola, Stephan, 251
Albert of Mainz, 56–58, 60, 61, 62, 64, 70, 103, 123, 130, 136, 146, 148, 153, 154, 158, 224, 227, 252–54
Aleander, Jerome, 121–24, 130–31, **132**, 136, 137, 139, 144–48, **149**
Alexander VI, 38
Alsace, 209, 213
Alstedt, 203, **205**
America, 22
Amsdorf, Nicolas, 166, **224, 226**
Anabaptists, 109, 200, 205–207, **220,** 221, 243, 245, 254, 294–96
*Anfechtung*, 31, 47, 262, 279, 283, *See also* Depression
Annas, 68, 143, **148**
Annates, 71
Anne, St., 15, 19, 21, 25, 302
Antichrist, 15, 84–85, 104, 120, 124–26, 128–29, 139, 151, 159, 166, 194, 258
Antwerp, 122
Apocrypha, 90–91
Apostles' Creed, 137, 233, 263, 270
Aquinas, Thomas, 24, 94, 169, 180, 183, 189
Aristotle, 20, 94, 97, 184
Art, 36, 161, 199, 206
*Assertion of All the Articles*, **127**
Assisi, 238
Assyria, 168, 185, **278**
*Asterisks*, 82
Astrology, 210
Athenians, 111
Attrition, 62
Augsburg, 69–70, 72, 74, 77, 95, 135, 242, 246, 247, 253–54. *See also* Diets
**Augsburg Confession, 99,** 253–54, 292

Augustine, 44, 47, 65, 89, 95, 102, 169–70, 180, 184, 186–87, 233, 266, 276, 301
Augustinians, 25, 33, 36, 37, 39, 65, 68, 70, 71, 74, 111, 152, 155, 156, 157
general of, Gabriele della Volta, 65, 111
cloister in Wittenberg, 39, **45, 47,** 157, 226, 227
Augustus, 189
Austria, 98, 141, 145, 207, **221**
*Auto da fé*, 122

Baal, 151, 193, 205
Babel, tower of, 37
Babylon, 75, 80, 127, 135, 143, 168, 179, 258, 259–60
*Babylonian Captivity, The*, 105–108, 137, 140, 141, 146, 153, 156
Bach, Johann Sebastian, 262, 267, **301**
Baden, 207
Ban, 67–68, 70, 77, 79, 98, 129
Banishment, 76–78, 203, 245, 246
Baptism, 106–107, 108, 109, 117, 287
Baptism, infant, **161,** 199, 200, 202, 207
Baroque, 258
Barth, Karl, 64
Basel, 73, 93, 149, 205, 247, **249**
Basel, Council of, 90
Bathsheba, 264
Bavaria, 121, 122, **195, 221,** 246, **269**
Beatitudes, 180
Becket, à, Thomas, **97**
Behemoth, 205
Belvedere, 258
Benedict, St., 24
Bernard, St., 155, 276
Bethlehem, 18, 170, **276**
Bible
authority, 31, 33, 68, 69, 73–75, **125,** 127, 138, 144, 147, 161, 288
canon, 259
chair of, 45
inspiration, 259
translation, 152, 163, 255–62, **301**
*see also* Word of God
Bigamy, 292–93
Blasphemy, 44, 63, 96, 124, 125, 135, 194, 243, 283, 295
Bohemia, 70, 86, 89, 90, 92, 108, **112, 114,** 119, **138,** 215

Bohemian Brethren, 263. *See also* Hussite
Bologna, 82
Boniface VIII, 68
Brabant, 93
Brandenburg, 92, 122, 138, 185, 194, 252-53
Brenz, John, 66, 251
Brethren of the Common Life, 191
Brigitta, St., 36, 53
Bucer, Martin, 66, 103, 140, 249, 250-51
Bugenhagen, John, 155
*Bund*, 209-10, 215
*Bundschuch*, 146, 209-10
Bunyan, John, 301
Burgundy, 141, 145
Burning
  Luther's works, 111, 114, 116, 122-23, 133-34, 136, 148
  papal bull and canon law, 127-29, 135, 147

Caesar, appeal to, 121, 132, 139
Caiaphas, 68, 109, 148
Cain, 109, 236
Cajetan, 69-76, 77-81, 105, 107, 112, 164
Callistus, St., 36
Calvinism, 299
Campeggio, Lorenzo, 241, 252-53
Canaanite, 284
Canute, 53
Capitalism, 183
Carlstadt, Andreas, 81, 82, 86-88, 121, 149, 152, 154, 157, 160-61, 162, 166, 199-202, 204-205, 229, 265
Carthusian, 24, 33, 181
Carvajal, Cardinal, 112
Castelo de St. Angelo, 258
Castle Church, 39, 53, 55-56, 60, 79, 130, 152, 155, 157, 159, 192, 246
Catechism, 262-64
Catharinus, Ambrosius, 152
Celibacy, 119, 154-56, 234, 275
Celtes, Conrad, 21
Chancellor of Saxony, Brück, 250
Charlemagne, 136, 141
Charles I of England, 127
Charles V, 79, 98, 116, 121, 124, 126, 131, 134, 136-38, 141, 142, 144, 146-49, 194, 248, 251-53, 254, 293, 298-99
Charybdis, 198
Christ
  deserted, 47, 179, 290, 302
  example, 179
  incarnation, 45, 95, 107
  judge, 22, 25, 43, 47, 286
  kingdom of, 187, 242, 275
  love, 68
  mediator, 50, 51, 173, 263

  merits, 63
  revealer, 170-73, 297, 302
  Saviour, 45, 50, 53
  sinlessness, 35
  victor, 50, 242, 280
  *see also* Jesus, Passion
Christmas, 159, 171, 237, 274
Chrysostom, St., 53
Church
  allied with state, 109, 117, 187
  condition of, 238
  doctrine of, 51, 106, 108-10, 242-43
  gathered, 109
Cistercians, 23
*Civil Government, On*, 246
Clement VII, 247
Clergy, powers of, 106-108
Cloister
  life in, 27-28
  Luther's entry, 18, 25-27
Coburg, 252
Cologne, 110, 112, 125, 128, 129, 132, 242, 252
Columbus, 22
Communism, 207
Compostela, 288
Conciliarism, 112, 127
Confession, 34, 37, 40-42, 54-55, 59, 106, 152, 159, 162
Confirmation, 106
Conrad, Bishop, 220
Conscience, 144, 151, 249, 266, 275, 279
Consistory, papal, 111-14
Constance, 238, 247
Constance, Council of, 89-91
Constantine, 83
*Constantine, Donation of*, 96
Consubstantiation, 108
Contrition, 54-55, 59, 62, 66, 67, 106, 278
*Corpus Christi*, 86, 253
Corsica, 238
Council
  appeal to, 75-76, 114, 116
  authority of, 69, 79, 90-91, 92, 137, 144, 148, 288
Counsels of perfection, 33, 156, 175
Counter Reformation, 123, 149, 191, 193, 221, 301
Cranach, Lucas, 53, 120, 227, 256, 258
Cranmer, Thomas, 301
Creation, 167, 171, 182
Croesus, 228
Cromwell, Oliver, 214
Cross of Christians, 203
Crusades, 54, 70, 71, 79, 157, 183, 208
*Cujus regio*, 247
*Cum Postquam*, 78
*Curia*, 61, 77, 80, 101, 104, 110-11, 125, 127, 130-31, 134

Damascus, 46
Damnation, 48, 63, 150, 241
Daniel, 127, 159, 202, 204–205, 296
Dante, 188
David, 55, 111, 169, 202, 220, 257, 261, 264, 269, 283, 284
Death
  *Art of Dying*, 21, 280
  dance of, 22
  penalty, 187, 193, 207, 295
Decretals, 73, 75, 81, 83, 88, 91, 194
Degrees, academic, 201
Denmark, 53
Depression, 20, 25, 31, 42, 169, 281–92
Deuteronomy, 184
Devil, 27, 31, 33, 41, 50, 68, 139–40, 150–51, 155, 162, 164–65, 169, 170, 186, 190, 196, 204, 221, 225, 239, 241, 256, 264, 267, 275, 283–84, 287, 290, 293. *See also* Lucifer, Satan
Devils, 19, 22, 220, 242
Diets
  Augsburg (1518), 70, 72, 74
  Worms (1521), 70, 81, 130–48, 150, 164, 167, 185, 195–96, 204, 223, 246–47, 280, 298
  Nürnberg (1522), 162, 163, 166, 194, 246; (1524), 247
  Speyer (1526), 247; (1529) 248, 294
  Augsburg (1530), 246, 253
Diseases, Luther's, 34, 42, 152, 228, 283, 300
Divorce, 293
Doctor's degree, Luther's, 45, 65, 148, 259, 264
Dominicans, 55, 59, 66, 68, 74, 79, 103, 111
Domitian, 36
Dostoevski, 301
Doubt, 33, 38, 44, 70, 150, 286
Drinking, 233
Dürer, Albrecht, 47, 96, 99, 122, 148–49, 257

Easter, 34, 262, 271, 274
Ebernburg, 102–103, 130, 140, 164
Eck, John of Ingolstadt, 82–92, 101, 110–12, 116, 121–22, 124–26, 128, 131, 183, 253, 258
Eck, John of Trier, 141–42, 143
Economics, 183, 208–209, 215, 301
Education, 16–18, 20, 51, 182, 262
Edwards, Jonathan, 301
Egypt, 168–69, 206
Eisenach, 150, 296
Elbe, 39, 55
Elect, 203
Eleutherius, 97
Elijah, 150, 202, 296
Elisabeth, mother of the Baptist, 168

Elizabeth, St., 150
Elster Gate, 128
Emser, Jerome, 258
Endor, witch of, 108
England, English, 88, 93, 98, 101, 131, 140, 195, 208, 245, 297, 301
Epicurean, 137
Epiphany, 274
Equalitarianism, 210
Erasmus, 66, 96–99, 101, 105, 108, 110, 122, 123, 131, 132, 133, 136, 139, 149, 168, 175, 191, 195–99, 206, 232, 253, 263, 269, 302
Erbe, Fritz, 295
Erfurt, 18, 20, 24–25, 34, 36, 39, 66, 86, 110, 122, 139, 151, 228
Esau, 197, 225
Ethics, 174–90
Eucharist, 93. *See also* Mass
Europe, 53, 98, 183, 208, 293, 299
Evangelical experience, 45
Eve, 41, 235, 284
Excommunication of Luther, 74, 75, 97, 114, 115, 130, 132, 137, 147
*Exsurge Domine*, 112–15, 121, 124–25, 130, 137
Extreme unction, 106
Ezekiel, 261
Ezra, 179

Faber, John, 258
Faith, 49, 63, 107, 109, 110, 119, 120, 137, 159, 168, 173, 176, 178, 234, 245, 250, 253, 259, 296
Fall of man, 171, 182–83, 184, 242
Family, 182, 186, 207, 233–34
Fasting, 34, 159, 206. *See also* Mortification
Ferdinand of Austria, 98, 194, 207, 246–48, 250, 252
Ferdinand of Spain, 141
Folklore, 19–20
Forgiveness, 178, 274, 280
Fortuna, 96
France, French, 15, 77, 88, 93, 98, 101, 131, 140, 144, 148, 181, 191, 208, 225, 234, 248, 256, 297, 299
Francis I, 98
Francis, St., 97
Franciscans, 39, 111, 159, 184
Franconia, 121, 214
Frankenhausen, 96
Frankfurt, 103, 297
Fraticelli, 84
Frederick Barbarossa, 157
Frederick the Wise, 39, 53–55, 60, 65, 69–71, 75–77, 79–81, 99, 111, 114, 120, 122, 124, 129–34, 138, 140, 142, 144–47, 148, 149, 157, 158, 162–63, 192–95, 204, 216, 223, 246, 257, 260, 269
*Freedom of the Christian Man*, 105, 126, 138, 140, 146, 178–79

*Freedom of the Will, On the,* 196
Free will, 196-97
Freiburg im Breisgau, 73
Fritz, court fool, 130
Froben, John, 93, 96
Fugger, Jacob, 57–58, 61, 80, 183

Gabriel, 168, 227, 231, 286, 288
Galatians, 45, 96, 228
Galilee, 102, 276
Gamaliel, 146, 161, 254
Genesis, 229
Gentiles, 66, 90, 197
George, Duke, 82, 83, 86, 89, 92, 122,
   143, 146, 162, 164, 195, 198, 217,
   246, 258, 260, 269, 293
George of Brandenburg, 252
George, St., 86
German language, 18, 90, 98, 144, 148,
   153, 160, 255, 257, 261, 266, 272
German nation, 70, 136, 140, 143, 145,
   191
Germany, 16, 37, 53, 55–57, 61, 64,
   67, 69, 79, 80, 93, 100–103, 110–
   12, 114, 120, 130, 134, 141, 146,
   151, 208, 220, 231, 238, 246, 247,
   251, 262, 300
Gethsemane, 188
Glapion, 140, 141, 146
Glatz, Kaspar, 224
God
   absolute, 169
   abyss of, 43
   dualism, 187
   Father, 280
   hidden, 169, 187
   holy, 31, 33, 47
   justice of, 44, 290
   love of, 48, 173, 283
   majesty of, 30–31, 43–44, 47, 58,
      142, 161, 173, 197, 280, 302
   mercy of, 48, 49–50, 51, 63, 187,
      197, 302
   substance of, 108
   terror of, 25, 104, 142
   vengeance, 298
   wisdom, 269
   wrath of, 21, 41, 43, 49, 51, 126,
      187, 216
Goliath, 82, 111, 220
Good Hope, Cape of, 22
Gospel, 75, 104, 111, 115, 137, 148,
   188, 275
Gothic, 18, 54
Grace, 26, 29, 169, 271, 273, 276
Greece, 168
Greek Church, 88, 89, 99
Greek language, 67, 82, 87, 96, 99,
   121, 152, 206, 255, 266, 302
Gregorian chant, 268
Gregory I, 67

Hadrian VI, 191, 193–94, 196
Halberstadt, 56

Halle, 35, 153, 228
Hannibal, 225
Hapsburg, 56, 79, 101, 141, 144, 194–
   95, 207, 246, 248
Heathen, 268
Heaven, 43, 169, 231, 234, 269
Hebrew, 65, 87, 95, 121, 163, 165,
   255, 270, 279, 302
Hebrews, Epistle to, 261
Hedio, Caspar, 251
Heidelberg, 65, 103
Heinrich of Zuetphen, 282
Hell, 20, 22, 25, 38, 78, 169, 171, 241,
   279, 293
Henry VIII, 98, 195, 198
Hercules, 93
"Here I stand," 144, 302
Heresy, 69, 70, 71, 78, 111, 112, 126,
   144, 148
Heretic, 68, 75, 78–80, 92, 93, 114–15,
   120, 125, 134, 138, 141, 145, 195
Herod, 288
History, 22, 168
Hochstraten, Jacob von, 93, 94, 96
Hohenzollern, 56
Holbein, Hans, 55, 94
Holcot, Robert, 94
Holiness, 33, 201
Holy Roman Empire, 15, 79, 101, 111,
   141, 143, 254, 299
Holy Spirit. *See* Spirit
Holy, terror of, 30, 142. *See also* God
Hope, 41
Horeb, 150
Hours, canonical, 27, 152
Humanism, 95–96, 99, 101, 103, 121–
   22, 132, 136, 195, 206, 262
Hungary, 131
Hus, John, 78, 89–93, 113, 120, 128,
   136–38, 143
Hussites, 84, 89, 92, 108, 157, 191
Hutten, a, 189
Hutten, Ulrich von, 100–104, 115, 117,
   123, 130, 132, 134, 136–37, 139,
   146, 149, 164–65
Hymns, 270–71
   *Aus tiefer Not,* 271
   *Ein feste Burg,* 270, 290–91
   *Gelobest seist Du,* 237
   *Nu freut euch,* 50–51
   *Von Himmel Hoch,* 237

Images, 153, 160, 162, 201, 239
Individualism, 109
Indulgences, 22, 35, 53, 54–65, 66, 68,
   70–71, 75, 78, 81, 91, 96, 97, 98,
   110, 112, 119, 127, 136, 153
Inquisitors, 89, 134
Interdict, 134
Inwardness, 97, 187, 201, 203, 204, 288
Ironsides, 214
Isaac, 27, 209, 289–90, 300
Isabella, 121, 141
Isaiah, 170, 270

Ishmaelites, 168
Israel, 143, 206, 212, 284
Italy, Italian, 37, 55, 61, 77, 82, 101–102, 112

Jacob, 197, 256–57
James, Epistle of, 138, 259, 261
Janssen, Johannes, 210, 248
Jena, 204
Jericho, 119
Jerome of Croatia, 90
Jerome, St., 53
Jerusalem, 22, 63, 80, 140, 179, 276
Jesuit, 198, 271
Jesus, 53, 82, 125, 135, 148, 167, 194, 263, 268, 274. *See also* Christ
Jews, 66, 122, 125, 143, 176, 179, 197, 245, 255, 297
Jezebel, 150
Joachim of Brandenburg, 130, 194, 246
John Frederick, 204, 257, 269, 298
John of Saxony, 204, 216, 252, 268, 294
John, St., 36, 261, 271, 272, 282
Jonah, 41, 278–80, 288
Jonas, Justus, 156, 157, 237, 251
Joseph (Old Testament), 168
Joseph (New Testament), 169, 225, 276–77, 288
Josiah, 193
Jost, 237
Judaism, 174
Judas, 36, 274
Jude, 261
Judgment, day of, 22, 24
Julius II, 51, 57, 68, 76, 114, 127
Justification, 49–50, 261

Kappell, 251
Keys, power of, 61–62, 147
Kierkegaard, Søren, 301
Knights, 101, 150, 164
Kopp, Leonard, 223, 226
Koran, 185

Laity, 106, 112, 134, 147, 153, 194
Lang, Cardinal, 138, 148, 194, 241
Lapland, 19
Lateran Council V, 90
Latimer, Hugh, 301
Latin language, 18, 60, 67, 121, 144, 148, 160, 265–66, 270, 272
Latomus, Bartholomew, 152
Law
  canon, 79, 88, 104, 109, 128, 137
  civil, 17
  German, 208, 275
  Old Testament, 242, 259, 261
  Roman, 30, 208
Layman, Luther quoting Panormitanus on, 89–91

League
  Catholic, 207, 246
  Swabian, 220–21
Leah, 234
Legalism, 27, 199, 201
Leipzig, 83, 89, 95, 128, 164, 228, 239
  debate, 86–92, 102, 110, 141, 269
  University, 39, 82, 86
Lemberger, George, 257–58
Lent, 34, 97, 274
Leo X, 35, 55, 56, 58, 60, 65, 66, 71, 74, 80, 84, 121–22, 125–27, 194, 247
Leviathan, 205
Leviticus, 256
Liberty, religious, 99, 114, 120, 188, 193, 205, 207, 243, 245, 248, 254, 294–96
Lichtenburg, 124
Lie, 188, 293
Liège, 123
Lippus, 237
*Litany of the Germans*, 139
Literalism, 200, 249
Liturgy, 243, 254, 265–66, 269
Litzkau, 53
Lochau, 244
Lombard, Peter, 94
Lord's Prayer, 233, 235, 263, 280
Lord's Supper, 108, 166, 200, 205, 249–50, 265, 293. *See also Mass*
Louvain, 73, 110, 112, 122, 125, 149
Low Countries, 121, 141, 149, 268
Lucifer, 239, 240. *See also* Devil, Satan
Ludwig of the Palatinate, 145, 147
Ludwig of Saxony, 276
Luke, St., 37, 103
Luther, Martin
  birth, 16
  schooling, 16–18, 20
  early religious disquiet, 18–22
  entry into the monastery, 22–27
  novitiate, 27–28
  recurrence of disquiet; the first mass, 29–33
  self-help through mortification, 33–34
  the merits of the saints; trip to Rome, 35–38
  permanent residence in Wittenberg, 39
  influence of Staupitz, 39
  exploring confession, 40–42
  the inadequacy of mysticism, 42–43
  doubts as to the justice of God, 44
  blasphemy, 44
  appointment to the chair of Bible, 45
  the evangelical experience, 45–48
  justification by faith, 48–50
  commencement of reform in theological training, 51
  indulgences at Wittenberg, 53
  first protests, 53–55
  indulgence for St. Peter's, Tetzel, 56–60

Luther, Martin—*cont'd*
  *Ninety-Five Theses*, 60–64
  reported to Rome, 64
  Heidelberg Disputation, 65
  Dominican assault, 66
  attack on penance, papal primacy,
    the ban, 67
  reply of Prierias, 68–69
  case referred to Cajetan in Germany,
    69–71
  interviews with Cajetan, 71–75
  threatening exile, 75–78
  *Cum Postquam*, defines indulgences,
    78
  imperial election affords respite, 79
  Miltitz appointed to negotiate, 80–
    81
  arrival of Melanchthon, 81
  challenge of Eck, 82–83
  Luther suspects the pope is Anti-
    christ, 84–85
  Leipzig, debate, 86–92
  the endorsement of Hus, 89–92
  dissemination of Luther's writings, 93
  Renaissance and Reformation, 95–96
  Erasmus and Luther, 96–99
  Melanchthon and Luther, 99
  Dürer and Luther, 99–100
  German nationalism and the Refor-
    mation, 100–104
  Hutten, Sickingen, and Luther, 100–
    104
  respite and writing, October 1519–
    October 1520, 105
  *Babylonian Captivity* and the sacra-
    ments, 105–110
  persecution resumed, 110–111
  the bull *Exsurge*, 112–15
  Luther's attitude: incendiary and
    apocalyptic, 115–16
  appeal to the emperor, 116
  *Address to the Nobility*, 117–18
  publication of the bull, 121–22
  burning of Luther's books, 122–24
  *Against the Execrable Bull*, 125–26
  *Freedom of the Christian Man*, 126–
    27
  *Assertion of All the Articles*, 127–28
  Luther's burning of the bull, 128
  the German constitution, 130
  parties on the eve of Worms, 130–32
  hearing promised and recalled, 132–35
  Aleander's bungling of the prosecu-
    tion, 136
  violent temper at the Diet, 137
  Aleander's speech, 137
  invitation to Luther renewed, 138–40
  Glapion's attempt at mediation, 139–
    40
  Luther before the Diet of Worms,
    140–48
  the Edict of Worms, 144–48

Luther, Martin—*cont'd*
  Luther's trial compared to Christ's
    passion, 148–49
  at the Wartburg, 149
  depression and disease, 151
  literary labors, 152
  reformation at Wittenberg, 152–58
  *On Monastic Vows*, 155
  the mass, 156
  outbreak of violence, 157–58
  exploratory return to Wittenberg, 158
  tumult: Carlstadt and iconoclasm,
    159–61
  Luther invited to return, 162–64
  the return: plea for moderation,
    164–66
  Luther's theology, 166–74
  nature, history, philosophy inade-
    quate as revelation, 167–70
  Christ the sole revealer, 170–74
  Luther's ethics: the menace to morals,
    174–76
  the ground of goodness, 177–79
  the callings, 180–83
  economics, 183–84
  politics, 184–87
  church and state, 187–90
  conflict with the Counter Reforma-
    tion, 191–95
  recoil of the moderates: Erasmus,
    195–98
  insurgence of the Puritans: Carlstadt,
    198–201
  the revolutionary saints; Müntzer,
    201–205
  rival movements: Zwinglianism and
    Anabaptism, 205–207
  social unrest: Peasants' War, 208–22
  Luther's marriage, home life, *Table
    Talk*, views of marriage, 223–37
  dissemination of the reform by pam-
    phleteering, 238–42
  problems of Church administration,
    242–44
  the visitation, 244–46
  the protest at Speyer, 246–48
  attempt at Protestant alliance: Mar-
    burg Colloquy, 248–51
  Augsburg Confession, 251–54
  Bible translation, 255–62
  catechisms, 262–64
  liturgy, 265–66
  music, 266–70
  hymns, 270–71
  preaching, 272–80
  prayer, 280–81
  Luther's persistent religious difficul-
    ties, 281–92
  the bigamy of the Landgrave Philip,
    292–93
  the Anabaptists, 294–96
  the Jews, 296–98
  the emperor, 298–99
  estimate of Luther, 299–302

Lutheran, 248–50, 265, 293, 299
Lyra, Nicholas, 94

Maccabees, 90
Magdeburg, 25, 56, 224
Magistrate, 117, 182, 185, 187–90, 203, 244, 275
Magliana, 111, 114
Magnificat, 20, 152, 188
Mainz, 56, 123, 129, 134, 185, 231
Man
  depravity of, 88, 110, 163
  nature of, 42, 196
  *see also* Fall, Natural man
Manasseh, 55
Mansfeld, 20, 231, 300
Marburg, 249
Mark, St., 103
Marrani, 122
Marriage
  of clergy and religious, 119, 153–56, 162, 191, 195, 201, 223
  Luther's, 223–37
  Luther's views of, 233–36, 275
  sacrament of, 106
Martyrdom, 125, 136, 144, 149, 205, 225, 282, 298
Mary Magdalene, 21
Mary, Virgin, 21, 24, 28, 35, 37, 44, 52, 60, 73, 159, 168, 181, 203, 209, 239, 256, 257, 276–77, 288
Mass, 29, 107, 157, 158, 192
  both kinds, 108, 153, 157, 159
  canon of, 265–66
  consubstantiation, 108
  for the dead, 38, 153
  elevation, 157, 266
  endowed, 156, 192
  German, 162, 266, 268. *See also* Liturgy
  Luther's first, 29, 142
  private, 156
  reform of, 159
  sacrifice, 107, 156, 160, 265
  transubstantiation, 107–108
  at Wittenberg, 193
Master of Arts, 20
Matthew, St., 103, 152, 267, 272, 293
Maximilian, Emperor, 68–71, 79, 103, 121, 141
Medici, 56, 60, 71, 247
Meissen, Bishop of, 122, 162-63
Melanchthon, Philip, 81, 86, 95, 99, 108, 120, 128, 151, 152, 155, 161, 163, 175, 210, 231, 237, 244, 249, 250–51, 253, 263, 270, 295, 300
"Melancolia," 99
Merits, 35–38, 40, 53, 54, 62, 63, 75, 78, 175, 234, 261, 263
Merseburg, 122
Middle Ages, 19, 20, 33, 79, 84, 129, 183, 208, 234, 262, 269, 297
Middle Way, 199

Midianites, 220
Miltitz, Carl von, 79–80, 124, 126
Ministry, 212
  lay, 201
  Luther's, 299–300
Moab, 198
Mochau, Anna, 155
Monasticism, 16, 24–25, 33, 107, 180, 184, 234, 239
*Monastic Vows On*, 156, 158
Morals. *See* Ethics
Moravia, 297
Mortification, 33
Moses, 16, 31, 36, 53, 180, 216, 255, 257, 302
Muelhausen, 216
Münster, 296
Müntzer, Thomas, 200–205, 206–207, 209, 214–21, 266, 296
Music, 161, 199, 206, 266–71, 285
  choral, 268
  not contentious, 269
  in despondency, 284
  modes, 267
  polyphonic, 268, 269
Mysticism, 42–43, 285

Naples, 88, 141
Nationalism, 15, 98, 100–104, 143
Nativity, 276–78, 288
Natural law, 176
Natural man, 185, 188. *See also* Man
Nature, 167–68, 197
Nazareth, 181, 276–77
Nebuchadnezzar, 204–205
Nehemiah, 179
Neighbor, love of, 179, 186, 235, 275
Netherlands. *See* Low Countries
New Testament, 96, 152, 175, 199, 244, 255, 257, 259–61, 263
Nimrod, 70
*Ninety-Five Theses*, 60–64, 67, 93
Nineveh, 278
Noah, 100, 134, 231, 261
Nonresistance, 104, 115, 164, 213, 299
Novitiate, 27
Nürnberg, 21, 66, 75, 84, 95, 98, 121, 195, 224, 226, 242, 246, 247

Oaths, 207
*Obelisks*, 82
Occam, William, 94, 169
Oecolampadius, John, 249, 251
Old Testament, 47, 91, 179, 203, 255–56, 259, 261, 293
Ordination, 106–107
Orlamünde, 166, 200, 204
Osiander, Andreas, 251
Ovid, 147

Pacifism, 207. *See also* Nonresistance
Paduska, John, 92
Palatinate, 138, 145, 147, 195, 214

Palestine, 256, 297
Palm Sunday, 139
Pamphleteering, 238
Pantheon, 37, 258
Papacy
    antiquity, 75, 83, 88, 136
    infallibility, 68, 75, 97, 191
    primacy, 88, 127
*Papacy at Rome, The,* 105
Paradise, 24, 60, 231, 288
Paradox, 197
Paris, 73, 86, 110, 121, 152, 242
Pascal, Blaise, 301
Passion of Christ, 148, 257, 290
Pastor, Ludwig von, 56
*Pater Noster,* 28, 36, 38. *See also*
    Lord's Prayer
Patmos, 148, 149, 152
Paul, St., 36, 44, 45, 49, 57, 58, 66,
    82, 83, 95, 99, 111, 114, 127, 137,
    175, 180, 184, 197, 206, 233, 259–
    61, 272, 273, 299, 301
Peasants, 19, 66, 101, 146, 243, 265
Peasants' War, 205, 208–22, 224, 229,
    247
*Pecca Fortiter,* 175
Penance, 40, 43, 61, 66, 67, 78, 106,
    110
*Penitence, On,* 93
Pentecost, 271, 274
Perfection, unattainable, 33, 175, 185
Persia, 168
Perugia, 239
Peter, Epistle of, 261
Peter, St., 21, 36, 42, 57, 58, 61, 75,
    83, 88, 114, 125, 131, 134, 148,
    181, 209, 259, 273
Peter's, St., basilica of, 37, 57–59, 61,
    102
Pfefferkorn, John, 95–96, 297
Pharaoh, 141, 143, 153, 200, 212
Pharisees, 111, 149
Philip of Hesse, 216, 247–50, 252–54,
    293–94, 299
Philosophy, 48, 170
Pilate, 36, 38, 68, 148–49, 190
Pilgrimages, 22, 36–37, 97–98, 120,
    288
Pinturicchio, 37
Pirkheimer, Willibald, 95–96, 121, 140,
    195
Pius II, 114, 127
Political theory, 184–90, 298–99. *See
    also* Magistrate, Resistance, Non-
    resistance, Liberty, Revolution
Poor relief, 160, 162
Pope
    authority of, 68–69, 73, 78, 83, 88,
    97, 288
    contrasted with Christ, 120
    *see also* Papacy
Portuguese, 122
Prague, 92

Prayer, 43, 151, 159, 280
Preaching, 273-81, 300
Predestination, 89, 196–98. *See also*
    Free will
Prierias, Sylvester, 68, 70, 93, 95, 112,
    115
Priesthood of all believers, 106, 112,
    118–19, 191, 210
Protestants, 198, 199, 203, 223, 248,
    253–54, 293
Protestation at Speyer, 248
Prussia, 19, 235
Psalms, 47, 51, 152, 161, 206, 262,
    264, 270–71, 288
Pubelsberg, 19
Purgatory, 20, 35, 38, 53, 58, 60–64,
    67, 78, 79, 83, 90, 110, 137, 288
Puritan, 127, 198–201, 213, 299
Pyramus, 161

Quakers, 201

Rachel, 234
Raphael, 286
Reason
    inadequate, 44, 48, 96, 169, 172,
    196, 197, 261, 278, 279
    right, 73, 128, 144, 185, 196
Reformation, the, 93–95, 98, 160, 209,
    211, 220, 239, 270, 272
Relics of the saints, 35, 37, 53, 58, 80,
    157, 192, 231
Renaissance, 15, 18, 20, 21, 37, 95–
    100, 109, 183, 191, 234, 258
Rent, 212
Repentance, 48, 67
Resistance, 188, 298–99
*Resolutions,* 67, 93
"Respectively" in papal bull, 90, 113,
    125
Restitution, 199, 207
Resurrection, 116, 280, 290
Reuchlin, John, 95, 103, 111, 122
Revelation, 89, 167–74, 202, 283–91,
    297
Revelation, book of, 152, 255, 257, 258,
    261
Revolution, 138, 159, 188, 190, 195,
    201–205, 216, 295. *See also* Re-
    sistance
Rhaw, Georg, 82, 269
Rhine, 121, 122, 130, 209
Riario, Cardinal, 104, 111
Richard of Greiffenklau, 81, 111, 146,
    164
Rink, Melchior, 296
Romans, of antiquity, 196
Romans, Epistle to, 45, 49, 51, 184
Romantic love, 234
Rome, Church of, 67, 68, 71, 73, 75,
    77, 80, 83, 88–89, 99, 101, 104–
    106, 110–111, 114, 119, 121, 125,
    137, 148, 165, 191, 195, 198. *See
    also* Papacy

Rome, city, 36, 38–39, 53, 61, 63, 65, 66, 68, 69, 73, 74–78, 80, 92, 93, 101, 132, 134, 168, 225, 241, 288
Rose, golden, 80, 130
Rotterdam, 195
Rozdalowski, Wenzel, 92
Rupf, Conrad, 268

Sabbatarianism, 200, 264
Sachs, Hans, 241
Sacraments, 38, 40, 51, 97, 106–108, 147, 174, 191, 199–200, 206, 234. *See also* Baptism, Lord's Supper, Mass, Confirmation, Marriage, Penance, Extreme unction, Ordination
Safe conduct, 70, 83, 114, 134, 139, 145, 147
Saints
 All Saints', 53, 54, 57, 60, 65, 157, 192
 canonization, 120
 cult, 263
 despised, 168
 intercession, 22, 44
 *see also* Relics, Merits
Salvation, 63, 89, 97, 174
Salzburg, 77
Samaritan, 48
Sanballat, 195
Sarah, 289–90
Satan, 104, 116, 124–28, 134, 151, 169, 230, 241, 284. *See also* Devil
Satisfaction, 54
Saxony, 89, 91, 104, 122, 179, 193, 203–205, 215, 229, 242–43, 247, 248, 257
 ducal, 82
 electoral, 53, 57, 76, 82, 138, 243, 244, 249, 253, 255
*Scala Sancta,* 36, 38
Schedel, Hartmann, 21
Scholasticism, 93, 108, 109, 122, 128, 169
Schongauer, Martin, 257
Schools, 17–18, 20, 182, 262. *See also* Education
Scotus, Duns, 94
Scripture. *See* Bible
Scylla, 198
Seal, Luther's, 172, 277
Sedition, 294. *See also* Revolution
Senfl, Ludwig, 269
*Sermon on Good Works,* 150, 180
Sermon on the Mount, 34, 186, 207
Sermons, 67–68. *See also* Preaching
Sex, 34
Sicily, 238
Sickingen, Franz von, 101, 103, 115, 122, 130, 140, 152, 164–65
Simony, 137
Sin, mortal, 66
Sinai, 31, 286

Sins, seven, 41
Sixtus IV, 60
*Sleep Well,* 123
Sodom, 115
Soldiers, 182
Spain, Spaniard, 79, 88, 93, 101, 110, 122, 130, 134, 137, 140, 141, 145, 191, 208, 297, 301
Spalatin, George, 69, 77, 78, 104, 124, 139, 144, 151, 152, 157–58, 161, 223–26, 256
Spengler, Lazarus, 98, 121
Spirit
 general, 161, 199, 206, 249, 254
 the Holy, 106, 114, 203, 204, 269, 276
 versus letter, 199, 202
State, the, 110, 188. *See also* Political theory
Staupitz, John, 40, 41, 42, 43–45, 66, 67, 72, 74, 77, 80, 111, 135, 151, 175, 198
Stotternheim, 15
Strassburg, 66, 152, 205, 246, 247–49, 253–54
Sturm, Caspar, 139
Swabia, 239
Switzerland, Swiss, 93, 165, 206, 221, 242, 247–50, 253

*Table Talk,* 17, 230–33, 295
Tarshish, 278
Tauler, John, 276
Ten Commandments, 41, 57, 175, 180, 189, 233, 263
Tetzel, John, 59–60, 64, 67, 68, 81, 83, 112
Thankfulness, 178
Theocracy, 199, 203
*Theology, A German,* 102
Thief, the penitent, 21
Thisbe, 161
Thuringia, 18, 39, 150, 165, 214, 257, 296
Tithe, 212
Torgau, 53, 122, 223, 244
Transubstantiation. *See* Mass
Treasury of merits, 35, 62, 72–74, 75, 78, 112. *See also* Merits
Trebonius, 18
Trinity, 82, 83, 147, 169
*Trinity, The Roman,* 101
Turks, 70, 90, 113–14, 125, 127, 143, 161, 176, 185, 196, 202, 231, 248, 278
*Twelve Articles,* 212
Tyndale, William, 301
Tyranny, 126, 143, 188

Ulfilas, 255
Ulm, 242, 247
Ulrich of Württemberg, 189
Unamuno, 301

Uniasts, 191
*Unigenitus,* 72
Usury, 82, 184, 215, **275**

Valla, Lorenzo, 88, 96
Vatican, 71, 79, 93, 127, **131**
Venice, 225
Vergil, 20, 288
Veronica, 36
Vienna, 82,122
Violence, 136, 147, 157–8, **162,** 165, 189, 193, 194, 203, 213
Violence, Luther's, 115, 138, **147,** 194, 216
Visitation, 162, 244–45
Vocation, 16, 156, 181, 190
Vow, Luther's, 16, 25, 28, **74**
Vows, 138
Vulgarity, 231-32, 292, 298
Vulgate, 67, 96, 255, 256, **270**

Walther, 268
War, 186, 207
Wartburg, 150–51, 152, 153, **157, 158,** 163, 166, 223, 252, 255
Watts, Isaac, 301
Westminster, 301
Westphalia, 296
William of Anhalt, 25, **33**
Wise Men, 53, 136, 288
Witchcraft, 95–96

Wittenberg, **34, 39, 53, 55–56, 57, 60,** 65, 67, 75, 77, 79, 82, 86, 96, 103, 120, 121, 152, 156 ,157–58, 162–66, 179, 191–93, 195, 198, 200, 205, 215, 221, 223, 224, 239–42, 246–47, 252, 256, 263, 265, 268, 269, 272, 275, 300
Concord, 250
University of, 40, 56, 65, 72, **75,** 76, 78, 81, 122, 132, 154
Word of God, 104, 108, 141, 144, 166, 167, 174, 193, 212, 216, 246, 248, 254, 258, 264, 267, 268, 272–73, 295
Works, good, 40, 178, 259, 261
Worms, Edict of, 116, 146, 147–48, 211, 247, 248. *See also* Diets
Württemberg, 66, 189
Würzburg, 220
Wyclif, John, 89–90, 120, 138, **143**

Zionism, 297
Ziska, 214
Zulsdorf, 228
Zürich, 164, 205, 207, 249
Zwickau, 161, 200, 201
Zwilling, Gabriel, 152, 155, 157, 160, 163, 166, 244
Zwingli, Ulrich, 93, 200, 206–207, 243, 245, 248–49, 250–51